Liquid Assets, Dangerous Gifts

Liquid Assets, Dangerous Gifts

Presents and Politics at the End of the Middle Ages

VALENTIN GROEBNER

Translated by Pamela E. Selwyn

PENN

UNIVERSITY OF PENNSYLVANIA PRESS
Philadelphia

The Middle Ages Series

Ruth Mazo Karras, Series Editor
Edward Peters, Founding Editor

A complete list of books in the series is available from the publisher.

10 9 8 7 6 5 4 3 2 1

Published by
University of Pennsylvania Press
Philadelphia, Pennsylvania 19104

Library of Congress Cataloging-in-Publication Data

Groebner, Valentin.
[Gefährliche Geschenke. English]
Liquid assets, dangerous gifts : presents and politics at the end of the Middle Ages / Valentin Groebner ; translated by Pamela E. Selwyn.
p. cm. — (The Middle Ages series)
Includes bibliographical references and index.
ISBN 0-8122-3650-5 (cloth : alk. paper)
1. Switzerland—Politics and government—1499–1648. 2. Bribery—Switzerland. 3. Political corruption—Switzerland. 4. Misconduct in office—Switzerland. I. Title. II. Series.
DQ116.G7613 2002
364.1'323'0949409024—dc21
2001052540

Frontispiece: Detail from the Master of the Holy Family, *Legend of Saint Anthony*, ca. 1460. Alte Pinakothek, Munich.

Contents

Introduction: Speaking of Gifts

A gift is a transaction that assumes a particular rhetorical form. A gift is a gift because it whispers (or shouts, depending upon the circumstances), "I am for you alone, and you don't have to do anything." Whether this is true is at least doubtful, but what is clear is that at the moment of giving the giver cannot demand an explicit quid pro quo if he or she does not wish to endanger the efficacy of the entire transaction. Gifts possess seductive power, eloquence, and the capacity to transform social circumstances because in these circumstances they are as far removed as possible from calculation and self-interest: an effective gift is thus one that evokes ambiguity.

Our concern here will be with gifts in the urban societies of the late Middle Ages and the early modern period, with things that changed owners and with the terms used to describe them. When speaking of gifts, the people of the fifteenth and sixteenth centuries associated them and the effects attributed to them with concepts of legitimacy, purity, and visibility. This book will explore the means by which gifts were rendered legitimate or illegitimate, visible or invisible, (ac)countable or unspeakable.

The emphasis on naming is intentional: a gift is simply whatever contemporaries call a gift—*schenck* in the case of medieval and early modern German. The term strongly emphasizes how removed the gift is from any return services. This emphasis would mark the terminology for a very long time—Zedler's *Universallexikon* of 1735 still offered this definition: "Gifts are those things whose ownership one transfers to another without recompense. The rational basis of gifts is a surplus."[1] Surplus or not, from the fourteenth century onward, gifts fill long columns in municipal and private account books, chronicles and memoranda, treatises on politics, household management, and etiquette, and they appear very powerful. "What is there that gifts cannot do?" exclaims Lionardo in Alberti's *Libri della famiglia.* "They can win you new friends, certainly, but they can also reconcile and recall even men filled with serious malice and hardened hate against you."[2] As efficacious as these gifts may have been in the eyes of contemporaries and as carefully as they were recorded, they assumed—in contrast to the donations and legacies found in notarial files and testaments—no fixed legal form. Instead, they remained within the indeterminate sphere of general sociability and everyday relations. The gifts in Swiss and South German cities that will interest us here were transactions between living persons in the here and now, and in a secular context. We will thus not be concerned with alms, *caritas*, religious foundations, and pious works or with transgenerational transfers or testaments. Our topic here will be gifts in the strict sense of the word—acts of secular largesse and generosity, tokens of regard, extras.

The temporal framework will be the end of the Middle Ages and the first decades of the sixteenth century, a period that begins around the Council of Constance and ends with the great conflicts surrounding the imperial election, Luther, iconoclasm, and the Reformation, a period, generally speaking, not of ending or decline but of reform and new beginnings.[3] The geographical framework will be the political space that stretches from what is today eastern France through southern Germany and Switzerland. Basel, with its extraordinarily detailed surviving sources, will form the center of the analysis. The Basel municipal account books, which exist practically complete beginning in 1371 as an official register of gifts given, the Basel town council records, oath formulas, memoranda with their stipulations on permitted and forbidden giving, and the Basel chronicles with their stories of venality and conflict constitute the backbone of this study. These sources have been supplemented with material from Zurich, Bern, Strasbourg, Sélestat, and Freiburg im Breisgau, as well as more distant South German cities such as Nuremberg and Augsburg. This urban landscape will be treated as a common political framework connected by rivers of information. This flow of news in the form of letters, manuscripts, and pamphlets connected such far-flung city-states as Strasbourg, Nuremberg, and Bern in an intensive exchange of ordinances and missives; it made the wars against the duke of Burgundy in the 1470s into a media event in the German-speaking realm and, as we will see, produced a great similarity in the polemics and justifications for the toppling of the allegedly corrupt mayors of Augsburg and Zurich.[4]

Those who pick up this book expecting to find out who influenced whom and which gifts led to which political services may be disappointed. I am less interested in proving who gave what gift to whom and when than in placing these gifts and their functions in a broader context and locating them within the conditions of municipal record-keeping, the political struggles between the Holy Roman Empire and the Swiss Confederacy, and the formation of political elites. I would like to take a closer look at the dividing lines between legal and illegal transfers, permitted gifts and forbidden bribes in order to pursue the ways of speaking that associated gifts with political legitimacy.

The gifts to be discussed in the chapters that follow are gifts recorded in account books, chronicles and memoranda, gifts between living persons, in this world, for secular purposes, and not as alms. The Bern town council records of the fourteenth and fifteenth centuries, for example, distinguish quite clearly between *schengki* (gifts) distributed by the city to diplomats, messengers, and its own officeholders and *spenden* (donations), pious investments in the form of candles for the churches or bread for the municipal poor.[5] Such gifts were material objects, that is, they were not benefits, emotions, or services of a physical or spiritual nature. They consisted of wine, food, clothing, money, and other valuables and were named and registered as such. The objects that will interest us here were also primarily gifts between men. They were presented by male persons to other male persons, almost exclusively, although we will examine a few exceptions. I will try to show that this circumstance had a decisive influence on how people spoke about these gifts and what terms were used to describe these transfers, with their positive or negative connotations. It is no accident that the dangerous gift offered to Saint Anthony on the frontispiece of this book, which comes from a fifteenth-century panel now in the Munich Pinakothek, is presented by women. And as familiar as these gifts—liquids and money—were to late medieval beholders, the givers are equipped with devilish attributes, such as the claws under their richly adorned garments. How could legitimate offerings be distinguished from such dangerous presents?

The gifts that will concern us here relate to bodies that were conceived of as male and were closely associated with notions of domination and order. These gifts in Switzerland and the region of the Upper Rhine in the fifteenth and sixteenth centuries and speech about gifts will be investigated as instruments of a political culture—instruments, however, on whose naming and use contemporaries by no means agreed at the outset—and as instruments in a conflict.

Historians have paid increasing attention in the past decades to the early and high medieval *dona, beneficia,* and *patrimonia,* the bestowing of land and valuables referred to as gifts and transfers to monastic institutions as part of a complicated network of aristocratic family strategies and social conflict resolution, but their research is based largely on sources from the period before the thirteenth century.[6] In recent years, important studies have appeared on gifts at the late medieval and early modern courts; the extensive material on gifts in the municipal notarial registers and accounting records of the fourteenth and fifteenth centuries, however, has received comparatively little analysis.[7]

The lists of officially bestowed *schenck* in the records of municipal administrations and in private journals and letters of the late Middle Ages and early modern period north of the Alps have been known to urban historians since the end of the nineteenth century, and an increasing number are available in published editions. Up until now, these gift registers have generally only been used to answer individual questions of prosopography or legal history and have not been studied in a broader context. This legacy of an intellectual tradition that has consistently associated gifts with older, oral, "embedded" local, social, and economic forms and assiduously distinguished them from the money economy, literacy, bureaucratic rule, and an economy characterized by a division of labor will be the subject of the final section of this Introduction. From this point of view, gifts as simple informal offerings could not play an important part in the expanding commercial and administrative centers of the late Middle Ages, even if recent works on patronage and administration have made clear the key role that must be assigned to gifts most particularly in the political networks of these administrative structures.[8]

The scholarly traditions surrounding gifts and giving clearly determine in more ways than one what we do or do not associate with such donations; they will be addressed in this Introduction. Those readers who prefer not to linger over social scientific model-building and its contemporary echoes are welcome to move on to the systems of recording that literally render the gifts visible for us. Chapter 1, "Liquids and Pronouncements," discusses the particular conditions of this registration in more detail. Gifts, the form in which they were registered, and the functions of their distribution were closely linked with the rise of administrative record-keeping and its functional differentiation in the later Middle Ages. Chapter 1 explores economic and ritual aspects of the gifts, the types of presents given, the costs of distribution, and the procedures according to which giving was orchestrated.

Despite all this emphasis on municipal generosity, the objects given as gifts speak very eloquently of their material value, their price. A work on gifts and how they were perceived at the end of the Middle Ages and the beginning of the early modern period thus risks confusing the reader, who may lose sight of the gifts among long series of figures in exotic currencies—whose value is difficult for us to imagine today—and equally unfamiliar terms for good or evil transfers. For that reason, wherever possible I have not expressed sums of money in the contemporary parlance of pounds, shillings, and pfennigs but converted them into pfennigs alone in order to make the amounts and their relationships, for example, to artisans' daily wages easier to follow. For the same reason I have decided not to convert sums of money in gold coins—Rhenish guilders, occasionally also French gold crowns and Italian ducats—into contemporary silver money. These gold coins were costly treasures and sharply distinguished from silver or copper pfennigs and shillings. Whether someone received a sum of money in gold coins or small change was important for fifteenth- and sixteenth-century people; I would like to retain and accentuate these distinctions in the perception and effect of monetary gifts.

The phenomena of this gift economy can be described as existing in a sort of intermediate, transitional space between "hard," clearly fixed, and explicit (political) rules and "soft," ambiguous, and implicitly expressed informal practice. Chapter 2 ("Offices") is thus dedicated to the protagonists of municipal authority, to the retainers and officials, the gifts they received, and the rules to which these presents were subjected. Following these two chapters, I will provide a brief summary of the first section of my study, which is devoted to legal, public gifts.

Those presents that the cities made to high-ranking visitors, travelers, couriers, and deserving citizens and registered so carefully had their dark and dangerous counterparts, which will be treated in the second part of the book. Chapter 3 examines representations of venality and corruption. It pursues the history of the term *miet*, which more than any other summarized for late medieval and early modern contemporaries the ambivalence and risks of gift giving, the forms in which it appeared, and the conditions of its use; for that reason this chapter is entitled "Manners of Speaking." Chapter 4—"Pensions"—is devoted to the political conflicts surrounding gifts and "dirty money" in Switzerland. It revolves around those payments and pensions that well into the twentieth century remained a neglected area in the history of the Swiss Confederacy. Chapter 5—"Pensions in Basel, 1501–1522"—takes us back to the Upper Rhine region. What role did pensions in Basel play in the political conflicts around proper and improper gifts and their designation and registration? Which constellations were responsible for the toppling of the powerful mayor Jakob Meyer zum Hasen in October 1521, and what could contemporaries read in and behind the pictures that Hans Holbein painted during those turbulent months in the newly built great council hall in Basel? The sixth and final chapter will take stock of the "Instruments" that present themselves for the description of these gifts and their functions; it will trace the recoding of this transfer in Reformation polemics and sketch some of the interactions between the gender order, the public sphere, and raison d'etat.

The kind of close-up I attempt in the present book necessarily draws our attention to details. It is the privilege of such a method that it allows the objects of investigation to appear alien and unfamiliar, as if they had just been rediscovered. It offers the possibility of reading them anew, beyond traditional attributions. Talk about gifts in the cities of Switzerland and the Upper Rhine between the fourteenth and sixteenth centuries reveals fundamental parameters of the political and their transformation: the recasting of the relationship between visibility and invisibility, *publicus* and *privatus*, representation and information at the beginning of the modern era.

Marcel Mauss in the Middle Ages

The term *gift* presents a transfer as selfless and voluntary, separating it as sharply as possible from other forms such as exchange, sale, and payment for work and portraying it as a generous gesture, an extra. In order to be effective as an extra, a benefit must appear to be voluntary and thus primary. Only those who purport to give first and "from the virgin soil of the soul" can use this instrument; Georg Simmel clearly notes the ambivalence of this process in his 1908 *Soziologie.* A gift must be abstracted as thoroughly as possible from the context of its potential effects; it is effective because, if only at the carefully staged moment of its bestowal, it is presented as a unique and isolated love offering, and for this one moment neutralizes—or at least appears to neutralize—the stubborn reality of mutual obligation. The ethnologist Maurice Godelier resorts to the trick of the double negative in order to emphasize this implicit tie of solidarity, asymmetry, and dependency between giver and recipient. In his definition, gift giving means voluntarily transferring something to someone that one believes cannot possibly not accept it.[9]

What has this got to do with late medieval bookkeeping, representation, and corruption? Historians explicitly and implicitly use social science models when they speak of gifts, and they tend to do so all the more when they define themselves as specialists in a limited area such as the Middle Ages or the Renaissance. Sociologists and anthropologists, in contrast, are quick to refer to supposedly self-evident "historical" points of departure or developments. Thus we shall begin here with some of these models—especially because everyone writing about gifts or offerings is in a certain sense involved in a conversation with the late Marcel Mauss, one of the founding fathers of modern ethnology and sociology. Even today, Mauss's 1923 *Essay on the Gift* continues to set the framework for scholarly debates on gifts and giving.

According to Mauss, in the gift the boundaries between persons and things are fluid: the gift assumes qualities of the giver, and this exchange of gifts and rendering of services (*prestation*) produces a social effect because it always demands requital and a return gift. The gift forges ties, and the powerful "total social fact" of gift exchange stood at the beginning of contractual relations, communication, and society more generally. While in 1908 Georg Simmel soberly noted that giving as social interaction par excellence creates society, even without exchange, Marcel Mauss, writing under the impression of the First World War, conceived of giving as *the* moment of social progress. In his work, the "total social phenomenon" of gift exchange is the counterpart to total war, and the gift represents the path of reason: It frees society from the stagnation and isolation of conflicts and creates culture because it makes possible contracts and communication by transfer and information. "Thus," Mauss writes at the end of his essay, "the clan, the tribe and peoples have learnt [through the exchange of gifts] how to oppose and to give to one another without sacrificing themselves to one another. . . . This is one of the enduring secrets of their wisdom and solidarity. There is no other morality, nor any other form of economy, nor any other social practices save these."[10]

When Giving Gifts Still Helped: Tales of a Lost Whole

Mauss's famous central question "Why does one give in order to receive?" brings together three acts: giving, receiving, and giving in return. It makes of all three a single object of study and reifies it as gift exchange. In his famous introduction to the 1950 edition of Mauss's sociological and ethnological works, Claude Lévi-Strauss gently suggests that the master had thereby ignored the religious aspect of gift giving and failed to recognize that relations surrounding gifts were about the symbolic origins of society itself. Transfers are raised here to a higher level of abstraction. According to Lévi-Strauss, it is more or less unimportant whether the circulation involves food, women, money, services, seeds, religious emanations, or children: *what* is given is immaterial; analysis should be devoted to the elementary structures transported by the transfer.[11]

In a process of displacement, the gift, which as gift exchange is already a "total social phenomenon" in Mauss's work, is turned from an object of study into a model. In "L'enigme du don," Maurice Godelier describes the gift as an essential element in the production and reproduction of objective social conditions as well as subjective personal relationships. What is more, gifts embody (Godelier uses the verb *incarner*) the whole of both persons and their relationships to each other. For that reason the gift contains and unites something that comes from the persons with what is present in their relationships, totalizing and symbolizing it in its practice as well as in the objects in which it becomes materialized.[12] It is, admittedly, a bit unfair to paraphrase such an elegant piece of French scholarly prose, but I cannot suppress a certain discomfort I felt while reading it. Godelier's formulation completely obliterates the persons who bestowed these objects (thereby making them gifts in the first place). If the gift so seamlessly welds together social and symbolic functions, what are social scientists actually investigating that they did not already know before and what are the results of their analyses?

Whether or not scholars refer to Mauss, the study of gifts appears to seduce them into speaking of totalities: it is quite literally an all-or-nothing proposition. Godelier's book treats relations of exchange among the Baruya people of Papua New Guinea, but he does not hesitate to make direct connections to French society of the present and to the contemporary discourse on venality, money, and the limits of relations of exchange. The category of "total social facts" becomes a sort of magic carpet with which the scholar can move at a brisk pace through time and space. Marcel Mauss understood his own synopsis of widely disparate phenomena as part of a moral commitment. In search of the gift as a basic ethical principle, at the end of his essay he expressed the conviction that in those non-European and archaic European societies that he had studied—Germanic societies up to the writing down of the *Edda*, Roman society before the Twelve Tables, Irish society "up to the creation of its main literature"—individuals "were less sad, less serious, less miserly, and less personal than we are. Externally at least, they were or are more generous, more liable to give than we are."[13]

Mauss's yearning for salvation from the contemporary profit economy by means of the archaic, voluntary gift is unmistakable here.[14] This utopian past of more real, more altruistic, and thus more "total" gift-giving relationships becomes the leitmotif of an emphatic reading of the gift, of a sociology of the no-longer in which the pure binding gift is the key fossil in a history of loss. It is in this intellectual tradition that we must place Georges Bataille's longing for the total exertion and self-abandon of a mythical past, which was destroyed and replaced by the "universal stinginess of bourgeois society," as well as Theodor Adorno's melancholy reflection that human beings have forgotten how to give gifts: "Even private giving of presents has degenerated to a social function exercised with rational bad grace, careful adherence to the prescribed budget, skeptical appraisal of the other and the least possible effort." Adorno published those lines in 1951. Unfortunately, he has little more to say about the precise temporal location of the era of proper, generous, and honest gift giving than that it is gone. In a sort of mirage, the pure, altruistic gift is located at once at an archaic distance and in an immediately recent past. All this talk of loss is more in a literary than a social scientific tradition of moralizing. The rise of vulgar calculation and the fall of liberality and generosity had already been lamented by the French lawyer Noel du Fail in his 1547 *Propos rustiques*, as well as by courtly authors of the twelfth century.[15] For several hundred years, the "genuine" gift had apparently always just recently disappeared.

Whether in literary treatises or social science models, such evocations of past genuineness, whose linear temporal decay is suggested by the words "still" and "already," never mention actual dates or concrete actors, but only broad "developments," which are at once the agents and the results of social processes. In this emphatic reading of Mauss's essay, relationships created by gifts are always at once "anti-market" and "anti-state" (as we shall see in more detail later). In such a macroperspective, there is plainly no place for any more subtle distinctions such as that between the high and late medieval doctrines on alms and usury, or between Catholic reciprocity and the Reformed insistence on liberality—after all, what is at stake here is nothing less than society and morality "as a whole." By speaking of the whole, one not only suggests an overview but also avoids a discussion of particular interests, paradoxes, and conflicts. Like authenticity, the whole is manufactured by removing practices from their use contexts and lifting them to a higher level of abstraction. This process of taking things literally produces serious, intense, and severe images of "total" meanings, in which the human actors become completely dissolved in a systematic whole or a purportedly homogenous gift mentality. Whether one grasps these transfers as the original source of contractual relations, a final expending of effort, a symbolic exchange, or a pattern for how a society communicates with the sacred or organizes gender relations, the notion that a total social meaning is always inscribed into gifts, their characteristics, and meanings appears to lend itself to circular thinking. Marcel Mauss's methodological legacy thus has its pitfalls. If all things social originate in the gift as a "fait total," the gift becomes a supersubject that creates social ties and integration in and through itself. Also in this tradition is Jacques Derrida's *Counter-*

feit Money, which provides a stimulating analysis of Mauss's essay but postulates rather firmly that every gift has a "nature that is excessive in advance." The gift articulates the "command to forget;" that which is surrendered dispenses with control, the offering must "always run over its borders."[16] Every gift? Always?

As valuable as Mauss's references to the intensive interweaving of gift, contract, and social conflict may be, gift exchange as a figure of reciprocity possesses two quite distinct functions that cannot simply be intermingled. On the one hand, the exchange of gifts as reciprocity constitutes a relationship that is basically oriented toward the "outside" and defines exchange between separate parties with differing interests. On the other hand, it functions as redistribution toward the "inside," which organizes relationships within a group—reciprocity does not function in the same way for everyone. Even seemingly altruistic relations of exchange prove on closer inspection to be the products of the participants' efforts to banish the self-interested aspect of the transactions from their social representation. The status of a transfer as a "genuine" gift is thus not confirmed by recompense, but rather always called into question and threatened. Thus (as Pierre Bourdieu has noted, somewhat ironically) cycles of reciprocity as a mechanistic machinery of mutual obligation exist only from the viewpoint of the omniscient and omnipresent beholder.[17] The relationship constructed by historians or ethnologists between the allegedly pure gift and reciprocity mirrors only too clearly the structures of their own societies—the models used to describe gifts and their functions rest on the inversion of modern European categories of commodity and purchase. Whether in the South Seas, the early Middle Ages or some other geographically or temporally distant Elsewhere, Mauss's gift exchange as a realm of freedom and solidarity is a specifically European social utopia born of the European trenches and the sociopolitical struggles of the twentieth century.[18]

Registration, Ambivalence, Representation

How can we study and write about gifts at the end of the Middle Ages and the beginning of the modern period without totalizing concepts? I would like to suggest three possible points of departure. The first relates to the sources. Any study of gifts in the late Middle Ages and early modern period must begin with the qualification that it deals only with gifts on paper—as temptingly "whole" as we may wish to imagine these gifts as being. Those transfers available to us, which permit description, analysis, and synchronic and diachronic comparison, are those that were recorded, usually in very concise form, in household account books, bills, memoranda, and chronicles. However eloquently they may have spoken to contemporaries, practically all other gifts have disappeared.[19] It is the written sources that create urban gifts for the reader and offer him or her a set of terms used to refer to them, and these terms are often vague and ambiguous.

This may sound rather obvious, reminiscent of the usual discussion at the beginning of historical works about the difficult and spotty state of the sources: the desired information is a scarce commodity to be gleaned drop by drop, as it were. This is not what I mean here.[20] The written documents available to us as sources on and products of the social reality of the fifteenth and sixteenth centuries are not simply the results of abstract discourses. In their time, they occupied a place that can be determined quite precisely, both as products of the social world and in relation to the linguistic tools prevalent in that world. They refer to both in complex (and conflictual) constellations. If we take seriously the conditions and practices of recording gifts in writing, then these texts on gifts reflect not pure concepts but their application—in short, the inseparability of material and discursive practices. And this is how the political language analyzed here should also be understood, as a socially powerful practice of labeling. Not everyone is involved in determining what will be registered as a gift and what will not.

My second point of departure relates to the ambiguity and multiple meanings of gifts. Mauss's archaic societies are utopian societies, not only in the sense of great temporal and spatial distance, but also because he described them as polarized places in which there are only two possible ways of behaving: total distrust or total trust, war or generosity. This is honorable, but such an ideal-typical situation in which one can choose from only two options is highly simplified at best. In practice, the participants always have several options at their disposal. They can hesitate and avoid, they can refuse to communicate with and face others, they can attempt to gain time and offer noncommittal signs of goodwill. Above all, they can act as if their gifts make peace and make promises that they do not intend to keep. Since one never knows enough about the true intentions of one's opponent, choosing the options of deceit and betrayal is a realistic middle way between total war and total trust. However unrestricted, altruistic, and voluntary the gift may appear to be, from the beginning it has, so to speak, an evil twin.

The third point of departure relates to the participants in these gifts. We have seen that the older social scientific tradition viewed gift giving as an "archaic" economic form that has (or at least should have) nothing to do with the money economy or a division of administrative labor. Gifts are thus understood implicitly and explicitly as against or outside the state because they do not resolve conflicts between quarreling parties to the benefit of a third higher power; in this view gifts are instead transformed into a direct relationship between two opponents. We will see that this description has precious little in common with actual conditions in the fifteenth and sixteenth centuries. Gifts were just as inextricably linked with the practices of the monetary economy as with the rise of centralized administration and the early modern state. In their particular rhetorical form—the gift mode, as Natalie Davis has called it—however, gifts represent economic transfers of a specific kind. They underline the autonomy of giver and recipient and throw into relief their difference from the others: they cannot help but create preferred beneficiaries.

This means that neither giver nor recipient is alone, though. The offering always takes place before an audience that must be regarded not simply as a mute backdrop but as a participating factor: that of the nonrecipients, if you will, those who go away empty-handed. The transfer has only fulfilled its function when it successfully confirms (that is, enforces) the position of the two "self-evident" partners, the giver and the recipient. The gifts must always present themselves in such a way as if they were dyadic, only related to two people, and occurred freely and without cost. This is the rhetorical form and the rules of the game of representation, and the participants are well aware of this. Thus the traditional debates about gifts always revolve around the nonmaterial gratitude of the recipient and not his or her polite and correct return gift; on the contrary, the return gift threatens a transfer's status as a gift and love offering.[21] The recourse to gratitude as an abstract principle is intended to help avoid the ever-present danger of deception and betrayal: the recipient of the gift is supposed to offer his or her grateful inner self in recompense. Talk about gifts revolves around this notion of identity with itself that surrounds the presence or absence of deception—the field of gift giving is a *regio dissimilitudinis* in the literal sense of the phrase.

It has often been remarked that the productive misunderstanding of the gift as a return gift is a precondition of its functioning. If the abstraction of gift exchange is made explicit, the pure act of giving becomes impossible. It is based on the fiction that there can have been no previous history and that this time, too, a gift was given for the first time, out of affection, and without expectations. This is not "false" but rather perfectly proper consciousness because it renders the act possible in the first place. In reality, everything cannot be given to or accepted from everybody, and the participants know it. The paradox of compulsory choice is helpful in describing such behaviors: the subject chooses the rules of the game to which he or she is already subject. The field of the implicit and explicit rules of gift giving is never completely closed, and not everything is already predetermined. Instead, it contains a point of "proper" behavior that one must not necessarily, but should be allowed to, reach. Put another way, the rules of gifts are structured in such a way that they contain a choice, which is a metachoice: those who make the wrong choice forfeit the opportunity of choice itself.[22]

Historians' usual manner of writing about the legally binding or customary character of gifts thus misses the very field in which these transfers are supposed to function. In the societies of the Middle Ages and the Renaissance, gifts were efficacious because they could *not* be demanded by law, because although their advent was not unexpected, it was always uncertain as to size, quality, intention, and interpretation. One could "reckon with it" but one could not, and must not, depend upon it. It was apparently the ambivalent gift between unequal parties that had the greatest effect.

Late medieval authors explicitly emphasize this ambiguity of transfers. In his bestseller, *The Ship of Fools*, which appeared in 1494, the Basel jurist and municipal official Sebastian Brant adds a special passage on gift giving and regrets. One should give gifts with good cheer, joy, and a smiling face, he admonishes (thereby paraphrasing Seneca's *De Beneficiis*). At the same time, Brant makes it clear that the game of giving also has less amiable aspects. Refusing a gift is terribly rude (*gar zu grob*), he writes, and "One should not force anybody to give." In a sermon on *The Ship Of Fools* that he gave in Strasbourg cathedral in 1498 or 1499, Brant's commentator, the popular preacher Geiler von Kaysersberg, stresses more strongly the limited choice and dangers of gift giving. Gifts received must not be immediately requited, he reminds his listeners: "For if you do so you disgrace him from whom you received the gift." A doubly requited gift is no gift at all, he adds, but rather only a loan (*geliehen gut*) and thus devilish usury. It was even worse not to recognize gifts as such, to scorn them, or, worse still, to mistake them for misdeeds and assaults.[23]

It is precisely the relationship to the return gift that made gifts appear so ambivalent in the eyes of these fifteenth-century men and threatened to transform them into misdeeds, insults, and attacks. Alberti's Lionardo, whose emphatic invocation of the power of the gift I have quoted, said something quite similar, albeit in a positive form. A gift can contain a threat: some powerful men were so generous, to paraphrase a saying one encounters in several late medieval texts, that they gave away not only their own goods but also those belonging to others. It is no accident that Baldassare Castiglione adopted this point of view in his own *Book of the Courtier*, along with a warning: Not all those who give many gifts are generous.[24]

1 *Liquids and Pronouncements*

Writing as Self-Control

What did it mean for authors of the fifteenth and sixteenth centuries—a Basel town clerk, the secretary of a Basel bishop, an Augsburg merchant involved in long-distance trade, a Nuremberg painter—to keep careful records of their spending on gifts in their household ledgers, accounts, or memorandum books? They noted to whom they gave something on which occasion, what the gift was, and also who delivered something to them from which third party. I would like to suggest that we not simply understand this recording as the mere registration of a transfer, but also study it as an activity in its own right.[1] Under what circumstances and for whom were gifts registered?

In 1416 the Nuremberg patrician Walpurga Kress began a special book in which, until 1438, she carefully recorded all gifts to her friends. This term referred to relations in the broad sense of the word, encompassing families bound by neighborhood, godparent-hood, and marriage. The author noted meticulously what she and her husband gave to whom on which occasion—christenings, entry into a convent or monastery, marriage, moving into a new house: costly dishes, silver objects, drinking vessels filled with wine. On January 20, 1431, she recorded the death of her husband Conrad Kress in this gift book, using the same form. He had left her with five daughters and four sons, whose names she lists. "God let me raise them all with love and to praise him. Amen," she ends the list, only to continue seamlessly with the next gift entries—bedding and furniture for her son. The text unites private memorandum book, pious memorial, family chronicle, and a precise registration of gifts and their prices within a network of urban relationships.[2]

The late medieval civic literacy to which we owe our information about these gifts, the occasions for them, their costs and recipients, was shaped by commercial practice. Any treatment of private writing in the first-person singular necessarily leads us to the condensed written form of merchant account books, *ricordi, Jornalls.*[3] This recording practice was organized according to the principle of self-control and never-ending vigilance. Fifteenth-century authors on household economy emphasized that each paterfamilias must maintain records and be constantly accountable to himself.[4] Many were negligent, noted the Augsburger Matthäus Schwarz in his 1518 instructions on proper bookkeeping. They overestimated themselves, tried to keep everything in their heads, and did their accounts on scattered and disorderly pieces of paper. Rather than making a little effort, such poor bookkeepers preferred to lose their overview, he adds ironically, and when they finally went bankrupt, they could not understand how it had happened. The bookkeeping specialist in the service of the Fuggers never tired of admonishing his readers to forget nothing, record each transfer, and keep themselves thoroughly informed about their own affairs.[5]

The principle according to which Schwarz, who had been trained in Italy, organized his model bookkeeping—the multiple recording of sums in various account books and other memorandum books—can be traced, down to the smallest detail, in the notes of his contemporaries. In the private household journal he maintained from 1507 to 1517, the Nuremberg merchant and banker Anton Tucher kept precise records, in separate registers, on all gifts received and given. In a first volume, entitled *hawßpüchlein* (little household book), he noted what he spent and took in for his kitchen and wine cellar. He also used it to record what gifts of food and drink he received, such as a cask of Franconian wine given to him by the elector of Saxony on January 6, 1508, or a barrel of herb beer from Torgau that Duke Frederick had sent to him on June 23 of the same year. For both gifts he noted precisely and unsentimentally the size and contents, just as he did for the wine he bought himself for household consumption.[6]

The gifts that Tucher himself bestowed are recorded in a second, separate register. Here he noted, for example, the cost of the eight large trout he presented to the patrician Jörg Fütterer on June 11, 1508, the wine and the hundred lemons he sent to a kinswoman who was taking the cure, or gifts to council members, friends, foreign guests or members of his family who were returning from a journey—wine, fish, spices, exotic fruits, costly fabrics.[7] Tucher's trading company also maintained such a separate account book. He mentions it in an entry of June 1512 in which he remarks that he had had his expenses for New Year's gifts recorded in the main account book for the beginning of 1512. These included a total of 33 florins for saffron, figs, almonds, and dates. Such gifts at the beginning of a new year are well documented for the late fifteenth century, together with printed greeting cards.[8] Another register was exclusively devoted to Tucher's servants. It recorded their wages and debts and the presents he gave them; a further book noted his payments of the municipal excise tax on wine and beer. A final, separate register contains notes on his family and children.

The household book is thus only part of a far more extensive written registration of expenses and income divided into separate areas in which business and family records overlap.[9] This becomes even clearer in the particular manner of recording employed by a colleague and contemporary of Tucher and Schwarz, the Augsburg merchant Lukas Rem. His notes, which the editor has entitled, somewhat misleadingly, a diary (*Tagebuch*), encompass ten such separate registers that contain entries for the years 1495-1541, documenting, among other things, his business trips, illnesses, taxes, business profits, and the wedding presents he received upon his marriage in 1518. A further register lists the gifts he gave others after 1518. The two last-mentioned lists are extremely concise memorandum books, containing nothing more than the names of the giver or recipient and sums of money. The bookkeeping specialist Rem also insisted on drawing up a balance sheet; adding up the value of all the gifts he received for his wedding—422 florins—he noted that his own gifts to others came to something over 309 florins.[10]

Such a dry calculation of love offerings according to their monetary value was not specific to Rem. The careful registration of who gave gifts of what value can also be found in the more politically than commercially organized notes of Sixtus Ölhafen, *secretarius* to Emperor Maximilian and the imperial administration that was established in Nuremberg in 1500. Writing of his 1501 wedding, Ölhafen proudly reports which illustrious guests were seated at which table and that the archbishop of Mainz had danced with his bride. The entire second half of his account is devoted to the wedding presents and their givers, with eighty-two names in all: from a gold chain from Duke Frederick of Saxony to silver and gold-plated cups, numerous rings, costly household objects and textiles, silk fabric "for an underskirt" for the bride (a gift from the Basel canon Hanns von Halstat), and plain cash. Worms sent forty florins, and the small imperial city of Isny sent six. We should not imagine that all of these gifts were wholly voluntary: "May God alone be honored" (*Allein Got sey geehret*), Ölhafen ends his list somewhat disingenuously, "Amen."[11]

All these forms of recording were not merely temporary memos or notes that have come down to us by accident; they were set down deliberately and over long time periods. It was important to register gifts received or bestowed in a permanent form. As both Ölhafen's and Rem's records make clear, the presents themselves were anything but informal. The practice of recording them intensively and precisely was also not limited to merchants. During his journey to the Netherlands in 1520, Albrecht Dürer noted the costs of the ship's passage through the Main and Rhine rivers, the meals he ate, and his provisions on board. He had trouble even keeping up with the names of the many people who gave him presents, such as the Cologne goldsmiths and painters who favored him with bottles of wine upon his departure.[12] Whatever such gifts may have been intended to achieve in an individual case, for contemporaries it was apparently important to record them, along with the names of the giver, in a specialized and condensed written practice: gift bookkeeping.

The City's Gifts

This gift recording applies not only to private and commercial accounting. Public bookkeeping north of the Alps begins quite literally with gifts: the first lines of the earliest surviving Basel municipal accounts of weekly expenses and intakes carefully register the city's spending on gifts. Visitors from the neighboring city of Rheinfelden cost the council 96 pfennigs *pro vino* on July 5, 1371, notes an entry on the first page of the weekly accounts of the *Dreierherren* (Committee of Three), the council members responsible for the town treasury.[13]

The Basel weekly account books survive almost completely intact from 1371 throughout the late Middle Ages and the sixteenth century. Under the rubric *Schenckwein* (gift wine), they record meticulously from week to week the names of recipients not only of municipal presents of wine, but also of official extras more generally. Presents of money to messengers and minstrels appear in the lists along with compensation for those wrongfully arrested.[14] Mentions in the yearly account books for Basel reach back even further, to 1361, summarizing total spending on these ritual gifts. If the recipients were prominent enough, the information was more detailed. The amount spent on gifts of wine to the kings of Cyprus and Denmark and other princes and cities came to more than 45,000 pfennigs, the balance sheet for fiscal year 1363-64 notes.[15] Beginning in the mid-fifteenth century, a special rubric for gifts appears in the annual accounts, registering in detail the most important occasions and recipients. The margrave of Baden, for example, received a salmon on his visit to the city, as was noted in the accounts for the years 1458-59; a blind man from Nuremberg was given wine and money; and a silver drinking vessel costing almost 14,000 pfennigs was presented by the city to the new bishop of Basel, Johann von Venningen, at his investiture.[16] The registration of gifts served as a current political memorandum book.

Gifts were politics. In his "Council Poems," a long set of rhymed instructions on the proper administration of a city that was written in the last decades of the fourteenth century, the Erfurt town clerk Johannes Rothe described gift giving as the most important task of municipal treasurers. They were the city's "hands," who should gladly and generously spend money on gifts to the benefit and honor of the town, while it was the job of the town scribe, as the city's "eyes," meticulously to record and register all municipal business and transactions. The municipal officers, according to Rothe, must care as much for the city's gifts as for the condition of its towers and walls.[17] Basel followed this advice, and it was not alone in doing so. From the middle of the fourteenth century on, we possess information from numerous South German and Swiss cities about specialized registers and gift account books in which presents of money, wine, and other things to high-ranking visitors, diplomats, couriers, or other particularly worthy citizens were recorded.[18]

The precise registration of gifts given was not, however, limited to the municipal authorities.[19] In his own household ledgers, the Basel bishop Johann von Venningen, about whose investiture gifts the Basel municipal accounts inform us so precisely, kept careful records of the costs and recipients of his own generosity. In the household ledger that he began upon assuming episcopal office, alongside his spending for messengers, clothing, shoes, artisans, and scribes, he carefully noted on the first page that he had given one florin as a godparent gift upon the baptism of the child of a certain Claus Schnyder; he gave a further florin to a blind man from Nuremberg. We have already encountered this blind man: in the same month of June 1458 he also received a gift from the Basel council before visiting the bishop's residence.[20]

That we can locate this blind man again so readily is not necessarily a coincidence: the gift bookkeeping of the fifteenth and sixteenth centuries was designed to make it easy to identify recipients. Bishop Johann von Venningen kept such careful records of his expenses and income not only because his bishopric was in financial straits, but also in order to recall the associated names and circumstances more readily.[21] Similarly, the council records of Upper Rhenish cities note some incidents and the names of the participants with the express remark "this should not be forgotten." The point was to facilitate placing the entry in a political context.[22] And in the municipal registers, gifts of wine, expensive delicacies, valuables, or money were accompanied strikingly often with remarks on the procedure to be adopted for the visit or the purpose of the recipient's sojourn in the city. The gift account books were compiled not for lower officials but for the political leadership.[23]

The issue of who was authorized to make official gifts in the city's name, however, aroused heated conflicts in the towns of the late Middle Ages, and the written registration of municipal munificence reflects these power struggles just as the normative texts on gifts and giving did. If a 1401 ordinance in Sélestat authorized the mayor to make the ultimate decision about who would receive what gift in the city's name, despite the council members assigned to him for this purpose, we can assume that this was preceded by a struggle over just this competency. In the constitutional battles in Strasbourg at the end of the fourteenth century this same right of the highest municipal officer to make official gifts out of the town treasury became the subject of bitter disputes, and the reforms of the city's statutes between 1405 and 1433 place particular emphasis on this point. Henceforth no municipal officer could make gifts on his own authority. All officials were to submit their accounts to the council, and all municipal spending had to be recorded in the council books.[24] The meticulous written records of gifts, like the contemporaneous regulations concerning who should be given presents how and when, were thus no simple documentation of a "social practice." The documentation itself was produced by the conflict surrounding the control of these practices, and thus cannot be used as a neutral source for their sociability and their unifying circulation.

The Politics of Recording

Because of the richness and accessibility of the material, it is easy to regard municipal and private account books of the late Middle Ages as a direct, "realistic" point of entry to municipal administrative practice. Since accounts emerged from the immediate work of administration and were accessible only to a small circle, it is often argued that one can ignore the factors of historiographic intention and subjective choice.[25] To be sure, account books are a relatively objective source genre when compared to the oath formulas and political treatises or polemics of the fifteenth and sixteenth centuries. But just as late medieval inventories by no means list every single object in a household, account books also do not reflect the entirety of income and outlays. Only account-worthy items were registered, gaps were smoothed over, and care was taken that the figures added up at the end of every page.[26] A second qualification must be taken even more seriously. Who kept the account books, and who had access to them?

A municipal treatise of 1476 counts it among the chief duties of a mayor that he should receive all who visit his house "kindly and not entertain them too meagerly, to the honor of the city and his own good reputation."[27] Anyone who came should see how generous the city and its officials were. The written registration and counting of this generosity, however, occurred for the eyes of only a few select men. However publicly gifts may have been bestowed, gift bookkeeping was an affair carried on behind closed doors.[28] The extensive municipal government accounts in the archives have become so self-evidently available to scholarly readers since the nineteenth century that it is easy to forget that at the time when they were written (and long afterward as well) they were open only to a few members of powerful council committees and sworn clerks. The oaths sworn by town clerks and finance officers emphasized the duty of lifetime secrecy. In Basel, council members as well as municipal officials had to swear to maintain absolute secrecy about everything that was discussed or read out in the council that had to do with outlays and receipts. A council resolution of the late fifteenth century even set the penalty for breaking council secrecy at death by beheading; the subsequent stipulations of 1506 and 1521 are scarcely less ominous.[29] Municipal gifts were a secret matter; in the correspondence of the city of Nuremberg, for example, gifts to high-ranking advocates of the city at the imperial court and the identity of the recipients were cautiously shrouded in code. "We need more nails," the city's envoys wrote from Augsburg in April 1500, for example, and requested that 2,000 florins be sent as quickly as possible. They had "nailed down" the "blackbird" (the archbishop of Mainz) so successfully, they wrote a week later, that it had begun to sing quite sweetly.[30]

The accounts of the city of Basel used no such poetic code words but were written in perfectly plain language. They were, however, strictly official secrets and in their written form accessible only to a very small group within the council. Since the fourteenth century, the city's highest finance committee was the so-called Seven (five council members and two guild masters). In the mid-fifteenth century a new body, the Committee of Three, was established as a permanent organ of the financial administration, and it prepared the weekly, quarterly, and annual accounts. The Basel weekly and annual accounts that have come down to us are a selection compiled by the town clerk from the internal account books of the Committee of Three. They represent a carefully edited political overview of the city's finances with especially highlighted individual items produced expressly for justification purposes when it was read out at the close of accounts to the two municipal councils, whose members took an oath every year not to discuss municipal finances with anyone outside the council chambers.[31]

These accounts could be consulted only by a few influential councilors. The mayor, the administrative head of the guilds, members of the Committee of Three, and the town clerk compiled these weekly and yearly accounts, not only by manipulating figures, which were intended to influence council decisions, but also by the highlighted and accentuated details of which gifts were given to whom.[32] These municipal accounts are, above all, political texts that refer to particular concepts of "proper" gifts to the "proper" people. A German textbook for Italian merchants written in Venice in the first half of the fifteenth century pithily sums up the principles according to which this writing practice was organized: "El taser non se puo scrivere—silence cannot be written [down]."[33]

Municipal gifts were thus created in the first place by specialized registration, and the account books accordingly contain numerous extras and gifts to the clerks and officials who were responsible for keeping them. After the Imperial Diet held in Freiburg in 1498, which had yielded extensive gifts for the assembled dignitaries, the Basel town council rewarded the clerk delegated for this purpose with a substantial gift of money for his effort and labors in distributing presents.[34] What sort of gifts, then, did the city bestow, and according to what rules were they distributed?

Gifts of Wine as Municipal Legitimacy

In the fourteenth, fifteenth, and sixteenth centuries, as in present-day usage, the German verb *schencken* meant both to bestow a gift and to pour a liquid. When the word appears in the Basel municipal accounts, something was usually actually flowing; many of these municipal gifts were quite literally liquid. In 1517, Antonio de Beatis, secretary to Cardinal d'Aragona, noted in his account of a journey over the Alps and through southern Germany that in all the free imperial cities and the two Swiss cantons that the cardinal passed through, delegates of the authorities had called upon him and given him gifts of wine, bread, and fish. The same treatment was shown to all visiting secular and clerical dignitaries. Two generations later the manservant of another distinguished visitor described the procedure of this municipal munificence in more detail: "The council [of the city of Basel] did Messieurs de Estissac and de Montaigne the honor of sending one of their officials to welcome them with wine. This was accompanied by a long speech at table, to which Monsieur de Montaigne responded in another long address. During this whole time they stood bareheaded, in the presence of several Germans and Frenchmen who were dining with them. Their host served as interpreter. The wines there are very good."[35] What apparently mattered here was less the drink itself than its formal ceremonial bestowal: an everyday ritual that foreign travelers (or their employees) deemed worthy of preserving in writing.

We generally associate gifts—particularly in the form of alcoholic beverages—with personal, informal relationships. The gift wine of the early modern period was, above all, a political liquid. The role that wine and its demonstrative distribution and consumption played in the political self-representation of the late Middle Ages and the early modern period awaits detailed study.[36] For all the symbolic functions of gift wine (to which we will return later), its primary role was economic. As in other cities of the Upper Rhine, in Basel the excise tax on wine, together with the grain or mill tax, was the most important source of income for the municipal treasury. If one adds fees and customs duties from the wine trade, one could say that in the late Middle Ages the city was financed to no small degree by the wine whose cost it inflated at the expense of the consumer. In contemporary perceptions this may have further intensified the effect and taste of municipal liquid offerings.[37]

Wine gifts were also inextricably linked with the demonstration of political legitimacy. No formal political event took place at which wine was not present—the Basel authorities served wine not only to foreign visitors but above all to themselves. The Basel accounts for wine gifts document liquid presents for council meals in the banqueting halls *zum Sufftzen* and *zum Brunnen*,[38] in the houses and halls of the increasingly influential Basel guilds, to officials during the inspection of the salt stores, and to the town crossbowmen.[39] Gifts of wine accompanied the visits of council committees to the city's abbeys, meetings at the town hall,[40] the completion of accounts regarding the municipal salt supply, as well as consultations between the mayor and guild masters with delegates from other cities. Gifts of wine to the *Stuben* (meeting places of the local elite), guildhalls and above all to the ruling municipal *houpter* (lords) were an expression of increased political display and ritual regulation. The council of neighboring Freiburg im Breisgau made this very clear in an ordinance of 1501, which stipulated that after the election of the mayor councilors had not only to accompany the new officeholder to the patrician *Stube*, but also to remain there during the distribution of his wine gifts and not go home beforehand because to do so would detract from the reputation of their office.[41] The presentation of gifts of council wine was not necessarily a simple sign of merry sociability, but rather entailed obligatory attendance.

Wine gifts represented legitimacy, and the carefully orchestrated distribution of pitchers of municipal wine accordingly accompanied the city's central political ceremonies on St. John's Day, when the council was formally elected. The gift ordinance of 1477 stipulates that for the annual installation of the council and mayor four jugs of wine were to be sent to the episcopal court on the cathedral hill. Additional pitchers were sent to the mayor and guild masters and a whole series of further liquid gifts to the various guild houses, where the newly elected were received and entertained.[42] When the councilors went up to the town hall after the actual election process, two pitchers of wine were carried behind each of them; they were sent four more jugs of council wine for the round of drinks and the meal that took place on the following Sunday morning.[43] It was literally the gift wine that made the official. Finally, with all this ritual drinking, the council ordinance of 1506 also took the consequences into consideration: "Furthermore, if it comes to pass during the council session that one of the councilors needs to go into the courtyard to make water," he should return afterward to his proper place in the council chamber and not retire to one of the back benches to nap.[44]

Political Liquids

The role of these gifts of wine in the city's own rituals of display provided the framework when, under the heading of *Schenkwein* (Gift Wine), the amounts of wine presented to various people were read out to members of the two Basel councils every Wednesday. In the week of June 24 to July 1, 1452, for example, recipients included messengers from the city of Cologne, traveling officials such as the Strasbourg mayor (*Ammeister*), local officials, and two Basel guild masters who had returned from a journey.[45] Standardized figures were mentioned, which were calculated according to the price per pitcher: In the 1450s this was always 64 pfennigs or some multiple thereof, a decade later 80 pfennigs, and so forth.[46] The number of jugs presented depended upon the rank of the visitor and the occasion. The detailed list of how much wine the council should give on which occasion, which was compiled in 1477, stipulates, for example, that a man who had just earned his baccalaureate at the

University of Basel should receive two pitchers of wine from the city, a *magister* four (the same number offered to the bishop when he was in the city), and a new doctor of philosophy eight jugs—exactly the same number due to a papal orator.[47] The rector of the university was also officially honored with council wine when he gave his inaugural banquet; similarly, other of the city's clerical institutions were presented with wine on various occasions.[48] The city also gave wine to its citizens: gifts of one or two pitchers of wine to high-ranking persons as an official token of condolence upon the death of a family member appear in the records beginning with the early 1470s. Similarly, the council sent a guild master two jugs of wine on the marriage of his son or described the gift more generally as congratulations on a wedding or the birth of a child.[49] In late November 1496, the citizen Hans Kilchmann was greeted on his safe return from a pilgrimage with several gifts of council wine.[50] Famous scholars also received gifts of wine: on November 16, 1521, the weekly account book for expenses mentions 160 pfennigs for wine for the reception of *herrn Erasmo Roterodamo*.[51]

When the visitor was of especially high rank, the value of the wine was expressed not in pitchers but in casks at varying prices. In 1471 a papal legate received an entire cask as an honorary gift; that same year councilors of the duke of Burgundy who traveled through Basel received a tun of wine worth 1,724 pfennigs.[52] The names on the gift wine lists compiled for presentation in council always carried current political undertones. Intensified diplomatic relations in the early 1470s with Basel's menacing new neighbor, Burgundy, found expression in these lists. On Whit Saturday 1473, for example, the Basel council hastened to present the father confessor of Charles the Bold with two pitchers of wine when he passed through town. The council lists continued to reflect the city's role in the war against the Burgundians in the years that followed. In January 1477, before the battle of Nancy, Basel presented the Swiss troops who were marching through with 120 jugs of wine.[53] The internal Swiss holiday and visiting diplomacy with its extensive gifts of wine, into which Basel entered after 1501, can be traced in the gift wine accounts, as can a formal ritual gift of wine to a cardinal who passed through Basel in 1520.[54]

These visitors in official functions made up the largest proportion of names on the lists of wine gifts. They were almost exclusively male, with women appearing only rarely.[55] Pitchers of council wine accompanied every appearance of the bishop within the city walls. The list of council gifts that was maintained after 1477 stipulated that every time he rode into the city or appeared personally before the council he should receive four jugs of wine.[56] However precarious the bishop's political power in the city, he was presented with wine on every conceivable occasion, so that "our gracious lord of Basel," as the accounts for 1515 called him, was the individual most frequently mentioned in the gift wine lists of the fifteenth and early sixteenth centuries. Despite residing outside the city, the Basel bishops themselves were strikingly involved in municipal rituals even in the late fifteenth century, such as the memorial banquet held for the late mayor of Basel in the council hall in 1470.[57] On Shrove Tuesday, 1504, Bishop Christoph von Utenheim sent several casks of Alsatian wine, malmsey, and game to a holiday delegation from Zurich, an expensive and not wholly voluntary gift—at any rate not according to a contemporary polemical letter penned by the Alsatian humanist Jakob Wimpfeling.[58]

In Basel, as in other cities of the Upper Rhine and Switzerland, the dispatching of municipal gifts to their recipients was generally the job of the town guards. In the fifteenth century their oath of office expressly bound them to deliver exactly the wine entrusted to them to precisely the persons named: they were paid extra for this task and could also expect a tip from the recipient.[59] Who, in which function, and on which occasion, was considered worthy of this municipal wine could vary considerably. An ordinance on gifts of wine that was entered into the council's Little White Book in 1457 states that gentlemen or messengers passing through should only receive council wine once per journey and not every time they stopped in Basel during the same trip. Officers of the surrounding territories who traveled through Basel on their own business rather than in an official capacity were not to receive wine at all, except for officials of the Austrian and Württemberg territories, with which Basel wished to remain on especially friendly terms.[60]

The gifts presented by the city also differed greatly according to whether the visitor's role was official or private. The Strasbourg authorities, for example, relied on the duty of hosts to provide information in order to discover whether visitors to the city were there in an official capacity or "on their own business." Only in the former case was wine sent to them in municipal pitchers in the name of the city.[61] The municipal gift in any case clearly marked whether someone entered the city in a private or official capacity.

These gifts of wine were presented in specially made pewter pitchers bearing the municipal coat of arms, which were returned to the city when empty. Their number could be quite substantial: the 1464 inventory of housewares and kitchen crockery from the Nuremberg town hall mentions 200 large wine jugs with bases decorated with the municipal coat of arms. The Basel wine pitchers also bore the city arms, and the municipal accounts note numerous outlays for their cleaning, repair and replacement.[62] To modern ears "pewter pitchers" sound rather banal, but in the perception and cost calculations of the fifteenth and sixteenth centuries the city sent its gifts of wine in valuable objects for whose prestigious material it spent its own money.[63] After the extensive banquets and receptions that marked the city's ceremonial entry into the Swiss Confederacy and the subsequent inventory, the town clerk noted with some resignation in the weekly account book on March 18, 1502, the item of 312 pfennigs for two such municipal vessels: they ended up missing when the city went Swiss and bestowed gifts upon its new Swiss confederates.[64]

The replacement of lost pitchers may have been an extra cost for municipal generosity, but even the normal expenses for all these liquid gifts could reach heady proportions. An entry in the Basel council's ordinance book for summer 1503 notes that presents of wine entailed substantial costs, which in the long run could not be financed out of public funds. For that reason the council resolved that in the future the city would no longer bestow wine on anyone who came to the city on his own business rather than as an official representative of some authority, with the exception of pilgrims and merchants on their way to the Frankfurt fair from towns allied with Basel.[65] A further entry of July 1503 states more precisely that municipal wine should be given first of all to persons of high rank to whom the city wished to show its goodwill: "Men of honor, whom the city can enjoy."[66]

Eloquent Objects: Fish, Drinking Vessels, Liquid Money

The boundaries between persons and gifts seem to disappear in the words of the Basel council—who attained enjoyment by giving what gifts to whom?—but wine was only one element of the municipal gifts mentioned in the council accounts. On St. John's Day in 1469, for example, the council heard of the outlay of 30,456 pfennigs for the wine, bread, *and other things* given to the troops of the Swiss Confederacy—rather threatening guests in this case, who marched past the city on their way to plunder Alsace—along with the costs for wine and fish presented to the margrave of Baden and his son (to the tune of 10,476 pfennigs).[67] In the late Middle Ages, an edible fish was a prestigious, rather expensive, and accordingly effective present.

In the course of the 1450s, an additional column appeared in Basel's annual municipal accounts. Under the heading "bestowed" (*verschenckt*), this rubric summarized outlays for those gifts that had nothing to do with wine. The category became increasingly detailed and voluminous with the years and was compiled from the weekly and quarterly accounts.[68] In this rubric the mayors and guild masters presented to the assembled councilors what they wished to portray as extraordinary municipal generosity. The annual accounts for 1439-40, for example, proudly detailed what the recently elected pope, Felix V, received upon his solemn entry into the city. Apart from the equivalent of 340 liters of wine he and his son received a precious object costing 102 florins, or some 28,400 pfennigs.[69] The orchestrations of the visits of princes, like the contemporary chroniclers of these entrances, place the publicly bestowed silver or golden vessel, the centerpiece of municipal gifts, at the heart of the ceremony. When Frederick III entered Basel on September 3, 1473, the council presented him with a gilded silver goblet, one hundred sacks of oats, and fifteen casks of wine.[70] In these rituals, the ceremonial drink and cash underwent a marriage of a peculiar kind because the gilded or silver bowls for the emperor and his son were filled with gold coins—1,000 for Frederick and 500 for his son, the Basel chronicler Knebel tells us. In a manner of speaking, the city offered the ruler potable cash.[71]

It would appear logical to read the fixed gifts of wine and oats that the late medieval cities presented so visibly to arriving princes as the core of the ritual, a legal tradition and "residue" of older municipal obligations to offer hospitality, and to understand transfers in cash as their monetarized, stunted form, and German legal history has long done so.[72] In a sense, the Basel council itself said something similar in its internal records of 1477, when it stipulated that a visiting prince should receive a cask of wine and eight sacks of oats, a papal legate the same, a papal orator eight jugs of wine, and so forth, according to the "old custom," as the entry assures us.[73]

On closer inspection, however, this "old custom" turns out to have been quite flexible. During Maximilian's repeat visit to Basel in 1493, he received grain, several casks of wine, and a drinking vessel of respectable size, this time containing only 400 Rhenish gold coins, however.[74] Measured against the expenses for the goblet plus its contents, the Basel council managed to find a rather cheap means of maintaining the alleged old custom. The wine presented to Maximilian in 1493 cost the city treasury less than 6,800 pfennigs, while the drinking vessel cost 40,870, plus the 400 florins inside it (110,400 pfennigs by the official exchange rate). The gift ordinance of 1477, however, does not mention the silver or gilded goblets at all. There was no "old custom" concerning the size and extent of the truly expensive gift. The Basel town council, like that of neighboring cities, decided from case to case what was necessary in order to "enjoy the men of honor." When Charles V arrived in Augsburg for the Imperial Diet in 1530, the Augsburg council presented him with not one but three gilded drinking bowls filled with 2,000 new Augsburg florins and covered with a silk cloth in the city colors. He also received two *Eimer* (a vessel holding about 90 liters) of red wine and two tubs of fish. The official council memorandum on these gifts places great emphasis on the fact that, in contrast to earlier visits, the emperor was the only person to receive money in bowls. In the final paragraph of the ordinance, the Augsburg council also noted that so much had changed recently in the giving of gifts that the authorities should be permitted to increase or decrease the city's official munificence as they saw fit; presents constantly needed to be adapted to new conditions.[75]

The combination of goblet and wine was, incidentally, not reserved for the monarch. In the course of the fifteenth century, this combination became the usual form assumed by formal diplomatic gifts. The annual accounts for 1483–84 mention spending 90 florins on a goblet presented to Duke Sigismund of Austria, which was filled with an additional three hundred florins. Augsburg also gave similar coin-filled goblets, together with wine and fish, to the Bavarian dukes, with whom the city maintained the same volatile relations as Basel did with the Habsburgs.[76] Drinking vessels of precious metals were ceremonially presented to lesser dignitaries as well. When the municipal accounts were read out on St. John's Day in 1472, the Basel councilors were informed that the city had honored the newly installed Burgundian bailiff of the neighboring provinces, Peter von Hagenbach, with a small silver tankard with a lid worth 23 florins (about 6,350 pfennigs at the official exchange rate).[77] A similar offering to an influential outsider whose goodwill the Basel town council hoped to ensure appears in the accounts for 1503–4. In this case, the recipient was the Bern town clerk and council jurist Thüring Fricker, to whom the Baselers gave a goblet valued at 50 florins, or 12,000 pfennigs.[78]

Such vessels were representative gifts in the literal sense, splendid presentation objects of aristocratic and urban wealth, and they were displayed on specially made stands at noble feasts and receptions, as municipal council silver, in combination with relics such as the Basel cathedral treasures, or as a demonstration of patrician wealth, as the chronicle of the barons von Zimmern emphasized in a famous description of the wedding silver of the patrician Wasserfaß family in Cologne.[79] These goblets or bowls of precious metal speak eloquently of their own worth. The silver goblets or tankards were intended not only to announce their value but also to say something about the persons involved, and to do so as explicitly as possible. Many of these bowls were ornately marked as gifts. The Basel bishop Johannes von Venningen notes in the income side of his household account book that he received forty florins in a silver goblet from the convent of Klingenthal, which had been embellished for this purpose with the arms of his family and his bishopric.[80] Basel too made an effort to label its costly gifts appropriately for the occasion. The annual accounts for 1504–5 note not only the price for the silver goblet that the city bestowed upon the papal legate Peraudi—an expensive piece worth 14,592 pfennigs—but also the fee of the goldsmith who personalized it.[81]

These careful marks did not prevent the goblets—in either contemporary perception or economic practice—from being made liquid again, both literally and figuratively. Inventories and household account books generally note their weight in silver or gold, and some pieces have the weight of the valuable metal engraved inside the lid or under the base.[82]

In the practical esteem of the late Middle Ages, all that glittered was, in a sense, gold, but enormous improvements in silver-plating and gilding techniques at the end of the fifteenth century increasingly challenged this equation. Beginning in the second half of the 1480s, municipal ordinances frequently warned of false silver-plated and gilded objects *aus abentheurer*, as the ordinances refer to them (literally, "of adventure")—that is, made of dubious and inferior materials—that were so cunningly worked that even goldsmiths took them for silver.[83] Were the demonstratively proffered silver or gilded goblets really worth as much as they appeared to be? In his diary for March 1491, the Florentine chronicler Luca Landucci describes the triumphal entry into the city of the son of Lorenzo de' Medici, who had just been invested as cardinal. On his way to mass at Santa Maria del Fiore, the signoria presented him with a gift of silver dishes, including goblets, bowls, plates, and basins, which it took thirty men to carry. Landucci reports that they were valued at more than 20,000 florins, although he considered this improbable (he did not think well of the Medici). The claim had been made *per publica voce e fama*, however, and for that reason he recorded it.[84]

North of the Alps these opulent gift giving ceremonies tended to be described with less ironic undertones, but their effect was similar: what counted was the demonstrative presentation of the precious and costly object. For the great majority of urban spectators, the value of the large silver goblets or drinking vessels that the city bestowed upon high-ranking visitors represented several years' work. Such a silver bowl was literally old age insurance, the aim of a lifetime of saving and a successful economic foundation. It was no mere abstract luxury item, but rather proclaimed its value so loudly that one could not always tell whether it was genuine.

Elastic Traditions and Ominous Offers

Whether the offering in question consisted of wine, costly fish, or gleaming vessels, the account books and detailed descriptions of such extravagant presents in chronicles or council memoranda inform us in retrospect about successful gifts. Sources on the preparations for gift giving rituals themselves are rather scarce. The city archive of Freiburg im Breisgau preserves a large paper brochure bound in parchment and written in the hand of the town clerk, Jakob Mennel, that was dedicated to the 1498 Imperial Diet, which was held in the city. Mennel not only recorded the negotiations and their results but also offered an equally thorough account of the Freiburg town council's preparations for the meeting.[85] They were intended to ensure that the common good of the city would be increased and promoted in the face of such numerous and noble guests.[86] In its argumentation, Austrian Freiburg was indistinguishable from the neighboring free or imperial cities. The town clerk was concerned with the key concept of urban self-understanding, the common good (*gemein gut*), a term he cites twice in his preface.

How did Freiburg prepare for its illustrious guests? In a first bundle of measures, the town council sought to secure reasonable prices for food and services for those attending the Imperial Diet. Security was a second concern. The numbers of guards in the city towers and nightly patrols were increased, and the city gates were closed at night and equipped with a special sentry for each (which apparently was not normally the case). The entire population was admonished, under pain of penalties, not to use any unseemly or angry words toward courtiers or other persons, "either secretly or openly." Finally, the council set down formal regulations on gift giving, which stipulated the exact size of gifts for the king and queen, the electors, the dukes of Bavaria and Wurttemberg, the margraves of Baden and Brandenburg-Ansbach, and the archbishops and bishops who were expected to attend.[87]

At the same time, the mayor and the head of the guilds were given the right to increase or decrease these gifts as circumstances required, and a number of amendments explain why. Duke George of Baden, for example, was to receive a whole rather than a half tun of wine and double the stipulated amount of oats because he was an intimate of the queen's and had great influence over her. Count Heinrich von Fürstenberg, too, was to receive gifts not simply in his role as marshal. He was also to be honored with special attentions because of the city's particularly close relationship with him—but this should occur in secret. The city also began to maintain a separate gift register.[88]

Finally, the town clerk provided extensive descriptions of the entries of dignitaries into the city at which he himself had been present. When the bishops of Würzburg and Eichstätt arrived in the city on June 2, he was there to meet them together with the mayor and master of the guilds and to offer them eight pitchers of wine. Mennel not only confidently writes "I," but also repeats the lengthy and carefully phrased greetings with which he handed the jugs to the bishops and provides their replies verbatim, not without an unmistakable pride in his own role in this ceremony.[89] Here the notes of the industrious clerk end. Because of other pressing business, he was unable to participate in the reception of further dignitaries, he states with obvious regret. The man who so precisely recorded the elaborate ceremonial language of the gift transfers and signed the transcripts self-importantly "Jacob Menel [*sic*] of Bregenz, at present town clerk" did not remain in the service of Freiburg. Two years after the Imperial Diet, he became chief secretary to the grand prior of the Knights of Malta in Heitersheim; from there he managed the leap to the court at Vienna. During the Imperial Diet he had handed Maximilian a learned treatise on the usefulness of chess; in 1503 he once again dedicated a work to the emperor, this time an illustrated book on prodigies and miracles. Beginning in 1505 Maximilian employed him as a historian and genealogist, and against bitter competition he became an influential specialist on the glorious and apocryphal ancestry of the imperial dynasty, a remarkable scholarly career.[90]

Jakob Mennel and his rise demonstrate not only that gifts functioned as a central element of municipal self-representation in the political practice of late medieval cities, but also that the figure of the presenter and intermediary played a special role here—especially since the Freiburg town clerk united two functions in his person, the written registration of municipal gifts and their ceremonial distribution. The description of these ritual gifts as urban "tradition" or "custom" is at any rate insufficient. The municipal authorities of the late Middle Ages were always only as traditional as appeared expedient to them. The form was elastic: gifts were fixed politically, not ritually. The cities' investments in gifts refer in an almost ironic manner to entertaining with wine, in the form of drinking vessels and potable money. The liquid remains present, more strongly than we are aware of when we skim over the word *geschenckt* (given and poured).

In 1495, three years before the ceremonies Mennel described, the Freiburg town council decided to give a gift to Junker Hans Han, bailiff of the city, because he had obtained full confirmation of the city's rights and freedoms from King Maximilian at the Imperial Diet in Worms; for this service he was to receive twelve florins. Han resisted. He ultimately accepted the money, not as a gift, but as compensation for unnamed valuables destroyed in a fire in Worms. He appears expressly to have refused any further presents.[91] Not everyone could—or wished to—accept every gift.

Such news of presents that misfired or were refused are rare indeed.[92] Despite the municipal rhetoric of "old customs," there were no fixed tariffs regarding how expensive a gift had to be in order to be useful to the city in a given instance. The question was decided differently by the city authorities from case to case. In Basel on September 9, 1482, the council records noted that it had been resolved to give Duke Philip of Savoy an "honorable reception" upon his arrival, including a gift of eight pitchers of wine, six sacks of oats, and a salmon. The council was plainly not quite certain of the proper amount in this case, because the clerk scratched out the original figure of six jugs and increased it to eight.[93]

The Freiburg records reveal not only similar political adaptations of the "traditional" rules (and the secrecy surrounding the reasons for them), but also, with their extensive security measures, reflect an uncertainty of another kind that overshadowed municipal rituals and princely visits. The visiting dignitary may have accepted the city's gifts gratefully, but how gratefully and politely were the armed horsemen who entered the city along with him likely to have behaved? We catch a glimpse of this problem in a note in the Basel annual accounts for 1454–55, which states that the city had been compelled to spend 1,536 pfennigs to replace table linen and bowls lost after a visit by the duke of Burgundy.[94] Less harmless was the visit to Augsburg in June 1470 of the newly elected bishop Johann von Werdenberg. The day before his formal entry Werdenberg informed the Augsburg town council that, contrary to his earlier announcements, he would take office accompanied by 1,800 armed horsemen. The Augsburg chronicler Hektor Mülich describes the hasty preparations for the visit that ensued. Within half a day, all of the side streets leading to the agreed route had been barricaded, the gates, guild houses, and public buildings had been occupied by armed men, and the reception committee had been issued suits of armor. Neither men, women, nor children were permitted on the streets, the mayor Ulrich Schwarz added in his chronicle, because "We were afraid." While the city's highest officials welcomed the visitors outside the city walls, the city gates were closed behind them, just in case, and they hastily had the bishop take an oath on a mandate listing the conditions for his visit. When Werdenberg finally rode into the city, accompanied by two Bavarian dukes, the bishop of Eichstätt, and more than 2,000 horsemen, his route through the town was demonstratively lined with armed men and all but two of the city gates were kept closed for the two days of the visit.

However worried and fearful Augsburg may have been, as Schwarz writes, the liquid gifts flowed in streams. During the visit more than 900 quarts of Italian wine were distributed, the chroniclers report, and the bishop received a gilded drinking bowl worth 100 florins that was filled with 200 florins in coins. The two accompanying dukes were given similar coin-filled drinking vessels, along with wine and fish, and the newly installed bishop and his armed men departed without incident. In this case, the gift bestowed upon the bishop had a special meaning. It was so valuable because, as both chroniclers report, he had recently interceded on the city's behalf in a conflict with Duke Ludwig of Bavaria. The drinking bowl was Werdenberg's gift as the new bishop, while the 200 florins inside were a reward for his services as an intermediary, as was the money presented to the dukes who accompanied him, and Schwarz comments sarcastically: "What good they did only God knows."[95]

The surprise attack on the free imperial city of Mainz by its bishop in 1462 was still fresh in the minds of the South German cities. Behind the polite rituals of municipal gift giving, we catch a glimpse of something else: the carefully orchestrated threat that such a visit could also take an altogether different (and very violent) course. This threat in turn combined the blunt and unrefusable demand for suitable payment of intermediary services with a demonstration of political power within the city walls.[96] The Augsburg notables themselves regarded the gifts that the city was compelled to offer during the visit of the bishop and his companions as the settlement of a political debt. In addition to the cash and the gilded vessels presented to the princes, the city had to provide their entourage with wine and fish, complained Ulrich Schwarz, who thought that the city paid all too dearly. Not only the costs but also the risks of such a transfer were too high.[97]

It is doubtful that Mayor Schwarz's advice about gifts fell on receptive ears. We will meet him and the silver goblets again later. The accounts of the Freiburg Imperial Diet of 1498 and the bishop's visit to Augsburg in 1470 should, however, encourage us to view rituals in the late medieval and early modern cities, with their somewhat pompous apparatus of compliments and honors, as more than just legal traditions and prestigious displays that functioned quasi-automatically. These displays also represented a constantly renegotiated balancing act between reluctant and sometimes rather uncooperative participants, who emphatically (and menacingly) reminded the other side that they could act quite differently if they chose.

Pronouncements: Adventurers, Heralds, and Political Music

At the beginning of this work, I noted that every gift involves more than two parties. In the cities of southern Germany and the Upper Rhine at the end of the Middle Ages, gifts were legitimate in the eyes of contemporaries because they were presented before an audience in the form of those publicly proffered offerings of wine and money we dealt with in the previous sections, as well as being announced as official *schenck* by being read aloud to the town council. The gifts mentioned in the Basel municipal accounts were linked as closely as possible with relationships to the outside. Beginning in the 1450s, the costs of gifts were noted at the head of the account sheets with the outlays for council correspondence and administration and read out together to document the council's activities. Their presentation placed them emphatically at the center of urban self-stylization—and, as we will see in what follows, municipal information policy as well.

The dignitaries upon whom such official municipal gifts were bestowed occupied various noble ranks. The Basel annual account for 1470–71, for example, notes a gift of six florins to a gentleman from Constantinople; "further, 1 florin to a Greek" was recorded in the annual account two years before. The long list of gifts to ambassadors, noblemen, musicians, and heralds during the past fiscal year was summarized for the councilors in the annual account: "bestowed upon all manner of gentlemen and adventurers" a total of 83,703 pfennigs.[98]

Fifteenth-century political treatises pragmatically registered such outlays under what we would nowadays call public relations: learned men, merchants, and travelers should be honored and provided with gifts, admonished the widely disseminated treatises on princely education. This promoted one's "good reputation in foreign lands and also at home."[99] Municipal gifts to such exotic dignitaries and picturesque travelers were not always simply alms to the needy or pilgrims. The Basel weekly record of outlays for February 20, 1473, mentions the gift of one florin in gold to a knight who had been a prisoners of the Turks, and one month later, on March 20, it notes that a foreign nobleman from Negrapont had been presented with 240 pfennigs. The city did not have that kind of money for the ordinary poor.[100] Befitting his duty as a merciful prince of the church, in July 1468 the bishop of Basel also gave 24 pfennigs in alms to a man making the pilgrimage to Jerusalem who claimed that he had been robbed. In March 1470, in contrast, the bishop mentions having given one florin (more than ten times as much) to an old man passing himself off as a herald of the pope in Rome, although he actually hailed from a village on Lake Constance.[101]

Amusing performances were apparently rewarded along with the spectacular and miraculous. When in the spring of 1471 the Basel accounts mention that a learned boy had been given one florin, we may assume that the wunderkind put on some sort of show for the town council, a sample of his talents, like the nameless *astronimo* a year later upon whom the council bestowed one gold florin.[102] Other travelers were offered money for what they did not show, like the woman "without female attributes" who received 120 pfennigs from the city fathers. What did "Hanns Trittherfúr (literally 'Jack Stepforward') the sorceror," who appears in the annual accounts for 1487-88, show the council? It must have been pretty convincing because he received 2,400 pfennigs, the equivalent of one hundred days' wages for a journeyman tailor, while two mendicant monks mentioned in the same section of the accounts managed to garner only 240 pfennigs.[103]

It might seem appropriate to describe these quaint strangers as traveling folk or vagrants and to consider them part of the large group of late medieval and early modern "marginal groups," but I would recommend caution here. The information about these people in the account books is very sparse. The Basel accounts mention the exotic knights, astrologers, and sorcerors not as curiosities but rather as worthy recipients of the city's munificence, who were accordingly registered and presented officially when the accounts were read aloud. If gifts of money to picturesque strangers and exotic dignitaries became less frequent in the weekly and annual accounts around 1500, this was a result of changes in the means of conveying information, and this change becomes particularly clear when we examine the role of heralds and musicians as recipients of official gifts.

In the detailed list in the Basel council records of the gifts given to Emperor Frederick III and his entourage during his 1473 visit, the presents to the imperial chancellery and various servants are followed by the substantial sum of four florins for the herald Kilian.[104] Heralds were not simply court experts in heraldry and ceremony, but also, under Frederick III and Maximilian, increasingly came to be used as diplomatic go-betweens and specialist messengers.[105] They thus traveled not only with the emperor, but also alone, like their colleagues from the Austrian, Württemberg, and other princely courts. The Basel town council accounts mention them as the recipients of official gifts according to a standard tariff, usually one florin in gold. The same sum went to the envoys whose name sounds so much less impressive, and who appear in the records as *gokelmann* (buffoon) or *parcifal* (knight errant).[106]

This nominally fixed gift of gold indeed changed in character in the final third of the fifteenth century. Beginning in 1473, all princely heralds or knights errant received only silver gifts from the city, no matter which princely name they bore.[107] In the years immediately preceding and during the Swabian War, gifts to imperial envoys decreased rapidly; after Basel's entry into the system of the Swiss Confederacy in 1501 they disappear from the accounts altogether.[108] During the first two decades of the sixteenth century gifts to heralds and specialists in coats of arms occasionally appear in the accounts, but without specifying their political connections; it was apparently no longer of interest for the names of their lords to be read out to the town councilors.[109]

The lines between the spoken presentation of knights errant, heralds, and traveling court poets and the performances of court musicians were fluid in the fifteenth century. Throughout the Middle Ages, gifts to musicians were the classic demonstrations of official generosity, and the sums mentioned in connection with them are often strikingly high.[110] At the Regensburg Imperial Diet of 1471, the Basel bishop Johann von Venningen gave more than twelve florins to imperial and princely musicians, among other gifts, even though the Basel chaplain Johannes Knebel considered him a thrifty gentleman; other chroniclers mockingly called him *Johannes de Pfenningen* (John of the Pfennigs), and to judge by his household accounts he was anything but a spendthrift.[111] Venningen also proved generous to minstrels under other less spectacular circumstances, but he did not give indiscriminately. While the piper of the counts of Katzenellenbogen received a mere 144 pfennigs from him in 1459, in February 1464 he was prepared to give almost four times as much—two florins or 552 pfennigs—to the piper of the count palatine, with whom he and his family were closely allied politically.[112]

The Basel town council also splurged on gifts for princely minstrels: it is no accident that the accounts read to the council especially highlight gifts of gold coins. In the fifteenth century, the florin was not just any coin; it was sharply distinguished from the smaller silver or copper and silver coins. It was its own, particularly durable, and valuable kind of money. In the second half of the fifteenth century the purity and exchange rate of silver coins circulating in the Upper Rhine region fell dramatically in some cases, and owners of silver money had to pay increasingly high fees to exchange it into florins. There was a very real difference between receiving a sum of money in florins or in the official equivalent of silver coins. Town councilors and high-ranking officials of the city of Basel made sure that they were paid in gold coins that would retain their value.[113] The florin *in gold*, which the city bestowed upon the trumpeters of the margrave of Baden on December 19, 1472 was thus worth a good deal more than the official exchange rate of 276 Basel pfennigs—and a qualified Basel journeyman artisan had to work at least ten days (and a maid-servant nearly a month) for even that sum. This may help us better to appreciate the five florins that the city gave the count palatine's pipers for their performance on February 6, 1473—no small sum, and demonstratively bestowed in the much coveted gold coinage.[114]

The conspicuous golden gifts that the city gave to heralds and musicians from certain courts in the early 1470s, and above all in 1473 and 1474, were thus demonstrative diplomatic investments.[115] They were part of Basel's integration into the coalition system directed against Burgundy. In 1473 the city borrowed an unusual amount of money and used it to buy large stocks of grain, muskets, and gunpowder and to recruit mercenaries and military commanders.[116] In fiscal year 1474-75, the city presented the count palatine's pipers with six florins and the imperial trumpeters with four (both times in gold) on the occasion of the campaign to Neuss. A year later pipers in the service of the dukes of Austria and the margraves of Baden were honored with gold coins.[117]

Gifts and war were rather closely allied. After the coalition victory over Charles the Bold in 1477, the golden gifts to both musicians and heralds disappeared, suddenly and virtually completely, from the Basel account books. Total outlays for gifts fell substantially, and their bestowal was more tightly and restrictively organized by the gift ordinance of 1477.[118] Henceforth musicians received their gifts in cheap silver coins and at falling rates.[119] When the Basel town council stipulated in 1477 that musicians from other cities should be given gifts according to where they came from, this had less to do with the geographical than with the political situation. Were relations between Basel and the other city such that they gave each others' musicians gifts? Like heralds, all of these musicians were sign bearers in the literal sense of the term. Dressed in the colors of their lords or cities and frequently equipped with special coats of arms (*schilten*), they unmistakably marked political alliances.[120]

Throughout the Middle Ages, moralizing authors used the topos of gifts to itinerants and musicians as false and pointless openhandedness, and in his 1498 novel-cum-treatise on statecraft, *Agatharchia*, the humanist Jakob Wimpfeling could point to long lists of old authorities when he warned against excessive gifts to *histriones et pantomimi*.[121] The increasing regulation and restriction of these gifts to traveling musicians is quite evident.[122] It is fitting in this context that the Basel council, which in 1476 had still permitted its own musicians to play for foreigners, resolved in 1498 that only minstrels from the Swiss Confederacy could play at the town hall in order to receive gifts. On the eve of the Swabian War between the Confederates and the Austrian Empire, this regulation carried a clearly political flavor.[123] When the city joined the Swiss Confederacy in 1501, the Basel Committee of Three did its best to ensure that readings from the weekly and annual accounts to the assembled Greater Council would contain above all gifts to musicians of Swiss origin, a policy that played an indispensable role in inner-Swiss ceremonial diplomacy; presents to minstrels from abroad became significantly less frequent. In 1511 and 1514 Basel dismissed its own municipal pipers and council trumpeters.[124] When musicians appear in the accounts their places of origin are not mentioned, and the amounts of money offered as presents are lower.[125] The compilers of the Basel accounts found musicians increasingly less suitable for presentation to the assembled councilors as recipients of municipal munificence.

It is not a question of "marginal groups" here (even if some entries in the accounts contain at least overtones of the classic definition of alms), but of representation and display. While heralds, reciters, and musicians played an important role in the fourteenth and fifteenth centuries in the spectacular pronouncement and visualization of diplomatic presence—the municipal trumpeters, in particular, appeared as a sort of acoustic heraldry, loud and clear symbols of municipal jurisdiction and genuine power—they increasingly lost this function at the end of the fifteenth century and with the beginning of the age of printed mandates and pamphlets. But if these traveling communications experts appear in the gift registers ever more seldom and with gifts of declining value, which communication media took their place?

Part of their role was taken over by the diplomacy of holiday visits in which Basel became integrated after its entry into the Swiss Confederacy. We have already heard about the military pomp of the visitors from Zurich on Shrove Tuesday in 1504 and the mixed feelings of the Alsatian Jakob Wimpfeling, who remained loyal to the emperor. The Basel town council records devote a detailed description to a similar Shrovetide visit, the playful abduction of a straw man known as *Fritschi*, allegedly the oldest citizen of Lucerne, by Baselers in 1507 and its recapture and return by a large festive party from Lucerne and delegations from Uri and Schwyz in 1508.[126] According to the records, the visit cost the city of Basel 199,344 pfennigs or some 650 florins, including around 170 florins for wine and fish. The city spent a further 37 florins for gifts to messengers, minstrels, and jugglers.[127] The municipal gifts to local and outside marksmen, who played a significant role in these festivities and were the subject of extensive descriptions by the chroniclers of the participating towns, also belong in this context.[128]

Directly following Basel's entry into the Swiss Confederacy, a new group of municipal gifts appears in the Basel accounts. On January 15, 1502, the scribe notes that "a clerk named Tielen received a gift of 900 pfennigs for a window"; 720 pfennigs went to Mayor (*Ammann*) Wagner from Schwyz for the same purpose, and on February 5 the provincial clerk (*Landschreiber*) of Underwalden received 720 pfennigs for such a glass window, or rather, for the presentation of the Basel coat of arms as a window pane.[129] The Basel coat of arms was not intended to adorn churches alone. The annual accounts for 1502–3 mention two such municipal presents of 720 and 873 pfennigs respectively for windows in Zurich taverns, and this was only the beginning of an uninterrupted series of such gifts.[130] These window gifts were not random; the sum was standardized at between 720 and 900 pfennigs, without any apparent fundamental distinction between the Basel coats of arms on the windows of churches or taverns.[131]

The window gifts, analogous to other obvious religious investments, which contemporaries interpreted politically, were quite literally illuminated political advertising. Around 1500 they began, together with the marksmen as bearers of municipal symbolism and the Swiss custom of ceremonial visits on holidays such as Shrovetide, to take the place of gifts to picturesque diplomats, heralds, and traveling musicians. The official gifts presented to the town council speak of the forms of municipal representation and their transformation—and not least of the accelerated changes in political communication and media at the end of the Middle Ages.

Messengers and Signs

The traveling sign bearers discussed in the previous section—the heralds and musicians—like the exotic adventurers drew a substantial portion of their incomes from gifts. This they had in common with a fourth group of recipients of official gifts who are less readily labeled as marginal figures in medieval society, although they were also mobile bearers of announcements, earned part of their income in gifts, and appear in the municipal accounts in close proximity to members of the above-mentioned professions—these were the couriers (*lauffer*) or messengers.

Late medieval account books virtually overflow with mentions of presents to the deliverers of services, news, or gifts. The Schaffhausen messenger, for example, who brought the Basel hospital the yearly interest due on its title-deeds in Schaffhausen, always received 60 pfennigs as a gift or tip. Similarly, the bishop of Basel reciprocated the presents of gingerbread and spices that he received every year from the nuns of Klingental with gifts to the servants who delivered them.[132] Johann von Venningen also repaid other small tokens in this way: for the cheese and cake that the mayor of Basel sent him at New Year's 1461 he presented the boy who brought them with 6 pfennigs. It was apparently important to send the bishop such little gifts, and he proved himself generous to those who delivered them.[133] If a gift was expensive enough and the giver prominent, these gifts to messengers could reach substantial sums. In October 1467, upon receipt of a chandelier from Duke Sigismund of Austria for the great hall in the bishop's palace at Porrentruy, Johann von Venningen presented the servants who delivered it with a tip of one florin; the messengers who brought him a gift horse from the duke a year later received two florins. The Nuremberg patrician Anton Tucher gave a tip of four florins to the men accompanying the duke of Saxony when they delivered a cask of Franconian wine in November 1514—a sum that corresponded exactly to the yearly cash earnings of his maidservant.[134]

Gifts to subaltern present-bringers did not simply serve as return gifts but were meant to underline and make public the demonstrative act of transfer—the legal character of these small tokens and tips will be discussed in more detail in the next chapter. This pattern is clearest when the person receiving the token was delivering not local produce, gingerbread, or wine, but something immaterial—information. Fifteenth- and sixteenth-century messengers could expect a substantial gift from the recipient if their news was considered sufficiently weighty. The Basel bishop Johann von Venningen, for instance, was willing to pay a good deal for word of an important legal decision; in his household account book for April 1466 he noted that he had given one florin to the manservant of Hans von Randeck who brought him the information. The florin that the Basel town council gave on July 6, 1471, to a messenger from Colmar who had just arrived from Regensburg was apparently connected to news from the Imperial Diet. Similar generous gifts in gold coins that the council gave to messengers from Strasbourg and Breisach in the week before Palm Sunday 1473 were associated with the visit of Frederick III in the Upper Rhine region.[135]

Even messengers conveying more mundane information could expect gifts of money, with the amount varying according to the circumstances and the sender. The courier sent on a mission from Heidelberg to the episcopal court in October 1470 with information and papers received 108 pfennigs as a gift—four days' wages for a journeyman artisan. In July 1490 a messenger from Colmar with news for the Basel town council even received 168 pfennigs. The envoys who brought news from the pope regarding pensions to the Swiss Confederacy meeting in Zurich in July 1520 received an even larger gift. The Baselers gave them six French gold crowns, about 2,448 Basel pfennigs—an investment in political communication in several respects that will be examined more thoroughly in the following chapters.[136]

In fifteenth- and sixteenth-century usage, the word *botten* (messengers) referred to papal diplomats as well as simple municipal couriers. In Basel, councilors entrusted with diplomatic functions were known as *Boten electi* or *rats botten*.[137] When the municipal account books speak of gifts to *botten*, we should keep this double meaning in the back of our minds—we will hear more about the Basel officials and the gifts they received below. What interests me at this juncture are the gifts that the city gave to information carriers from outside; we should imagine most of these messengers to be simple postmen who brought letters and news. Considering their importance as conveyers of information, we know relatively little about these municipal messengers of the late Middle Ages and the early sixteenth century. After at least the fourteenth century, the southern German cities had an organized system of municipal couriers, and the administrative sources from the second half of the century record special titles for regularly employed delivers of information.[138] Surviving municipal letter-books and missives from the 1470s document increasingly intensive correspondence. In order to maintain contact with its troops outside Neuss, the Strasbourg town council sent them over fifty letters during a five-week period, and during the wars with Charles the Bold the Bern chancellery sent up to fifty-six letters in one night. The recipients of municipal news and announcements could number one hundred and more.[139]

The speed of information was clearly important. In his 1476 treatise on the duties and administration of a mayor, the Görlitz town clerk Johannes Frauenburg stressed the importance of speed in a tone that sounds oddly familiar to modern ears. He strongly urged the mayor to receive and listen to all messengers immediately and to open all official correspondence to himself or the council quickly. Had Julius Caesar taken this approach, the town clerk noted, not without a certain drama, he would never have fallen into the hands of his murderers. It was equally important not to let writings and letters to the council go unanswered, even if there was no explicit request for a reply, because this was a challenge to the attentiveness and quick reactions of the municipal authorities.[140] The rapid processing of information is described here as an essential criterion for the common good of the city and a test of quick reflexes. The long lists of gifts to arriving messengers that fill the Basel weekly accounts are also witness to this.

In the fifteenth century, Basel had at least four sworn, permanently employed letter carriers, who were paid a fixed annual sum of 1,200 and later 960 pfennigs; they also received fabric and occasionally winter clothing. Their actual payment is recorded in a table attached to the weekly account books for 1462-73, which stipulates their fees according to distance. The transportation of news to frequent ports of call was paid according to a series of flat rates; if the messenger had to wait at his destination, he was paid 24 pfennigs for every whole day he spent there. The wages were not particularly high, and for most messengers the work was simply one sideline among several.[141] The oath taken by Basel municipal messengers accordingly made the couriers promise not to take on private commissions without council permission, not to ask more than the fixed rate, to present themselves at the town hall every morning for possible commissions and not to gamble during working hours. A rider to the second oath formula from the mid-fifteenth century also admonishes them to keep secret what was said to them verbally during their work; they were also forbidden to borrow money from anyone. Finally, the messengers were ordered to report all gifts they received to the town council.[142]

Most importantly, though, the messengers had to be recognizable as such. The ordinances laid great stress on the municipal symbols that were to identify the bearers of the city's news. Messengers were obliged to display the colored coat of arms prominently on their outer clothing, and the official messenger cases were also embellished with the municipal arms.[143] The Basel authorities were increasingly eager to ensure that their messengers actually wore the cloth in the city colors of black and white that they received as part of their remuneration.[144] The issue here was clearly a visual pronouncement, the programmatic visibility of municipal order and authority.

Beginning in the first decade of the sixteenth century, the city colors gained increasing prominence in the weekly readings of the Basel municipal accounts to the council. In 1511 the couriers Jacob Thurler and Severin Durlach were expressly presented with clothing in the Basel colors. Gifts to messengers of clothing in the city colors became more frequent in the context of the Swiss Confederacy's wars with France. The messengers who brought news of victory from Novara and Dijon in 1513 and 1514 were rewarded with black and white fabric at great expense.[145] Costly gifts in the Basel colors were, however, not necessarily tied to news of victories. The Zurich messengers who delivered news of the calamitous Swiss defeat at Marignano in 1515 were also presented with such striking gifts. Similarly expensive presents in black and white fabric were given as premiums to survivors of the battle who had rescued the city's banner during the catastrophe and brought it home again.[146] These presents of cloth are linked to the colored pictograms of rule that in the political cult of flags became a part of Swiss self-representation with the Burgundian wars.[147] During the major remodeling of the Basel town hall in 1511, a colorfully painted larger-than-life figure of an armed municipal standard-bearer was demonstratively placed over the façade of the building. Its counterpart, erected at the same time inside the town hall (originally in the corridor linking the front and rear wings), was the figure of a courier bearing a messenger's case and dressed in black and white, a conspicuous connection between outside and inside, military power, and information clothed in the city colors.[148]

Outside the forms of municipal representation, however, neither the symbols nor the news were ever quite that unambiguous. In the everyday communication system of the South German and Swiss cities in the early sixteenth century, intercepted or assaulted couriers and lost letters were common enough. In the autumn of 1511, an attack by French troops on two Swiss messengers unleashed the so-called Cold Winter Campaign. The robbing and disappearance of couriers and letters frequently occupied the attention of the Basel town council. The commanders of the Basel contingents during the military campaign at Novara informed the town council on July 2, 1513, that they were "distressed" to have heard no news of the arrival of their courier, whom they had sent to Basel with messages.[149] The yearly accounts for 1516–17 record a gift of 600 pfennigs as compensation for the municipal courier Damian Ertzberg, who had been robbed.[150] We thus might do well to describe the gifts given to messengers by the recipients of information as a sort of success premium.

These gifts for couriers were, ultimately, rewards for speed. That current information can never be complete and current enough was no secret to early modern Swiss town councilors. The treacherous drawback to the need for an ever faster flow of information was also familiar to them; by the late Middle Ages, disinformation by means of deliberately spread rumors was already making life difficult for the authorities. In his Swiss chronicle, Heinrich Brennwald included the tale of the three false couriers who burst in upon the trial of the toppled Zurich mayor Hans Waldmann on April 6, 1489, with the news that the emperor and his troops had crossed the Rhine and were marching on Zurich to rescue Waldmann. They had taken care to wet their clothes

Figure 1. Messenger in the Basel town hall, early sixteenth century.

in a fountain beforehand, the chronicler added, "as if they were sweating," and the news was intended to effect Waldmann's immediate execution. False news of attacks from the other side of the Rhine was not uncommon. In 1495 the treasurer of Solothurn noted that the "adventurer" who had warned the townspeople of an alleged Austrian assault had received food and cash worth 15 shillings. The word *adventurer* (*abentürer*), which is now familiar to us as a term for exotic travelers, apparently also carried associations of goods for sale and precious metals of dubious purity. The 1484 Strasbourg law concerning messengers laments the hiring of "many careless servants," who then went about carrying the municipal messenger cases. The courier who appears in Sebastian Brant's *Ship of Fools* is a liar who drinks so much wine that he forgets his message and reports instead gossip he has picked up or made up on his journey.[151]

If the news was not genuine here, at least the messenger was. At the beginning of the sixteenth century, Paracelsus posed the rhetorical question, "Why does a courier carry a case or have an emblem hanging on his mantle if not so that one may see he is a messenger?"[152] In doing so, he raised the issue of the unambiguousness of visible symbols. Was the courier, however, always in the service of those whose symbols he wore? Beginning in 1513 the above-mentioned Basel courier Damian Ertzberg appears regularly in the Basel yearly accounts as the recipient of gifts of clothing. The new jacket in the city's colors that he received in 1522 did not prevent him from looking around for other employment. In July of that same year, he was released from jail in Basel after taking an oath of truce, having been in custody for entering papal service as a mercenary soldier despite an official prohibition. He continued to work as a courier for the city, however, in spite of his illegal military service.[153]

Genuinely false couriers, or rather couriers wearing false colors, were all too familiar to contemporaries. A Swiss envoy who delivered an urgent appeal to levy new troops for the Italian campaign in June 1515 found to his astonishment that he had been preceded by a mounted postman who had announced everywhere in the name of the assembly of the Swiss Confederacy that it was unnecessary to go to Italy and that the mercenary soldiers should all turn back.[154] How could the true deliverer of news be distinguished from his doubles? Perhaps we are too quick to imagine the societies of the fifteenth and sixteenth centuries as defined by "face-to-face interactions."[155] In a world without the possibility of photomechanical reproduction, it was difficult to know for sure which face belonged to which name. Well into the sixteenth century we encounter a bewildering coexistence of family names, occupational designations, and nicknames, all applied to the same person. The municipal elections of this period stipulated an elaborate procedure in which the identity of the councilors in attendance was to be ascertained and recorded by clerks in special, annually renewed lists.[156]

How, then, could one tell who someone was? The "wanted" posters and lists of the late fifteenth and early sixteenth centuries offer only scant descriptions of faces for the establishment of identity. Instead, the distinguishing marks resided on or in the clothes of the person in question. In 1475, for example, the Bern town council described a man sought in connection with adulterated wine as "tall fat Martin Walliser" who was wearing a silk jerkin.[157] Michael von Dinkelsbühl, who denounced the leaders of an alleged peasant uprising (*Bundschuh*) to the Baden authorities in 1517, offered no details on the faces, sizes, or ages of the conspirators but did describe their clothes. Their leader, the famous Jos Fritz, could be recognized by his black and brick-colored French coat and fashionably slashed red breeches; the only indelible distinguishing mark mentioned was a dark mole on his left hand. The conspirators used itinerants as couriers, the informant continued; one of them was known as Heinrich of Strasbourg, was a reciter (*sprecher*), carried a conjuror's bag (*gaukelsack*), and was dressed in red and yellow. These details come from the letters sent by the dukes of Baden in November 1517 to the Strasbourg authorities with the request that these persons be arrested as soon as possible. They make particular mention of a stylized letter "H" that, at least according to Michael von Dinkelsbühl, all participants in the uprising had sewn on or into their clothing. Together with the cry "Saint George!" (*sant Jörg*), this was one of the secret signs they used to recognize each other, and the authorities too could use these signs to identify the conspirators.[158]

Identification was possible then, after all: in this mode of perception, garments, as expensive personal valuables of which most people possessed only a few, became part of the person, the equivalent of facial features. As gifts they could, conversely, also become the mark of the informer. Lux Rapp, who reported an earlier *Bundschuh* conspiracy to the authorities in Speyer in 1504, was rewarded with an official court-dress from the bishop.[159] The presentation of official municipal gifts from Basel to couriers in the form of conspicuous clothing clearly points to the significance of colors and symbols —primarily, of course, conspicuous official symbols. Other symbols or signs that were secret were clearly also in circulation alongside these, and like their official counterparts, they aided in placing and identifying individuals.[160] The man who delivered official news occasionally had a mirror-image, a sort of evil doppelgänger. We will encounter similar constellations and fears in connection with other gifts.

Gifts as Media

This sketch of bookkeeping on gifts by the Basel town council from the second half of the fifteenth century to the 1620s has taken us from gift wine, the spectacle of princely visits, and the functions of heralds and musicians to the more or less professional information couriers and their doubles. In the Basel account books, they appear in a context we may refer to as pronouncements: the conspicuous presentation of municipal public relations.

The registration of gifts in Basel proves to have been pragmatic. It was less a form of commercial registration than a functional political mode of utilitarian writing. In the guise of weekly and annual accounts read aloud to the town councilors, it served the propagation of consensus within the councils and at the same time acted as a political memorandum book for a few initiates. The forms of writing, like the presentation of these gifts, were inextricably linked with the changing military and political commitments of the city, situated between its alliance (known as the *Niedere Vereinigung*) with Austria in the wars against Burgundy in the 1470s and its growing ties to the Swiss confederate system. While many elements remained constant—the coding of the transfers as "fluid," the careful adaptation of purportedly "traditional" gifts to the appropriate current circumstances—the decades between 1450 and 1530 reveal definite shifts in the municipal politics of gift giving. Prominent forms of communicative performance lost in importance; heralds, reciters, and minstrels from outside the Swiss Confederacy forfeited a large part of their role as symbol bearers, and the politically important sumptuous gifts to the musicians of neighboring lands became mere alms to "foreign trumpeters." After Basel's entry into the Swiss Confederacy, new types of prestigious political presents such as stained glass windows appeared in churches and taverns as the luminous reproduction of municipal symbols. At the same time, gifts of clothing in the town colors and presents rewarding military merit began to appear in the Basel account books.

As far as we can tell from the terse entries, the terminology of the municipal accounts also changed at the beginning of the sixteenth century and became more strictly associated with municipal bureaucratic authority. The Basel mayors, guild masters, and town councilors became "my lords." Beginning in 1515, and increasingly after 1520, special gifts also appear without any attribution except "according to the judgment of the council." These were official gifts of honor without any explicitly mentioned occasion: more discreet presents, separated from the gifts offered as pronouncements that have concerned us here. In what follows we will expand our investigation to include a second area—fifteenth- and sixteenth-century Basel officials not only as distributors but as recipients of premiums that were referred to and recorded in highly diverse ways. What were the connections between official function, payments, and gifts?

2 *Offices*

From the earliest surviving volumes on, the Basel account books are filled with references to gifts presented to local municipal officeholders. Beyond their established salaries, public servants received money or valuables "for their labor" that the records particularly single out as gifts. The occasions and amounts varied, ranging from the substantial sum of 20 florins to the guild master Jakob Ziboll in recognition of his services in the successful acquisition of the neighboring town of Kleinbasel in 1392 to the gift of 60 pfennigs to the town guards in February 1477 for capturing a wolf.[1] These were not alms for the needy but bonuses associated with the recipients' efforts on behalf of the city.

Municipal officers also received a number of gifts from other quarters than the city administration. Every year at Christmas the household account book of the bishop of Basel mentions two florins as a New Year's gift to the two highest-ranking town guards, which the bishop's secretary formally presented to them. Similarly, the city itself was constantly giving gifts to the officials of other governments, as we have seen, whether in the framework of diplomatic missions or more discreet political contexts, and these gifts could attain quite respectable sums. In 1491, Basel gave the imperial tax collector a gift of 3,600 pfennigs in cash; we have also already heard of the precious silver goblet that the city presented to the influential Bern councilor and former town clerk Thüring Fricker in 1504.[2]

Over the course of the Middle Ages, the South German and Swiss cities built up an increasingly tight network of officially appointed and publicly remunerated municipal "civil servants." A similar process occurred in the territorial states. The term *office*, at any rate, was increasingly separated from the man who held it, depersonalized, and associated ever more closely with the field of activity involved.[3] This process has been described frequently, with direct or indirect reference to Max Weber's important definitional colon—"For in everyday life political rule (*Herrschaft*) is primarily: administration." In German-language historiography, "office" (*Amt*) and "administration"

(*Verwaltung*) are weighty concepts, carrying with them extensive methodological assumptions and an equally voluminous heuristic apparatus.[4] What did administration and gifts have to do with each other?

Gifts as an "Anti-State" Phenomenon: An Excursion into the History of Bureaucracy

In the autumn of 1875, Gustav Schmoller gave a lecture at the University of Strasbourg entitled "Strasbourg at the Time of the Guild Struggles and the Reform of Its Constitution and Administration in the Fifteenth Century." Only with the major reforms of 1405 and 1433, he explained, were efficient institutions of city government created in Strasbourg. The administration of the *Ammeister* (mayor) and other municipal offices was subjected to fixed regulations and above all to the obligation to maintain written accounts, and the city's previous "great barter economy," which had given rise to "intrigue, waste and all manner of abuses," was abolished. "Out of the shipwreck of excessive self-administration," asserted Schmoller, "modern bureaucracy emerged in fifteenth century Strasbourg, still half-wreathed in fog, but then in ever clearer contours."[5]

Schmoller wrote his account as a Prussian civil servant in newly Prussian Strasbourg. The municipal reforms of the fifteenth century were a point of departure to which he would return repeatedly in his later studies of the German bureaucratic state and his major work on political economy. His 1875 account makes explicit his hope to discover that late medieval Strasbourg was ruled, as he wrote, by a "breed of municipal politicians, by capable town clerks nourished at the breast of the ancients, by jurists both learned and practical," who had generated that "dawn of a new education." No other group of historical protagonists inspired the bourgeois historians of the nineteenth century to view them as kindred spirits, predecessors, and distant brothers the way the burghers of the late Middle Ages did. The line of development from the German "burgher city" of the fifteenth and sixteenth centuries to the Prussian bureaucratic state of the nineteenth century was one that the older scholarship delighted in tracing; Georg von Below is the best-known example.[6] Schmoller, however, knew his municipal sources far too well to fall prey to such analogies. The reforms of 1405 and 1433 reflected desires for the future, not social reality, he emphasizes, precisely tracing the far less orderly details of practice.[7] He was concerned, though, with the principles underlying those stipulations that referred to the keeping of written records and the conduct of municipal officials in regard to gifts. "Official duties and official controls," Schmoller concluded, tamed gifts and thus formed the beginning of the "modern state."[8]

In this narrative, gifts function as a negative leitmotif: according to Schmoller, the roots of forward-looking modern administration must always be sought where the power of gifts was rigorously restricted. After him, Max Weber described on a few classic pages these gifts, perquisites, and revenues of office as aristocratic powers appropriated by subordinates with the attendant opportunities for skimming and profit, and he closely associated them with taxes paid in kind and the nonmonetary economy, but above all with the absence of regular salaries paid in money. The chapter on traditional or patrimonial rule, in which he treats these perquisites of office, at least suggests the categorization of particular elements of remuneration as forward-looking and "modern" and others as "traditional" remnants.[9] And although Weber himself firmly insisted that he did not wish to see his typology read as a historical succession, these passages have been used as a sort of sociological catechism of administrative history, which is supposed to provide the proper terms and relations for the description of the transition from randomly and heterogeneously remunerated traditional administration to demonstrably regulated and precisely rewarded legal administration—with the blessing of the authority of a classic. However vehemently the classic author may have warned against this in *Economy and Society*, it did precious little good.[10] When gifts appear in studies of late medieval and early modern bureaucracy written by scholars of legal and administrative history, they accordingly describe them as antistate—traditional waste products and remnants within a modernizing administration.

More recent studies no longer trace such a line of development (the municipal officials of the late Middle Ages as forerunners of modern administrative institutions) without warning us about the anachronistic distortion of late medieval and early modern conditions contained therein.[11] In these accounts, gifts nevertheless continue to appear as an archaic, pre- or antistate element. Whether or not they refer directly to Schmoller and Weber, the authors of these works tend to regard the very bracketing together of the prohibition on gifts with the command to keep written records as the bridge to modern normativity.[12] German historians seem unable to dispense altogether with equating small-"a" *amt* (medieval and early modern office) with capital-"A" *Amt* (modern bureaucratic office). Late medieval administrative office is thus on the one hand wholly different from its modern counterpart, but on the other must appear in handbooks and overviews as its early or pre-form.[13]

This may reflect a specifically German professorial longing for origins, roots, and long duration. Outside German-language historiography, studies of patronage, simony, and the clientele system have arrived at quite a different picture. Recent works have drawn our attention to the informal networks and mechanisms of patronage and clienteles, which the emerging central bureaucracies made possible in the first place, but which were created and padded with gifts.[14] In the work of Giorgio Chittolini, it is precisely the late medieval state administration's capacity to integrate private interests and familial systems of patronage and clienteles that made it so effective in asserting itself. From this perspective, the rise of the early modern state and administration literally rested on gifts, which were more or less freely given.[15]

What, then, did "office" (*Amt*) mean at the end of the Middle Ages and the beginning of the modern era? The older Latin legal texts that discuss the problem of gifts and bribes generally use the term *munus*, a word that can refer both to the office itself and to the income from that office, including gifts and bribes. In his *Policraticus*, John of Salisbury replies to the question of whether public officials may accept gifts with a quotation. There is, he writes, an old proverb (in reality a legal maxim from the late antique digests): Not everything, not from everyone, not always. For, he continues, it would take superhuman strength to refuse every gift but to accept anything without exception is iniquitous. It thus appears to be choice that distinguishes between good and evil gifts, and the multipurpose word *munus* can refer to either.[16]

In the vernacular sources of the fifteenth and sixteenth centuries, though, we encounter not the word *munus*, but rather *amt* (office), *gab* (offering, gift), and *schenck* (gift). The fact that the late medieval and modern terms sound the same is not unproblematic; there is a tendency within German-language legal and constitutional history to treat political and legal terms as autonomous units and to abstract them from the social contexts in which they acquired meaning and functioned.[17] This extraction is an operation with rather serious implications. Such a method encourages us to mount the historical lifeguard's tower and try to spy out embryonic forms, predecessors, and major lines of developments from up there. The object of study is largely reduced to the history of the term as a lexical stem, and it is easy under the circumstances to lose sight of the diverse practices to which a term was attached by contemporaries in various circumstances.[18]

Legal and administrative history refers to the sources—late medieval official or administrative regulations—from which it draws the answer to its problem of the evolutionary change but also fundamental continuity of the terms *office* and *official* in the period between the late Middle Ages and the eighteenth century. These sources include municipal constitutional reforms, oath formulas, sermons, memoranda, mirrors of princes (treatises on statecraft, often in fictional form), political tracts, and moral exempla, in which a "civil service ethos" formed during the late Middle Ages and the early modern period.[19] The historians working in these fields thus not only ignore less formalized written sources such as municipal accounts and chronicles, in which, as we have seen, gifts were stylized as a ritual expression of municipal legitimacy, the scope of the norms set down in "official regulations" also remains open. It is patently obvious, writes one of the authors of the history of German public administration, that some catalogs of demands and some official regulations remained purely programmatic. Especially from the perspective of forms of payment, late medieval conditions by no means flowed straight into modern civil service law; the coexistence of "medieval" and "modern" legal forms characterized the system of remuneration until the end of the eighteenth century.[20]

Does this mean that there were no lines of connection after all, no rosy Schmollerian dawn of the civil service in the fifteenth century, but only a very long and rather messy Middle Ages, an epoch of dysfunction and corruption that ended only with the age of Enlightenment? Faced with this dilemma, another author tries to take the bull by the horns and refers to corruption in the *Handwörterbuch für Rechtsgeschichte*, a dictionary of legal history, as the "historical rule" in the history of public administration. He suggests that we view "honest administration" as an "exceptional case" and "probably only a temporary exceptional case at that."[21] Such a depiction of corruption as an ahistorical, all-too-human failing is not very satisfying. The moment that all premodern administrative activity, without exception, falls under corruption the term ceases to signify anything more than bewildering disorder in a murky past.

Let us try a different approach. The normative texts of the fifteenth and sixteenth centuries insist on the separation of office and person and repeatedly demand it in the light of a vague and slippery municipal reality. Was this repeated, (re)written, paraphrased, and invoked so often only to be ignored by contemporaries with a shrug of the shoulders or a cynical remark? The texts aimed to put the world in order; with their authoritative and literary tricks, superimpositions, and omissions they created an orderly internal reality, and as fictitious as these textual edifices may have been, they proved powerful. There is something like a parallelism of interests between the medieval government officials who wrote these texts and the modern historians who would prefer to find orderly (and describable) structures.[22] They are united by the desire to believe in the norms, even if both are perfectly aware of the far more incoherent reality of practice. And in order to be effective, must not a norm be equally capable of seduction and discipline? The point here cannot be to provide a definition of disorder or corruption and then apply it to fifteenth- and sixteenth-century conditions.[23] We will take a closer look at the components of the incomes of lower and middle officeholders—municipal civil servants in the sense that their oath of office gave them a particular legal obligation to the city. I would also like to bring together some material on the terms (and their establishment and connotations) that contemporaries used to refer to the relationship between offices and gifts. In what context did these terms appear, and exactly what practices were they supposed to describe?

Gift-Giving Practices: Tokens of Transition, Second Incomes, and Compensation

In what follows, the word *official* will be used to refer to those persons who were appointed by the town council as the local authority and had a direct relationship to it. Their particular status was created by the oath of office, which set down their duties. As much as their ranks differed, this special legal status united high functionaries such as mayors and magistrates with customs officers and town guards. I am concerned here not with the personal availability of the holders of influential political posts and their payment but rather with the broad mass of municipal public servants.

The sworn holders of municipal offices such as town guards, tower guards, customs officers, and the like received only a small weekly salary as we understand the word. The regular Basel town guards, for example, were paid 48 pfennigs a week between 1414 and 1560, and their immediate superior, the chief town guard, 78 pfennigs. These sums are significantly lower than the wage rates paid to qualified journeyman artisans during the same period. They represent only the base income from this office, however.[24] This sum was supplemented by yearly benefits in kind (in the case of the town guards, for example, half an Easter lamb and cloth) and further fixed bonuses at particular dates, such as the quarterly payments known as *fronfastengelt*, an annual gift at year's end, and another on St. John's Day (June 24), when a new council was elected and the town guards renewed their oath.[25] All these wage components had in common that they were terminologically separate from the official remuneration of the position. They had nothing to do with the actual work performed but instead constituted the special contractual relationship between the city and its officers, analogous to very similar gifts that the bishop of Basel gave to his officials.[26]

These gifts were all the more effective or, if one prefers, legally binding, the more regularly they were bestowed. They confirmed and renewed the contractual relationship between employer and employee, which not coincidentally recalls the fifteenth- and sixteenth-century institution of *leitkauff*, a gift, usually in the form of wine, that served to close and affirm a contract. A German textbook for Venetian merchants, which was written in the mid-fifteenth century by a Nuremberger, places this wine offered at the close of a contract at the center of a didactic dialogue between business partners during the sale of expensive bales of cloth. It was a custom among the Germans always to demand an "extra," complains the Venetian vendor; and they thought that they had not closed a deal if they did not receive such a bonus. In the model dialogue, this extra is only the first of several gifts with the aid of which the business partners finally reach an agreement.[27]

Much the same procedure seems to have prevailed in the work contracts (or contract extensions) of municipal or episcopal officials. In his household account book, Bishop Johann von Venningen carefully recorded the gifts he gave his employees in connection with the making or renewal of their yearly contracts. He paid his servant Stoffel 1,695 pfennigs as his agreed yearly wage, he notes in 1466, and gave him a further 39 pfennigs as a gift. The popular terms for these extras, *leitkauff* or *weinkouff*, suggest the proximity of such gifts to liquid transfers, and Venningen frequently paid his employees one or two quarts of wine as a *weinkauff* when they entered into a contract.[28] The gift did not create the contractual obligation but instead made public the parties' mutual agreement. It is at this point that the small bonuses paid to episcopal employees intersect with the costly silver-sheathed "long knife" worth 25 florins that Johann von Venningen presented in 1478 to the war-hardened old campaigner Oswald von Thierstein when the latter entered his service.[29] Gifts upon taking and leaving office were the rule. When an old watchman gave notice, for example, Venningen presented him with 72 pfennigs as a parting gift, and when the city dismissed its pipers and drummers in January 1521, they received 720 pfennigs "as a gift of honor."[30] These tokens of transition also include the already mentioned gifts given upon the closing of accounts, which appear frequently in episcopal and municipal bookkeeping, as well as compensation for those who applied for but did not receive posts.[31]

The income of late medieval officials thus consisted, first of all, of such gifts and a regular salary, in gold or silver money depending upon the post. What these regular payments have in common is that they were ritually fixed, paid independent of work done (i.e., also to some retired officials), and made up only a small portion of the person's total income. A number of Basel officeholders, chief among them the town guards, received such regular gifts of money not just from the city but also from third parties. The account book of the saffron guild notes a quarterly gift of 240 pfennigs to the town guards; I have already mentioned the bishop's annual gift to them of two florins, and the council account books mention a whole list of institutions from which the guardians of public order received money at the New Year, including the provost of St. Alban, the convents at Klingenthal and Gnadenthal, the Carthusians, preachers, and the district of Kleinbasel. Taken together, these New Year's bonuses represented two months' wages for a journeyman artisan.[32] The town guards were, to a certain extent, gift experts, as we shall see. They also delivered official gifts of wine to their recipients; a municipal ordinance admonished them to share the tips they received for this service among themselves.[33]

A second source of income was regular but not temporally fixed benefits from third parties. When the lessee of the municipal brothel took his annual oath and extended his lease with the city, he had to give the chief town guard one florin or a pair of breeches. When a criminal was caught and executed in the city, the town guards had a right to his clothes and the cash he had been carrying on his person; they also had a right to one-third of the income from the *Kohlenberggericht*, an institution of self-administration for beggars and prostitutes (named after the Kohlenberg district of Basel), and a portion of the fines levied for disturbing the peace, carrying weapons, and gambling (the guard involved in the incident, however, had to share these amounts with his fellow town guards). In addition, anyone who called in the authorities when there was a disturbance of the peace had to pay the chief town guard a fee of 12 pfennigs; people recently admitted to citizenship had to pay him the same amount.[34] Thus although late medieval officeholders took their oath of office to a specific institution, which constituted them as officials, they drew their actual income from a variety sources.

Apart from the fixed salary independent of work performed, a third and far more substantial portion of the remuneration of these officials consisted of their share of the administrative income, fines, or fees that they collected. This was true not just of the town guards, but also the Basel bailiffs, the officials of the municipal court, and most of the fee-collecting officials such as warehouse clerks and customs officers.[35] The municipal oaths of office and mandates of the fifteenth and sixteenth centuries accordingly repeat with great regularity that those officials who collected money should not pocket their own portion but instead put the monies into the designated receptacle in the presence of the paying clients. It is in this context that we must understand the stipulation in the oath taken by the Basel magistrates according to which they should accept no fines or fees, either in their own homes or elsewhere, except in the presence of a second municipal official.[36]

These officeholders were particularly authorized providers of paid services in the name of the city, in other words, subcontractors of the authorities rather than civil servants in the usual sense. They accordingly offered not just municipal services, but also their own. Lower municipal officials such as couriers, gatekeepers, tower guards, and night watchmen continued to work at other trades as well.[37] The chief town guard of Basel, for instance, also made money from the sale of the clothes of executed criminals, which came to him as a perquisite of office.[38] In 1482 and 1483 the Basel town guards were permitted to confiscate belts and cloaks that violated the city's sumptuary laws and to keep or sell them. Similarly, we know of the Strasbourg executioner that his wife had her own stand at the secondhand clothing market there, at least in the years around 1509. In 1496 the town guards of Freiburg im Breisgau were forbidden to act as private debt-collectors alongside their official duties.[39]

For higher officials, the coexistence of municipal and private services was the rule in any case. The oath of office taken by town clerks admonished them to particular secrecy and obedience to the council but left it up to them whether they accepted private commissions. The multiple and not wholly uncontroversial functions fulfilled by the Augsburg town clerk Konrad Peutinger as the employee of several political authorities in the first decades of the sixteenth century were not unusual from the perspective of the late fifteenth century.[40] In connection with the mixed form of income drawn by late medieval officeholders, in which official salaries made up only a fraction of the total, many officials were expressly permitted to accept gifts for their services. As Erasmus noted with some bitterness in his 1518 *Institutio Princeps Christiani*, a situation in which officeholders earned such a large salary that they were not compelled to supplement their incomes was a lost ancient ideal.[41]

It was quite legitimate to demand gifts. His contract of appointment authorized the Strasbourg town clerk Spatzinger to ask for a gift when the text required of him was particularly elaborate, and with the mayor's permission, he could accept private gifts at any time. The most widely disseminated and popular fifteenth-century legal handbook for laymen, the so-called Legal

Summary of Brother Berthold, an alphabetical encyclopedia of canon and secular law, authorized not just those employed by the courts as assessors, messengers, and guards to request small gifts from people who came before the court, but also permitted the judge himself to accept such tokens, as long as he did so in moderation.[42] The practice was not necessarily limited to holders of high office. The four town guards who delivered official gifts of wine from the council were forbidden, to be sure, from directly demanding anything in return, but they were naturally permitted to accept what people offered them voluntarily. In 1483 the Bern council even issued the town executioner with an official certificate allowing him to walk about the city requesting New Year's gifts.[43]

Offers of Mercy

In the fifteenth and sixteenth centuries, the word *schencken* did not just stand for presents and liquids but also carried a third meaning in connection with officials. Municipal regulations and oath formulas repeatedly admonished municipal officials not to offer anyone a reduction (*zuo schenckhen oder nachzulassen*) on the charges or fines owed to the city treasury. An entry in the Basel ordinances for July 1486 sharply emphasizes that wrongdoers must always pay the full fine for breaches of the public peace and explicitly protests against the practice of agreements between officeholder and plaintiff to reduce the fine by one-third. This reduction doubtless affected one of the thirds due to the municipal treasury, not the third claimed by the officeholder: This was not the proper way to *erkennen*, or decide, the council stated, and to make this clearer the word *erkannt* was placed in quotation marks.[44]

Before rushing to diagnose corruption and malfeasance here, we should examine matters more closely. Neither regulation prohibited the practice as such, but the right to grant such reductions was reserved to the council alone. The issue was thus who was authorized to make such offers. Despite these formulaic and oft-repeated regulations, a partial reduction or deferment of payments was the rule in many areas of municipal administration. In the case of citizenship fees, monetary fines for violating market regulations, or penalties for assault, municipal accounts show that in many instances the stipulated charges and fines were not paid at the full official rate, but only in part. In other cases next to the name of the person in question and the sum owed, we find only the word *dabit* or *debit*, that is, payment was deferred. Historians have long regarded this as a vagueness in the sources, for which social and criminal historians need to correct in their calculations and tables. In light of the erratic availability of cash in the fourteenth and fifteenth centuries and the very limited means of law enforcement at the disposal of municipal authorities (in which the written recording of the demand, complete with names, played an important role), this purported lack of precision is more likely to have been a pragmatic strategy for eventually collecting and enforcing fees and fines in a highly confusing legal landscape. When accordingly in 1506 the Basel ordinances record that the councilors had, at the request of the magistrate of Lucerne, let off two journeymen artisans from Kleinbasel who had fallen foul of the law, this was no mere demonstration of official mercy. As an act of grace, it was a political ritual for handling escaped criminals and the authorities of neighboring towns.[45] The refusal to impose sanctions was an indispensable instrument of integration, and the municipal authorities were unwilling simply to delegate this instrument to the subordinate providers of municipal services.

Power Relations and Euphemisms

Whether these acts of clemency and gift giving always arose exclusively from mutual affection ("because of our amicable love," as the common formula ran) and had no strings attached, as the written records insist, is doubtful at best. In February 1477 the household account book of the bishop of Basel, Johann von Venningen, notes the receipt of 200 rhenish florins from his bailiff in St. Ursanne in the matter of two men condemned to death who had been granted clemency. It is unclear where the money that the episcopal administrator of St. Ursanne paid came from and what its connection was with the reduction of the sentence. How gratis was grace? In 1489 the toppled mayor of Zurich, Hans Waldmann, and his town clerk stood accused, among other things, of demanding a large sum of money in exchange for an official request for clemency on behalf of a doctor imprisoned in Milan. At the time, the town clerk had allegedly claimed that Zurich's official intervention could only be had at the price of 200 florins for Waldmann. The desperate prisoner had at first offered 40 florins, without success, and then 100, until the official letter from Zurich to Milan materialized and he was released. In addition to the money, he had had to give the mayor and one of his aides costly fabrics and a silken cloak.[46]

Was this a mere invention designed to sully the name of the deposed mayor's town clerk? False accusations can tell us just as much about late medieval perceptual patterns as true ones because they refer to a fabric of rules and a framework of the plausible that was familiar to all concerned. In the language norms concerning the relationship between gift and office in the cities of the fifteenth and sixteenth centuries, municipal officers appear as providers of official services equipped with special concessions who drew part of their income directly from the public. The degree to which the charges for these services were paid voluntarily could vary. When the Basel town guards arrested someone, he or she had to pay them a certain fee, known as *Bindgeld*.[47] If these persons were unlucky, this was only the beginning of a whole series of payments they had to offer to these personifications of municipal authority.

The guardians of public order in Basel were not necessarily pleasant company. The municipal *Urfehdenbücher* (legal records containing the promises of those released from prison not to exact vengeance) recount a series of cases of town guards arrested and then released by the town council. The reasons mentioned for their arrest include misappropriation of municipal funds, disturbing the peace, and violence, as well as the capricious punishment of offenses. In 1517, Caspar Scheffer, described in the sources as a town guard and torturer, was placed in the tower because he had accepted a bribe in exchange for turning a blind eye to a crime, and when the court messenger Peter Widerstein was released from jail, he had to swear that he would repay one florin to a woman from whom he had apparently extorted money.[48] Conditions were similar in other cities of the period. The Nuremberg town council repeatedly criticized the town guards for using undue violence and forbade them on several occasions from demanding gifts or tokens from innkeepers or other citizens.[49] In Freiburg im Breisgau, the town watchmen were warned in a series of regulations in the 1490s to curb their use of violence and personal caprice. Their oath of office, renewed in 1495, admonished them to return lost property to its proper owners and not to demand more than a quart of wine in return. With conspicuous frequency, municipal ordinances also prohibited the lending of money to officeholders in any form whatsoever. The representatives of municipal authority could, after all, be particularly convincing in their requests for money, and in 1496 the Freiburg town guards were expressly forbidden to pressure and arrest debtors on behalf of private individuals without orders from the mayor.[50]

Such extras as part of the income of office were apparently also due in those cases where it was a matter not of direct but of indirect authority—of access. At the end of the fifteenth century, the Basel authorities stipulated that any Jew sojourning in the city had to apply for a special permit. Such a permit cost 60 pfennigs per day, to be paid to the chief town guard, according to a 1490 entry in the town council records. In order to apply, though, Jews first had to pay 12 pfennigs to the gatekeeper.[51] Such payments from private individuals to officials were widespread and applied not only to the Jewish minority. We might call them access fees; the people of the late Middle Ages and early modern period nevertheless insisted on referring to them as gifts (*schenck*). An addition to the oath formula of the Basel town guards in the fifteenth century stipulates that they must not accept money from anyone with business in the offices that employed them. In 1456 the guards in Strasbourg town hall had to take an extra oath promising not to ask the citizens who appeared as petitioners for money: if, however, someone offered them a "modest tip" they could keep it.[52] Similarly, the town guard who acted as porter at Nuremberg town hall was warned several times by the town council not to demand gifts from people who came to petition the council. Naturally, he could accept what people gave him voluntarily, the council minutes note.[53]

It was not generally forbidden to ask for such gifts. Rather, one gains the impression that these access fees were tolerated as long as they did not overstep a certain limit. Municipal officials themselves had to offer such gifts when they traveled on behalf of the city, for which reason they often appear in the account books. Johannes Wal of Cologne, for example, who sojourned in Basel in 1433–34 in order to negotiate with Emperor Sigmund on behalf of his city, noted rather bitterly that he had had to pay the doorkeepers of the imperial chancellery one florin simply to gain admittance and find out to whom he needed to speak. He had had to give the chancellor 49 florins and the marshal a gilded goblet worth 31 florins. In addition to the substantial issuing fees, he had finally been obliged to offer the clerk half a florin to ensure that he would not abridge or alter the municipal documents requiring notarization.[54] In 1451 the city of Basel paid 400 florins for the imperial affirmation of its freedoms and privileges; the municipal envoy, however, had to lay out a further 151 florins for clerical fees, seals, and gifts to the chancellery, musicians, and doorkeepers—a nice list of the various costs of acquiring connections and access at court.[55] During the spectacles of princely visits, the cities gave the imperial doorkeepers separately registered gifts, which were then read out to the council as special municipal expenses—perhaps an ironically ritualized reflection on this general practice.[56]

In oath formulas, ordinances, and municipal account books, such access fees were referred to quite self-evidently as gifts. Poems and moral tracts of the same period strike a rather different note, however. *The Devil's Net* (*Des Teufels Netz*, a poem composed about 1430 in the region of Lake Constance) laments that a poor man desiring an audience with his lords must first pay the gatekeeper and grease his palm. Those who fail to do so soon find themselves outside the gates, with no possibility of obtaining justice.[57] In his treatise on the miserable life of courtiers, the Italian humanist (and future pope) Enea Silvio Piccolomini embroiders on the theme, complaining that it was just bearable to be forced to give gifts to persons of high rank. At court, however, one constantly had to approach the lowest and most common people with gifts and entreaties, above all the watchmen, who admitted only vain flatterers and violently slammed the prince's door in one's face. However often and richly one bestowed gifts upon the doorkeepers, one remained outside.[58]

To put it another way, late medieval officials represented a measure of not just abstract, but also quite concrete, personalized violence. Medieval Roman and canon law used the term *concussio* to refer to extortion in office.[59] The word appears nowhere, however, in our municipal sources. Even the numerous orders to municipal officials and guardians of order not to demand gifts from the population never directly mention the illegality of such fruits of official force. The designation of a transfer as a gift clearly signals a good deal of ambivalence.[60] The configuration of municipal offices and gifts in the late Middle Ages and the early modern period is well-nigh impossible to grasp using the terminology of office and corruption. We are dealing here with euphemistic (and occasionally cynical) designations, and it is this ambivalence in referring to a fee as a gift that constitutes the efficacy of the term. Fifteenth- and sixteenth-century officials were in a position to make offers that citizens could not refuse, and contemporaries referred to the responses to such offers as gifts, gratuities, or tokens of gratitude. In reality, there was no reciprocity (as the term *gift* seeks to evoke) between the providers of such official services and those who were obliged to negotiate with them. Even if it was in reality a supplementary income, protection money, or an extra profit squeezed from power relations, it was important that the gift be staged as a voluntary love offering. A German dictionary of the late sixteenth century accordingly translates the ambivalent French term for a gratuity (but also a bribe), *pot-de-vin* (literally, jug of wine), enigmatically as "What one gives to a person who brings us something that was lost."[61]

Gift Narratives

Let us take stock of what we have learned thus far. If we take the account books of the city and bishop of Basel and the town clerks and chroniclers at their word, what terms did they use to present gifts and what did they associate them with in their narratives?

Gifts were, first of all, represented as liquids. When the word *geschenckt* appears in the registers, something was usually flowing, and when the bestowed objects were not literally fluid but were gratuities (the German word means "drink money"), cups, or drinking vessels filled with money, they were still presented as liquid, with an explicit or implicit reference to wine, the ritual political liquid of the late Middle Ages par excellence. Liquid gifts of money were also omnipresent in an everyday form: Basel's saffron guild used a gilded and painted goblet to collect the annual New Year's gift of money from its members. These potable funds are even more obvious in the florin-filled drinking vessels that were ceremonially presented to princes and dignitaries when they entered the city. The emperor, however, could reverse the game when he wished. In his efforts to convince the Swiss to support him against France in 1507, Maximilian made them not only a series of fantastic promises but also had their envoys presented upon departure with gilded silver dishes containing money.[62]

However much such presents may seem mere bagatelles to the modern reader, in the eyes of contemporaries they were very serious business indeed. A gift given in the name of the public demonstrated legitimacy. As strongly integrated as they were into the municipal rules of courtesy and as ritually fixed as they may appear to have been in contemporary perception and economic registration, gifts were a central political agenda of the authorities in which they invested substantial amounts of money. It is no accident that the highest annual sum ever spent on gifts in Basel during the period in question was in the dramatic year 1473–74, the prelude to the fateful military conflicts between Burgundy and the governing authorities of the Upper Rhine and the Swiss Confederacy.[63] Although the wording of certain council decrees emphasizes that the gifts given in connection with a certain event had been bestowed according to "habit" and "ancient custom," in the cities of the late Middle Ages ritual gifts proved to be carefully orchestrated gestures that were continually being readapted to current needs. They were far more evocative of tried and true political skill and the adaptability of local diplomacy than of unchanging traditional legal forms. Gift giving was work, and after the Imperial Diet of 1530, the city of Augsburg accordingly rewarded those of its officials who had been entrusted with the apportionment and distribution of official municipal presents for their efforts.[64] The written records of these gifts, themselves protected as a municipal secret, are a deliberate, current, politically determined selection of what the city bestowed. They are no mere financial registration of municipal liberality but rather a reference work, a political text produced by certain concrete actors—the councilors responsible for the accounts and the town clerk—for other municipal actors; they tell stories.

Third, as legitimate gifts, all these gifts referred to a public sphere—more specifically to a legal public sphere. Analogous to the small gift of wine customary at the closing of a commercial deal, such gifts confirmed employment contracts with municipal servants and officials, and we may assume that this meaning at least resonated in the carefully orchestrated bestowal of gifts to princes and diplomats, as it did in the elaborate holiday and visiting diplomacy of the cities of the Swiss Confederacy. Late medieval town dwellers were not so naive, however, as to attribute such a magical quality to the acceptance of a gift that it created an automatic obligation. In fifteenth-century cities, contracts—whether for sales, employment, or political treaties—were sealed and made binding not by shared wine but by legal guarantees, witnesses, written agreements, official control institutions, and a sophisticated system of sureties and mutually accepted arbitrating jurisdictions. Gifts alone did not create a legally binding status, but they were designed to make commitments and legal relationships public.

However much gifts may have been stylized as pure signs of affection, their character was not wholly voluntary—but then are legal relationships ever that? The Burgundian governor Peter von Hagenbach, whom the Baselers gave large gifts on several occasions, had demanded that his wedding guests arrive with fitting gifts, at least according to the Basel chronicler Johann Knebel, who was not well disposed toward him. Conversely, in his *Descriptio Helvetiae* written between 1500 and 1504, the Milanese envoy Balcus reserved some very plain words for the gift-giving rituals of the Swiss. Foreign ambassadors received wine as a greeting and with their meals from the Swiss authorities, he writes, but also had to give one or two coins to the men who delivered the wine. During meals (Balcus was no friend of Swiss cuisine and speaks of *barbara condimenta*, barbarously seasoned dishes), the musicians and players expected gifts, regardless of one's opinion of their performance. The envoys were virtually besieged at table, Balcus continues, and were compelled to feed and bestow gifts upon members of the rabble, lest they be pursued with hatred and malice.[65]

In short, one gave gifts in public for the sake of one's public reputation. It is in this context that gifts also appear in the municipal regulations concerning municipal spending. The great Basel ordinance from the mid-fifteenth century that sought to regulate the cost and the number of candles and guests at funerals, the value of gifts to the newly baptized, and the number of courses at the New Year's banquet of the guilds brought together all of these ceremonies, whether they took place in the open air, in churches, or in guildhalls, under the rubric of *schenck*, an umbrella term for demonstrative services more generally.[66] In a late medieval city, the public was not an abstract homogeneous arena in the modern sense, but rather a mixture of coexisting and intertwined urban publics, in the plural.[67] Gifts served as media within these social spaces, as means of transmitting and multiplying information.

The fourth point relates to the referentiality and ambiguity of gifts. The meanings of *schenck* described in the preceding chapters—prestigious liquid, conspicuous display, legitimate administrative act, a euphemism for potentially menacing offers that one could not refuse—resist sharp distinctions. On the contrary, they are mutually reinforcing. When mercenaries from Bern and Solothurn passed through Basel in August 1445 on their way home from the Breisgau campaign, the first thirty of them received one florin each as a welcome gift; the council also gave them several casks of wine. This did not, however, prevent the soldiers from storming and sacking the town houses of several noblemen in Basel, with the apparent approval of a segment of the local guilds. The town council barely succeeded in averting open warfare in the streets, and only further generous gifts of wine could convince the plunderers to leave the pillaged houses and the city.[68] A generation later the Basel chaplain Knebel also described involuntary gifts of wine and menacing guests in his chronicle. When the victorious Swiss troops marched into Basel on their way back from the battle of Nancy, a few citizens encouraged them with gifts of malmsey wine and sugar to pillage the houses of the canons and curates.[69] Gifts of malmsey and sugar also appear in Knebel's chronicle as the means of persuasion used by an elegant confidence man who appeared one year later in Basel. By forging the secret seals of great Nuremberg bankers and merchant houses, he managed to fleece a number of gullible people in Basel.[70] In the work of this urban chronicler, no friend of the Swiss Confederacy, presents of costly imported wine appear as highly ambivalent liquid gifts. Perhaps we may even regard the six quarts of malmsey that the town council presented to the courier of the Swiss Confederacy in 1504 during the solemn announcement and invocation of the Swiss prohibition on pensions as a subtle reference to this history of gifts, which linked wine as a political liquid with Basel's relationship with the Swiss Confederacy and ambiguous gifts.[71]

Gifts talk, then. Some, like the expensive silver goblet embellished with a coat of arms and little figures that the city of Basel gave to the papal legate Peraudi in 1504, do so conspicuously and unmistakably. Others are more discreet, and we only hear of them because the extent of the investment itself aroused controversy. In a memorandum of 1511, Gabriel Gesser, a Vienna-based clerk in the Ravensburg trading company, described to his superiors the means used by the Viennese partner Heinrich im Steinhaus to extricate a debtor from prison in Ofen (Budapest) and get him out of a lawsuit involving sureties. Heinrich had given many gifts for the purpose, Gabriel reports, including gilded drinking vessels to Count Lienhart and a certain Doctor Cryspyon, along with cash and an expensive fish dinner. And while he, Gabriel, had believed matters would end there, the count had returned from Ofen and demanded a silk jerkin as a fee for his successful efforts. Heinrich had also agreed to this, remarking that he had gotten off quite cheaply.[72] Gabriel Gesser accordingly asked the head office for additional funds to purchase silk garments for similar gifts; in particular, fabrics threaded with gold were needed so that "gentlemen might be served with them to our advantage." This sounds rather ironic, and with a sort of deep sigh the merchant recapitulated that in Hungary, as elsewhere, "the noble gentlemen do nothing for free."[73]

It is unclear whether one partner here was trying to blacken the name of another because he had bestowed overly generous gifts. What is clear is that with such gifts, cost effectiveness was difficult to establish. The offer always had to be reasonable (*wolfayll*), just as the gifts had to announce their value quite audibly. Whether Heinrich actually gave the exact gifts Gabriel Gesser describes is less interesting than the fact that they inscribed themselves in a code of efficacious gifts that was apparently familiar to contemporaries. For that reason they also seem strangely familiar to us. We have already encountered similar silver cups and costly fabrics in the Basel accounts and in the expensive cloaks that the blackmailed Zurich prisoner had to give his benefactor Hans Waldmann in exchange for his release. We will encounter a few more before we are through, gleaming bowls and silky gifts such as the piece of cloth with which a robber and murderer allegedly purchased his release from prison in Augsburg in 1475 from the mayor Ulrich Schwarz.[74] These were no mere fictions; it was quite possible to bribe someone with clothing. In a lengthy 1494 ordinance against abuses in the wine trade, the Strasbourg town council tried to prevent the officially appointed wine brokers from receiving garments or other tokens from their preferred business partners. Middlemen expected gifts. Within this logic of offerings, access, information, and gifts were inextricably linked. The chronicle of the counts von Zimmern recounts the tale of the abbot of Fulda who sought an audience with the emperor at the Augsburg Imperial Diet and after a long wait approached the court jester Conz von der Rosen to act as his intermediary. The abbot believed that Conz would deliver his request free of charge, but, remarks the chronicler ironically, Conz wanted his palm greased. He saw the abbot's costly silk-lined marten cloak lying on the table, donned it, and said, "My lord, if I am to accomplish anything with the emperor I must be properly dressed, otherwise I will be taken for a fool." And then he vanished, taking the cloak with him. That was the last the abbot saw of either.[75]

In discussions of gifts in the cities of the late Middle Ages and the early modern period, talk about *schenck* became condensed into tales and microplots that provided contemporaries with familiar set pieces. They were not unambiguous and "true," but rather appropriate and plausible because they transported the ambiguities, euphemisms, and power relations that were inherent in these transfers. In fact, it was not just the gifts that were eloquent, but sometimes also the names of those involved, even in the more sober kinds of texts. The figure of the middleman who makes an offer one cannot refuse appeared several times in the preceding sections. Sometimes he too had a name. When Frederick III visited Augsburg in 1442, the city set up a register as a memorandum for gift giving during later visits by monarchs. Aside from gold, wine, and fish for the king and his retinue, it also mentions 21 florins for four silver goblets that were presented to a particular member of the royal court whose goodwill the city needed, a certain "Chamberlain Disgrace" (Camermeister Ungenad).[76] The victim of the Zurich mayor Waldmann's extortion, who was forced to buy his way out of prison in Milan with 100 florins and a silk cloak, bore a wonderfully appropriate name: Andreas Schenk, doctor of jurisprudence.[77]

What, ultimately, was the connection between municipal offices and these eloquent offerings, between administrative duties and ambiguous gifts? The fifteenth- and sixteenth-century sources reveal officeholders as *personae mixtae*, dual but insufficiently separate figures in which official and private incomes and functions overlapped in a complex manner. Legal and constitutional historians have described these phenomena as weaknesses of the early modern state and as corruption. This interpenetration of official and private arenas does not, however, reflect any fundamentally deficient selectivity on the part of contemporary terminology. On the contrary, the wine bestowed by the city was an official distinguishing feature that indicated whether someone was in the city in an official or a private capacity. (The gifts provided by cities during princely visits have accordingly even been used as a statistical basis for determining more precisely the size of late medieval courts.)[78] It was in no small part through gifts that officials were situated, confirmed, and variously remunerated in their posts: the town guards who delivered the city's official gifts embodied municipal power in more than one sense. The gifts of the fifteenth and sixteenth centuries literally created officials and official powers.

Which half of the officeholder's dual persona accepted the gift in a given instance, and which one kept it, remains unclear. Gifts of diverse provenance played a prominent role in the income of municipal officials, as we have seen. The oath taken by the Basel couriers explicitly authorized them personally to retain gifts from the recipients of their messages; they had to swear, however, to report what gifts they had received and from whom.[79] In Basel, though, the word *botten* referred not just to simple messengers paid by the mile to carry letters but also to persons of far higher rank, members of the town council or its various committees who were entrusted with diplomatic missions as *ratsbotten* (council envoys). We know a good deal about them because they were required to provide careful bookkeeping of their expenses and outlays, and their reports are thoroughly documented in the council's weekly account books.[80] They too were dual persons; the council ordinance of 1506, which set new rates for expenses and reimbursement for council envoys, forbade them to combine diplomatic missions with their own private business.[81] Just as the city of Basel gave gifts to foreign diplomats, its own official ambassadors also received presents on their missions. Prohibitions of such tokens to municipal couriers appeared early,[82] but in fifteenth-century practice the Basel regulations emphasized the duty to report gifts. What exactly happened to these gifts and according to what key they were distributed between the two halves of the dual official remains obscure. What is clear is that such missions could be extremely lucrative.[83]

During the first century after Basel's entry into the Swiss Confederacy, a radical change appears to have taken place in either the perception of these tokens in the city or the actual size of diplomatic gifts. The new council ordinance of 1506 set a new framework of expenses for officials who had to leave the city on municipal business and subjected them to stricter reporting procedures.[84] An amendment of January 20, 1507, continued to permit municipal envoys to accept gifts but required them to hand over whatever they received because it was "common property." Only when the gifts that envoys brought home exceeded municipal expenditures could the council decide to give them the surplus or some part of it. A supplement of February 1511 extended this strict regulation to the servants and mercenary soldiers who accompanied municipal diplomats.[85] The handing in of gifts did not always go smoothly, it seems. A decree of November 1512 complains that gifts to municipal envoys had led to quarrels in the town council; an entry of March 1513 further intensified the duty to turn over gifts.[86]

Clearly, notions of what kind of gifts these were, who had a right to them, and what relation they bore to officials' duty towards common property—one of the central concepts of municipal legitimacy and political self-representation—differed widely. All the gifts so carefully registered in the municipal written records discussed here thus far, whether they involved liquids, political display, acts of administrative clemency, or the irrefutable demands of menacing middlemen, had one thing in common: visibility. In 1507, when the Basel town council introduced the strict requirement that municipal diplomats turn in gifts, the town clerk added in the margin of the municipal ordinance book "secretly or publicly" (*heimlich oder offenlich*). Behind the demonstrative gifts that assumed such a central place in urban political display, another, more discreet form of transfer began to emerge. What did the one have to do with the other?

3 *Manners of Speaking*

Venality and Its Terminology

The rules to which gifts were subject in the late medieval and early modern periods were second-order rules, intended to regulate not the acts themselves but rather talk about the rules. Behind the rhetoric of honoring (*eren*) local or foreign officials with presents and the voluble demonstrations of political munificence, hints of other stories and other gifts emerge. The narratives about these *schenck* contain a number of ambivalent and negative elements, and it is these elements that will concern us here. If the official presents of the fifteenth- and sixteenth-century cities concentrated so strongly on wine and were depicted as liquid and public, what can we say about other less easily controlled and more dangerous transfers?

In fourteenth-century municipal ordinances, legal texts, and chronicles, a term for gifts began to appear that had—or supposedly had—nothing to do with the liquid tokens for prominent travelers, presents for the wearers of foreign coats of arms, demonstrative offerings at receptions and weddings, and the various *schenck* directed at municipal officials themselves that we have encountered to this point. This term was *miet*. On July 13, 1372, the Basel town council resolved that in the future, each councilor should swear before the saints that henceforth he would accept no *miet* from anyone connected with the council members or the court, on pain of one year's banishment from the city and a lifetime exclusion from all municipal office. The complete oath formula was inscribed in the city's parchment Red Book and also in the paper White Book. In July 1385 the prohibition was entered into the council records once again, and the threatened punishment raised to five years' banishment.[1]

All Basel officeholders swore to uphold this prohibition. The formula promising that they would do their best for the city, unhindered by friendship, enmity, fear, envy, or *miet* (nor by the expectation or promise of such a gift), was read out unaltered every year during the council election. Into the seventeenth century, the records showing the composition of the council, which are preserved from 1436 on, repeated the oath before the yearly list of the councilors' names.[2] These gifts were, apparently, dangerous in the extreme. The oath formulas no longer existed merely on paper but were reflected in concrete cases. In 1420 the Basel *Leistungsbuch* records the trial of a high municipal official, the magistrate Jakob Boumli, for accepting *miet* (he was, however, permitted to convert the penalty of five years' banishment stipulated in his oath of office into a monetary fine). In 1421, two more officials were sentenced to heavy fines for the same offense and permanently ousted from office.[3]

The Basel ordinances had some trouble defining the precise character of *miet*, though. They mainly describe what it does *not* mean. Judges, councilors, and guild masters were permitted to accept horses and other things as gifts, notes the 1372 ordinance, but they had to declare publicly from whom they had received them and to leave the council chamber during any deliberations that concerned the giver. The ordinances of 1372 and 1385 and their successor stipulations of the fifteenth century continued to ensure that the holiday gifts that the butchers or other guilds, the municipal convents and monasteries, and the Jews had traditionally given to the mayor and councilors were not covered by the law, and neither were presents of game, poultry, gingerbread, or spices.[4] The Strasbourg ordinance on council elections and the municipal administration enacted in 1433 began by stating that all forms of *miet* were forbidden and anyone accepting them would have to pay the city the hefty sum of 24,000 pfennigs, would be considered a perjurer, would be banished from the city for five years, and could never serve on the council again. "We define as *miet*," the ordinance then goes on, "horses, clothing, suits of armor, coins, gold, silver, salt, any kind of game meat, victuals and other things, small or great, in money or cash value, that is liable to soften a man and is used to prevent the city from doing something or to promote or disadvantage certain persons."[5]

As strict as this definition may sound, not every gift to every municipal official fell under the prohibition. Like other authorities, the Strasbourg town council in the fifteenth and sixteenth centuries did allow its officers to accept gifts, even those of money or costly precious metal objects. It expected to be asked for permission first, though.[6] *Miet* is not a class of negative gifts that is easy to delimit either qualitatively or quantitatively. Instead, in South German usage it appears to have been *the* key term for forbidden gifts to officials, whether in Nuremberg, Bern, Sélestat, or the Austrian city of Freiburg im Breisgau. The term often appears in tandem with the more neutral words for gifts that we have encountered already, thereby lending them a negative flavor. Neither "*miet* nor *gab*," so the stock phrase went, should keep the officeholder from his duties, and in this form the term soon appeared in the influential supraregional legal codes of the late fifteenth and early sixteenth centuries, the Bamberg *Halsgerichtsordnung* of 1495, its printed edition of 1507, the various versions of Ulrich Tengler's *Laienspiegel* of 1509–14, and the imperial *Constitutio Criminalis Carolina* of 1527, which was valid throughout the Holy Roman Empire.[7]

Invisible Transfers

Miet was not simply the late medieval German word for bribe. The word's history points in a direction that at first glance has nothing to do with administration and officials—the price of the body. In texts of the High Middle Ages, it appears as a neutral term for gifts, payment, and compensation for services rendered, albeit with a strong emphasis on the dependency of the recipient of *miet*. From the late twelfth century on, it appears as ransom money (in the epic poem *Erec* by Hartmann von Aue), as hush money, and above all as a reward for treachery. In the Middle High German versions of the *Chanson de Roland*, Genelûn delivers the hero Roland into the hands of the pagans for *miet*, and Judas's recompense was, naturally, also *miet*.[8] This traitor's reward was closely associated with false judgment and fraud when the word was used for self-servingly inflated court or procedural fees. Older German legal texts such as the *Schwabenspiegel* and the *Deutschenspiegel* combine warnings against corrupt judges with those against deception and betrayal.[9]

In this tradition Judas appears as the omnipresent evil patron saint of gifts: bodies had a price, and it was called betrayal. The early fifteenth-century satirical and moralistic epigrammatic poem *The Devil's Net*, in which a dialogue between Satan and a hermit sketches a hellish sociology of the individual estates and their sins, reserves a place in the devil's deepest sack for unjust judges who allow themselves to be swayed by *miet*. The author uses the same word for deceiving advocates and false witnesses in court. The anonymous reformist text, written between 1441 and 1443, describes conditions in the Strasbourg episcopal courts and complains of the *miet* that court couriers and advocates extorted from the poor and calls for thoroughgoing prohibitions.[10] In Michel Beheim's somewhat later epigrammatic poems, the term appears closely allied with greed, whether as the reward of a traitor who has sold his kinsman or brother to his enemies for *miet*, or as the fruit of usury. The language of contemporary Bible translations corresponded quite precisely to this use of the word.[11]

Figure 2. Judas points out Jesus to the soldiers. Detail from Stefan Multscher, Sterzinger Altar, ca. 1470, Multscher-Stadt-Museum, Sterzing.

According to the definition of the Strasbourg town council of 1433 cited above, almost anything could be *miet*, as we have seen, from horses, suits of armor, and cash to salt and foodstuffs: anything that could "soften a man," as the ordinance rather oddly put it. The term may seem vague, but it was pivotal in the particular legal relationship that the oath of office created between the city and its officials, and it was for this reason that the Strasbourg ordinance placed so much emphasis on the strict distinction between legal and illegal transfers. Ecclesiastical livings and curatorships did not fall under the regulation, the ordinance adds; similarly, it was not *miet* when one received gifts from close relatives. If presents were exchanged by non-kin, the ordinance continues, then such gifts should be bestowed publicly before the mayor and the town council, who had to then decide whether the gifts were lawful or not.

The choice of words is decisive. The council speaks here not of *miet*, for it differed from other gifts (*gifft und gob*) by being offered secretly, in sharp contrast to the city's official gifts of wine and other things, which had to be presented to their recipients before witnesses in a tavern, as another ordinance of the same period stresses.[12] *Miet* was the dark and hidden counterpart to the demonstrative public gifts that were so much the focus of municipal self-representation and political registration, and such transfers were all the more menacing for being invisible.

Body Parts for Sale: The Hands

We are faced with a paradox: How can a gift that is by its very definition invisible be made visible and identifiable? The learned traditions of the Middle Ages offer a number of pithy sayings for such corrupting presents. Michel Beheim opens his epigrammatic poem "Von Miet und Gab der Richter" with the biblical quotation about the *miet* that dazzles the eyes of judges and renders them blind and dumb: according to Beheim, the powerful threatened to devour their subjects if the latter did not stuff their mouths with money. In a moralistic poem of praise to the city of Nuremberg written in 1492, Kunz Has depicts the secret doughnuts and devilish sweets that deceitful lawyers and intercessors accept at court and accuses venal judges of cooking two kinds of porridge in a single pot—classic set pieces gleaned from a long tradition of food metaphors for evil gifts that can be traced back to the rhetoric of the High Middle Ages.[13]

Dangerous gifts were described and rendered visual even more directly on the body itself because the common good or *gemein gut*, the central term for the well-being of the city, was itself a body, as the town clerk Frauenburg put it in his 1476 instructions on the proper running of a city. In his early fifteenth-century council poems, the Erfurt town clerk Johannes Rothe uses John of Salisbury's famous dictum on the officials and judges as the hands of the state when he assigns these hands of the city the duty of bestowing money and gifts for the good and honor of the community, under the guidance and supervision of the clerks, who represent the eyes.[14] These hands not only give, however, but also take. Do not allow your palms to be greased, Rothe warns municipal officials, adopting another of the classic metaphors that medieval learning provided for gifts offered with evil intent.[15] The game of literary references and variations turned the greased palms of the Franciscan sermon exemplum into the "pfennig salve" that worked wonders and softened the hands (and hearts) of hardened officials. In 1474 a journal of the Ravensburg trading company notes pragmatically of a legal transaction that, before it encountered any great delays, "we must quickly grease the people's palms with gifts," and in his 1497 *Spiegel des Regiments,* Johann von Morsheim has a servant cynically congratulate an official on his new dignity: the more his palms were greased, the faster he would become a rich man.[16]

In these sayings, hands appear eminently suited to entering into close relationships with gifts of dubious purpose. The Strasbourg Bible of 1467 translates Jesus' reply to the questions of his disciples in Matthew 26:18, according to which he had announced that one of them would betray him: "He who places his hand in the bowl with me will betray me."[17] In his council poems, Rothe was not satisfied merely to refer to greasing when he personifies the parts of the municipal body. "If thine eye offend thee, pluck it out, and cast it from thee," he quotes from the Bible; it is better to enter heaven with one eye than hell with two. It was just the same with hands, he continued: it is better to cut one off than to come to a bad end with two.[18] In fifteenth-century German illustrated catalogues of virtues and vices, Justitia actually appears as a blind woman with arms amputated below the shoulder. She is flanked by two men holding banners. "How beautiful she would be if she had eyes and hands," reads the banner on her left. "She is most beautiful as she is," replies the text on her right; had she eyes and hands she would be hideous (*turpissima).*[19] Leaving out the allegorical reference to Justitia, political treatises of the late Middle Ages down to the *Institutio principis* of Erasmus of Rotterdam streamline this portrayal to focus directly on the male person of the official or judge. Referring to Plutarch, they provide a description of the statue of an official without hands that was erected in Rome in praise of incorruptibility. The representation of this handless official appears both in the images of justice on late medieval town halls and in Andrea Alciati's *Emblemata*, printed in 1531. In the various editions of his *Schelmenzunft* of 1512, Thomas Murner directly ties this representation, as the sin of venality, to Judas: a woodcut (Figure 3) shows a bound and naked man on a bench whose hands and arms the axe-wielding executioner severs from his body.[20]

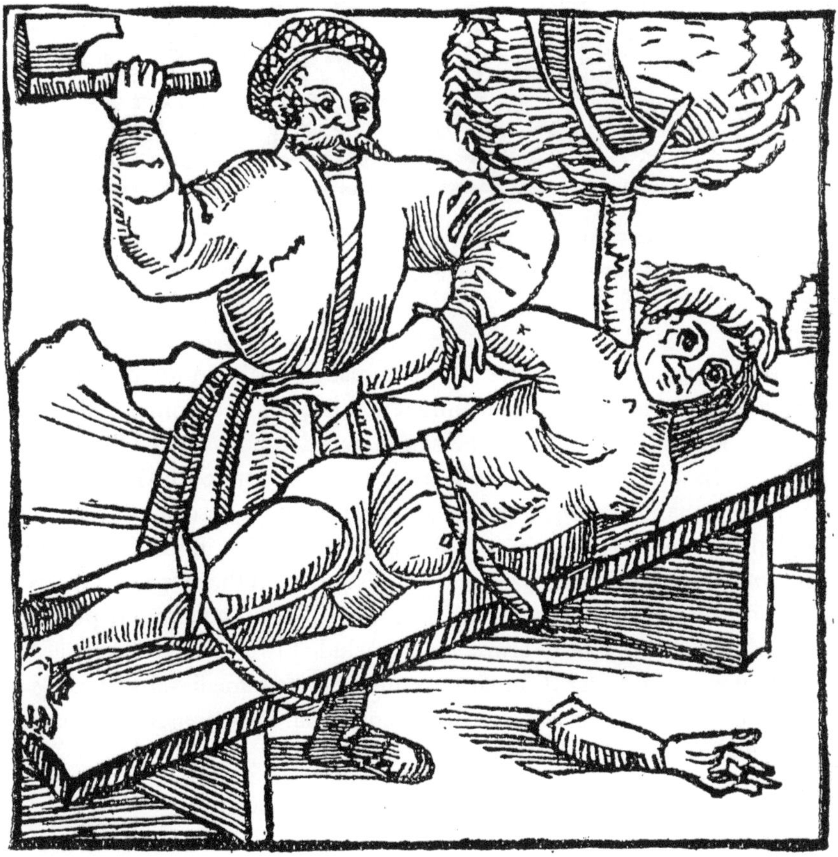

Figure 3. The traitor's hands are chopped off. Woodcut from Thomas Murner, *Der Schelmen Zunfft*, Strasbourg, 1512, Öffentliche Bibliothek, Universität Basel.

Figure 4. The handless judges. Representation of Justice. Woodcut illustration by Jörg Breu in Andreas Alciatus, *Emblematum Liber*, Augsburg, 1531, Öffentliche Bibliothek, Universität Basel.

Were these simple pictures or words made visual? In the fifteenth and sixteenth centuries, a common phrase for dropping criminal charges in exchange for gifts stated that the person in question had "looked through his fingers."[21] In fact we have evidence from a number of South German cities that severing hands or fingers served as punishment for corrupt officials. This mutilation points so plainly to venality and betrayal that in his rhymed *Buch von den Wienern*, written in 1463 on commission from the emperor Frederick III against the insurgent city of Vienna, Michel Beheim polemically provided the city with a new coat of arms, which included two severed fingers at the center, along with other defamatory symbols.[22] Late medieval sayings were clearly not intended to be exclusively metaphorical. They transported the gory threat that they could be taken quite literally.

The Judge's Skin

An early fifteenth-century illustrated South German manuscript collection on the virtues and vices combines the depiction of justice as a handless figure with the allegory of the corresponding vice of avarice. On the same page, it is brought together with another representation that, like the hands of the incorruptible official, refers directly to the body, albeit in a far grislier manner: the judgment of Cambyses.[23] The tale of the corrupt judge Sisamnes, whom the Persian king Cambyses had flayed alive in order to use his skin to cover the judge's seat to which Sisamnes' son then acceded, was originally told by Herodotus. In the transmission of Valerius Maximus, it appeared in chronicles, medieval encyclopedic works such as the *Speculum historiale* of Vincent of Beauvais, and collections of exempla from the thirteenth century onward. When medieval authors cited the story and referred to Herodotus and Maximus, they reversed the original moral, however. In Herodotus, the cruel verdict illustrated Cambyses' madness and horrific tyranny; the medieval tradition, in contrast, portrayed him as a sage who acted justly in making a public example of a corrupt officeholder. In this version the tale found its way not just into catalogues of virtues and vices but also into widely disseminated texts such as the vernacular versions of the "chess book" of Jacobus de Cessolis and the *Gesta Romanorum*.[24] Similarly, it appeared as a menacing allegory in numerous fifteenth- and sixteenth-century depictions of justice. Gerard David's painting *Judgment of Cambyses* in the Bruges town hall is the most famous example; one finds similar representations on medals, stained glass windows, frescoes, and the façades of both private houses and public buildings.[25]

This was naturally an eloquent punishment: in these images the late medieval expression according to which lords and officials skinned (*schinden*) their subjects appears reversed and reflected as an ominous example. The anonymous author of *The Devil's Net* complains that officials rob their subjects of "skin and hair" (*hut und har*) and also relishes the moral thrill of knowing what punishments await the holders of secular power in the hereafter, where God would "flay the evil officials." In Morsheim's *Spiegel des Regiments* (Mirror of Government), the author's eloquent laments about greased palms and corrupt officials are followed by Cambyses' order to "flay the official alive" and stretch his skin over the judge's seat.[26] What was Sebastian Brant referring to in his 1494 *Ship of Fools* when he inserted Ovid's motif of Marsyas skinned alive by Apollo into a representation of contemporary municipal justice? In the late medieval prose versions of the *Ovide moralisé*, Marsyas appears as an embodiment of vanity and hypocrisy who was subjected to a terrible punishment for his dissimulation.[27] During the ceremonial entry of Charles V into Augsburg for the Imperial Diet of 1530, tableaux

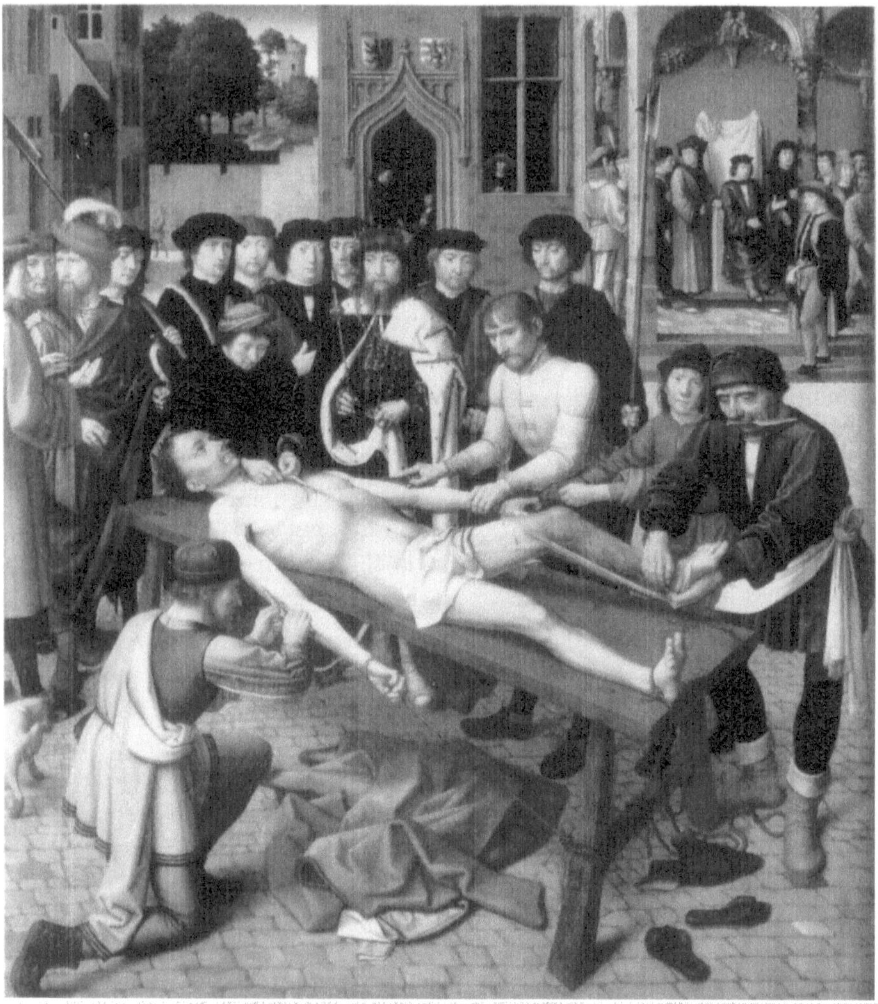

Figure 5. Gerard David, *The Judgment of Cambyses*, Groeningemuseum, Bruges.

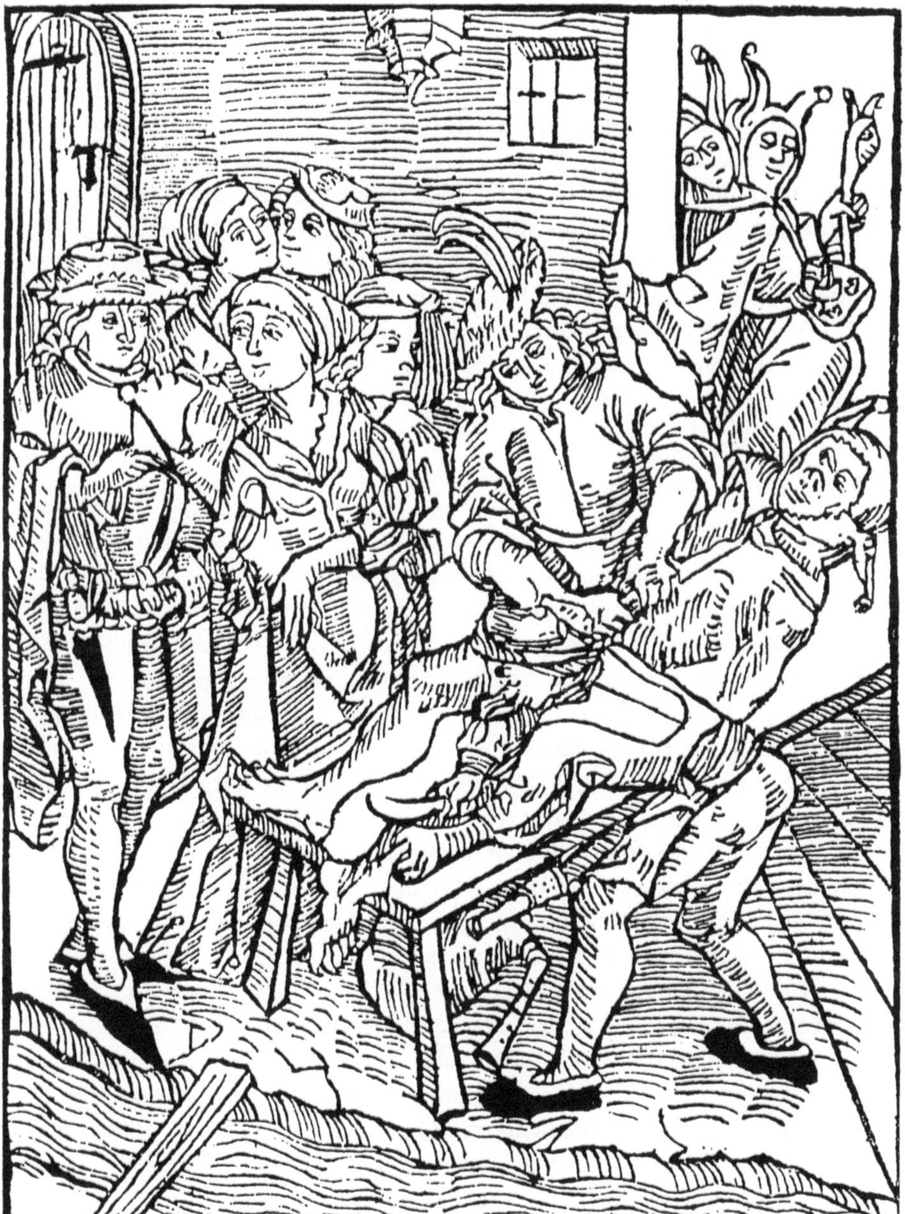

Figure 6. Woodcut illustration, *The Flaying of Marsyas*, in Sebastian Brant, Das Narrenschiff, Basel, 1494, Öffentliche Bibliothek, Universität Basel.

vivants taken "from old histories," as a chronicler put it, were performed for the local population and visitors to the Diet at various locations in the city. The ominous example of the corrupt judge and the merciless forces of order was also invoked here. As the author notes with some awe, "a man was skinned alive" on the stage.[28] Just as deceitful officials and judges skinned the poor, the punishment meted out to Sisamnes was performed on them in turn; that which is interior and invisible will be made visible, and peeling back the skin will reveal the true nature of lawbreakers. Also in the mid-sixteenth century, medals appeared in the Swiss Confederacy that depicted the corrupt flayed judge Sisamnes on one side and the coats of arms of the Reformed cantons on the other: ammunition in the political battles over gifts that will concern us in the sections to follow.[29]

Secrecies

The expressions for evil gifts and the allegories that reflected their mingling with deception, betrayal, and fraud did not only point to the body. They could also be combined with each other. Enea Silvio's famous polemic on courtiers and court life, for instance, is shot through with such linked meanings, and the printed German translation of his work attempted to convey for the audience of the 1520s the game of assigning biblical quotations, political classics, and popular expressions when it recounts the dangers of eating at court. "Just look," wrote Enea, "how many hands grasp at the meat in the bowl, and how many try to spear a piece with their knife." At such a meal, he adds, it was highly advisable to don one's iron gloves. The many hands that dipped into the common bowl were not merely the hands of the hands of state and the potential hands of Judas. They also wielded knives. No wonder, so the moral of the story, that some hands and fingers were lost in the process.[30]

In the Middle Ages and Renaissance, body metaphors highlight not simply political unity and integrity but also, at the same time, the internal hierarchy of individual body parts. The use of body metaphors thus always included the possibility of the dissection or disintegration of this "one" or whole body. The more explicitly it sought to exclude the danger of fragmentation and incoherence, the more clearly it confirmed them. The ambivalence was inherent in the use of the metaphor itself; it literally created those monsters that represented disorder, tyranny, and "false government." However much unity and order were invoked, the body metaphor always also contained an evocation of the dangers that the body represented for itself.[31]

Even more than food, hands, and skin, the genitals were predestined to shift these risks to the foreground. Gifts as pledges of love between men and women play an extraordinary role in the courtly literature, and in the erotically charged present, the boundaries between gift and person become fluid: "A woman who accepts a gift sells herself; a woman who gives a gift, gives herself." It was not for nothing that the women offering liquid gifts to St. Anthony on the frontispiece of this book were given diabolical attributes by the late fifteenth-century Cologne master who painted them. Against this background, medieval moralists not only warned women not to accept gifts from men but also conceptualized gifts from women to men as a dangerous and monstrous reversal of the moral order.[32] At the same time, however, the medieval tract literature portrays the risks of accepting gifts as risks for a body that was conceived of as both political and explicitly masculine. In his *Policraticus*, John of Salisbury speaks of the court and gifts at court as being like the fountain of Salmacis, which robbed men of the qualities of their nobler sex, turning them into monstrous hermaphrodites.[33] The German translator of Konrad von Megenberg's political bestiary *Buch der Natur* likewise juggles with the similarity between the words capon (*Kapaun*) and chaplain (*Kaplan*). He compares the castrated rooster, who, robbed of his genitals, is tasty but infertile and incapable of protecting his hens, with the wicked clerics who bring forth no spiritual works and no longer care for their flocks. "Oh you accursed shepherds!" he exclaims, because they accept *miet* and forget their duties. Now that the wolf was upon the sheep the castrated priests and prelates ran for the hills. They were good for nothing but the devil's kitchen—and he knew many such fat birds.[34] The expression concerning the shepherds who accepted *miet* is a biblical quotation (John 10:11-13), which the author embellishes with his reference to castration. To refer to someone as castrated was a common insult in the late Middle Ages; the fifteenth-century Italian-German textbook cited above virtually plays upon this derogatory (and rather risky) expression for municipal officials.[35] But what did this have to do with *miet* and evil gifts?

Warnings against effeminate, flattering, and corrupt officials and advisers who lubricated matters with gentle words and poured lies like poison are a commonplace of medieval tract literature. John of Salisbury's *Policraticus* links the theme of flattery as poison with the constantly repeated warning against milksop courtiers who acted *more meretricantis*. In his work, the price for the body is emphatically sexualized; in the *Policraticus* corrupt judges and false advisers alike are prostitutes who adopt the whorish trade of deceit and vice.[36] The mixture of corruptibility, lies, deceit, and unmanly sexuality runs through the various fourteenth- and fifteenth-century mirrors of princes, down to Jakob Wimpfeling's 1498 *Agatharchia* and the great texts of the sixteenth century. Erasmus's *Institutio* features it, as does the great best-seller of the Renaissance, Baldassare Castiglione's *Book of the Courtier*.[37]

These texts draw their warnings against effeminate advisers, emasculation, and entrusting secrets to women or men with feminine characteristics from an additional source, the *Secret of Secrets* (*Secretum Secretorum*), or, as it was called in late medieval German translation, the *Haimlichkeit des Aristotelis*. The fictive didactic dialogue between Aristotle and Alexander on the art of government, which is of Syrian provenance and was first translated into Latin around 1150 and into German in the early fourteenth century, was one of the most influential and widely disseminated political tracts of the Middle Ages.[38] Like scarcely another text, the *Secretum*, with its advice on dress, self-presentation, dietetics, physiognomy, male cosmetics, and the use of poisons, focuses on the body of the ruler. In order to protect his physical integrity, the prince must not confide his secrets to any woman, paraphrases one fifteenth-century version, lest he fall victim to poison and treachery. Excessive sexual intercourse sapped male strength and engendered effeminate habits and tempers, according to the illustrated German translation of the *Haimlichkeit* produced in Basel in 1476. For that reason the monarch should trust no one, advice that applied not just to women, but also to his councilors and servants. He should, instead, make use of covert informants. To be sure, one could not have absolute faith in such secret couriers, who often betrayed their masters for money.[39] Finally, the author uses an example to summarize the entire complex of poison, gender, gifts, and the reading of hidden signs. Remember the gifts sent to you by the queen of India, Aristotle admonishes Alexander, "many richly ornamented precious objects and lovely tokens." They had also included a beautiful young maiden, who had been fed snake venom from earliest childhood. Had he not looked at her closely and noticed that her gaze and her touch were deadly, Aristotle continued, and had he not signaled this to Alexander by secret signs, the latter, once his passion for her had been awakened, would surely have died.[40]

The tale of this poisonous daughter of the South is an oft-repeated motif signaling the evil gift in medieval and Renaissance exempla.[41] The *Secretum* is not only closely allied to contemporary discourses on gifts; the text also underlines the strong sexual connotations of the word *heimlich* (secret). In a carnival play of the mid-fifteenth century in which men and women denounce each other before an ecclesiastical court, the wife accuses her husband of neglect. She had long "suffered a secret lack" while he courted other women. The man, in contrast, denounces her reluctance to perform her marital duties, which drove him to other women in the first place, to whom he lamented his "secret infirmity." The allusion to the nature of this deficiency or infirmity would not have been lost on contemporary readers—the adjective "secret" (*heimlich*) points firmly below the waist. Thus in his 1497 *Spiegel des Regiments,* Johannes Morsheim could denounce the "secret" tricks and agreements of the prince's deceitful advisers as procuring, and in a collection of sermons compiled around the same time and printed in 1521, Geiler von Kaisersberg admonishes his audience ambiguously to beware of great lords confiding their secrets because this could imperil their souls: one would become mixed up in their worries and business whether one liked it or not. He preferred to remain silent on their other sins, he adds suggestively; one must flatter and consent to evil.[42] In the 1521 German translation of Petrarch's *De remediis utriusque fortunae,* Joy boasts in a dialogue of her wealth of "secret" gardens, to which Reason replies by alluding to the disgracefulness of the secret pleasure gardens of Emperor Tiberius and pondering the wicked use of words. "I am ashamed and vexed to know of this thing, to recount with what curses this old and craftily hidden or secret path has been poisoned."[43] Clearly, the voluptuousness and sins alluded to here were especially terrible and destructive, but they must not be named.

The search for expressions used to refer to the evil gift seems to have taken us far away from the municipal officials of the Upper Rhine. Let us return to *miet* and the figure of Judas. From the High Middle Ages on, the legend of Judas was recounted as a medieval Oedipus motif. Abandoned by his parents after a terrible prophecy, Judas was adopted, treacherously slayed the son of his adoptive parents, murdered his biological father after his return because of a court intrigue, and was married to his own mother by Pontius Pilate. The popular vernacular versions of his life story always duly emphasize the secrecy (*heimlichkeit*) of Judas's deeds.[44] In a moral poem written around 1460, Michel Beheim has a corrupt judge appear as Judas, who receives his reward for a body sold. As the personification of avarice, Judas thus becomes a figure uniting covetousness, usury, and simony.[45] The reward for betrayal is false money in the literal sense of the word. Johann von Morsheim accordingly complains in his *Spiegel des Regiments* that disloyalty and false money rule all the estates of the world.[46] The manner of speaking about this false money itself became quite literal: late medieval Passion plays painted in broad strokes the scene in which Caiaphas attempted to pay the treacherous Judas in counterfeit coins.[47]

This conglomeration of evil transfers surrounding Judas runs through the entire vernacular literature of the late Middle Ages. Bribery, fraud, usury, and simony were categorized as a conglomeration of closely allied hidden sins. According to the influential theologian Nikolaus von Dinkelsbühl in his early fifteenth-century commentary on the Ten Commandments, a usurer was not only a person who loaned money at interest, but anyone who loaned money in exchange for services or aid, for example, from officials, or in court. Fraud, bribery, and usury were the sins of concealment, Dinkelsbühl explained in connection with the seventh commandment because, as Isidore of Seville taught, they took place secretly and in the dark.[48] Under the sins caused by avarice, a Bavarian penitential book of the mid-fifteenth century accorded a prominent place to treason, after deceit and violence. Just as Judas betrayed Jesus Christ for thirty florins, the author wrote, people in his day were betraying each other in court with secret gifts to the judge.[49] The Latin-German *Speculum christianitas* that arose in a late fifteenth-century urban context accordingly names usury, deceit, treachery (*prodicio*), and spiritual usury or simony (*symonia*) as direct derivates of the sin of avarice.[50]

The word for Judas's reward can thus also be found in the late medieval German adaptations of the story that presents the evil gift par excellence: the tale of the fall of the city of Troy. Known throughout the Middle Ages and frequently used as the starting point of mythical genealogies, vernacular German romances about Troy enjoyed an extraordinary dissemination and popularity between the late fourteenth and the late fifteenth century. They refer, however, not to Homer's *Iliad*, but to the now less familiar versions by the late antique authors Dares and Dictys and the *Historia destructionis Trojae* of Guido of Columna based upon them. In this version of the story, Troy's downfall was brought about not by Greek cunning but by treachery: it was the Trojans Aeneas and Anthenor who facilitated the smuggling of armed Greeks past the city walls in exchange for the promise of rich rewards. In the fifteenth-century South German redactions and prose versions of Konrad von Würzburg's *Trojan War*, the name of the alleged turncoat who persuaded the Trojans to bring the horse into the city was, appropriately, Symon. In Ulrich Füetrer's *Adventure Book* of the 1470s, he then became "the scoundrel who accepted *miet*."[51] In his moral satire *Schelmenzunft* (Rogues' Guild), which appeared in Strasbourg in 1512 and was reprinted several times, Thomas Murner could thus count Judas, the fall of Troy, and Babylonian rule together as the classic cases of devilish treachery.[52]

I am concerned here not with the history of concepts in the strict sense of the term, but rather with the reconstruction of word clusters, with what con-

Figure 7. The figure of Judas (*right front*) is depicted with an erect penis and fashionable clothes; note the spilled wine at his feet and the fly in front of his mouth. Detail from Jörg Ratgeb, *The Herrenberg Altarpiece*, 1519, Staatsgalerie Stuttgart.

temporaries kept in mind and alluded to when the word for evil gifts appeared. The political slogans of the late Middle Ages, the arenas of their reception, and the concepts with which they were associated are not easy to grasp.[53] *Miet* is not simply an old-fashioned word that officeholders repeated and declaimed every year in their traditional oath formulas. This recourse to the word for forbidden gifts points to the religious connotations of usury and simony in vernacular Bible translations, catechisms, and municipal legal texts as well as instances of deception and betrayal in exempla, romances, and moral and satirical epigrammatic poetry. What all of these gift-sins had in common was that they occurred invisibly and secretly—in the dark, as Nikolaus von Dinkelsbühl put it.

Familiar Quotations

The late medieval term *haimlichkeit* bore both a menacing and an intensive relationship to its opposite *gemein nutz* (common good).[54] The author of the *Reformatio Sigismundi*, which was written in Basel in the mid-fifteenth century, thought he recognized the source of all that was wrong with his age in avarice and the "great simony," which like usury had poisoned all the clerical estates: the word for evil gifts runs through the entire reform text. The mendicant orders had bribed cardinals from their ranks who pestered the pope day and night with gold and silver, the author lamented. Many priests were "secret sodomites," and the bishops were bribed with *miet* to tolerate the sins of the clergy. Uneducated priests and corrupt bishops and cardinals permitted themselves to be diverted from their official duties by *miet*, he continues, and donations to the convents were not passed on to God via the poor but went straight to the devil by way of the rotten gifts (*miet*) from monks to the mighty.

The *Reformatio*, which emerged from the circles of the Council of Basel and was disseminated in the urban milieu of the Upper Rhine and South Germany, unites this specifically expanded and very political notion of simony with complaints about avarice, sodomy, and evil gifts.[55] The 1476 printed version of the *Reformatio* further intensified the formulations, which were taken up again in the radical *Book of the Hundred Chapters*, which was composed in 1508, also in the Upper Rhine region.[56] The reform biblicism of this so-called Upper Rhine revolutionary alluded to the broad field of meaning of "silent sin," usury, treachery, and bribery, which was all too familiar to contemporaries—transfers in the orbit of usury, fraud, and deviant sexuality. "Many gifts were given to her," wrote the Augsburg chronicler Wilhelm Rem in 1518 of the pious professional faster Anna Laminit, now unmasked; she had received many treasures from foreign lands, and yet she had cheated, counterfeited, procured, made her house available for peculiar sexual practices, found homes for "secret" children, and murdered her husband with poison.[57] In his chronicle some years later, the painter Jörg Bräu, a passionate partisan of the Reformation in Augsburg, offered a briefer version of the dealings between Anna Laminit and certain patrician families. These included procuring, he writes, arranging erotic encounters, getting rid of unwanted children, money-lending, and, finally, accepting and distributing gifts and *miet*.[58]

The gifts with which social and political relationships and alliances were so conspicuously proclaimed in the cities of the late Middle Ages and early modern period had their dark counterparts. Contemporary townspeople persistently associated these negatively connoted transfers with body metaphors and invisibility, and the word *miet* functioned as a key term for such covert connections in which bodies and money mingled in a highly specific manner.[59] In a homage in the prologue and in a remarkable gloomy prophecy at the end of his tract, the anonymous author of a radical reform treatise of 1508, the so-called "Upper Rhine revolutionar," invoked the classics of high medieval body metaphor. If the abuses prevailing in the administration were not stopped, he threatened, "I tell you that the common man in the Black Forest will follow the teachings of Policraticus" (*der ler policrati*)—that is, the political doctrine of tyrannicide.[60]

John of Salisbury in the Black Forest of 1508: a tale well told could clearly cover great distances in time and space. The authors of the late Middle Ages recombined narrative elements from the *Secretum Secretorum* and the *Policraticus* as the basis for a political pathology of a very special kind—the evocation of those evil gifts that aimed at the body. These traditions—the metaphors of the body politic and its sexual pollution through venality—are not etymologies or roots in the sense of genealogies in the history of ideas. They are more a collection of set pieces, possible choices, and expressions available to late medieval people, which could be used and adapted as the need arose. This need was current, pragmatic, and political. Where did the word for evil transfers appear in the Upper Rhine region and the Swiss Confederacy in the late Middle Ages, and how was it used?

4 *Pensions*

The Mayor Falls

The term for invisible gifts can already be found in oath formulas and municipal chronicles of the late fourteenth and early fifteenth centuries, as we have seen. Beginning with the great conflicts between the Swiss Confederacy and Burgundy in the 1470s, however, it was used with increasing frequency and prominence as a political slogan and battle cry. In 1474, Rudolf Montigel of Lucerne composed a political song praising the alliance between Austria and the Swiss against Charles the Bold in which he accused segments of the nobility of having sold themselves to the Burgundians for *miet*.[1] The outraged participants in the illegal military campaign who arrived armed at the outskirts of Bern after Shrove Tuesday 1477, having marched from central Switzerland, sought not merely to collect (and redistribute) the monies owed by Geneva to the Swiss confederates, but also to punish the Swiss military commanders whom they held responsible for the absence of payments because they had accepted secret funds—*miet*. That, at least was what envoys of the insurgents claimed in a tumultuous debate with a delegation from Bern's Great Council.[2]

Miet also featured in the spectacular downfall of the Augsburg mayor Ulrich Schwarz in April 1478. The official pronouncement of judgment on the executed mayor declares that Schwarz had abused his offices to the detriment of the common good, accepting gifts as a broker and arbitrator in conflicts, extorting money from prisoners of the city, and always demanding a high *müet* for appointments to municipal office.[3] The labels applied to the mayor, the favors he bestowed, and the gifts he accepted have a familiar ring. When his municipal adversary Hans Vittel returned to Augsburg in 1477 from a diplomatic mission to the court at Vienna, the mayor, "with the underhanded malice of a false Judas," greeted him with a gift of six jugs of wine but shortly thereafter had him (unjustly) executed for high treason.[4] The text of the confession that was circulated after Schwarz's execution in 1478 provides further details. During his time in office, the text reports, Schwarz had extorted over

2000 florins in *miett.* He had not only poisoned his father-in-law, but also planned to attack and plunder the city's clergy and to have a number of former town councilors murdered in their beds; in addition, he had had secret copies made of the keys to the city. Finally, Schwarz, who had not gone to confession for many years, had not merely forged the city seal, but had also sold apple and pear cider as wine. The text ends with an inventory of the mayor's confiscated household effects. Apart from the enormous sum of 15,000 florins in cash, no fewer than three hundred silver goblets and forty gilded and two solid gold drinking vessels, which the mayor had received as gifts, had been found in Schwarz's house.[5]

How true were such fantastical accusations, whose descriptions of the evil liquid fruits of power mix murder, silver goblets, missed confessions, poison, the keys to the city, and the adulteration of wine? Much as the actual sequences of events and political contexts differed, the downfall of the Zurich mayor Hans Waldmann in April 1489 reads like a parallel narrative to the execution of his Augsburg colleague. Here, too, secret transfers and invisible crimes were involved.[6] Waldmann, the successful head of a mercenary army in the war against Charles the Bold and one of the great military entrepreneurs of the Swiss Confederacy in the 1480s, was arrested in the town hall during an uprising of Zurich's rural communes, which culminated in a virtual siege of the city by insurgent peasants. The provincial estates had risen up against the mayor's unpopular measures, particularly the new poll tax, an official salt monopoly, new appointments to the courts, the forced settlement of artisans in the city, and a new sumptuary edict introduced the previous year.[7] Waldmann's opponents in the city brought forward quite different accusations. The mayor had raped the wives of pious citizens and forced them with terrible oaths to remain silent, read the official charges; he had accepted bribes from foreign powers and betrayed Swiss military secrets in exchange; in addition, he had extorted gifts of money, textiles, and silver goblets from the citizenry. Above all, according to the rumors circulating in early April 1489, Waldmann had planned to have a number of town councilors murdered and to hand the city over to the German emperor Frederick III, whose army was on the march. To this end he had had copies made of the keys to all the towers and gates; the emperor's disguised and bloodthirsty partisans stood ready to begin their assault on Zurich as soon as they received a secret sign—two crossed fingers and the cry "Sankt Niklaus!"[8]

What sort of secrets was a supporter of Waldmann's who was arrested and interrogated in Lucerne referring to when he desperately denied having had anything to do with the mayor's political activities, stating that he had

had no secrets (*heimlichkeit*) with Waldmann?[9] After his arrest the deposed mayor was incarcerated in the Wellenberg, the municipal prison tower, in the cell of a *ketzer* (the fifteenth-century South German term for a sodomite),[10] and contemporary chronicles report at length on how he was forced to eat from the *ketzer*'s bowl. Under repeated torture Waldmann refused to admit to the sexual offenses of which he was accused. In the subsequent trial against the mayor, these accusations were tacitly dropped. On April 6, in an edifying religious procedure in which he asked those present to pray for his soul, Waldmann was beheaded before a crowd of several thousand spectators. His property was publicly assessed, inventoried—the lists especially highlight his silver and gilded goblets and drinking vessels—and sold. Following negotiations and rich gifts of wine and victuals, the insurgent peasants retreated. Eight weeks later, on Ascension Day 1489, the envoys of the communes were generously fêted as a sign of official reconciliation with the provincial estates, and new appointments were made to the offices and governorships on Lake Zurich. The new mayor and the new head of the guilds received the usual gifts of wine—a fine example of how close the forms of legitimate and illegitimate gifts could sometimes be.[11]

What Was a Pension?

In order to understand this close relationship between visible and invisible gifts, the use of the metaphors associated with them, and the contemporary allusions, we will need to look more precisely at political events in the Swiss Confederacy in the late fifteenth and early sixteenth centuries. It is a complex history of war and mercenary economies, battles, treaties, and rapidly changing political alliances, and a brief overview may be in order here.

In connection with the toppling of Hans Waldmann, a term for political transfers appears that, beginning with the last third of the fifteenth century, would dominate talk about gifts, offices, and political publics in the Swiss Confederacy for quite some time: *pension.* In its original meaning in canon law, a pension was the right accorded a person to draw a certain portion of the income from a benefice. Strictly speaking, only clerics were eligible; laypersons required a papal indult.[12] At the end of the Middle Ages, however, the word came to be used for regular annual payments more generally. The above-mentioned written complaint about the state of affairs in the ecclesiastical court at Strasbourg in the 1440s, for example, particularly stressed that the judges of the episcopal court should accept pensions or annuities from no one; a distinction was no longer made here between clerical and secular sources of pensions. The term *pension* was increasingly closely associated with the emerging central administrations. Whether constable, seneschal, or *bailli*, wrote Jean Juvénal des Ursins in 1445, there was no royal official who did not try at all costs to attain a pension in addition to his normal salary.[13]

In the usage that became established in the late fifteenth century, pensions were official (if often confidential), regular and contractually agreed payments to individuals, officials, councilors, and political corporations.[14] When the chronicle of the city of Zurich notes tersely in connection with the Burgundian wars, "and much money came into the land," it is referring not just to the booty and soldiers' wages of the victorious Swiss, but also to such annuities. The high sums that the French king Louis XI paid to Bern and other cantons in 1475 are well known, but we can document substantial Austrian pensions as well. Nikolaus von Diesbach (d. 1475), at any rate, proudly announced on his gravestone that he had brought his home city *pensas magnificas*.[15]

Diesbach, however, accepted large sums not just on behalf of the city of Bern but also for his own private coffers, and not all of his contemporaries regarded these payments as wholly glorious. In his chronicle of Bern, Diebold Schilling, himself the discreet recipient of Austrian monies, notes of the French pension payments of 1474 that the common man had suspected that "the city of Bern, its land and people had been sold."[16] Starting in 1474, the Swiss Assembly (*Tagsatzung*), composed of envoys from the confederated Swiss cities and cantons that met regularly, attempted on numerous occasions to limit or prohibit such payments altogether. At the Assembly meeting of October 21, 1474, just before the outbreak of the Burgundian Wars, the eight members of the Swiss Confederacy forbade the acceptance of donations and annuities from Duke Sigmund of Austria. In late February 1475, a renewed attempt was made to prohibit not just Austrian but all annuities and pensions because they "harmed" the Swiss Confederacy—the attempt was not successful, however.[17] An April 1475 entry in the minutes of the Lucerne town council documents the rumor that Waldmann and others had accepted money at the signing of the coalition treaty between Louis XI and the Swiss on October 26, 1474.[18]

What terms did contemporaries use to discuss such payments? The prohibition of 1474 used the word now familiar to us for invisible and dangerous gifts and boldly and clearly called these transfers *miet*. This word carried considerable political weight. When the authorities of the city of Bern resolved in 1474 to work together with the French king, the Inner Council ordered that the oath formula promising not to accept *miet*, which was usually publicly declaimed once a year at the council elections at Easter, no longer be read out—apparently as a preventive measure against accusations of perjury.[19] In letters, council resolutions, and chronicles, official Bern assiduously avoided referring to the French monies by anything other than the neutral terms "pension" or "annuity" (*Jahrgeld*); the passage from Schilling's Bern chronicle cited above was stricken from the official version. The French payments were officially and expressly referred to as gifts, which were legal because they demanded nothing in return. A Bern council resolution of 1477 explicitly permitted the councilors to accept pensions and New Year's gifts from the French king. The council members would certainly not allow this to influence their speeches or resolution, because they were bound to the king neither by oath nor by word of honor, the text of the council resolution noted artlessly, and some councilors noted just as artlessly that they would not object to the king giving them even more.

These regulations were linguistic ones: it *did* matter which terms were used to refer to the payments. When the Bern town council renewed the permission to accept French payments in 1479, it added the threatening amendment that anyone who slandered the councilors because of this would be arrested and severely punished.[20] Such people indeed existed. In 1487 a certain Rudolf Sidler was arrested in Lucerne for saying loudly on the street that honest men were recorded in the municipal *Schelmenbücher* (literally, books of rogues, the city's record of criminal offenders) rather than the miscreants who accepted pensions. Sidler was sentenced to death for this offense but appealed and had his sentence commuted to a monetary fine. He also had to make public amends and declare that he had only honorable things to say "about all those who accept pensions or payments."[21]

Similar expressions appear in the contemporary documents concerning the foreign pensions paid to Waldmann. They portray the pensions as reflections of a particular closeness between the giver and the mayor of Zurich, as gifts given out of affection or gratifications for Waldmann's selfless efforts. In an official pension letter of August 1476 from Duke Sigmund of Austria, for instance, he appears as "our dear, loyal Hanns Waldmann," who in the future would receive 100 rhenish florins annually for the "loyal advice and assistance" he had provided the duke concerning the coalition with the Swiss Confederacy. A letter of November 1477 from Louis XI promised Waldmann a yearly pension of 600 livres tournois *pour consideracion de pluseurs bons, grans et agreables services.* In 1482 he was mentioned on a further list of drawers of Austrian pensions, and in 1487 Maximilian chose the mayor of Zurich as the person who would accept and distribute the 4000 florins in pensions for the entire Swiss Confederacy because of his particular "love and loyalty." He was accorded a private pension of 400 florins a year for his efforts.[22] A letter of April 11, 1488 from Waldmann makes clear what "efforts" meant. He complained that the king had not yet sent any of the announced sum (Maximilian was in difficulties and imprisoned at Bruges), so that he and the Austrian chargé d'affaires had to raise and advance the money themselves. Waldmann also acted as a pension distribution broker for the Tyrolean duke Sigmund.[23] Finally, as a special *amico* of the duke of Milan, he not only received personal gifts and a yearly pension but was also responsible for the further distribution of Milanese funds—substantial sums of several thousand ducats in coins and costly silk fabrics. In his letters to the duke, the Milanese ambassador Moresini documents the description of payments as love offerings as well as their secrecy. "May I ask your lordship to give him, if possible, something as a reward for his love, but secretly," he wrote to Milan on December 8, 1487 (*Ge domanday, come poria esser, se ben V. S(ign.) volesse dare qualche cossa a costor per amor suo, che al fusso secreto*), while at the same time in Zurich Waldmann threatened him intermittently with arrest and open violence if the promised funds failed to arrive.[24] Pensions, it appears, were love offerings of a very particular kind.

Swiss chronicles of the early sixteenth century already portrayed Waldmann as the recipient par excellence of "many pensions and annuities."[25] For nineteenth- and twentieth-century Swiss historians, his rise and fall, and his contradictory character—he was depicted, alternately, as a warlike Swiss self-made man or a corrupt tyrant—served to crystallize the controversies surrounding pensions and political morality in the Swiss Confederacy during the transition from the Middle Ages to the early modern period. Like the figure of Cardinal Matthäus Schiner, Waldmann was described as hero or antihero at different periods and with shifting political undertones.[26]

But while the older patriotic historiography of the nineteenth and twentieth centuries (not unlike its late medieval and early modern counterparts) employed colorful metaphors for pensions, such as "widespread disease" (*Volkskrankheit*), "political degeneration," and "urges run wild," the economic historians of recent decades have emphasized that the significance of these payments for late medieval and early modern Switzerland can scarcely be overestimated. Pensions shaped the Swiss political elites as well as local systems of patronage and appointment; they placed the administration of the individual members of the Swiss Confederacy on a completely new footing and facilitated the rise of a class of wealthy Swiss notables and military entrepreneurs. The political structures of the early modern Swiss Confederacy emerged along with and by means of these payments.[27] Briefly put, the early modern political elite of the Swiss Confederacy was created with French, Italian, and Austrian funds.

Rumors and Revolts

The Zurich mayor Hans Waldmann thus did not stumble over his own lucrative activities as a drawer and distributor of pensions; on the contrary, they were part of his power base. His undoing was a series of domestic policy errors vis-à-vis the self-assured peasant communes around Lake Zurich and his municipal adversaries and rivals around the powerful former mayor Heinrich Göldli, himself a successful pension broker and war entrepreneur. After Waldmann's death, Göldli apparently took over his role in the distribution of monies; in the early summer of 1489, the Zurich town council was still writing a number of letters to the executed mayor's out-of-town pension providers demanding payment of all the pensions promised to him.[28]

The pensions shaped the Swiss Confederacy's internal conflicts in the late Middle Ages and early modern period as scarcely any other force did, and in what follows we will address these conflicts over outside funds in the years between 1490 and 1530. The conflicts were determined by widely varying political constellations; the resistance of local elites against official taxation policy and political modernization played a role here, as did the rivalries and distribution struggles between military entrepreneurs. What they had in common, however, is that they were conflicts over gifts—dangerous, invisible, and corrupting gifts—and over political legitimacy. In fact, these were conflicts over the public sphere and sovereignty, over the authority to enforce concepts and appellations.

Waldmann's fall in 1489 unleashed a wave of unrest in the Swiss Confederacy in which the political demands of the rural communes mingled with furious attacks on the recipients and distributors of foreign annuities. Faced with riots and threats from the communes, the town councils of Lucerne and some central Swiss cities felt compelled to issue formal prohibitions on pensions. By late April, Bern already feared the spread of the revolts, and called special sessions of the city's Greater Council on pensions (without results), and in early May the city agreed to adopt joint measures with Solothurn and Biel to stop the unrest in the countryside. On April 25 and May 20, 1489, the

Swiss Assembly debated a general prohibition of all such payments (now referred to, once again, as *miet und gab*) but did not institute it.[29]

Three months after Waldmann's execution the Zurich town council issued a sharply worded mandate according to which no citizen of Zurich would be permitted to accept pensions or annuities from anyone whatsoever. Council envoys to political negotiations were required upon their return to present the council with anything that they had received beyond their regular pay while out of town. The familiar word for evil gifts appears nowhere in this mandate, and yet was so plainly implied that a correspondent from Bern tersely summarized the prohibition on pensions as follows: the Zurichers had all had to swear "not to accept *miet* from anyone."[30] This official prohibition remained in force for only seven years. In November 1496, when the city joined the alliance between the Swiss Confederacy and the French king, the council decided to lift the mandate because the other members of the Swiss Confederacy did not obey it either.[31]

Rumors of substantial payments to individual town councilors had already been circulating months earlier, in the winter of 1495. The Zurich authorities summoned a number of persons whom they accused of alleging that Mayor Schwend had accepted money. The accused said in their own defense that they had heard such talk only from strangers in taverns; for example, that a donkey carrying gold was on its way to Zurich, or that 5,000 or 12,000 ducats had arrived in Zurich, Lucerne, and Bern. They had not realized who the subject of discussion was and were certain that the speakers had only meant the other two cities, and they themselves had naturally never believed the crude talk they heard in the taverns.[32] Rumors of Italian and French monies paid to Swiss officials worried other authorities as well. In June 1495 the Bern town council was disquieted by rumors of extensive secret payments of money that had supposedly moved the Swiss to intervene officially in Italian entanglements on the side of Milan.[33] That same year the Swiss Assembly addressed a proposal to forbid all pensions and gifts as well as foreign mercenary service, but without reaching any agreement. A renewed proposal in October 1496 concerning officials lining their pockets, pensions, *miet und gab*, and enlistment in foreign mercenary armies was put aside for further consideration, that is, deferred.[34]

In March 1499 the city of Bern, which had previously supported Milan and Maximilian and been integrated into a system of Venetian, Milanese, and imperial pension payments, changed sides and declared itself prepared, together with Schwyz and Unterwalden, to join the coalition of Swiss cantons and the French king. On April 1, 1499, the Bern authorities solemnly pronounced a prohibition on all public and private pensions, which was renewed and underlined in council decrees of February and March 1500.[35] The ultimately uncontrollable recruitment of Swiss mercenaries by the belligerent parties in Italy and the differing political stances of the Swiss cantons provided the background to the Swiss Assembly's deliberations of February 1500 on foreign mercenary service; pensions were mentioned only in passing. Plans for a much farther-reaching prohibition of all pensions were discussed at the subsequent sessions of March 23 and 31, and a draft of April 7, 1500, extended the prohibition to secret pensions (*heimlich pension*).[36]

The dates of these resolutions are not insignificant. Pensions were forbidden when the political management of the flow of foreign monies and their controlled distribution by official brokers were no longer guaranteed. Before 1500 the Swiss cantons did not have complete control over who provided soldiers to whom for money. In 1494, after several unsuccessful mandates, the Zurich town council sent the councilor Ruedi Schmid as an official envoy to Bellinzona in order to effect the return home of the mercenaries from Zurich, who had been recruited illegally for France in violation of the express prohibition of the town council. A few days after his arrival in Bellinzona Schmid declared in a letter to the town council that he himself would remain with the mercenary soldiers as an officer and go to war against Zurich's ally Milan. The council had no choice but to accept this. An entry in the council manual notes with resignation that it was better for the mercenaries to serve under a Zuricher than under a foreign commander; the boundaries between "official" and "private" functions proved highly fluid. Alongside official representatives of Swiss cantons such as Waldmann and his successors, that is, mayors, magistrates, and influential council members, private individuals also acted as military entrepreneurs and providers of mercenary armies, often in opposition to the official coalition policy at a given time. They were frequently close kin to representatives of the authorities and were treated with corresponding indulgence. The rapid shifts of political constellations—with Austria, then against Austria with France, and later against France again—meant that there were always new recipients of foreign monies who, despite official prohibitions, promised and delivered the expensive and much sought-after Swiss mercenaries in exchange for pensions. In most Swiss cantons, pro-French as well as pro-imperial brokers and liaisons who accepted gifts from abroad for further distribution were active both inside and outside the political decision-making bodies.[37]

The dates of the prohibitions on pensions are also significant because they preceded rather than followed political catastrophes. On April 9, 1500, the (pro-imperial) Swiss mercenaries under the duke of Milan, Ludovico Sforza, who was encircled in the walled city of Novara, refused to fight the attacking Swiss troops in the pay of the French and, after negotiations, turned the duke over to the French. Disguised among his Swiss mercenaries, who had been assured safe passage, Ludovico tried in vain to make his escape. He was betrayed, unmasked, and arrested, and the event was loudly exploited in the contemporary political literature as the treason of Novara and a perfect example of the venal, dishonorable, and greedy behavior of the Swiss.[38]

On May 5 the Swiss Assembly saw itself compelled, because of the "defamatory remarks" against the Swiss Confederacy, to order a strict investigation.[39] Apart from the search for the guilty parties, extensive interrogation of the Swiss military commanders involved, interviews of witnesses, and the 1503 execution of Hans Turmann of Uri, who had allegedly pointed out the disguised duke to the *bailli* of Dijon for 200 crowns, the main consequences of Novara were a number of suits against individual mercenary leaders and efforts at general prohibitions of pensions.[40] The envoys of the Swiss cantons who attended the Swiss Assembly meetings of May and June 1500, however, disagreed on whether all annuities should be forbidden. Some representatives preferred to play a waiting game and refused to swear an oath on the ordinance—some because they preferred to retain public pensions in favor of the town treasuries and others because they were holding out for a general prohibition. Throughout 1501, and despite ever-new negotiations and drafts, this stalemate continued to block any decision.[41] Meanwhile, foreign mercenary service and payments to the cantons and the pension brokers continued. Under pressure from the provincial estates, in January 1501 the Bern town council once again enacted a general prohibition on pensions, declared that it would accept no French money in future, and had several mercenaries and illegal recruiters executed. In July 1501 three hundred armed men gathered at the Swiss Assembly in Lucerne and openly threatened the delegates with violence. In the summer of 1502, the Zurich town council initiated an investigation against a priest who had preached against the pensions and annuities paid to the town councilors and had called upon the communes to take action.[42]

The "treaty on pensions" finally agreed upon at the Baden Swiss Assembly on July 21, 1503, which prohibited all forms of pensions, donations, annuities, gifts, and *miet*, was never ratified by all the cantons at any one time. Conflicts over the formulation of an additional clause of August 1503 and the demand that all members of the Confederacy must accept the regulation were used by several representatives as an excuse to refuse to swear the oath upon the ordinance as a whole. Pointing to the refusal of Zurich and Solothurn, Lucerne and then Fribourg withdrew from the agreement in the autumn of 1505. In November of the same year Bern also conducted a solemn ceremony exempting itself from the prohibition on pensions that it had sworn to just as solemnly six years before. The council and citizens kneeled and received absolution from the bishop of Lausanne and immediate permission to accept such gifts of money again.[43]

At no point do the majority of Swiss cantons and the representatives of their authorities appear to have stopped drawing pensions. On August 1, 1501, for example, Diebold Schilling of Lucerne sent a humble request to Maximilian for annual gifts of money in recognition of the political services he had shown the emperor in his town. The polemics that followed in the wake of the war between the Swiss Confederacy and the Holy Roman Empire frequently picked up the motif of the venal Swiss. In the spring of 1502, the Basel town council had a Swabian university student arrested for a satirical poem mentioning the vain hopes of the Swiss for golden gifts from the French king. In his Swiss chronicle, completed around 1516, Heinrich Brennwald even presented the year 1501 as the year of French money par excellence. The purse of the *bailli* of Dijon (who had always been particularly prominent in diplomatic dealings with the Swiss Confederacy), the leaping dolphin, and the lilies on the French gold crowns were the emblems he used to compose the date 1501. From this date and by these emblems, the chronicler noted, the reader should understand when (and whence) the "unrest" had begun.[44]

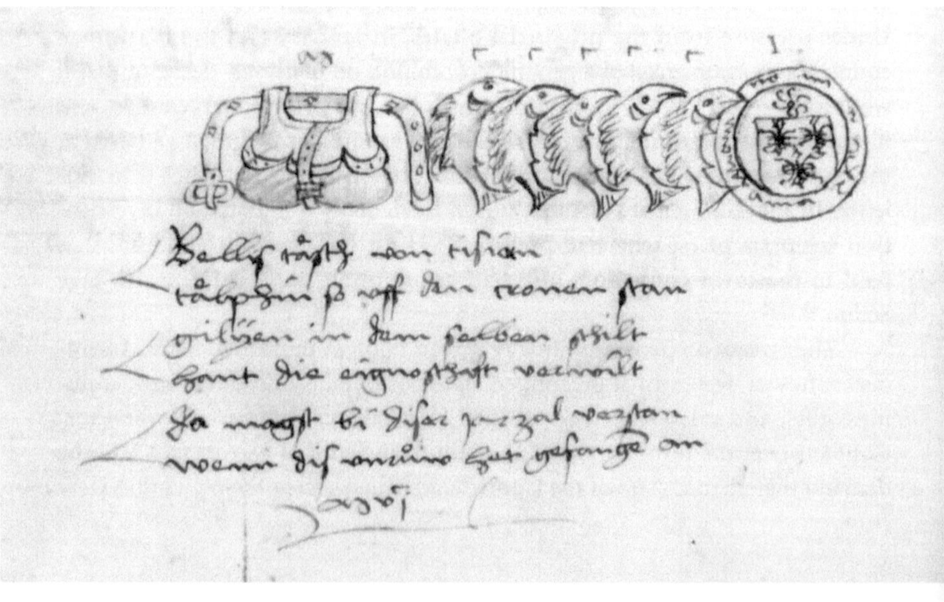

What did Brennwald mean by "unrest"? After 1509 the Swiss Confederacy turned away from France once again and renewed its coalition with the emperor and the pope. Even if the French king continued to possess a substantial number of Swiss partisans (and mercenary contingents), the general mood in the Confederacy became increasingly anti-French. After the Swiss military victory against France at Novara in 1513, revolts broke out in Lucerne on June 20 and then in Solothurn. On June 26 some three hundred armed peasants gathered during the fair at Köniz near Bern and forced their way into the city. Calling for "Swiss Frenchmen" and "crown eaters" (after the French gold coin), the crowd stormed and plundered the houses of known French pension brokers. Although the peasants retreated after negotiations, an open revolt of the provincial estates broke out in the days that followed. On June 29 bailiffs, town councilors, and citizens of Bern publicly swore to a renewed prohibition on all pensions, annuities, and *miet*, but this did not satisfy the insurgents. On July 2 a secret list containing the names of the recipients of 2,100 French crowns was read out publicly, and all the town councilors mentioned therein had to swear to pay the money into the city treasury at once. A number of them were also expelled from the town council. The town councilor Anton Hetzel was arrested, tortured, and lynched, Ludwig von Diesbach's castle was plundered, and two alleged French agents were killed as the revolt spread. Several thousand armed peasants massed before the cities of Lucerne and Solothurn, demanding that high municipal officials be handed over to them. Under threats from the peasants, Lucerne had the accused tortured and the bailiff Fehr and one councilor executed. The Bern innkeeper Michael Glaser and a second broker were beheaded on July 23, and a number of town councilors sentenced to heavy fines. In the wake of the unrest, Zurich too was compelled to introduce a sharply worded prohibition on pensions.[45]

The provincial estates were concerned with more than just the punishment of pension recipients among the urban elites, however. The demands of the insurgents and the administrative inquiries that Bern conducted in the weeks after the uprising—clearly to pacify its subjects—included the abolition of recently introduced excise taxes and fees, the preservation of the rights of communes, and a restriction of the powers of government officials.[46] In the autumn of 1513, allegations that high Swiss military commanders and negotia-

Figure 8. A purse, gift fish, and a French gold coin. Illustration from Heinrich Brennwald, *Schweizerchronik*, Ms A 56, Zentralbibliothek Zürich.

tors had been bribed were rekindled when the campaign against Dijon was broken off in October after military successes and extensive concessions by Louis XII—prematurely, many contemporaries believed. According to rumors, the envoys of the Swiss Confederacy, that is, the official diplomatic negotiators, had accepted money from the French. Before the peace treaty was signed, three of the Swiss military commanders had entered the besieged city secretly and wearing masks, and the French had distributed 50,000 crowns in all among the leaders of the Swiss troops in order to persuade the army to retreat.[47] In queries to the communes in the autumn and winter of 1513, the Bern authorities were compelled to protest against the Swiss envoys' acceptance of money at Dijon and asked whether a regulation should be introduced that would require Bern's ambassadors to hand over all gifts from princes and lords. The answers of the communes were as plain as they were menacing. Henceforth, all gifts to couriers and envoys should flow into the municipal coffers; the president of Villeneuve, who was being held hostage in Bern, should be tortured in order to gain reliable information on the bribery of ambassadors and to punish those responsible—the allusion to the executions of Bern officeholders forced by the peasant uprising was loud and clear.[48]

Unrest erupted again after the crushing defeat of the Swiss troops at Marignano by a French army in September 1515. The Bern patrician Albrecht von Stein was accused of corruption and treason; in December 1515 armed peasants massed outside Zurich and demanded that a number of high municipal officials and town councilors be tried for desertion, taking pensions, and accepting French bribes. Threatened with an assault on the city, the Zurich town council had a number of people arrested, tortured, and sentenced (although most sentences were later revoked); on January 12 the communes encamped outside the city gates forced the issuing of the so-called Milanese Treaty, which confirmed the rights of the provincial estates.[49] At a special session in March 1516, the Swiss Assembly called for another extraordinary session to decide upon a universal prohibition of pensions. Once again no such prohibition could be resolved.[50]

However impressive the forms assumed by the opposition to pensions or their modes of distribution may have been, surviving receipts and lists of names would seem to suggest that annuities continued to be paid even in the years of the revolts. A register in the papers of the Imperial Chancery in Vienna lists the Swiss recipients of Maximilian's *provision* in the years 1513 to 1515 by canton, one hundred names in all. In some cases the register points out that pensions were forbidden at the moment, for example, in Bern and Zürich. It was left up to the recipients to decide whether they wished to take the risk of continuing to receive the money, a note adds; people would have to be paid later for the years in which it was officially forbidden in any case. Next to the names of a number of officeholders, the Austrian ambassador Reichenbach also noted that they apparently took gifts from both sides, and he commented ironically on the entry for Daniel Babenberg of Solothurn: "May God ensure that he earns it honestly."[51]

In May 1515 the same Dr. Reichenbach wrote an urgent letter to Maximilian's chancellor Serntein requesting the immediate provision of substantial funds for himself and his intermediaries. He needed 300-400 florins for wine, food, and gifts to the Swiss communes so that he could draw their attention to the corruption of the Swiss Assembly by the French; once the common man knew what was going on, the fire would be ignited in earnest.[52] Two years after the Zurich revolts, in October 1517, the papal legate Antonio Pucci delivered a list to Cardinal de' Medici naming the most influential personalities in the city who should receive gifts to the ultimate benefit of the Holy See and the emperor. Johannes Berger, who had enjoyed a high reputation since the uprising of Zurich's rural communes and was very influential, Pucci noted, figured prominently on this list.[53] The revolts against pensions, it seems, allowed new aspirants to such payments to emerge. Switzerland teemed with rivals to Reichenbach and Pucci in the form of recruiters and agents of the French king, for example, a certain Burkart Sässeli, who was arrested in January 1515. Sässeli was active both as a distributor of pensions and as a sort of French public relations agent. Witnesses questioned in Lucerne, Zurich, and Basel reported that Sässeli had announced in country inns that the king of France intended to keep the agreements he had made with the Swiss at Dijon and send the promised money. To be sure, Sässeli allegedly said, the French monarch was subject to extortion by the Swiss authorities and military commanders: in their greed, they wished to garner so many pensions for themselves that even a king could not pay for them all. For that reason the king desired to reach an accord with the "common man"; what *he* asked for would surely be paid.[54]

If Sässeli really said all this—after all, to whom were the witnesses interviewed in Zurich and Lucerne actually speaking?—then it was an elastic and wonderfully self-referential argument. Gifts were inseparable from talk about gifts. Polemics and revolts against covert gifts were supposedly promoted by more covert gifts; popular opponents of pensions thus rose to the status of pension holders. Rumors about pensions and their corrupt and covetous recipients were intended to make the communes themselves receptive to such monies.

The Price of Blood and the Sale of Flesh

When people talked about such payments as tainted transfers and evil gifts, whether they did so in polemics of an imperial, papal, or French tendency, or in the struggles of council factions or of the provincial estate elites with the cities, a number of elements remained constant in the thirty years between 1489 and 1519. Pensions were, first of all, always of foreign provenance. The insurgent peasants called the drawers of French pensions crown eaters after the common French coin. In fact, though, payment was not always in crowns. In tense situations, such as the payment of the Swiss mercenaries after the hand-over of the duke of Milan in April 1500, the origins, quality, and exchange rate of the money quickly sparked conflicts. Dissatisfied at being paid in Italian money, Swiss mercenaries assaulted the *bailli* of Dijon and other envoys from the king directly after Novara and threatened to kill them. After the Swiss forced the new duke of Milan to pay them an additional 50,000 florins in the spring of 1515, their envoys complained that the duke had had worthless counterfeits of Swiss coins minted in Milan and was trying to pay them with these. Bern even sent its municipal mint master along with the courier who went to pick up the money, so that he might test its quality on the spot.[55] Contemporaries drew a direct connection between the invasion of counterfeit or inferior coins and pensions; Basel instructed its envoys to the Swiss Assembly of February 1507 to demand consultations regarding the worthless bad florins coming in from abroad; in 1520 there were calls for a prohibition on counterfeit coins from Milan.[56]

A number of polemics against pensions accordingly played on the double entendre engendered by the similar sound of *valsch* (false) and *walsch* (Italian or French) money. They also linked the motif with a second element, treachery. In his chronicle of the year 1500, Brennwald complained that the Swiss mercenaries "shamefully betrayed" the duke at Novara not just once, but (like Peter in the case of Jesus) three times.[57] In January 1514 the Swiss Assembly called an extraordinary session to discuss how to handle the current disloyalty and treachery in the Swiss Confederacy; in the unrest after the battle of Marignano in 1515, Albrecht von Stein of Bern was accused of "multiple treason."[58] The widow of the Bern town councilor Anton Hetzel, who had been tortured and executed during the Köniz uprising of 1513, put it even more dramatically in a letter to her son Hans, who also stood accused of treason and accepting French monies. He had, she wrote, sold his father in the same way that Judas had delivered God to his death.[59]

Venality elicited graphic descriptions. In 1496 the Bern authorities protested against French pensions with the argument that they did not wish to be regarded as a city that "sold its subjects for gold and money and, as some people say, drove them to the slaughter." The (biblical) image of the slaughter (*die Fleischbank*, literally, butcher's stall) also appears in the negotiations conducted outside Novara, when the Swiss abandoned their Milanese allies.[60] In 1503, Cardinal Schiner tried in a grand speech to persuade the Zurich town council to accept a prohibition on pensions. This money, he argued, caused not only bloodshed, violence, disobedience, and perjury, but also sold "babes in their mothers' wombs." We have seen how self-evidently Thomas Murner's *Rogues' Guild* combined the motif of the severed hands with Judas's betrayal of Jesus and the image of the slaughter. Erasmus of Rotterdam formulated this quite similarly in his popular collection, *Adages*; every reader knew whom he was talking about when he wrote of compatriots who were hired like butchers to slaughter (*veluti carnifex quispiam ad lanienam precio emptus*). Accepting pensions was tantamount to "selling flesh and blood" protested Lenzburg in an administrative enquiry undertaken by the city of Bern in 1516, and in a sermon of 1521 the Zurich reformer Huldrych Zwingli reduced the same motif to the famous formula of the red hats and cloaks of the Roman cardinals. When one shook them, ducats and crowns fell out; when one squeezed them, the blood of one's own sons, brothers, fathers, and kinsmen streamed from them.[61]

Zwingli's combination of money, blood, and the sale of bodies was such a success not only because he formulated the familiar Judas motif in a fresh and sharp manner but also because he so pithily brought the conspicuous colors of blood and red hats together with foreign money—money that was otherwise colorless and invisible. It was precisely the invisibility and secrecy of pension payments that increasingly became the focus of conflicts and polemics. Around 1500 the ordinances of the Swiss Confederacy began to distinguish sharply between pension payments to the municipal treasuries as "public" (*gemeine*) pensions and annuities to private individuals (*geheime oder sundrige pension*).[62] The Swiss Assembly heard in 1509 that secret agents and distributors of French monies had been arrested; disguised as monks, they had "secretly" recruited mercenaries. In February 1510 the minutes of the Swiss Assembly mention once again that the cessation of secret pensions had been discussed, and in January 1514 they not only point with concern to an increase in treachery but also urge a joint prohibition on secret pensions. During the renewed debates in June 1519, representatives of Uri defended the position that secret pensions must be forbidden at all costs.[63] The same metaphors of concealment, dissimulation, and liquid gifts appear in a rumor that circulated in Zurich that same year and occupied the authorities. Mayor Schmid, it was rumored, shrouded himself in a white cloak to conceal his identity (apparently this was sufficient disguise) and secretly entered the house of the bailiff, where he drank a "nightcap" with the French and made secret agreements with them.[64]

Unspeakable Relationships

Betrayal, secrecy, invisibility: in addition to the cannibalistic turns of phrase around butchery, the opponents of pensions deployed a number of other robust metaphors referring to the body. The chronicler Brennwald called the Bern town councilors who accepted gifts in exchange for dropping charges against mercenary soldiers "those who look through their fingers." The French king's purse not only became a person in its own right but was also wittily and ambiguously assigned a gender and family role when some representatives of the communes at the Swiss Assembly of March 1508 explained to Emperor Maximilian's envoys, who had demanded that the Swiss Confederacy call its mercenaries home from Italy, that the (French) king was their father and his (money) sack *(sin seckel)* was their mother.[65] Dangerous transformations and bodily fluids were just as readily invoked: pensions were poison and disease, pronounced the insurgent subjects of Zurich in the winter of 1515; the Swiss Confederacy would surely perish if its abscesses were not lanced and the pus drained.[66]

The conflicts surrounding Swiss pensions at the beginning of the sixteenth century invoked a further chain of associations for covert gifts and their recipients. After the wars against Maximilian at the turn of the century, polemics loyal to the emperor attacked the Swiss as oath-breakers, traitors, and renegades. The rhymed chronicle on the Swabian War written by Heinrich Bebel around 1499 not only calls the Swiss confederates rats, but also compares them to the worst enemies of Christendom, the Turks. As shedders of Christian blood, the Swiss were, to be sure, even more terrible than these infidels. While the Turks were at least declared enemies, the hypocritical and deceitful Swiss violated treaties and peace agreements, attacked secretly, falsified symbols and seals, betrayed their allies, and generally behaved like treacherous *ketzer*.[67]

This last invective did not allude to heretics, as it would in the modern sense, but rather to sodomy, following the late medieval usage of *ketzerey* as a "crime against nature" (*crimen contra naturam*). In the late Middle Ages, it was popular and common to vilify the Swiss as sodomites, especially among their neighbors north of the Rhine, and these denunciations reached a high point during the Swabian War. In his chronicle ten years later, Brennwald was still complaining that the Swiss had not only been referred to in disgraceful terms, as sodomites and worse than the Turks, but had even been depicted in paintings having sexual intercourse with cows.[68] In the South German linguistic region, *ketzerwerk* was the most widespread term for sodomy: it alluded not just to the hindquarters of cattle, but also to the backsides of men, particularly foreigners. In 1475, captured Italian mercenaries in the pay of Charles the Bold were burned at the stake in Basel for *ketzerei*; the accusation of sodomy was a stock element in the anti-Burgundian and anti-Italian propaganda of the 1470s. In the confession he made before his execution in Zurich in 1482, the Strasbourg knight Richard Puller von Hohenburg described having committed sodomy with several boys.[69]

This metaphor could be adapted particularly well to accusations of the sale of flesh, sexual misconduct, and venality in the discussions surrounding pensions, and the attempts to make the deposed mayor of Zurich Hans Waldmann into a *ketzer* after his execution should be viewed in this context.[70] During the conflicts over the 1495 French treaty with the Swiss Confederacy that arranged for the provision of Swiss mercenaries in exchange for French pension payments, allegations were made against the mayor of Zurich, Schwend, that alluded menacingly to his predecessor in office. Since Waldmann's death, each of the two Zurich mayors had received 400 florins in annual pensions, an innkeeper in Lucerne had allegedly announced. A subject of the city of Zurich was denounced by neighbors for having commented on rumors of high payments from Milan with the remark that he was worried that money was "being stuck into their assholes behind and their eyes in front." In other words, the Swiss were being simultaneously blinded and sodomized by these gifts of money.[71]

Invisible money and unspeakable practices made a powerful combination. In a Lucerne tavern, a certain Peter Jos claimed that the duke of Milan was a bugger (*arsbrutter*) and that the bailiff Peter Seiler, who had accepted money from him, should be burned together with the other man. The Bern town council minutes for 1496 record the conversations supposedly conducted in Freiburg and Solothurn. The Bernese had attached themselves to the German buggers and had taken money from them; a nobleman of Freiburg had cursed a town councilor, saying that if he himself was a Bernese, then "he [the councilor] was a Lombard and, by your leave, a bugger "; and a third man had told them to kiss the Roman king's (i.e., the emperor's) behind.[72] The stereotype of Italians as sodomites could be employed quite flexibly: one moment it was the duke of Milan who was meant and the next his imperial ally. When necessary, any reference to Italian conditions would do, as in the case of one Jakob Nadler. In May 1514 he proudly announced that he was a partisan of the French, for he would prefer to serve the French than buggers like Schiner; he also said the cardinal of Valais, who wished to be pope, was a hypocrite and used boys in the Italian manner. According to Nadler, the pope should not meddle in politics but bless holy water, and the Lombards were buggers and sodomites whom he would never serve.[73]

Who the sodomites were in a given case was a matter of one's viewpoint, which, as we have seen, could change quickly, but venality, an Italian context, invisibility, and betrayal were always part of the pattern. One and a half years later, after the defeat at Marignano, the Bernese commander Albrecht von Stein had to defend himself against charges that he was a traitor and a *ketzer*, had long "buggered" his way around Italy, had betrayed occupied cities to the French king for money, and had "led all the Swiss to the slaughter."[74] Secrecy and venality, body metaphors and their intersections with treachery, and the unmentionable vice of sodomy were made to coincide as closely as possible here. These noisy accusations were not concerned with concrete sexual behavior, either in the case of Mayor Schwend, the Bernese commander Albrecht von Stein, Matthäus Schiner, or Waldmann, who was dragged to the cell of a convicted sodomite, as we saw at the beginning of this chapter. The testimonies of witnesses against the mayor of Zurich mention no spilled male bodily fluids. In a decisive phase of the revolt, Waldmann was to be marked as a *ketzer* (a clear allusion to the Alsatian knight Richard von Hohenburg, who had been burned at the stake for sodomy in Zurich seven years previously, in 1482);[75] these charges were dropped without a trace at the later trial.

For contemporaries, the exchange of such dangerous gifts and bribes was always unseen and unseeable, an invisible something that had to be made visible at all costs. The term *miet* was so useful for political denunciation because it was paradoxical: it alluded to silent secrets that must by definition remain invisible, like the catalogue of mute sins in the vernacular catechisms of the fifteenth century in which simony and sodomy functioned side-by-side as sins that were at once mute and cried out to heaven. In the political language of the Swiss Confederacy and the Upper Rhine, this bundle of metaphors with a particular emphasis on the invisible *welsch* (Italian or French) sin was the strongest symbol of the power of that which one cannot see. The only fluid spilled in these invisible liaisons was ink. The invisible drew its power in the first place from vociferous defamatory talk. The denunciation of pension recipients as sodomitical traitors was so effective because of the breadth of possible meanings of *ketzer* and "traitors." The description of pensions and annuities as *miet*—at once a battle cry and a word for the traitor's reward—was intentional and effective because the word did not have a clearly delineated field of meaning, but rather a diffuse and extraordinarily negative one. It could be used to evoke all manner of unspeakable crimes.

Making Meanings: The Terms and Their Usage

The repertoire of terms for evil gifts remained rather constant between the Burgundian wars and the Reformation: I would, however, warn against drawing simple conclusions about a continuity of underlying attitudes or "mentalities" from the repetitions of these narrative patterns and sayings. Central terms are central because their interpretation is neither coherent nor unanimous. One of the most common slogans invoked against pensions was the call "to rid ourselves of all foreign lords," a demand constantly reiterated in the minutes of the Swiss Assembly and repeatedly and menacingly brought forward by the rural subjects of the cantons and communes, in particular. But this same argument was invoked by Bern in 1497 to exhort the cantons of Schwyz and Obwalden to resist French offers and maintain their alliance with Milan and the emperor and to draw annuities from both.[76]

Even more widespread and all-encompassing was the concept of "the common good," which had allegedly been violated by the deposed mayor Ulrich Schwarz with his reputed craving for power and gifts, as well as by his colleague Hans Waldmann. "The common good" has been read as *the* key term of premodern rule, not only as a legitimation of authority but also as a reified form of the body politic more generally, a central concept for early modern political thought and just rule, in contrast to which its negative complementary term, self-interest (*aigen nutz*), stood for the illegitimate appropriation of goods.[77] The common good was, however, not simply an abstract "oppositional key concept," but was used pragmatically, an abstract category that could just as easily be interpreted cynically or taken literally with a vengeance. In the summer of 1507, while French envoys were busy doling out rich gifts to recruit mercenary soldiers and supporters in the Swiss Confederacy, the French bishop of Rieux was preaching in Bern that it would be extremely foolish of the Swiss to refuse the money. "The common good," he stated, "means that the common man has money, not the municipal treasury."[78] And this very same *gemein nutz* was the battle cry of the mutinous

Swiss mercenaries outside Pavia in July 1512, when they demanded the immediate distribution of booty and a return home.[79]

Neither of these uses deviated from some "proper" use of the term. A basic concept is not central by nature, but only becomes so when it represents a socially contested projection of diverse—that is, ambiguous and nonidentical—views of society. The names given to pensions and gifts from foreign powers were so frequently repeated because contemporaries were constantly adapting them to new conditions, and it was from this breadth of meanings that they drew their efficacy. Which interpretation of the word for dangerous gifts was the Bern town council trying to prevent in 1474 when, after making a pact with Louis XI, it ordered that the publicly sworn promises not to accept *miet und gab* would henceforth no longer be read out at the annual council elections at Easter? Which term was used to refer to the transfers in a given case, or, to be more precise, what the authorities permitted a word to mean in a given instance, was decisive.[80]

On June 21, 1514, the decision in a dispute over the use of clerical rights was recorded in the Bern town council manual. The council's jurists had been consulted, the official journal notes; they had reached the unanimous opinion that no German word for *stipenden* and *pension* could be inserted into the disputed Latin document. They were clearly keen to avoid a politically controversial and loaded vernacular term: the storming of the city of Bern by insurgent peasants a year before was still fresh in the participants' minds.[81]

It was thus a matter of permitted meanings, and this incessant political work of adapting (and, when necessary, transforming) the terms is useful for a definition of tradition and continuity in political speech. Traditional narrative elements are those that can always be adapted anew to altered conditions: they are vehicles—*metaphorai*—not for long-standing contents but for those newly taken on board.

This chapter has addressed those gifts that lent the greatest political impact to talk about *miet* in the period between the Burgundian wars and the Reformation—pensions to the member cantons and functionaries of the Swiss Confederacy. Contemporary polemics described pensions as a source of unrest and inner conflict, a symptom of a bewildering present characterized by ambiguity, simulation, and dissimulation, in glaring contrast to a noble, simple, and godfearing Swiss past before the Burgundian wars, which was seen as a lost age of clarity. This model was organized by the older tropes of illegitimate reciprocity, (sexual) corruption, usury, and treason. Beginning in the 1520s, it was adapted and further developed in Reformation polemic, and these transformations of invisible dangerous gifts will occupy us below. From the perspective of social history, however, it becomes clear that these flows of money from outside promoted the installation of solid administrative structures and the emergence of a homogeneous group of urban political elites. Pensions caused not a crisis, but rather the cementing and rounding off of political structures.

The insurgent subjects of Zurich, Bern, Lucerne, and Solothurn appear to have understood this very well. They rose up in 1489, 1513, and 1515 against the crass injustice that ensured sure profits to the patrician brokers of mercenary armies while the sons of peasants and artisans, whom they recruited for an uncertain wage, bore the murderous risks of slaughter. Attacks on corrupting gifts and their recipients were instrumentalized here in defense of the rights to self-determination of the provincial estates against patrician domination.[82] But not all unrest was directed against gifts as such. In the armed revolts, local elites seem to have been trying, at least in part, to secure by armed force their own access to pensions and the lucrative business of providing mercenary soldiers, or to defend it against the monopolies of urban and territorial authorities. Local Swiss military entrepreneurs had access to powerful fighting forces, who could seriously challenge the authorities' monopoly on power in certain places. It would at least be hasty to assume a fundamental opposition between "private" war entrepreneurs and the patrician authorities because both acted as recipients of foreign pensions and providers of mercenaries in a private as well as a public capacity. Official, "state" pension holders in high municipal office often had close family and client ties to their private competitors that render any sharp distinction impossible. At the end of the fifteenth and in the first two decades of the sixteenth century, the politically ambitious could invest simultaneously in careers as town councilors and military entrepreneurs, and they certainly grasped the opportunity. The situation of independent war entrepreneurs declined markedly after 1520, though; only at this time were the Swiss authorities truly in a position to enforce their claims to a monopoly on providing mercenaries and on the receipt and distribution of foreign "gifts."[83]

At any rate, in the decades between 1470 and 1530, officeholders had the best chances of making their way as political brokers, pension recipients, and distributors if they filled official diplomatic functions as couriers and envoys. Viewed from this perspective, there is a certain ironic quality to the unsuccessful decades-long debates of the Swiss Assembly over a prohibition on pensions, which were conducted by the very same protagonists (the envoys of the Swiss cantons) who used these gifts as the basis for their own power.[84]

In the decades of the late fifteenth and early sixteenth centuries, extraordinarily large sums of money flowed into the cantons of the Swiss Confederacy. Contemporaries were aware of their unusual size; we know of Philippe de Commynes's (exaggerated) figure of one million French gold crowns. The effect of all these monies was, however, at least uncertain, even to those who paid them. Whether the *amico* and *cavaliere* Hans Waldmann or his successor Schwend really did as much as they claimed for the duke of Milan in Zurich, and whether they loved him as much as they pretended to, is questionable. The letters of the Milanese ambassadors leave some doubt about Waldmann's loyalty and portray him as a brutal and boastful extortionist—perhaps also in order to explain away the disappointing results of their own gifts of money. Dr. Reichenbach used similar language to describe his Swiss clientele to Emperor Maximilian. But payments apparently continued to be necessary, and a number of powerful men in the Swiss cantons received such sums over a long period of time from several—sometimes rival—European courts.

However much contemporary polemics and the older Swiss historiography ultimately may have described pensions as invisible monsters and cancers on the body politic, the forms in which they were transferred and registered were determined quite simply by the same procedures that applied to the usual demonstrative political gifts. At New Year's 1513, the French pension broker in Bern, Michael Glaser, owner of the Lion Tavern, placed a folded piece of paper (*ein zedelli*) with sixty French gold crowns in the hand of one of the city's four highest officials, saying (or so, at least, a witness later testified) that it was a New Year's present because he had not yet given him anything—an allusion to the preprinted New Year's cards with pious motifs that became popular in the last quarter of the fifteenth century.[85] On January 13 the Lucerne chronicler Diebold Schilling wrote to Maximilian that he wished to inform the emperor "as a New Year's gift" that Lucerne had ratified the agreement with him. After some further items of news about deliberations at the Swiss Assembly, he thanked the emperor profusely for the silver drinking vessel that he had heard would be coming his way. At the end of his letter, he was, however, compelled to broach an unpleasant subject. Unfortunately, he had not received the annual gift promised to him for two years, despite always having done his best for the emperor in his commune.[86]

New Year's presents, drinking vessels, fluid words, and insecurity: a characteristic tension persisted between the demonstrative and clandestine aspects of these gifts. On the one hand, secrecy was always writ large—the letters of Austrian diplomats to the Imperial Chancery repeatedly stressed the reluctance of recipients to appear in person for the distribution of monies or for consultations. On the other, pension holders were concerned to appear consistently as successful multipliers of their benefactors' interests, as recruiters, brokers, and distributors of their golden gifts, and for that reason tended to highlight their personal influence and large following.[87] When it came to efficacy, talk about gifts could easily prove just as useful as the gifts themselves. In particular, the secret, invisible gifts permanently pointed to pronouncement and publicity. In 1495 the Lucerne council courier and chronicler Petermann Etterlin, the recipient first of Austrian and Milanese and then of French monies, boasted in a tavern that he need not fear losing his influence with the town councilors: "For he knew too much that he had heard about them with his own ears."[88] Elsewhere, this very exhibition of the invisible could become a weapon. In Zurich in 1509 "secret letters" were nailed onto the church doors in which named individuals were accused of having pledged themselves more to the king of France than to the city and the Swiss. In July 1513, insurgent peasants forced the reading aloud of Michael Glaser's secret list of recipients of French pensions before the assembled population in front of Bern town hall. In May 1520, the Bern town council forbade, on pain of corporal punishment, the writing on window shutters or doors of slogans denouncing the inhabitants or owners of the houses as partisans of the emperor or the French. In the form of political graffiti, the invisible gifts wandered onto the exterior walls of houses.[89]

5 *Pensions in Basel, 1501–1522*

I began with the demonstrative legal gifts with which the city of Basel represented legitimacy in the late Middle Ages, in public gift-giving rituals as well as in the political documents that document these transfers. What traces did the Swiss debates over invisible gifts leave in the municipal economy of gifts? The older historiography on Basel prided itself on portraying the city as untouched by the "excesses" of pensions, that is, by the conflicts surrounding the acceptance and distribution of foreign annuities. Basel's stance toward pensions has been depicted as a model of integrity and a unique exception within the Swiss Confederacy.[1] In these accounts, the city of merchants and humanists appears far removed from the bloody controversies surrounding mercenaries, pensions, and violence.

Let us take a closer look at the municipal sources. When the city joined the Swiss Confederacy in 1501, the question of pensions was a constant theme at sessions of the Swiss Assembly. The Basel town council ordered its delegation at the Assembly in September of that year to vote for a prohibition of annuities to private persons. In the case of *gemeinen pensionen* (communal pensions), it was more reticent. The council was of the opinion that they too should be forbidden, but if the majority of the Swiss decided to continue to permit them, the envoys should concur.[2] The instructions to the envoys to the Swiss Assembly of July 1502 were more cautiously worded still. If pensions were discussed, the envoys should remain silent. Basel had accepted neither communal nor private pensions up until that point but would adhere to any resolutions that the Swiss took on this matter.[3]

Secret and Public

As restrictive as these regulations sound, Basel was nevertheless quite prepared to accept payments of money from outside when the political framework was right. In an instruction of January 1503 on French pension offers, the council ordered that no agreement on payments should be entered into if the French negotiators did not reach an accord regarding Bellinzona; if, however, an agreement were reached, then the Basel envoys should seek a promise of French pensions.[4] Six months later the council exhorted its envoys to consult with (unnamed) intercessors for Basel on how best to obtain pensions; in any case they were to ensure Basel's inclusion in any new coalition between the French crown and the Swiss Confederacy.[5] This was not without a certain irony because the official prohibition on pensions in the Baden Accord, which had been sealed by the delegates from Basel (among others), had gone into effect on July 21. The town council had the prohibition publicly sworn to and confirmed with an ostentatious liquid gift: on this occasion the city solemnly presented the envoys of the confederated Swiss cantons with a barrel of wine, as was emphasized when the annual accounts for 1503–4 were read aloud.[6]

The city thus instructed its delegates to agree to the prohibitions on pensions (while at the same time urging them to secure pensions for the city treasury), signed the prohibition of all pensions with its allies, and proclaimed it ceremoniously with liquid gifts, gifts that the assembled town councilors then had read aloud to them as part of the annual accounting process. These rather diverse modes of treating foreign monies also underline the role that annual accounts played as political information and pronouncements. The Basel accounts do not necessarily tell us whether and in what amounts the city accepted pensions. For the year 1507, for example—a year when a contingent of Basel mercenaries in French service, commanded by Ludwig Kilchmann, was camped outside Genoa[7]—the annual accounts mention no foreign payments whatsoever. In February of that same year, Basel instructed its delegates to the Swiss Assembly, which was debating a prohibition on pensions yet again, to vote to permit pensions for the public coffers but to forbid those to private individuals.[8] Two weeks earlier, on January 20, 1507, a supplementary ordinance to the council statutes impressed upon the city's envoys that they could accept gifts—both secretly or publicly (*heimlich oder offenlich*), as the clerk added—but they must deliver them to the council upon their return to Basel. This process does not appear to have gone smoothly. An undated amendment insists that these gifts must be handed over to the city treasury just as they had been received, without any alteration, probably an allusion to coinage or foreign currency.[9]

Clearly, a special relationship existed between such gifts and pensions. When the Swiss Confederacy sealed its coalition with Pope Julius II in March 1510, payments unmistakably identified as pensions appear in the municipal accounts. Following the agreement, the city received one thousand florins in gold as a pension "from our most holy father the pope," a transaction the two councils heard announced in almost triumphant tones on St. John's Day, 1510. An additional 200 gold florins were distributed as personal gifts to the town councilors; the servants to the papal envoys who delivered the money were in turn presented with 756 pfennigs from the city.[10] In February 1511 a treaty on military support in exchange for pension payments was signed with Emperor Maximilian, which promised an annual pension of 200 florins to every canton in the Swiss Confederacy. As a participant in a special coalition of eight confederate cantons, in 1512 Basel also started receiving 200 florins as an official annual pension from Charles of Savoy, and in October of the same year the duke of Milan promised to pay the Swiss 40,000 ducats, which they could distribute among themselves as they saw fit.[11]

Not all of these monies are directly documented in the accounts. Sometimes payments were made late and only after repeated inquiries.[12] At any rate, before its admission to the Swiss Confederacy, Basel was clearly concerned to become integrated as thoroughly as possible into the system of political payments to the confederate cantons. The total income of the city treasury, which fluctuated between 4,320,000 and 7,200,000 pfennigs in the decades from 1490 to 1510, increased dramatically thereafter. The Three (*Dreierherren*, councilors entrusted with the accounts) took in more than 10,584,000 pfennigs in fiscal year 1515–16, and in 1517–18 the sum rose to 13,826,160.[13]

Expenses, however, had risen markedly as well. At the close of accounting in June 1512, the Three undertook a cost-benefit analysis regarding the altered intake. The municipal treasury had received gifts to its envoys amounting to 48,552 pfennigs, the Three reported to the assembled councils. In contrast, the city had been obliged to spend 27,847 pfennigs on gifts and 132,966 for diplomatic missions in the previous twelve months. The city had taken in a total of 671,800 pfennigs "in pensions" from the pope and the emperor, they continued. If outlays for military expenses were weighed against pensions received, the deficit became even greater; the city had spent 384,000 pfennigs more on military enterprises than it had received in pensions.[14] A similar reckoning was read out with the annual accounts in 1515; now the deficit was almost twice as high as three years previously.[15] These memoranda in the municipal accounts underline more than just the close connections between diplomatic gifts and pensions. They also document the open dissent within the council over these monies. A number of council members demonstratively refused to accept their share of the 200 florins that were supposed to be distributed among the town councilors as an extra gift from the pope.[16]

Foreign Gifts and Municipal Experts

The names of these reluctant town councilors went unrecorded. Beginning in 1511, though, the annual accounts list in increasing detail, in a separate rubric alongside the pensions, the names of those official municipal diplomatic couriers who had accepted gifts in the course of negotiations with foreign powers. The city's envoys received increasingly rich and lavish gifts in forms that sound familiar to us. During his mission to Emperor Maximilian in Trier, for example, the emperor himself presented the mayor Peter Offenburg with a silver drinking vessel filled with gold coins. This liquid gift was worth 72 florins, or 21,960 pfennigs, calculated the town clerk, adding himself, not without pride, to the list: "further, 25 lbs. which his imperial majesty presented to the town clerk."[17] Neither the mayor nor the town clerk was permitted to keep these treasures, however, but had to turn them over to the city (which is why they appear in the municipal accounts). In February 1511 a special council resolution noted the regulation regarding the handing over of all gifts to envoys, which had been introduced four years previously, and extended it to the town guards and armed escorts who accompanied municipal couriers.[18] In November 1512 the council felt compelled to repeat its insistence on a complete delivery of all gifts received during diplomatic missions. Some envoys believed that they had a right to get back the gifts they had turned in, the ordinance noted. This had led to much quarreling and disunity in the council, which the authorities sought to limit by introducing new and stricter regulations. An entry of March 5, 1513 reiterates that municipal envoys had been recently delivering gifts to the council in the belief that they would receive something back. In late March 1513, after lengthy debates, the council finally confirmed the strict stipulation of the previous autumn, and in November 1515 this regulation was also extended to all the city's military commanders.[19]

These repeated council resolutions reveal not just the wealth of gifts—the wars in Italy made the Swiss sought-after coalition partners, and they were literally showered with presents—but also a certain disquiet. This disquiet related to the relationship between pensions paid to the municipal treasury, the increasingly large and frequent gifts to diplomats (which also had to be delivered to the city), and those foreign payments to municipal officials that did not fit into either of the first two categories. We have encountered these diplomats, bookkeeping experts, and military functionaries several times already; they included Lienhart Grieb, Peter Offenburg, Lukas Zeigler, Ulrich Valckner, Heinrich Meltinger, and, not to be forgotten, Jakob Meyer zum Hasen, standard-bearer of the Basel contingent during the Genoa campaign of 1507 (on the French side), commander of Basel's forces during the Italian campaigns of 1510 and 1512 (on the papal side against the French), and a busy and successful municipal envoy.[20] In January 1512 he attended the solemn enthronement of the duke of Milan, Massimiliano Sforza, as Basel's official representative. He brought home a certificate postdated July 23, 1512 that promised him an annual pension of 100 rhenish florins for his particular services in recapturing the duchy, and in March 1512, Meyer petitioned the Basel town council for official permission to receive this annuity, not just for himself, but also for "several other members of this council," who remained nameless. The council resolved, however, that such payments were deleterious to government and the common good. Henceforth it was expressly forbidden to accept any pension (the clerk first wrote "person," then scratched the word out) from any foreign power.[21]

This confusion on the part of the clerk between *pension* and *person* is understandable because the city of Basel itself accepted pensions through the mediation of Jakob Meyer. One year later, on April 26, 1513, the council decided to grant Meyer fifty florins for his efforts in securing the Milanese "secret pension," to be subtracted from the first installment of 500 ducats. What is more, Meyer was promised the same proportion of the Milanese money for all subsequent years.[22] In the annual account for 1512–13, dated June 24, 1513, this sum is declared as a formal gift. Jakob Meyer zum Hasen had delivered fifty florins to the municipal treasury, which he had received from Cardinal Matthäus Schiner, and according to the accounts, he received the same amount back "for his trouble and labor" in acquiring a secret pension for the city from Milan.[23]

On this Feast of St. John in 1513, the city of Basel was already aware of the revolts against pensioners of the French king that had broken out in Lucerne and Solothurn. In a letter of June 20, the council pledged the bailiffs and military commanders by their oath to keep news of the uprisings absolutely secret. On June 28 the guild master Hans Kuttner informed the council of the assault of the Köniz peasants on the city of Bern and the devastation and pillaging of the house of the *Venner* (a high administrative official) Hetzel, and on June 30 two members of the Lucerne town council reported even more worrisome news from Bern in an express letter to the Solothurn council, which reached

Basel on July 2. It was rumored that peasants from the Bernese Uplands were marching towards Bern. "Distinguished gentlemen," the Lucerne councilors warned, "the insurgents are growing stronger by the day." They urgently recommended that measures be taken to deal with possible unrest and to adjust as well as possible to the altered situation.[24]

The Baselers certainly had no trouble adjusting. Within a week the authorities had proclaimed a radical about-face in their policy regarding foreign money. The passage on Meyer's portion was crossed out in the municipal records. An addition dated August 9, 1513 explains that Jakob Meyer zum Hasen had declared before the assembled councils his grateful relinquishment of this pension; he preferred for his portion to contribute to the common good.[25] The Basel council's official line on the debates on prohibiting pensions throughout the Swiss Confederacy, which the Swiss Assembly conducted repeatedly (and vainly) after the violent uprisings of spring 1514, sounds correspondingly familiar. Basel instructed its delegates to the Swiss Assembly held at Zurich in March 1514 to announce that the city had never permitted the acceptance of pensions and would maintain this policy in future. At the same time, the Basel envoys naturally continued to pursue official pensions for the municipal treasury.[26] After the unrest died down, the city tacitly returned to its earlier agreement with Jakob Meyer zum Hasen, which had been declared invalid in August 1513 under the influence of the uprisings. In June 1515, the municipal treasury paid Meyer fifty florins as his part of the papal money for that year.[27] In 1516 he became the first mayor of Basel to come from the guilds rather than the patriciate, and it is in this context that his outward appearance has become familiar to us. On the occasion of his accession to this new office, he commissioned a portrait of himself and his wife, posed in an elegant attitude, from Hans Holbein the Younger. The coin in his left hand is usually interpreted as an allusion to the city's right to mint its own gold coins, which was granted in 1516. But was the coin necessarily from Basel?

After the Swiss reached an agreement with France in that same year, French payments joined the official pensions from the pope. The instructions given to the municipal envoys Valckner and Truttmann in November 1516 even expressly prescribed that they should stress Basel's earlier services in the conquest of Genoa in 1507 and the city's loyal "service to the crown"—a nice play on words (the French gold coins were called crowns), given the fact that Basel had been at war with France during the previous six years. After the peace with France, Valckner and Truttmann should try, the instructions continued, to secure back payment of earlier annuities, and if this proved possible—the council clearly had its doubts—they should demand an installment.

Figure 9. Hans Holbein, *Portrait of Jakob Meyer zum Hasen*, 1516, Öffentliche Kunstsammlung, Basel.

The envoys should also endeavor to expedite the negotiations because of the *heimliche pension.*[28]

What did *heimliche pension* mean here? We have seen that from the beginning of the sixteenth century, the debates and agreements in the Swiss Assembly distinguished between public, communal (*gemein*) pensions, and secret (*geheim*) pensions paid to private individuals.[29] In Basel the receipt of the latter was forbidden, but there were nevertheless candidates for these payments. In March 1512, Jakob Meyer zum Hasen applied for permission to draw private pensions, not only for himself but also for other, unnamed, council members. Payments from Milan and Rome *pro pensione privata* are documented in 1512 and 1513, at least for the mayor Peter Offenburg.[30] Also in 1512–13 the pope paid 525 florins as a "secret token of honor," in addition to the promised annuities, and as we have seen, Meyer zum Hasen received an extra gift for having made this special income available to the city in the first place.[31] The word *heimlich* here is the German translation of the Latin *privatus* and signifies the personal right of an individual recipient—it was no accident that the clerk confused *person* and *pension* when recording Jakob Meyer's application for such a payment. The efforts of the Basel delegation under Ulrich Valckner to reach an agreement with the French in late autumn 1516 were ultimately successful. Basel joined the Perpetual Settlement with France, and in May 1517, Jakob Meyer zum Hasen could sign for 11,520,000 pfennigs in gold crowns *pro nostra pensione privata.*[32]

It was not self-evident that the municipal treasury could simply claim such payments *nomine privata* for itself. Even after its accord with France, Basel continued to pursue payments from other sources. In autumn 1516, acting on behalf of the pope, Cardinal Matthäus Schiner offered the city of Basel substantial sums of money in addition to its regular pension. An anonymous letter of September 2, 1516, from Zurich to the town councilor Ulrich Valckner informed Valckner and the new mayor Jakob Meyer that all of the other cantons except Zurich had accepted these secret pensions. These monies were, however, intended only for distribution to individuals, the informant writes: the papal negotiators were not prepared to pay pensions to municipal treasuries. He warned them emphatically that Basel was in danger of receiving nothing if it insisted on its current practice.[33] Finally a compromise was reached. Instead of 1200 florins to individuals, Basel received 500 extra florins from the pope in addition to its *gemein pension,* so that there might be no doubt about the holy father's goodwill, as the German translation of Schiner's letter put it so nicely, and so that Basel's envoy did not have to return home empty-handed.[34] The receipt for this payment, signed by Ulrich Valckner and dated that same September 13, survives in the Basel Stadtarchiv, but as a draft and with a telling alteration: as the reason for the payment, the words *heimliche pension* have been crossed out and replaced, in another handwriting, with the more neutral "as a gift" (*fur ein vererung*).[35]

The word *heimlich* could thus be used to refer both to payments to private persons and to discreet gifts to public treasuries that simultaneously drew pensions from the political opponent, and at the same time it naturally also continued to mean invisible and covert. Because of its officially anti-French stance, Basel was spared the violent assaults on genuine or presumed crown eaters or flesh-sellers in the revolts of 1513 and 1515. Jakob Meyer's demonstrative rejection of a guaranteed portion of the city's *heimlich pension*, however, makes it clear that in Basel too there was cause for caution. Rumors of astronomical bribes to Swiss military commanders during the march to Dijon in the autumn of 1513 could be heard quite loudly on the Rhine as well. Jakob Meyer zum Hasen had served the Basel contingent as a deputy commander, and the administrative head of the guilds, Lienhart Grieb, had served as commander. A mercenary soldier named Hans Mürer was arrested in Basel in January 1514 for "speaking maliciously about the pious gentleman Lienhart Grieb," accusing him of having "accepted money from the French on the march to Dijon" and using "other evil words against him."[36]

Latin Liquids

What kind of words were Mürer's "evil words"? Evil gifts and foreign money played an interesting role in the political literature of the Upper Rhine region in the early sixteenth century. In the spring of 1513, the Strasbourg printer Matthias Schürer published a long anonymous tract entitled *Die Welsch Gattung* (The Latin Fashion). The work sets its portrayal of current political ills within the framework of a chivalrous epic with fantastic elements—the narrator is carried off by a bearded hermit to an impenetrable forest, where he finds himself in a cave, facing a tribunal of wise masters. The author is anonymous, but his printer maintained connections with the circle of Upper Rhine humanists that included Brant, Beatus Rhenanus, and Wimpfeling. As in Johann von Morsheim's *Spiegel des Regiments*, which appeared fourteen years earlier, the wise men complain eloquently of corruption in the empire, avarice, discord, pride, unpunished tyranny, and violence, officials who "see through their fingers" and venal judges, of usury and simony. They warn that all these sins must be stamped out, lest Christendom fall prey to the cruel Turks.[37]

The Latin Fashion differs from older reform texts such as Brant's *Ship of Fools* or the Upper Rhenish *Book of the Hundred Chapters* because of its very current references to *welsch* (French or Italian) money. A warm wind was blowing from the South, bringing poisonous vapors to the Rhine, wrote the author, "invisible poison, mixed with sweets." Along with the deceitful arts of dissimulation and usury, the Latins had also introduced the worst vice, the "secret sin" of sodomy to Germany.[38] These complaints of moral ills and warnings against accepting gifts of plundered property were combined with very concrete political references. France sought war and despotism by means of deception and fraud and had paid the Swiss "large pensions" in order to subjugate Milan. The hunger for French money carried the seeds of invisible ruin, and these gifts were poison mixed with honey. The poem closes with gloomy allegorical images of "evil games," conspiracies under the sign of Scorpio, and warnings of the French arts of trickery and dissimulation: the French had murdered Swiss couriers (an allusion to an attack in 1511)[39] and everywhere sought to establish their influence through covert agents and bribery.[40]

Poison and sodomy, the Swiss and the Rhine, French money and "evil games" can also be found in a political poem that the Basel printer Pamphilus Gengenbach published in the autumn of that same year of 1513 in the form of an allegorical game of cards. Beware of the mendacious crowing of the Gallic cock, warns Gengenbach in the preface. This bird lies when it opens its mouth, he adds, as had recently been revealed at Dijon, where the Swiss troops had been duped and betrayed.[41] The contemporary references to the pension revolts could not be plainer. He exhorts the preservation of the common interest (*gmein nutz*) because otherwise discord would erupt between the communes and the authorities, as could be observed everywhere. The root of this evil was secret money, which ruined body and soul. Gengenbach also leaves no doubt about the origins of this *miet*, which dazzled the town councils and made them forget their honor; the cock's influence must be put to an end.[42] His fall had been prophesied by Cyril and Methodius, the Cumaean Sybil and St. Paul: a people without a head would rise up and support the eagle that came flying from the German lands. Then "the great simony would be abolished" in terrible wars.[43]

The printed pamphlet combines these menacing political prophesies of autumn 1513, which link *miet*, pensions, and simony, with the somewhat earlier text of a "card game" between the emperor, the pope, Venice, France, Milan, and the Swiss Confederacy, which traced the shifts and tricks of the Milanese wars, ending with the expulsion of the French from Milan in December 1512. Gengenbach has the French king Louis XII announce his impending return in threatening tones, and his ambassador Gruyer adds: "Of crowns King Louis has his fill / with which to do whate'er he will (*Küng Ludwig hat der kronen vyl / damit schafft er was er wil*). This too had a current and local background: this was the same Gruyer whom the Basel town council had arrested as a French agent and expelled in late March 1513.[44]

Gengenbach was only one of many political writers who lamented the Italian wars with their rapidly changing alliances, tricks, and diplomatic about-faces and portrayed the warring parties allegorically as animals. In 1510, Huldrych Zwingli penned a similar rhymed pamphlet in which he warned of the cunning and gifts of the leopard and his allies, the cats, who dazzled the (Swiss) oxen and smeared their muzzles with gifts (*gab*). In another allegorical tract, *Der Labyrinth*, presumably written in 1516, which laments the confusion and opacity of political circumstances, Zwingli also depicted France as a cock.[45] Gengenbach's epigrammatic poems, prints, and Shrovetide plays of the following years returned repeatedly to the theme of corrupt French money. His play *Der Alt Eidgenoss* (The Old Swiss), written in 1515 and printed in spring 1516, contrasts the virtues of the old Swiss with the vices of the new. The old Swiss had accepted no pay for their services, while the new casually sold themselves to foreign princes, particularly the deceitful French. "I've given you a pension great / and bestowed many a gift of weight" (*Ich hab dir geben gross pension / und manch grosse schenck gethon*), Gengenbach's Frenchman says, while Maximilian promises, "I do not seek to lead astray / I don't do things the Latin way" (*Ich will dich nit verfüren / so bin ich nit der welschen art*); it was not his intention to butter up the Swiss: "No Latin is well disposed towards the Germans" (*Kein welscher ist dem teütschen hold).*[46]

The same anti-French and antipapal motifs also appear in Gengenbach's Shrovetide play *Der Nollhart* (The Lay Brother), which was performed in Basel in February 1517 and printed that same year. A pious brother explains to the emperor St. Methodius's prophecy that he would drive the "fleur-de-lis to the West" and put an end to simony. The king of France jokes that as long as he has money this prophecy need not concern him; a Swiss man appears and laments that lords "with their evil money and gold" and their secret bribery were destroying and defrauding the country.[47] In the poem "The Ten Ages of Man," printed in 1518, in which each age corresponds to certain sins, Gengenbach has the sixty-year-old appear as the representative of avarice in a dialogue with a pious hermit. The former describes the imaginary kin of Judas; they take money secretly (*heimlich gelt*), thereby betraying their country and people.[48]

The Basel printer's polemical attacks on French pensions and secret money referred to current events in Milan and Dijon, to French agents on the Upper Rhine and Switzerland, to the revolts in Lucerne, Solothurn, and Bern, and apparently also directly to conflicts in Basel over pensions and diplomatic gifts. Gengenbach additionally charged his allusions to bad gifts, poisonous mone,y and the unspeakable sins of sodomy and simony with furious rhetoric attacking *welsch* fraud, lies, and dissimulation. This vigorously anti-French and proimperial political author was the son of a printer and himself a former journeyman printer and owner of a press, and he clearly knew a thing or two about pamphlets and their political impact. In 1517, at the end of *Nollhart*, the poet addressed his audience and declared that he had not written this play to harm anyone, especially now that so many disgraceful poems were in circulation, inciting people to partisan struggle, envy, and hatred.[49]

October 1521: A "Pension Storm"?

The city of Basel in which Gengenbach published his complaints about the influence of foreign money indeed accepted substantial sums from foreign powers in the years between 1517 and 1521. According to the reports that the Three collected for the reading of the accounts to the joint council meeting on St. John's Day, the gifts received by the city's diplomats nearly quadrupled between 1518 and 1521, from 45,093 to 165,516 pfennigs. The city received 1,500 florins in public and 500 in secret pensions annually from the pope, 200 florins each from the duke of Savoy and the Holy Roman emperor, a regular pension of 1,000 gold crowns from the king of France, and, starting in 1518, additional *heymliche* pensions of 2,000 and 1,000 crowns.[50]

On the Feast of St. John in 1521, the Three were able to present even higher figures. In the context of the new coalition, the town councilors Ulrich Valckner and Hans Galizian had received an additional 4,430 crowns, or 1,692,600 pfennigs, in pensions and gifts from the French embassy in Bern, in addition to the usual 2,000 French gold crowns.[51] On St. John's Day of that year, however, the procedure of submitting accounts took place under dramatically altered circumstances. The council had given notice that it would terminate the centuries-old *Handfeste*, its constitutional treaty with the bishop; on this June 24 the annual election of officials no longer took place at the cathedral, but instead on the square in front of St. Peter's Church, at quite a distance from the cathedral, and without the bishop's participation.[52] Six weeks earlier, on May 7, 1521, the city of Basel had joined the alliance with France in which all of the Swiss cantons, with the exception of Zurich, participated.

Basel's municipal authorities had clearly changed their attitude toward gifts and pensions. The instructions to the Basel delegation at the renewed deliberations on pensions at the Swiss Assembly of spring and summer 1519 had still stressed that private citizens in Basel did not accept annuities, which always meant pensions to officials as private individuals.[53] The day that Basel joined the French alliance, however, the town council made a change in the previous practice of municipal envoys handing over gifts to the city. It had been customary up until then for envoys who traveled on behalf of the council or the common good to turn in all gifts they received. This would not change. In the future, though, if one or more officials were dispatched on behalf of an individual rather than the council and they were given something, they would no longer have to deliver it to the city.[54] On August 29 the joint council resolved further that each council member should receive 15 crowns privately every year in addition to the public pension paid to the municipal treasury; the town guards and official couriers should also receive two crowns yearly from the French king. Some council members had refused to accept the money, the document notes: the council regretted this and would add the sums to the common coffers. The names of these refusers were recorded in the official collection of the council's decisions.[55]

What happened in the summer and autumn of 1521? Diplomatic gifts and pensions—or, more precisely, private shares in pensions—were closely linked here. The phrasing in the council resolution of August 29 carefully avoids referring to the 1,500 crowns that were distributed among the council members as royal payments intended specifically for these persons. They received the money as part of the official French payments to the city, and only as long as the pension was paid. This was the same procedure according to which the city had already distributed a papal gratification to all town councilors in 1510, and Jakob Meyer zum Hasen had secured a (substantial) personal share of the municipal pension in 1512–13. At the same time, the Basel town council continued to seek payments from the pope, who was conducting a war against France in Italy. On August 4, 1521, the *comes apostolicus* Guilhemus de Falconibus noted the arrival of a letter from the council and mayor of Basel in which "they demand pensions from me which they call private pensions" (*in quibus a me petunt pensionem suam quam dicunt privatam*), and on August 19 he confirmed the payment of 600 gold florins *pro pensione privata*.[56] Basel thus not only accepted but actively demanded money from several sides.

In that same year, 1521, as in previous years, the Basel authorities prohibited, and threatened severe penalties for, the private recruitment of mercenaries and the illegal enlistment of soldiers for the papal troops in the Italian theater of war, albeit without much success. Basel military entrepreneurs such as Heinrich Isenflam, Anthoni Dichtler, and Jakob Baumgartner participated in the military campaigns throughout the year with mercenary contingents on both the French and papal sides. The same Anthoni Dichtler attended the Swiss Assembly in Lucerne in August 1521 as the official council envoy in order to obtain an immediate payment of 825 florins of *heimlicher pension* for the city. In Basel, too, private engagement as a mercenary commander could be combined with the work of a municipal diplomat.[57]

When a new session on pensions was set for late September 1521, Basel armed its delegation with extensive justifications. Basel, it was claimed, had refused for many years to accept pensions, which had made it the laughing stock of the Swiss Confederacy. For this reason, the city had decided to accept payments this year like the other members of the Confederacy, but it would naturally do without them should a general prohibition be resolved.[58] It is this passage that is usually cited in connection with the events of 1521 in Basel.[59] *Pension* is understood here exclusively as a payment to a private individual, which is how the Basel town council (which, as we have seen, had been accepting pensions for the public coffers for twenty years), could write in this manner. Above all, however, the Basel council sought to avoid a debate on pensions at this juncture. The envoys were to inform the Swiss Assembly that the city found it a highly inopportune moment to treat the matter at all; in the future, when circumstances had become "somewhat calmer," the topic should be raised again.

The circumstances alluded to here included not just the tense relationship between Zurich (which had kept out of the 1521 alliance with France) and the rest of the Swiss Confederacy. They also related to internal conflicts. In the summer of 1521, an ordinance was introduced, along with a resolution on the distribution of French monies, that stipulated that only men born in Basel could hold council office. At the same time, the town council stripped the bishop of Basel of his power. All these developments produced tensions and political polarization. There was open conflict between French and papal mercenary commanders and their supporters, wrote the anonymous Basel chronicler of these years. The Baseler Fridolin Ryff noted in his 1529 chronicle that in 1521 there had been arguments, insults, and bloody street fighting between supporters of the French and papal parties in the city.[60] The conflicts between the municipal factions on the town council and the "outcry over secret money and pensions," as Ryff wrote, reached a climax on October 14 and 19 of 1521. After dramatic sessions of the Greater and the Inner Councils, the head of the guilds, Ulrich Valckner, and the mayor, Jakob Meyer zum Hasen, were arrested. Hans Galizian fled the city, and his property was confiscated. Along with Valckner, Meyer, and Galizian, four other councilors were permanently barred from municipal office. The council solemnly returned to its previous regulation on pensions and abolished the ordinance introduced in August according to which only men born in Basel could serve on the council.

Historians have referred to the events of October 1521 as a "pension storm." "Floods of *welsch* money" (when it comes to corruption, liquid metaphors are rarely far behind) and the victory of the French party had been followed by an "uprising of the citizenry against pension holders," a "purge" and a shift of power on the town council.[61] The expression "pension storm," however, is a twentieth-century invention, coined, as far as I know, by the historian Rudolf Wackernagel. The events of autumn 1521 are mentioned in no Swiss chronicle from outside Basel. One cannot speak of a fundamental shift of power. The municipal parties that were to play a central role in the Reformation movement eight years later did not participate: the "storm" was a compromise that merely led to a redistribution within already established leadership groups.[62]

At any rate, strikingly few contemporary sources on the events of autumn 1521 have survived. The permission for and subsequent abolition of pensions, which were registered in the council records and dated October 19, are from 1539, not 1521. A surviving older copy of the ordinance from the chronicle of Fridolin Ryff was produced no earlier than 1529.[63] The text of the *Urfehde* (oath of truce) that the deposed head of the guilds Valckner had to swear to upon his release on October 23, 1521, takes us closer to the events. He admitted to having given the council false information about the Lucerne Swiss Assembly at which the alliance with France was debated; he had erroneously said that all members of the Swiss Confederacy accepted the pensions, for which reason the city of Basel had broken its laudable "old custom" (the term sounds familiar). In addition, he had received a large sum of money from the French ambassador to be distributed as a "particular and secret pension" (*zu sonnderer und heimlicher pension*) to certain councilors and influential citizens. He had also received a gift of 250 crowns, which he had not turned over to the municipal treasury but kept for himself, and, finally, had caused discord and unrest in the council on several occasions. He had to swear immediately to deliver to the city treasury all money and valuables that he had received as pensions or gifts from the French king beyond from the permitted 15 crowns.[64] The problem here was not the French crowns distributed to the councilors at the end of August; on the contrary, this sum was expressly recognized as legal, the only payment that Valckner was allowed to keep. The focus here was, rather, on other, secret and covert monies that he received in part for distribution to others and in part for himself and referred to in his confession as *sonndere und heimliche pension.*

What constituted such a forbidden secret pension and what did not was by no means clearly defined, as we have seen. In early sixteenth-century Basel, it was determined by municipal realpolitik. When the city could secure such payments for itself, it did so; if it proved necessary to distribute portions to individuals (to brokers from other members of the Swiss Confederacy, or from Basel, or to all town councilors), then it did that too. As the texts of the annual accounts as political pronouncements show, both options were possible within the limited political arena of the Inner and Greater Councils and found majorities, despite the occasional "no" vote. In 1512–13 and 1516, the pope had already offered extensive private pensions to the municipal elite groups—we need only recall the attempts of Jakob Meyer zum Hasen or Ulrich Valckner, whom Schiner and his unnamed Zurich agent threatened with the cutting or stoppage of payments if all monies were paid into the public treasury.

After the signing of the alliance with France in the summer of 1521, these same influential town councilors—both of whom clearly owed their rise to the highest council positions precisely to their abilities as mediators and envoys—once again found themselves in a position similar to that of 1513 and 1516: the relationship between council *person* and council *pension* needed to be defined. Rumors of covert foreign gifts to councilors and municipal officials had already concerned the council in previous years. In August 1519 official investigations were instituted because of rumors about the town council clerk Heinrich Ruman, who allegedly told a man from Freiburg whom he met in a tavern in Nyon that some Basel councilors had accepted money from the French.[65] We have seen how Pamphilus Gengenbach managed in his writings to connect the French crowns with ever new and current allusions to bribery, simony, usury, betrayal, and venality. In some passages this even influenced the language of the annual accounts themselves. In 1514 the Basel town council bestowed a life-long pension of nearly 2,000 pfennigs a year upon a certain Jörg Trubelmann in recognition of his capture of an enemy flag at the battle of Novara. This sum was first incorporated into the yearly reading of the accounts on St. John's Day, 1515. In June 1520, however, the word *pension* was suddenly replaced by the more neutral annuity (*Jahrgeld*).[66] This was an apparent attempt to avoid reading out the loaded word to an already divided town council.

Words were never simple; beginning in November 1521 the municipal *Urfehde* books recorded a conspicuous increase in punishments for verbal abuse. On December 2, 1521, the Basel shearer Emmerich Würzgart was released from the tower after taking an oath of truce; he had been arrested for insulting Jakob Meyer zum Hasen, the council clerk, and other council members. In addition to his prison sentence, he had to promise to give satisfaction to the injured parties in court should they demand it. Should it be discovered that he had again used invective against the authorities, he could expect further corporal punishment and fines.[67] The entry does not tell us what Würzgart said about Jakob Meyer and the clerk to the town council, nor does it record the "seditious and inflammatory words" that the gardener Thomas Leberlin used against the council or the "multifarious words against our council authorities" uttered by the two Basel weavers Peter Lotterer and Jacob Zwaybecher.[68] On New Year's Day, 1522, a printer was also released from custody. During a dinner at the furriers' guildhall he had, together with two other men who were also subsequently arrested, made "some rash remarks" about the emperor, the pope, the French king, and the city of Basel, the court minutes note. They also tell us his name—Pamphilus Gengenbach.[69]

Hans Holbein Paints the Town Guard and Urs Graf Appears in Court

What were the consequences of this "storm"? The now familiar solemn prohibition of *miet*, to which the elected councilors and officials swore according to the newly introduced oath formula on June 24, 1521, on the square in front of St. Peter's Church, was amended in the autumn of that year to include the formulation that pensions to individuals would henceforth be forbidden in perpetuity.[70] The Basel town councilors were also reminded of evil gifts and their consequences in a second form, though. On June 15, 1521, twenty-three-year-old Hans Holbein was commissioned with the decoration of the newly completed great council hall on the second floor of the town hall. The contract was confirmed with the usual gifts of wine and food. Holbein apparently began work immediately and continued until September 14, 1521. He only resumed the project in April 1522, breaking it off again in November 1522 although he had not yet painted the rear wall.[71]

With the exception of a few fragments, Holbein's frescoes have not survived, but the individual images have, either as cartoons or as later copies. On the north wall of the hall, directly behind or above the mayor's chair, Holbein depicted the perils of wealth and power (the vanquished Croesus at the stake) and combined these pictures with a special series of images of Justice on the long wall. The first of these shows the suicide of Charondas; King Charondas, who had made a law forbidding anyone (on pain of death) to come armed to the public assembly, killed himself when he realized that he had violated his own law. The second depicts the mutilation of Zaleucus of Locri, who had decreed that anyone found guilty of adultery should lose both his eyes. When his son was discovered to be an adulterer, Zaleucus followed the law by having one of his son's and one of his own eyes put out. Between the two, Holbein placed a crowned David with a lyre, exhorting the councilors to judge justly.[72]

Together with the inscription accompanying a further picture showing Christ and the woman taken in adultery ("Let him who is without sin among you . . .") this decoration may also be read as an appeal for leniency toward those who had made the city's laws and were now punished according to them, such as Jakob Meyer zum Hasen, still Holbein's patron and protector.[73] This representation is complemented by the famous quotation from Anacharsis on human law as a spider's web whose filaments catch only the small and weak mosquitoes, while the fat flies rend it, just as the rich and powerful break the law with force.[74]

Adjacent to this image, on the right side of the long wall, Holbein portrayed the virtuous Roman Manius (referred to in the inscription as Marcus) Curius Dentatus in Roman uniform. He is being approached by a richly adorned delegation of Samnites wearing contemporary sixteenth-century dress. The first ambassador of the Samnites offers Dentatus a shallow bowl filled with gold pieces, the second a high silver tankard, and the third a document, apparently a receipt, for his signature. The inscriptions explain that the Roman preferred to stick to his turnips: what he had in his pots might be worse, he declared—according to Livy—but he ruled over those who sought to bribe him with money. Holbein further underlines the local relevance of the story of foreign diplomats proffering *dona* (and demanding receipts) with a painterly trick. In front of the picture of Dentatus and the ambassadors, he painted, in trompe-l'oeil manner, a portrait of the head town guard. We will recall that in Basel he was responsible for the city's gifts. Holbein painted him life-size. He looks out at the beholders—that is, the assembled town councilors—and raises his right hand to his cap in greeting; on his doublet he wears the emblem of the city, Basel's coat of arms.[75]

Depictions of Justice containing similar warnings about corruption and scenes from Valerius Maximus are familiar to us from many South German and Swiss town halls.[76] Such paintings were intended to provide allegories that permitted highly varied interpretations. Apart from the virtuous soldier, the untrustworthy-looking Samnite ambassadors, and the portrayals of impending punishment and bloody adherence to the letter of the law, contemporary viewers could find further points of connection to contemporary talk of gifts and pensions. In the hall Holbein also painted an allegory of Temperantia

Figure 10. Hans Holbein, *Marius Curius Dentatus and the Samnites*, fragment of the 1522 fresco, Öffentliche Kunstsammlung, Basel.

Figure 11. Hieronymus Hess, watercolor copy of Hans Holbein's lost fresco *Marius Curius Dentatus and the Samnites*, 1816, Kupferstichkabinett, Basel.

pouring wine from a large pitcher into a high, elegant goblet, above it the inscription: "He who wishes to allow himself more than his due seeks his own downfall" (*Qui sibi plus licere vult quam deceat sue studet ruine)*. The picture is a representation of temperance in the traditional catalogue of virtues but could also be read politically as an allusion to the dangers of brokering and distributing liquid offerings.

Finally, Holbein also placed the central pair of terms referring to dangerous gifts in the council hall. In the great council hall, Justitia points her index finger and the sword in her right hand at a large shield reading, "Oh you rulers, beware of the Private, and tend to the Public."[77] Holbein, protegé and patron of the deposed mayor, inscribed the official terminology concerning what was a public and what was a private gift onto the great council hall. Justitia's sword and warning index finger also make the limits of interpretation quite plain: not everyone may discuss what is *publicus* and what *privatus*, what is *gemein* and what *heimlich* in a given instance.

The Basel authorities clearly did not appreciate public debates about those town councilors who had been forced to step down. In the spring and summer of 1522, Jakob Meyer zum Hasen was no longer mayor, to be sure, but he was still quite capable of responding to accusations against him with heavy official sanctions. In the summer of 1522, he brought charges against the butcher Konrad Vorster and the "clerk" Joachim Schenkli, both of them Basel mercenaries, who had entered papal service in North Italy in October 1521 in violation of the official prohibition.[78] Schenkli stood accused of having said in front of other Basel mercenaries that Jakob Meyer bore sole responsibility for the fact that Swiss soldiers were fighting against each other in Italy because he "had accepted money from two masters" (which was true, at least in regard to the payments documented in Basel's political correspondence). In Milan, Vorster had also loudly proclaimed, in the presence of Jakob's cousin, that the mayor was a knave (*schelm)* and deserved to have his head laid between his legs. In August 1522 the two men were sentenced to a considerable fine and forced to recant publicly; they had to declare in court that they knew only honorable things about Jakob Meyer.[79]

Among those arrested and interrogated together with Vorster and Schenkli was the draftsman and illustrator Urs Graf, whom the records refer to as a goldsmith. These were not the first criminal proceedings against him in Basel, and he apparently held strong opinions about municipal justice and administration. In 1514, after participating in the march to Dijon, and after the subsequent conflicts over corrupt officials, Graf prepared a pen drawing of a female figure with downcast eyes and a peg leg. He drew her without arms,

Figure 12. Urs Graf, *The Girl Without Arms*, drawing, 1514, Kupferstichkabinett, Basel.

analogous to the motif of Justice without hands that one often finds in the late medieval catalogues of virtues and vices. [80] In the summer of 1521, after the conclusion of the coalition with France, Graf prepared another picture aimed

Figure 13. Urs Graf, *In the Guildhall*, drawing, 1521, Kupferstichkabinett, Basel.

directly at conditions in Basel. In the public rooms of a guildhall sit a German and a Swiss mercenary, recognizable by their clothing, a scholar, an artisan, a merchant, and a fool. At the table with them is an elaborately dressed man with his hand in a money bag adorned with the fleur-de-lis. The innkeeper pours wine into the Swiss soldier's cup from the right from a pitcher that he holds demonstratively high, and to the left Death enters the picture bearing a banner that reads, "I would like to listen for a while / to what you say under this rose."[81] This exchange of liquids, information, and money "under the rose" refers both to the oversized ceiling rosette hanging over the assembled men's heads and to contemporary parlance, which associated speaking sub rosa not just with secrecy, but also—as in Sebastian Brant's *Ship of Fools* and Thomas Murner's *Rogue's Guild*—with betrayal, deception, and dissimulation.[82]

The picture was probably drawn between the conclusion of the alliance with France (which united the confederated Swiss and German mercenaries under their new master) and Graf's illegal departure for Italy in August 1521. One year later, captured by his fellow countrymen and under tower arrest back in Basel, this same Urs Graf gave evidence about the evil words that had been spoken about the Basel authorities. When news of the arrest of Meyer, Valckner, and Galizian reached the troops in Milan at the end of October, he testified, many of the mercenaries had claimed that Jakob Meyer had accepted money from several sides, remarking that "It was a good thing that the lie came to light, so that the evil could be punished." Questioned more precisely, however, Graf played a close hand: he could not name any names.[83] Another Swiss mercenary arrested and interrogated together with Graf remembered more. When the news of Meyer's and Galizian's fall arrived at the camp, Konrad Vorster had shouted and made wild speeches which he, the witness, had, however, not understood. Vorster had said to one of his soldiers that he must become mayor now. Thereupon the other had cried out, "Then you must become *Zunftmeister* (master of a guild)." A third had then shouted, "Then I want to be a town guard!"[84]

All of these witnesses said more than they were asked. Thus Urs Graf wove into his statement about covert and secret gifts the thought that it would be a good thing for the lie, now revealed, to be punished—a rather risky sentiment for a man such as Graf with previous convictions to express to the judges of a Basel court in the summer of 1522. The second witness testimony alludes even more directly to conditions in Basel. The witness cunningly spun out a charade of reciprocal role assignments, which, moreover, he claimed guilelessly not to have understood properly. Like Holbein's frescoes in the council hall, these testimonies pointed to images and words for offices and gifts that could be read in many way and about which it was only permissible to speak ironically and figuratively. In these images and words, beholder and councilor, mayor and town guard, could easily switch roles.

6 *Instruments*

How can we categorize public gifts and their dark counterparts at the beginning of the modern era? When contemporaries spoke of liquid gifts, drinking vessels proffered, cloaks draped over shoulders or coins slipped to somebody, they referred to all of these things as real, tangible, and useful in the material sense. At the same time they referred to them as objects with a story to tell, as set pieces, allusions to or symbols of (legitimate or illegitimate) social relationships. In this final chapter, I would like to draw some conclusions from our research into visible and invisible gifts in the late Middle Ages and early modern period. What concepts and categories can be used to describe their functions? What roles were assigned by gifts, and in what narratives did they appear? In what form were these motifs reformulated in the religious upheavals of the Reformation? On the threshold of the modern era, gifts, I shall argue here, became part of a new paradigm of controlling and channeling information that quite literally helped bring the early modern state into being.

For an Economy of Information

In November 1521, when the mayor had just been deposed and Hans Holbein had begun his work on the frescoes in the town hall, the Basel municipal account books recorded an outlay of 160 pfennigs for four large pitchers of wine to a certain *herrn Erasmo Roterodamo*. This was an official welcome gift for the Dutch humanist, who had just settled in the city for the second time. Erasmus received wine, which the municipal accounts registered as a sum of money. Conversely, in the perceptions of contemporaries, gifts were frequently stylized as liquids and relationship-sealing offerings of wine, even when what was really at stake was the transfer of considerable sums of money. Both perspectives may seem picturesque and archaic to readers at the beginning of the twenty-first century. For the people of the fifteenth and sixteenth centuries, however, this stylization was no "traditional" ritual that repeated past processes. Instead, it represented a suitable and highly efficacious form of transfer. In order to be effective, gifts needed to be flexible, adaptable—and demonstrative. The presence of witnesses and onlookers was indispensable. Only in the eyes of those who received nothing did the objects bestowed become love offerings, gifts that demonstrated and expressed a particular relationship between giver and recipient.

Whether the two parties were really so well disposed toward each other as they appeared, and whether the gifts were really given so unconditionally as they pretended to be, remains an open question. For town-dwellers of the late Middle Ages and the Renaissance, *schencken* could be a rather ambivalent term, as we have seen. Asymmetries between giver and recipient and euphemisms for involuntariness and dependence become visible in the ways in which people used the word. This unease with gifts shines through in a letter that Erasmus wrote from Basel in 1515 to Pieter Gilles in Antwerp: "Friends of the common-place and homespun sort, my open-hearted Pieter, have their ideas of relationship, like their whole lives, attached to material things; and if they ever have to face separation, they favor a frequent exchange of rings, knives, caps and other tokens of the kind, for fear that their affection may cool when intercourse is interrupted." Erasmus presented his correspondent and himself, whose idea of friendship aimed at spiritual and intellectual communion and an immaterial exchange of ideas, as a contrast to this insistence on material gifts as compensation for distance. In confirmation he enclosed—"not without interest," as he adds ambiguously—a gift, "no common present, for you are no common friend, but many jewels in one small book."[1]

Erasmus was referring to the culture of gifts that arose in humanist circles at the end of the fifteenth century around the printing press. It took up and expanded the older custom of exchanging manuscripts and copies. With their combination of printed and handwritten dedications, these paper gifts shaped the relationships among scholars (and between scholars and their patrons) in the fifteenth and sixteenth centuries.[2] This particular kind of gift persists to this day in academia, as complex networking in the form of presentation copies and offprints. This paper gift can express respect or a patronizing gesture, the repayment of a debt, the exchange of information, or the initiation of a relationship. Erasmus's letters show us, among other things, how extraordinarily successfully and quite literally he engaged in self-fashioning by means of gifts, whether texts or painted portraits. In them he stylized himself repeatedly, and with ever new flourishes, as the very image of St. Jerome, who reaped nothing but ingratitude for his immaterial intellectual gifts. Erasmus was highly skilled at portraying himself as the victim of his own laborious textual work (here too he may have been a model for modern academics).[3]

The book that Erasmus sent as a present to Gilles in 1515 certainly speaks of gifts, in the form of proverbs. The text was his *Adages*, whose publication history is so closely associated with Basel. While the first of the adages elucidated there declares fittingly enough that friends have everything in common (*amicorum communia omnia*), he already qualifies the ambivalence of this liberality with a sarcastic quotation from Martial, which notes that this saying was often uttered by those who never gave but only took. Liquid gifts also reappear in the first book of the *Adages*: "To drink from the same cup" (*eodem bibere pocula*). Whereas nowadays we associate the expression with friendly sociability, in the sixteenth century, as Erasmus explains in his commentary, this meant to bear the same burdens and to be linked by the same gloomy destiny. He associates this cup not only with poison but also with violence and vengeance: "The same phrase remains in very common use in our own day in my native country," Erasmus notes, "for if they ever threaten to repay a man in his own coin, they say they will give him a drink of the same cup."[4]

The drinking vessels of precious metal that played such a prominent role in the presentation of public gifts in the fifteenth and sixteenth centuries thus had quite ambiguous connotations. In the logic of the public rituals, this issue had to remain abstract, however. The onlookers formed their own opinion in any case. The role of gifts here was to demonstrate that in this form they were fundamentally public and, ideally, impossible to overlook. They did not create social ties or legal positions, but rather publicized them. This was not the same thing, and we would do well not to equate the two functions. Gifts did this not least by their material magic, their ostentatious preciousness. This explains the great role that gifts of costly textiles played in contemporary perceptions, as well as the elegance of the combination of offering money as one might a liquid in silver or gilded drinking vessels. And for all their symbolism, the gifts themselves naturally remained valuables that could be turned back into a liquid resource as cash. Erasmus, for example, sold the gilded silver cup he received as a gift from Damiao de Gois in 1532 to his patron and supporter Amerbach.[5] Because well-placed gifts could eloquently mask the violent relations inscribed in them and because in a society dominated by material scarcity and merciless struggles over resources they could briefly evoke an artificial reality of effortless plenty, we would do well to describe them as media of communication.

Communication does not exist for its own sake, however. As effective as the terms may have been, the gifts did not wholly dissolve into appellations, turns of phrase, and word games. Relationships of power and dependency were inscribed on them. Present-day readers of the sparkling and elegant treatises of Baldassare Castiglione or Erasmus may be impressed by their emphasis on form, courtesy, and worldly wisdom and might be tempted, like their late nineteenth-century bourgeois predecessors, to admire the sophisticated legacy of these long-departed "beautiful societies" and to regret the loss of manners.[6] A closer examination of information, gifts, and violence in the late Middle Ages and the Renaissance, however, makes it clear that the people of the fifteenth and sixteenth centuries depended upon individuals for a number of services that we now receive through such institutions as the postal service, classified advertisements, telephone books, and official application forms (not to mention financial institutions, insurance companies, and unemployment offices), that is, for access to information. These individuals stood in widely varying relationships to the applicant or petitioner, and the degrees to which they could be helpful or cooperative also differed sharply. The web of small or large gifts known as gratuities, *leitkauf*, love offerings, or tokens of honor referred to these indispensable services: gifts may thus be understood as part of an economy of information.

The manners of speaking used by late medieval and early modern societies that we have examined here closely associated Judas and the thirty pieces of silver with the price of the body, venality. Judas received his reward not for turning over the body or person himself, however, but rather for something immaterial, for naming a place and time: for *intelligence*, to use a modern term. If taken seriously, a concept of information offers an approach to describing the manifestations and logic of gifts in the late Middle Ages and the Renaissance without recourse to a schematic model of reciprocity and relationship—a model, incidentally, that in any case has difficulty explaining the exchange of material versus immaterial payments and services.

Such a concept of information provides categories for describing the gifts and their recipients that we discussed in the previous chapters. A first group of recipients appears to have had no right of access to information; they merely conveyed it and received gifts in this function: these were the couriers and envoys. A second group, also with no access of their own to information, controlled the access rights of others and received gifts in this capacity; these were the porters or doorkeepers, whose outstretched hands were impossible to escape (Enea Silvio is as plain on this point as the minutes of the Freiburg, Strasbourg, and Basel councils). Once one had gotten past the doorkeeper, one next encountered the members of a third group. Their function was to sign for the incoming information, confirm it as authentic, and pass it on. They were accordingly authorized not to change it but to register it, and they too expected gifts; these were the clerks. Finally, the late medieval and early modern texts acquaint us with a further group of gift recipients, who were concerned neither with transportation, access, nor reproduction, but instead fulfilled a superordinate, essential, and correspondingly powerful role within the information economy. They provided information about information as agents, brokers, or middlemen.

For fifteenth- and sixteenth-century people, these brokers were familiar figures. Their colleagues at the town markets were officially sworn and known as subbuyers (*Unterkäufer*). In Strasbourg, for example, they had to be warned several times in 1494 to arrange the best goods and sales offers to customers from outside the city and not to demand excessive gifts or "love offerings" from them or local vendors. Their reputation was as dubious as their services were indispensable and their offers impossible to refuse. The aggressive and jocular dialogue between a merchant and a broker in the fifteenth-century German-Italian language textbook we encountered earlier brings together a complaint about the monopoly and power of these intermediaries with the gift: "*per amore*—so that he may come to you all the more gladly the next time." Was it mere chance that the Milanese negotiation partner of Zurich mayor Hans Waldmann used a very similar formulation in 1487?[7]

The whole point here is that every contemporary reader knew just what kind of *amore* existed between the broker and his customers.[8] The polemics against recipients of dirty gifts as procurers or procuresses of sexual services (which also belonged to this sector of the information economy) thus sounded perfectly natural and plausible to fifteenth- and sixteenth-century ears. Official documents, to be sure, used other words for these specialists in mediation. In both arenas the issue was dependency; the rhetoric of gifts was an expression of limited choices. Skilled brokers could thus maximize the payment for their services by offering flat rates, which included transportation and mediation. At the Swiss Assembly in October 1496, for example, one of the mayors of Fribourg offered to bring the French pension that was due on All Saint's Day from Lyon to Switzerland at his own expense and risk; his fee was one-half of one percent of the total sum.[9] When the Basel municipal accounts were read aloud before the two councils, they repeatedly listed, among the costly gifts that the city's envoys brought to the municipal treasury from their work elsewhere, the city's own gifts to brokers for initiating, mediating, and delivering payments from abroad. On St. John's Day, 1513, for example, the city solemnly presented Jakob Meyer zum Hasen with fifty florins because of the papal pension and an additional fifty for his services in securing the Milanese pension. The Lucerne mayor Jakob von Hertenstein received the same sum in 1518 as a "token, because he brought us the secret gift from the king of France"—a gift for a gift.[10]

Evil Words

I have used the city of Basel's bookkeeping on gifts as a point of departure for pursuing the registration of municipal gifts, their portrayal and instrumentalization in the various political publics of the Inner and Greater Councils, the shifting trends in total outlays for gifts, and above all the different appellations given to these premiums and bounties. Labeling proves to have been a complex process of the control and authoritative definition of powerful negative terms with dangerously proliferating connotations, which proved difficult to contain. The authorities of late medieval cities were eager to dissociate the gifts they gave or received from certain appellations and did so quite vehemently.

Evil words were a tricky affair. If one wished to distance oneself effectively and not be saddled with them, they could not be, or ever have been, spoken aloud. The authorities in Basel, Zurich, and Bern were very quick to threaten and impose severe punishments upon subjects who talked about dirty money and compromising gifts to officials in the political public sphere of guild meeting halls and taverns, and we have dealt with a number of examples here. The condition for leniency and release from custody was that the accused be prepared to swear a public oath that he knew nothing dishonorable about this or that official or mayor and nothing unfitting to a righteous and honest man. This was naturally a traditional legal formula, but it was accompanied by the threat of severe corporal punishment. In a testimony of 1461, a member of the Bern Greater Council complained that he had been punished and tortured for a few words; "many strange words were used in this matter in the city and everywhere in the country," as a municipal chronicler put it somewhat later. The Basel weavers Lotterer and Zwybecher had uttered "numerous words" against their local government, noted the city's juridical records in 1521. In the autumn of that same year, the printer Pamphilus Gengenbach spoke "many careless words" on the political situation in the guild meeting rooms and was imprisoned in the tower for it.[11] Such words were not, however, to be named and repeated.

These words referred to concepts and expressions surrounding dangerous gifts, which predated the gift-giving booms of the late Middle Ages and the early modern period. Venality, the reward of Judas, treason, body metaphors, and the dichotomy between self-interest and the common good had their roots in ancient literature and in the great systems of recording and exegesis that developed around the Bible. The gift that poisoned, the gift as sexual misconduct, disorder, and reversal, the images of severed hands and flayed bodies as visual representations of the corrupt official can be traced from the *Secretum Secretorum* and John of Salisbury to the encyclopedists of the High Middle Ages, and the collections of *exempla* from the circles of the mendicant orders to the vernacular literature of the late fourteenth and fifteenth centuries such as the collection of novellas in the *Gesta Romanorum* and the narrative complexes of the "chess books." These are unusual genealogies for a political topos. The late medieval word for an evil gift illustrates the power of literary narratives, of the momentarily suspended boundary lines between the fictional and the factual in political language.

The tales of tainted gifts, in which the lines between things and bodies became blurred and fluid, were so effective because they were fantastic. Like ostentatious ritual gifts, dirty, secret *miet* drew its political effect as argument from the fact that matters might be altogether different; that, for example, the Zurich mayor Hans Waldmann or the Bernese patrician Albrecht von Stein were *ketzer* bribed by the Italians and Matthäus Schiner not only "florenced" *welsch* boys under his cardinal's robes but had also learned the art of witchcraft from deceitful mendicant friars.[12] The stories that were conjured up by powerful expressions and made plausible, real, and "provable" in denunciations rested on the combination of older elements of talk about sins that cried to heaven or remained mute with continually adapted set pieces from the fields of usury, simony, and dis/simulation as the unspeakable vices of foreign neighbors. These stories could not deny their pleasure in the telling and in the garish assimilation and recombination of the well-known. These plots could be evoked and alluded to by the powerful words for dangerous gifts without having to be fully spun out—all the more so when these polluting and secret presents were conceived of (in contrast to demonstrative ritual gifts) as fundamentally efficacious *because* they were invisible.

Who would receive which gift from whom could not be predicted in advance. An imperial diplomat even commented upon the rapid about-faces of Swiss pension brokers during the Italian wars by invoking that embodiment of diabolical deception and imitation that late medieval theology otherwise relegated to the Last Things of the Passion. "The people turn with every hour," wrote the imperial diplomat Hans von Küngseck in March 1506 to

Maximilian I, a circumstance that he attributed to French money: "People speak of nothing else now, and if the Antichrist were to appear he could have every one of them if only he gave them golden gifts."[13] In the Upper Rhine region and Switzerland, the late medieval and Reformation discourse on venality and corruption was strongly influenced by the fact that talk about bribery was more effective than bribery itself. This talk was visual: it evoked hands, skin, and juices. Allegories functioned as open and in some cases threatening promises. They were so effective because the manner in which they were redeemed and taken literally was unpredictable; one was never sure of being on the correct and certain side of their meaning. Would they have been used to decorate town halls and courtrooms otherwise?

In the polemics on evil gifts—from the accusations against the Augsburg mayor Ulrich Schwarz or the Zurich mayor Waldmann to the Basel council's definitions of what distinguished "common" from "private" pensions—we repeatedly encounter the juxtaposition of legal gifts associated with the "common good" and illegal gifts associated with "self-interest." These definitions were elastic, though, as we have seen. They permitted public to be transformed into private and *gemein* into *geheim* (secret)—and vice-versa—according to necessity, offers, and political pressure. The common good and self-interest constituted central categories and basic concepts of talk about politics, office, and legitimacy in the late Middle Ages and early modern period. Basic concepts are not, however, a priori fundamental and central, but only become so when they represent a socially disputed projection of diverse—that is, not unambiguous and identical—views of society. Under certain conditions, the omnipresence of certain key words readily suggests the omnipresence of meanings, which easily serves to conceal how socially determined usage is.[14]

At the beginning of the sixteenth century, the German term *Eigennutz* (literally self-interest) was by no means limited to the purely economic sphere. It possessed a political component that was at least equally influential. We have seen that *aigen nutz* served as a slogan to link the misappropriation of public funds with usury, simony, and Judas's betrayal of Jesus.[15] The complementary terminology of the "common good" was useful not just for the cynical interpretation of the *bailli* of Dijon or the plundering and mutinous Swiss mercenaries, which we encountered in Chapter 4, but also for the constructions of the Basel town council, in which transfers of money from and to the pension broker Jakob Meyer zum Hasen always appeared as "public (*gemein*) pensions," no matter what direction they took. It was the current political constellations that determined what was public or private in a given case: from the definition of spring 1513 (Meyer secured for himself a guaranteed private share in the papal pension) to the redefinitions of summer 1513 (Meyer waived his share of the papal pension), summer 1521 (Meyer and other council members received private shares in the French pension), and autumn 1521 (Meyer had to take his hat, and private shares of the French pensions were always *miet* and thus illegal).

The terms thus appear to have been all the more effective the less precisely their meanings could be fixed. The history of political terms must thus be written as the history of their flexible and ambiguous deployment, adaptation and redefinition. As Robert Musil once wrote, sarcastically, "The imprecise has a great and uplifting power." This applies as much to the wild hermeneutics of bribery accusations as to the guiding and basic moral concepts of municipal authorities in the late Middle Ages and early modern period. Put another way, what precisely was meant by the formulas and terms to which mayors, guild masters, and town councilors swore publicly every year was defined by these men themselves.

Erasmus's Gifts

How then are we to grasp the connection between (political) power and gifts in the late Middle Ages and the early sixteenth century? The authorities, the public good, public office, and gifts—of a variously voluntary nature—were very closely associated in the minds of Renaissance people. Beginning in the mid-fifteenth century, the municipal memoranda concerning which visitors were to be offered gifts of official council wine noted with increasing precision whether the guest was sojourning in the city in a private or a public capacity. Whether it was a matter of gift giving to foreign visitors or the acceptance of gifts by local officials, in the recording and registration systems of the cities of the Upper Rhine and the Swiss Confederacy it was the gift that accentuated the dual nature of the public servant. One might say that it distinguished between official and private persons by being given to both.

These honorable gifts were, however, by no means as public as the municipal registers presented them. In other words, visibility, like invisibility, was something that, in the same way as the distinctions between outside and inside or public and private, had to be carefully manufactured and enforced politically. Contemporaries commented variously on these language games. The public good, offices, and gifts appeared not only in the tavern tirades, Shrovetide plays, and pamphlets that occupied us in previous chapters. When

Erasmus received the above-mentioned four pitchers of wine as a welcome gift in Basel in November 1521, it occurred in a political atmosphere in which the conflicts over visible and invisible gifts were fought out in street battles until the mayor was toppled.

Between the winter of 1521 and the summer of 1524, among other work, Erasmus revised and expanded his *Colloquia*, whose fourth edition was published by the Basel printer Froben in August or September 1524 under the title *Colloquiorum formulae*. Erasmus added a new dialogue for this edition—the "Convivium fabulosum," or story-filled banquet. Not unlike Holbein's frescoes in the Basel town hall, the dialogue treats the complicated relationship between office, the public good, and gifts of varying degrees of voluntariness. In the "Convivium fabulosum," wine is not simply offered as the reward for the best story; gifts are literally the red thread along which a chain of caustic anecdotes are strung. The tales that the guests tell each other range from an official of Emperor Maximilian who extorts excessive revenues in the emperor's name and goes unpunished because the other imperial councilors do the same thing, to the French king Louis, who receives a gift of 10,000 crowns. His avaricious courtiers hope that the money will be distributed among them. Louis, however, gives the present to his modest chancellor, the man among them who, when asked whether he needs anything, answers that his salary suffices. Finally, Erasmus presents the story of the same French king who, when brought a simple rustic gift by a peasant, rewards the latter with 1,000 gold crowns. When the courtiers see that the king is apparently in a munificent mood, one of them gives him a handsome riding horse on the spot, in the hope of an even more lavish return gift. Ah, says the king, what a precious gift; I must consider carefully what precious object to give in return. Thereupon he sends a confidant to his apartments to fetch the peasant's present and wrap it in silk. This he offers the courtier, adding that the gift horse seemed well compensated (in the original, *bene pensatum*) by such a treasure, which had been worth 1,000 crowns to him. Full of anticipation the courtier unpacks the silk-wrapped gift and finds—the turnip that the peasant had bestowed upon the king.[16]

It was also a turnip that Hans Holbein painted in the fresco depicting the story of Manius Curius Dentatus, which adorns a wall of the great council chamber in the Basel town hall, the turnip now placed, with caustic humanist wit, in a political context. In so doing he did more than merely allude to the conflict between the German emperor and the French king, which left its mark on Basel in these years. The relationship between private gift and public good and between gift and return gift was never simple reciprocity or "gift exchange," but rather always served to dramatize in no uncertain terms the inequality of power between the giver and the recipient. The stories may be read as arguments *against* reciprocity, which were intended to reveal talk of return gifts as both cynical and violent. In Erasmus, gifts dramatize relentless competition, not cooperation.

The Reformation of Gift Discourse and the Bodies of Women

The history of pensions and the multifarious manifestations of gifts in Switzerland and the Upper Rhine region does not end with the conflicts of 1521. On the contrary, in the spring of that same year in Zurich, Huldrych Zwingli preached against the Swiss military alliance with France, the enlistment of mercenary armies, and pensions from princes (the pope expressly included), and in this context he uttered his famous phrase about the cardinals' red hats and robes out of which fell gold that was in reality the blood of his listeners' brothers, fathers, and friends.[17]

Zwingli's argumentation is documented by a further sermon he preached against a renewal of the alliance with France in May 1522. He recalled old Swiss glories in battle and painted the dangers of ignoring divine law in the most vivid colors: pride cometh before the Fall, just as Sodom and Gomorrah were punished. The pension recruiters used diabolical lies and pretenses; war was the lawless rule of the stronger, which only bred violence and strengthened disobedience and discord in the Swiss Confederacy itself; the Zurich lay priest explicitly warned against a violent assumption of power by mercenaries in the service of foreign princes. If a foreign prince made a public (*offenlich*) pact with a town council or commune, Zwingli continued, but purchased the agreement of the responsible parties secretly (*heymlich*) with the aid of *myet* and these gifts were later discovered, then he was owed nothing and must be punished for fraud. This view could also be found in the articles of canon law concerning betrayal and dissimulation, Zwingli noted, finally referring to the punishment of Jugurtha, who had believed that he could buy anything with money and gifts—an unconcealed threat to the local pension brokers.

The third example Zwingli cited would ultimately determine subsequent Reformation discourse on pensions to a large degree. Foreign money, according to the Zurich reformer, corrupted morals. New clothing, new drinks, and new blasphemous words made their appearance along with pensions. Above all, however, the morality and decency of women were endangered. Women, who were by nature weak and attracted to pretty new things and jewelry, would be the first to succumb to temptation; voluptuousness, new apparel, and precious objects would then turn men too into women. Hannibal had been vanquished because he had allowed his army to grow effeminate (*erwybschen*). "What do you think," Zwingli asked his audience dramatically at this point, "will ultimately become of your precious shirts, your golden rings and your silken dresses?"[18]

Zwingli linked pensions with simulation and dissimulation, fraud and upheaval on the one hand and luxurious dress, evil oaths, and fornication on the other. He devoted not a single word to the events of October 1521 in Basel. Apparently, he did not find them useful as an admonitory example (with quite good reason, as we have seen). His sexualization of evil gifts took up some older narrative elements already familiar to us, in which male bodies lost their manly qualities through gifts, but aligned them in a new way. Gone are the unspeakable relationships between these male bodies; instead Zwingli stylized women as sites of fleshly wantonness and seduction through luxury, dress, and jewelry.

While the rural commune of Schwyz forbade pensions and the enlistment of mercenary troops immediately after Zwingli's sermon but rescinded this prohibition again in August 1522, Zwingli had more success in his hometown. In November 1522 the Zurich town council passed a new, strictly worded ordinance introducing the death penalty for the illegal enlistment of mercenary troops and the acceptance of secret pensions.[19] The following year a number of trials of mercenaries and recruiters were held in Zurich. All without exception were accused of violating municipal law by accepting such covert gifts (*mieth und gab*).[20] Zwingli expressed his Reformation reading of evil gifts more clearly still in his "faithful and ardent exhortation" to the Swiss of May 1524. Just as the Moabites had tempted the children of Israel with their beautiful women, the Swiss, Zwingli warned, were being lured by gifts to subjugate themselves to self-interest. From these gifts followed lavish clothing, idleness, gambling, and gluttony, and these led to the discord that threatened to tear the Swiss Confederacy asunder. Nobody wanted to work anymore. Instead they were greedy for cinnamon, ginger, malmsey, oranges, silks, and similar female delicacies (*weyberschleck*).[21] In a further sermon against pensions preached after the battle of Pavia in 1525, Zwingli sharpened even further his combination of a critique of luxury with the sale of flesh and blood. The pension lords sold their compatriots to Italy like cattle, and their commanders walked about dressed in silk, silver, gold, and damask. Zwingli closed his sermon with an only thinly veiled call to violence: these ill-gotten gains must be destroyed like molehills on the meadows and their beneficiaries punished as an example.[22]

With the polemics and pamphlets that surrounded the Baden disputation between representatives of reform and the Catholic clergy in the early summer of 1526, the old battle cry *miet* was tailored by the Reformation party to fit its orthodox opponents in order to denounce them as corrupt, dependent upon foreign powers, and traitors to the Swiss Confederacy. In the wake of a further sermon by Zwingli in September 1526, the Zurich town council initiated an official investigation into which of its citizens had received such invisible dirty gifts from foreign rulers. Zwingli gave a solemn deposition before the town council declaring all those who received pensions to be enemies of the Gospel who maintained dangerous secret connections to the enemies of the faith. Vice must be rooted out so that the city might be spared God's judgment. For that reason the authorities must proceed as severely as possible against the recipients of such gifts, in order to save Christian doctrine and the city as a whole. This was the prelude to a series of spectacular trials of mercenaries, pension brokers, and political opponents that culminated in the new stricter pension ordinance of December 13 and the execution of the councilor Jakob Grebel.[23] Grebel himself had little or nothing to do with the illegal enlistment of mercenaries. Rather, he was a former supporter of Zwingli's, one of Zurich's leading diplomats and a frequent envoy to the Swiss Assembly. In the reasons given for its judgment, the council stated that Grebel had accepted 4,000 crowns from unknown persons and secretly passed on information to the enemies of the true faith. By acquiring imperial and French stipends for his son Konrad during his studies in Paris, he had violated Zurich's prohibition on pensions and thus also his oath as a councilor—a further variant of letting the word *pension* mean whatever appeared opportune in a given situation.[24]

As deftly as Zwingli took up older terms, the expressions for evil gifts were reformulated here and extended in a particular direction. It was this reworking of the narrative patterns surrounding invisible gifts that was used by the reformed chroniclers of the 1530s and 1540s. When Johannes Stumpf wrote of the 1501 attempt to prohibit pensions in his *Chronicle of the Reformation in Switzerland* that these gifts caused babies to be sold in the womb, Christian blood to be shed, and the entire country to be robbed of its "manliest and most valiant" inhabitants, he was directly following Zwingli's argumentation. The same is true of his depiction of the Zurich uprisings of 1515.[25] While earlier chroniclers such as Ludwig Schwinkhart (died 1522) had described pensions soberly as a political business and emphasized their limited efficacy, Fridolin Ryff of Basel, for example, who wrote his chronicle under the immediate impression of the Reformation of 1529, portrayed the 1521 alliance with France as a diabolical pact with the heralds of the Antichrist that would tear the Swiss Confederacy apart. The city had "sold its own citizens daily." For Ryff, the pension riots of autumn 1521 represented nothing but discord and partisan battles unleashed by French money.[26]

The chronicle of the city of Bern that Valerius Anshelm Rüd compiled between 1529 and 1546 as an official history of the city reads even more colorfully. Conceived and written as a moralizing Reformation chronicle, Anshelm's work was consulted by German-language historians of the late nineteenth and early twentieth centuries mainly as an illustration of Swiss conditions before the Reformation. Corruption by French money is one of its leitmotifs. In Anshelm's teleological account, the introduction of the Reformation in Bern in 1528 was the event that at last enabled the city to put an end to the foreign entanglements it had acquired through pensions and polluting gifts, along with other vices.[27] In Anshelm's account, dirty French money (which he naturally refers to as *miet*) became a symptom of religious aberration that expressed itself politically. The chronicler thus devotes ample attention to the origins of this venality in the Burgundian wars. His chronicle recounts Waldmann's fall and the Italian wars in the moral terms of a political and religious language in which the past formed an immediate continuity with the present of the 1530s and 1540s.[28] Two Swiss diplomats, he reports, otherwise learned, honorable, and capable men, who were sent on a mission to France in 1516, had been "anointed with oil of lily [a reference to the fleur-de-lys on French gold coins], making them so soft and gentle" that they had signed a new alliance with the French king. However, Anshelm continues with the moral of the story, one of them died that same year, allegedly of poisoning, and the other a short while later on a pilgrimage. Thus both had "unexpectedly received their reward," he concluded sarcastically.[29] Women turned into prostitutes when French envoys mingled "in the baths and among the women with great wantonness and voluptuousness"; the same dirty French money had brought Swiss military commanders to offer themselves to foreigners "like whores." In Anshelm's chronicle, Italy not only grinds (*mahlt*, a verb with explicit sexual undertones in the sixteenth century) the Swiss but also devours them.[30]

Finally, Anshelm's chronicle links the motifs of the sale of bodies and blood with confessional conflicts around the sacrifice of the Mass and the veneration of the host. When a tower where gunpowder was stored exploded in 1526 in Basel after being struck by lightning, he explains, the orthodox interpreted this as God's punishment for the introduction of the new teachings. An Augustinian had preached that the misfortune was a warning sign from God against all those who doubted the doctrine of the real presence of Christ's body and blood in the Eucharist. If that were true, Anshelm continues polemically, then the Catholic clergy were the greatest merchants of bodies and blood anywhere because they offered the most sacred doctrine to the highest bidder. If God truly threw lightning bolts because of the new evangelical teachings, why did he not punish those Catholic town councilors who "saw through their fingers" (i.e., accepted bribes) and took blood money (i.e., foreign pensions)? As servants of foreign masters, they had sown discord among the Swiss with *miet und gaben*.[31] Anshelm recombined the older elements of talk about invisible gifts, the motifs of the traitor's reward, poison, and "greasing palms" and systematized them in a new context, that of the confessional conflicts and Reformation discourses on fornication of the 1530s and 1540s.[32]

In this new use of the language of evil gifts, the sexual imagery also underwent a reorganization. Corrupting invisible gifts no longer referred to the unspeakable relations between men and to sodomy as "secrecy," as had still been common in accusations against Swiss mercenary leaders only a few years before Zwingli. Instead, women's bodies, as perilous sites of seduction by luxury, dress, and jewelry, now came to represent dangerous gifts. The discourse on political venality in the Swiss Confederacy became fixated on discord and on luxury in dress and eating, and a newly formulated work ethic was marshaled against gifts and the trade in mercenaries. The associated connotations of female extravagance and unchastity were closely tied to the Reformation doctrines on fornication and marriage.[33]

Reformation polemics against gifts were integrated into extensive debates in which the reciprocity of the Catholic economy of the salvation of souls was contrasted with the reformers' insistence on voluntary devotion and irrecoverable and literally priceless grace, or the Catholic *do ut des* with Reformation "gratuitousness," as Natalie Davis has put it. The believer could not incur God's debt by offerings or gifts, the reformers taught. Like Judas, the Catholic priests sold the Holy of Holies, alleged radical reformed pamphlets of the sixteenth century, and any such transfer represented usury, theft, and dirty trade.[34] The elements of this line of argument and above all its metaphors did not, however, emerge from the close confines of scholars' studies in Zurich, Wittenberg, or Geneva. They originated in the reform movements of the fourteenth and fifteenth centuries and referred to an older vernacular tradition that, as we have seen, had long used the concept of evil rewards and negative, corrupting, and polluting reciprocity. In Switzerland

and the Upper Rhine region, *miet*, the word for gifts that implied tainted return favors, was an established political slogan throughout the last third of the fifteenth century and was associated with a number of dramatic narrative elements and denunciatory plots. The reformers did not hesitate to deploy these connotations. At the same time, they adapted and altered what the word meant to suit the political context and newly formulated moral code.

Making the Invisible Visible

Dirty invisible gifts literally organized these sixteenth-century reformed chroniclers' moral view of history. They portrayed a noble, simple, and god-fearing Swiss past before the Burgundian wars as a lost age of virtue that had been corrupted by illegitimate transfers and transformed into an era of internal conflict in whichdissimulation and vice ruled. Only the Reformation had put an end to this morally bankrupt epoch. Swiss historians of the period between the late nineteenth century and the end of the First World War were only to happy to adopt this dual image of the past with its tempting junctions for political and social analogies. In this context, pensions became a highly useful mirror of crisis. In a chapter of his influential history of the Swiss Confederacy entitled "Demoralizing After-Effects of the Burgundian Wars," Johannes Dierauer, for example, claimed that the "moral health of all strata of the population" had been seriously imperiled after the victories of 1477. In the years before and after the First World War, pensions appeared in historical accounts as "urges run wild," an "all-consuming creeper," "political degeneration," and a "widespread disease."[35] A military history of Switzerland published in 1933 offered the sober assessment that pensions merely highlighted the inner conflicts and contradictions that already existed in the Confederacy. At the same time, it deplored the attacks on official authority and the "rebelliousness" and "capriciousness of the masses." After the Second World War, the topic of pensions was treated only cursorily and negatively, as a marginal question in conjunction with the trade in mercenaries and the Reformation, but its confessional undertones remained evident. Typical here is a formulation of 1947, according to which pensions and mercenary service had led to "economic and moral decline." Only Zwingli "and the spiritual shock of his Reformation" had saved Switzerland from the abyss.[36] Parallels were drawn, however, to the neutrality, confessionalism, and traditions of "intellectual national defense" of the years following the Second World War. Polluting pensions became part of an all-encompassing management of memory in which the past was presented to the reader as a dangerously familiar message.

What all these accounts ignore is that the Swiss Confederacy emerged as a state at the beginning of the early modern period with and through these very payments. From the end of the fifteenth century, pensions placed the administration of individual cities and provinces on a wholly new footing and facilitated the rise of a stratum of wealthy notables and war entrepreneurs. They shaped the formation of local Swiss elites and systems of patronage and distribution of office in a way similar to what Sharon Kettering has described for early modern France. The early modern state was quite literally built on gifts. At the same time, however—and we could call this Zwingli's legacy — even at the beginning of the twenty-first century, to talk about dirty gifts is always to talk about politics and legitimacy. Gifts and the state—especially when the political past, as is the case in Switzerland, is instrumentalized as an integrative and heroic national Middle Ages—must always be separated as sharply as possible from each other.

The gift as information and pollution, as the intersection of the visible and the invisible, as a criterion of distinction and accentuation, and as a litmus test of *publicus* and *privatus* finally brings us to the altered character of political authority or the state at the end of the fifteenth and beginning of the sixteenth century, to the change in a paradigm of social ordering.[37] In the materials discussed here, we have repeatedly encountered the town guard, a figure who embodied the power of the authorities in a conspicuous and apparently generally quite unpleasant manner. It is no accident that chroniclers' accounts of the mayors Waldmann and Schwarz, who were deposed because of corruption, consistently emphasize the figure of the mayor's close associate, the detested town guard, who was also executed.[38] In their jokes about the downfall of the Basel war entrepreneurs and pension brokers, the Basel mercenaries captured and plundered at the camp outside Milan by their own compatriots portrayed this same town guard as a cynical model of municipal administration and careerism along with the mayor and the master of the guilds. It was this very multiple persona whom Holbein painted during that same autumn of 1521 on the wall of the great council chamber. There the town guard raises his hand to his cap in greeting and points out to the assembled councils the surrounding allegories depicting the complicated and, in places, bloody and violent relationship among profit, law, and official power.

I suggested above that the legal texts of the fifteenth and sixteenth centuries—oath formulas, ordinances, and mandates but also mirrors of princes (treatises on statecraft) and political tracts—should be read as a kind of matrix, a *doxa*, that does not claim to regulate practice completely but instead provides an authoritative vocabulary. In negotiating the question of what was a permissible or an impermissible gift in the cities of the late Middle Ages or the early modern period, a correct interpretation of the relevant legal texts was naturally important. At least as important, however, was the linguistic form in which the negotiation took place and in which the various forms of publicity and visibility played a decisive role. These rules imposed norms not on behavior, but on talk about behavior. They were, in short, rules of the second, not the first, degree; they did not exist in the abstract but were tied to concrete persons.

It is of these second-degree rules that the town guard spoke, and for that reason Holbein painted him greeting the beholder from the wall of the Basel great council chamber. He was the protagonist of the interpretation of gifts because he himself was capable of making offers that were impossible to refuse. This figure and the practices of municipal power associated with it allow us to avoid dwelling on the unfruitful distinction between municipal norms and practice and instead to understand the contradictions between the two as a field in which a rhetoric of definition developed. *Definition* is an honorable old academic word. In our cases, however, it is not a matter of unambiguous conceptual attributions. On the contrary, in order to use the fields as fields of action, we must define ambivalently and ambiguously. It is always the strategy of the speaker—an egotistical, present-oriented, and highly flexible strategy—that decides what is a gift and what is not, which offerings are tokens of love (including love of a very particular kind) and which are diabolical *miet*. In gifts, the lines between people and things indeed become fluid, as Marcel Mauss noted. Gifts were represented as fluid, political bodies were endangered by these liquids, and because all of this took place in secret ultimately anything could be an evil gift, regardless of whether something was actually bestowed, and if so, what. These secrets were localized in and on bodies. In contrast to our own accustomed mode of thinking, late medieval and early modern body metaphors appear to have served less to express and reveal something that one could see than to represent something that one could not.

Literacy and the principle of written record-keeping were essential forces in the production of this invisible. Bookkeeping on gifts in Basel, with its cautious interlocking of secrecy and publication, demonstrates how—to cite Max Weber—the exercise of power within the framework of bureaucratic rule was constituted through the economy of information and the establishment of official secrecy.[39] Hans Holbein painted this doctrine of official secrecy on the walls of the great council hall, together with the menacing images of punishment, suicidal and bloody justice, and humiliation. The principle was expressed here in a quotation from Harpocrates: "Whoever enters here shall maintain silence, as is fitting. For our law forbids us to reveal a secret."[40]

When the reformer Huldrych Zwingli solemnly declared on September 1526 before the Zurich town council that it had been revealed to him in strict confidence that the Zurich town guards (who else?) had been bribed with pensions to ensure that they would warn those who had incurred guilt by accepting and distributing dirty money in time to escape prosecution, he was doing more than just pointing out the association between gifts and the economy of information. Ultimately, he was demonstrating the particular conditions of visibility and invisibility that determined talk about gifts in the cities of the fifteenth and sixteenth centuries. The use of the terms for dangerous gifts reflects the complicated genesis of the concept of high treason and the history of those arcana with which states would be built in the century after the Reformation.[41] The talk about legal and illegal gifts offers a point of departure for pursuing the rise of the secret in early modern notions of the state, which was an instrument of a very special kind: the menacing and sublime paradox of the demonstratively invisible.

And that is perhaps what distinguishes our own talk about gifts most fundamentally from that of a humanist reformer such as Erasmus. To speak of gifts, I believe, is always to speak of utopia. An effective gift was (and is) one that produces ties through ambiguity. Nowadays, at the beginning of the twenty-first century, in a society with fundamentally different economic and personal commercialized market relations, we tend to regard gifts as purely positive—and perhaps even as a possible escape from commercial structures. A bit of utopia is apparently indispensable, though. As ironic as it may sound, the idea of a society without gifts and compulsory "gifts" was probably just as utopian for Erasmus and many of his contemporaries as the notion of a society without (wholly different) relations of economic dependency and dirty money is for us today.

Appendix

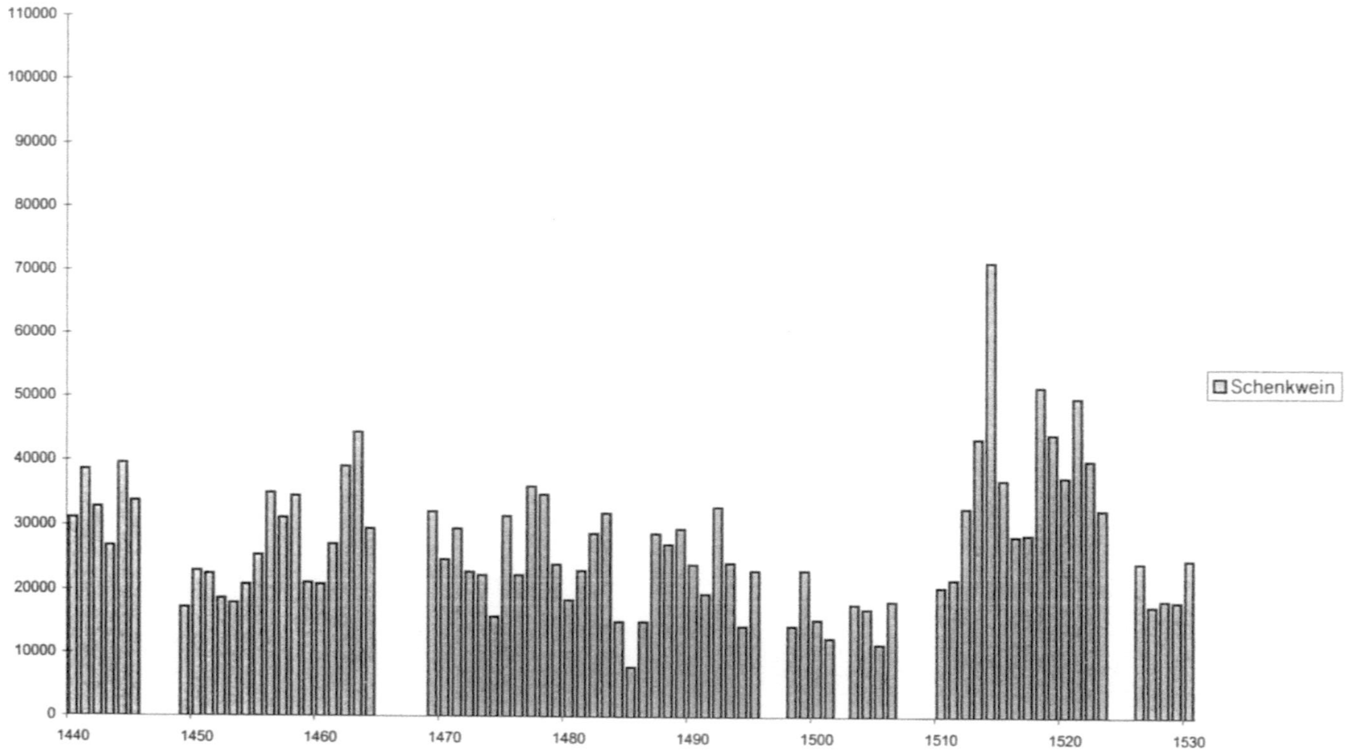

Appendix Figure 1. Spending on gifts of wine in Basel pfennigs, 1440-1530

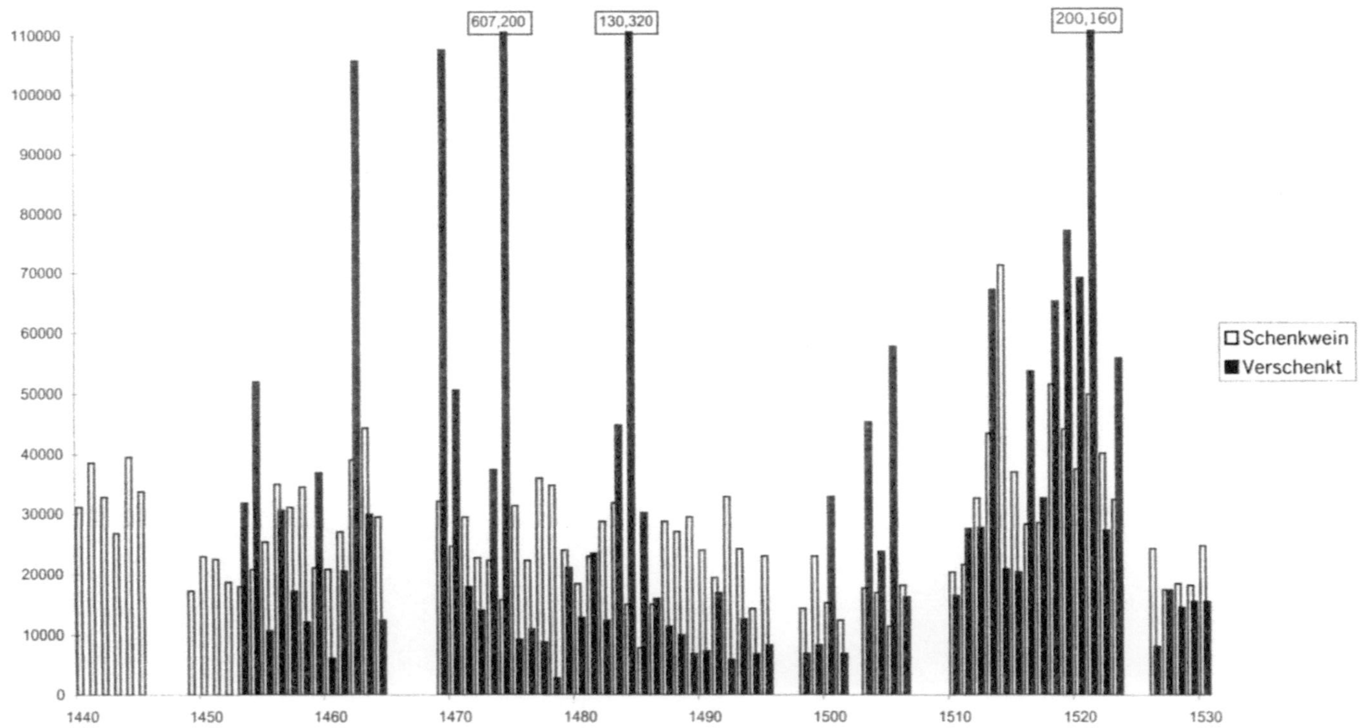

Appendix Figure 2. Spending on wine and other municipal gifts in Basel pfennings, 1440-1530

Abbreviations

AKG	*Archiv für Kulturgeschichte*
BChr	*Basler Chroniken*
BZGA	*Basler Zeitschrift für Geschichte und Altertumskunde*
d	Basel pfennigs
EA	*Amtliche Sammlung der älteren eidgenössischen Abschiede*, series 1245–1798
fl	Rhenish florins
GWU	*Geschichte in Wissenschaft und Unterricht*
HBLS	*Historisch-Biographisches Lexikon der Schweiz*
HRG	*Handwörterbuch der Rechtsgeschichte*
HZ	*Historische Zeitschrift*
JWCI	*Journal of the Warburg and Courtauld Institute*
MIÖG	*Mitteilungen des Instituts für Österreichische Geschichte*
MVGN	*Mitteilungen des Vereins für die Geschichte der Stadt Nürnberg*
PMLA	*Proceedings of the Modern Language Association*
StAB	Staatsarchiv Basel-Stadt
StadtAF	Stadtarchiv Freiburg im Breisgau
StAN	Staatsarchiv Nürnberg
StChr	*Chroniken der deutschen Städte vom 14. bis ins 16. Jahrhundert*
SZG	*Schweizerische Zeitschrift für Geschichte*
VSWG	*Vierteljahrschrift für Sozial- und Wirtschaftsgeschichte*
WAB	Wochenausgabebücher, Staatsarchiv Basel-Stadt
ZGO	*Zeitschrift für Geschichte des Oberrheins*
ZHF	*Zeitschrift für historische Forschung*
ZRG	*Zeitschrift der Savigny-Stiftung für Rechtsgeschichte*

Notes

Introduction

1."Geschenke nennet man eine Sache, deren Eigenthum man dem andern ohne Vergeltung überlässt. Der vernünfftige Grund derer Geschenke ist ein Überfluss." Jakob and Wilhelm Grimm, *Deutsches Wörterbuch*, vol. IV/1.2 (Leipzig, 1897), 3853–54; Johann Heinrich Zedler, *Grosses vollständiges Universal-Lexikon*, vol. 10 (Halle, 1735), 1218; on the far broader field of meaning of *Gabe* (gift, offering), see *HRG*, vol. 1 (Berlin, 1978), 1364–65.

2. Leon Battista Alberti, *The Family in Renaissance Florence: A Translation of I Libri della Famiglia by Leon Battista Alberti*, trans. Renée Neu Watkins (Columbia, S.C., 1969), book 4, 270.

3. See Hartmut Boockmann, "Das 15. Jahrhundert und die Reformation," in *Kirche und Gesellschaft im Heiligen Römischen Reich des 15. und 16. Jahrhunderts* (Göttingen, 1994), 9–25; similarly, see the introductory pages of Thomas A. Brady, Heiko Obermann, and James Tracy, eds., *Handbook of European History, 1400–1600*, vol. 1 (Leiden, 1996), xiii–xxiv; and Stephen Rowan, "Urban Communities: The Rulers and the Ruled," in the same volume, 197–212.

4. Thomas Brady, *Turning Swiss: Cities and Empire, 1450–1550* (Cambridge, 1985); Claudius Sieber-Lehmann, "'Teutsche nation' und Eigenossenschaft," *HZ* 253 (1991): 561–602.

5. Emil Welti, ed., *Die Rechtsquellen des Kantons Bern*, Sammlung schweizerischer Rechtsquellen II, vol. 1 (Aarau, 1902), 28, 134, 136.

6. With reference to Marc Bloch's attempt to pursue the institutions of gift exchange in nascent feudal society (Bloch, "The Rise of Dependent Cultivations and Seigneurial Institutions," in *The Cambridge Economic History of Europe*, vol. 1 [1941; Cambridge, 1966], 272 ff. Two influential works are Georges Duby, *The Early Growth of the European Economy: Warriors and Peasants from the Seventh to the Twelfth Century*, trans. Howard B. Clarke (Ithaca, N.Y., 1974), 48–76, and Philippe Jobert, *La notion de donation: Convergences 630–750* (Paris, 1977). Since then, a number of monographs have offered a more diverse picture; see, for example, Stephen D. White, *Custom, Kinship, and Gifts to Saints: The Laudatio Parentum in Western France, 1050–1150* (Chapel Hill, N.C., 1988); Barbara Rosenwine, *To Be the Neighbor of St. Peter: The Social Meaning of Cluny's Property, 909–1049* (Ithaca, N.Y., 1989), and Constance B. Bouchard, *Holy Entrepreneurs: Cistercians, Knights, and Economic Exchange in Twelfth-Century Burgundy* (Ithaca, N.Y., 1991).

7. Marcello Fantoni, *La corte del Granduca: Forme e simboli del potere mediceo fra Cinque e Seicento* (Rome, 1994), esp. "Il dono: liberalitá e potere," 97–137; Werner Paravicini, "Invitations au mariage. Pratique sociale, abus de pouvoir, intérêt de l'Etat à la cour des Ducs de Bourgogne au XVe siècle," *Académie des Inscriptions et Belles-Lettres, comptes rendus des séances de l'année 1995* (Paris, 1995), 687–711. On urban sources, see Christiane Klapisch-Zuber, "Le complexe de Griselda: Dot et dons de mariage," in her *La maison et le nom: Stratégies et rituels dans l'Italie de la Renaissance* (Paris, 1990), 185–213; Paul Baur, *Testament und Bürgerschaft: Alltagsleben und Sachkultur im spätmittelalterlichen Konstanz* (Sigmaringen, 1989); Martha Howell, "Fixing Movables: Gifts by Testament in Late-Medieval Douai," *Past & Present* 150 (1996): 3–45.

8. Alain Derville, "Pots-de-vin, cadeaux, racket, patronage: Essai sur les mécanismes de décision dans l'état bourguignon," *Revue du Nord* 56 (1974): 341–64, and "Les pots-de-vins dans le dernier tiers du XVe siècle," in Wim Blockmans, ed., *1477: Le privilége géneral et les priviléges regionaux de Marie Bourgogne pour les Pays-Bas* (Kortrijk, 1985), 449–71; Marc Boone, "Dons et pots-de-vin: Aspects de la sociabilité urbaine au Bas Moyen Age: Les cas gantois pendant la période bourguignonne," *Revue du Nord* 70 (1988): 471–87.

9. Georg Simmel, *Soziologie: Untersuchungen über die Formen der Vergesellschaftung*, ed. Otthein Rammstedt (Frankfurt am Main, 1992), 667–68,and "Dankbarkeit: Ein soziologischer Versuch," in Georg Simmel, *Schriften zur Soziologie* (Frankfurt am Main, 1983), 210–18. "To give is to transfer voluntarily something that belongs to us to someone whom one believes cannot not accept it," Maurice Godelier, *L'Enigme du don* (Paris, 1996), 20.

10. Marcel Mauss, *The Gift: The Form and Reason for Exchange in Archaic Societies*, trans. W. D. Halls (New York, 1990). On gifts and society, see Simmel, *Soziologie*, 663; the quotation comes from Mauss, *The Gift*, 82–83, under the heading "Conclusion Regarding General Sociology and Morality." On Mauss's political commitment under the influence of the war, see Godelier, *L'Enigme*, 89 and 292–93; on contemporary debates about Mauss's theory and also earlier discussions of the subject, see Patrick Geary, "Gift Exchange and Social Science Modeling: The Limitations of a Construct," and Beate Wagner-Hasel, "Egoistic Exchange and Altruistic Gift: On the Roots of Marcel Mauss's Theory of the Gift," both in Gadi Algazi, Valentin Groebner, and Bernhard Jussen, eds. *Negotiating the Gift* (Göttingen, 2002), forthcoming.

11. Claude Lévi-Strauss, "Introduction de l'oeuvre de Mauss," in *Sociologie et Anthropologie* (Paris, 1950), xxxviii. On this viewpoint, see Mary Douglas, "No Free Gifts," foreword to Marcel Mauss, *The Gift*, vii–xviii; for another view, see Godelier, "L'Enigme," 14–15; André Petillat, "Le don: Espace imaginaire normatif et secret des auteurs," *Anthropologie et Sociétés* 19 (1995): 17–44, 23; and Jacques Derrida's remark on the gift as a gift-gift, the poisoned gift, in his *Given Time: I. Counterfeit Money*, trans. Peggy Kamuf (Chicago, 1992), 69 n. 21.

12. "It is because it contains and unites at once something that comes from persons and something that is present in their relationships that it totalizes and symbolizes them in its practice and in the objects that materialize this practice." Godelier, *L'Enigme du don*, 145. The question of the gift is "the fundamental question concerning the nature of the social, of the essential components of all human society," ibid., 49.

13. Mauss, *The Gift*, 81.

14. It is here that one must also locate the works of André Caille, which promote parallel anti-utilitarian notions. See his contributions to the journal *Mouvement Anti-utilitariste dans les Sciences Sociales (M.A.U.S.S.)*, ed. André Caille et al., which was founded in Paris in 1988.

15. Georges Bataille, "La notion de dépense," in Bataille, *Oeuvres complètes*, vol. 1 (Paris, 1970), 302–20, esp. 312–14; Theodor W. Adorno, *Minima Moralia* (London, 1984), 42. A number of older examples can be found in Marian Whitney, "Queen of Medieval Virtues: Largesse," in Christabel Fiske, ed., *Vassar Medieval Studies* (New Haven, Conn., 1923), 181–215; on the topos of the munificence of the olden days in chivalric literature, see the overview in Maurice Keen, *Chivalry* (New Haven, Conn., 1984), 29–31; on Noel du Fail see Natalie Zemon Davis, *The Gift in Sixteenth-Century France* (Madison, Wisc., 2000), 43–44.

16. Jacques Derrida, *Counterfeit Money*, 38, 56, 70, 91. Derrida presents the fact that the word *percevoir* means both to accept and to perceive as fundamental philosophical proof that the mere recognition (*reconnaissance*) of the gift, even before the acknowledgement (also *reconnaissance*) of the gift assumes the form of gratitude, cancels out the gift as a gift. "The simple identification of the gift seems to destroy it," *Counterfeit Money*, 14.

17. Pierre Bourdieu, *The Logic of Practice*, trans. Richard Nice (Cambridge, 1980), 98–111 and 126. See also the same author's *Outline of a Theory of Practice*, trans. Richard Nice (Cambridge, 1977), 4–6, 12–15, 171–73, 190–97, and more recently, *Méditations pascaliennes* (Paris, 1997), 229–40.

18. Annette B. Weiner, *Inalienable Possessions: The Paradox of Keeping-While-Giving* (Berkeley, Calif., 1992), 6–44; Jonathan Parry, "The Gift, the Indian Gift and the 'Indian Gift,'" *Man* 21 (1986): 453–73; Nicholas Thomas, *Entangled Objects: Exchange, Material Culture, and Colonialism in the Pacific* (Cambridge, Mass, 1991); Alain Guery, "Le roi dépensier," *Annales E.S.C.* 39 (1984): 1241–69, 1260; N. Z. Davis, *The Gift*, 8 ff.

19. This remark applies above all to the urban context on which this study concentrates. In the cases of a number of surviving pieces of jewelry, precious metal vessels, cutlery, and art works from the court milieu, the function of the gift as well as the names of giver and recipient are known to us. See the examples in Herbert Seling, *Die Kunst der Augsburger Goldschmiede* (Munich, 1980); and Johann M. Fritz, *Goldschmiedekunst der Gotik in Mitteleuropa* (Munich, 1982). Jan Hirschbiegel (Kiel) is currently preparing a study of the New Year's gifts—so-called *entrennes*—at the Burgundian and French courts in the fourteenth and fifteenth centuries. On courtship and wedding gifts from an art historical perspective, see Michael Camille, *The Medieval Art of Love: Objects and Subjects of Desire* (London, 1998), 50–71.

20. The state of the sources must be difficult and spotty in order to permit historians to undertake their work of reconstruction. It is the gap, the missing information, that inspires the desire to know and renders it productive (even if historians are not always eager to admit this).

21. With references to passages in Aristotle, Seneca, and Augustine, see the extensive treatment in Thomas of Aquinas, *Summa theologica* 2,2, *quaestio* 106, article 3–5, and *quaestio* 117, in *Summa Theologiae*, vol. 41: *Virtues of Justice in the Human Commu-*

nity (2a2ae. 101–22), ed. and trans. T. C. O'Brien (Blackfriars, 1972), 88–101 and 220–39. Cf. the ironic acuity with which John of Salisbury treats the compulsory gifts to courtiers and the cynically dual nature of *liberalitas* as blackmail and deception in the fifth book of his *Policraticus*; John of Salisbury, *Policraticus*, ed. Cary Nederman (Cambridge, 1990), 85–90, esp. 87–88.

22. See Ronald Weissmann, "The Importance of Being Ambiguous: Social Relations, Individualism, and Identity in Renaissance Florence," in Susan Zimmermann and R. Weissmann, ed., *Urban Life in the Renaissance* (Newark, N.J., 1989), 269–80; Guy F. Lytle, "Friendship and Patronage in Renaissance Europe," in F. W. Kent and D. Simons, eds. *Patronage, Art and Society in Renaissance Italy* (Oxford, 1987), 47–61, esp. 56–61; for Elizabethan England, see Louis Adrian Montrose, "Gifts and Reasons: The Contexts of Peele's 'Arrayngements of Paris,'" *English Literary History* 47 (1980): 433–71, esp. 454 ff. In fact, what rules the game of gift and countergift is not reciprocity but expectation. See Davis, *The Gift*, 8 ff.

23. Sebastian Brant, *Das Narrenschiff: Nachdruck der Erstausgabe 1494* (Tübingen, 1968), 253; Geiler von Kaysersberg, "Predigt zum Narrenschiff," 545–47, in J. Scheible, ed., *Das Kloster*, vol. 1 (Stuttgart, 1845).

24. Baldassare Castiglione, *The Book of the Courtier*, trans. George Bull (London, 1976), 313.

Chapter 1

1. See Arnold Esch, "Überlieferungs-Change und Überlieferungs-Zufall als methodisches Problem des Historikers," *HZ* 240 (1985): 529–70.

2. Georg Kress von Kressenstein, "Das Schenkbuch einer Nürnberger Patriziersfrau von 1416–1438," *Anzeiger für die Kunde der deutschen Vorzeit*, NF 23 (1876): 37–42, 70–74, esp. 73–74.

3. Philippe Braunstein, "Towards Intimacy: The Fourteenth and Fifteenth Centuries," in *A History of Private Life: Revelations of the Medieval World*, ed. Georges Duby, trans. Arthur Goldhammer (Cambridge, Mass., 1991), 535–630, esp. 549–56.

4. Matthias Molitor, "Register von der hussorge und wy man sich dorynnen halden sol" (1463), Ms. Universitätsbibliothek Göttingen, f. 2r.

5. Alfred Weitnauer, ed., *Venezianischer Handel der Fugger nach der Musterbuchhaltung des Matthäus Schwarz* (Munich, 1931), 176, 270; Valentin Groebner, "Insides Out: Clothes, Dissimulation, and the Arts of Accounting in the Autobiography of Matthaeus Schwarz (1498–1574)," *Representations* 66 (1999): 100–121.

6. Wilhelm Loose, ed., *Anton Tuchers Haushaltsbuch, 1507–1517* (Stuttgart, 1877), 16, 18.

7. Loose, *Anton Tuchers Haushaltsbuch*, 63, 82–83, also 99. For further, similar, gifts, see, for example, 64, 70, 97, 101, 105, 108, 126, etc. For the reference to the entry in the trading company's *czornall* (journal), see 92. Natalie Davis mentions the existence of similar household books in sixteenth-century France; Davis, *The Gift in Sixteenth-Century France* (Madison, Wisc., 2000), 21.

8. See the reproductions of broadsheets with formulas such as *ain guot jar* (a

good year) in Paul Heitz, ed., *Neujahrswünsche des 15. Jahrhunderts* (Strasbourg, 1909).

9. In his edition, the editor of Tucher's notes changed the order of the registers regarding servants and taxes; on his abridgements, see Loose, *Anton Tuchers Haushaltsbuch*, 5 ff.

10. B. Greiff, ed., *Tagebuch des Lukas Rem aus den Jahren 1495–1541: Ein Beitrag zur Handelsgeschichte der Stadt Augsburg* (Augsburg, 1861), 50–52 (*Statt hernach, wer uns auf unsser und was Jeder gabett hatt*) and 52–55 (*Statt hernach wem Ich gab oder schenck auf hochzeytten etc. oder anders).*

11. Carl von Ölhafen, ed., "Eine Hochzeit zu Nürnberg zu Anfang des 16. Jahrhunderts," *Anzeiger für die Kunde der deutschen Vorzeit* 24 (1877): 242–47. For a stimulating account of demanded and forced wedding gifts, see Werner Paravicini, "Invitations au mariage: Pratique sociale, abus de pouvoir, intérêt de l'état à la cour des Ducs de Bourgogne au XVe siècle," *Académie des Inscriptions et Belles-Lettres, comptes rendus des séances de l'année 1995* (Paris, 1995): 687–711.

12. Albrecht Dürer, "Tagebuch der Reise in die Niederlande," in Albrecht Dürer, *Schriften und Briefe* (Leipzig, 1989), 57. For an account of the precise recording of the names, origins, and number of all guests who were hosted or given gifts in aristocratic household account books of the sixteenth century, see Felicity Heal, *Hospitality in Early Modern England* (Oxford, 1990), 49–57.

13. StAB Finanz E, f. 1.

14. StAB Finanz G 9, f. 12.

15. Bernhard Harms, ed., *Der Stadthaushalt Basels im ausgehenden Mittelalter: Die Jahresrechnungen 1360–1535*, vol. 2 (Tübingen, 1910), 3.

16. Harms, *Stadthaushalt*, vol. 2, 296 (1458–59).

17. Herbert Wolf, ed., *Johannes Rothes Ratsgedichte* (Berlin, 1971), 47–48, 71. On Rothe see George S. Williams, "Adelsdarstellung und adeliges Selbstverständnis im Spätmittelalter: Politische und soziale Reflexionen in den Werken Johannes Rothes und Ulrich Füetrers," in Paul U. Hohendahl and Peter M. Lützeler, eds., *Legitimationskrisen des deutschen Adels, 1200–1900* (Stuttgart, 1979), 44–60.

18. In Nuremberg such registers were kept as early as the 1340s. StaatsA Nürnberg Rep. 52b, Amts- und Standbücher 313 (1393–1422) to 321a (1619–1630). See also Paul Sander, *Die reichsstädtische Haushaltung Nürnbergs, dargestellt auf Grund ihres Zustands von 1431–1440* (Leipzig, 1902), 126–27, 615–25; Ernst Mummenhoff, *Das Rathaus in Nürnberg* (Nuremberg, 1891), 69–70; and Ernst Pitz, *Schrift- und Aktenwesen der städtischen Verwaltung im Spätmittelalter: Köln—Nürnberg—Lübeck* (Cologne, 1959), 167, 203–4. Separate lists of official gifts have also survived in the municipal account books for Augsburg, Bern, Lucerne, Cologne, Constance, Munich, Memmingen, Nördlingen, Obernai, Regensburg, Sélestat, and Schaffhausen.

19. There were close connections between commercial and municipal literacy and accountancy in the cities of the late Middle Ages, but the reference to commercial arithmetic as a purely urban phenomenon is misleading. The earliest surviving German account books from the mid-thirteenth century were, to be sure, influenced by mercantile literacy, but they come from the administration of territorial princes; municipal accounts began only somewhat later. On the oldest account books, see Wolf-Heino Struck, "Aus den Anfängen der territorialen Finanzverwaltung: Ein Rech-

nungsfragment der Herren von Bolanden, 1258/62," *Archivalische Zeitschrift* 70 (1974): 1–21. An Osnabrück account of 1285 is considered the oldest German-language example of municipal accounting. See Pitz, *Schrift- und Aktenwesen*, 278–83, and the remarks on municipal accounting in Eberhard Isenmann, *Die deutsche Stadt im Spätmittelalter* (Stuttgart, 1988), 166 ff. and 179 ff.

20. StA Porrentruy, Archives de l'ancien Evéché de Bâle, *Hofrechnungen, Hausbuch des Basler Bischofs Johann von Venningen 1458–1478*, f. 111 (henceforth referred to as Venningen, *Hausbuch*).

21. When Venningen's recently hired servant Huglin injured a horse in the summer of 1466, the bishop recorded the costs in his household account book and noted drily: *gedenck daran* (remember it). The unfortunate servant's contract was not renewed, and he disappears from the accounts; Venningen, *Hausbuch*, f. 323. See Gerhard Fouquet and Ulf Dirlmeier, "'Weger wer, ich hett sie behaltten': Alltäglicher Konsum und persönliche Beziehungen in der Hofhaltung des Basler Bischofs Johannes von Venningen (1458–1478)," in Werner Paravicini, ed., *Alltag bei Hofe* (Sigmaringen, 1995), 171–96 .

22. An example of 1495 from the council records of Freiburg im Breisgau makes this clear: a student stole a silver cup and fled his municipal persecutors to the freedom *(fryheit)* of the university, which, despite the city's request, turned him over for punishment not to the council but to the bishop. The university continued to demand that the council return the stolen property confiscated by the municipal authorities; the council thereupon resolved to lend *(verlihen)* the cup to the university but did not give it back. The clerk noted that this should be recalled (*Daran sol man gedencken*) and that one should not forget either (*des sol man ouch nit vergessen*) that the student, too, had not been properly punished; StadtAF B XIIIa, 4 a (Ratserkanntnisse, 1494–1502), f. 26r.

23. In Nuremberg all of these books were, not coincidentally, the files of the *Losungstube* (tax office), the direct registration department of the most powerful council office. See Pitz, *Schrift- und Aktenwesen*, 212. On the power position of the *Losunger* (tax officials) in the all-important Inner Council (*kleiner Rat*) in Nuremberg, see Christoph Scheurl's "Epistel über die Verfassung der Stadt Nürnberg," 1517, in *StChr*, ed. Karl Hegel et al. (Leipzig, 1869–1917), vol. 11, 781–804, esp. 792.

24. Joseph Geny, ed., *Schlettstadter Stadtrechte* (Heidelberg, 1902), 314; Karl Theodor Eheberg, *Verfassungs-, Verwaltungs- und Wirtschaftsgeschichte der Stadt Strassburg bis 1681*, vol. 1 (Strasbourg, 1899), 16, 17, 19. The classic work here is Gustav Schmoller, *Strassburg zur Zeit der Zunftkämpfe und die Reformation seiner Verfassung und Verwaltung im 15. Jahrhundert* (Strasbourg, 1875), 45. Similarly, in 1499 the Basel council sharply reminded the town of Liestal, which was under its jurisdiction, that it was the sole affair of the Basel authorities to make gifts to outsiders, and if Liestalers chose to ignore this they could expect severe punishment; StAB Ratsbücher B 1, f. 186v (1499).

25. On municipal accounts as historical sources, see the early study by Karl Bücher, "Der öffentliche Haushalt der Stadt Frankfurt im Mittelalter," *Zeitschrift für die gesamte Staatswissenschaft* 6 (1896): 1–19. See also Bernhard Kirchgässner, "Studien zur Geschichte des kommunalen Rechnungswesens der Reichsstädte Südwestdeutschlands

vom 13.–16. Jahrhundert," in *Finances et comptabilité urbaines du XIIIe au XVIe siècle*, ed. Centro Pro Civitate (Brussels, 1964), 236–54, and "Zur Frühgeschichte des modernen Haushalts, vor allem nach Quellen der Reichsstädte Esslingen und Konstanz," in Erich Maschke and Jürgen Sydow, eds., *Städtisches Haushalts- und Rechnungswesen* (Sigmaringen, 1977), 9–44; Hans-Joachim Behr, "Archivische Quellen zur bäuerlichen und bürgerlichen Alltagskultur vom 15. bis zum 17. Jahrhundert in Deutschland und ihre Auswertungsprobleme," *GWU* 36 (1985): 415–25.

26. On the key gaps in the household books of the bishop of Basel from 1458 to 1478, which make it impossible to reach reliable estimates based on the otherwise extraordinarily detailed notes on consumption in the episcopal household, see Fouquet and Dirlmeier, "Alltäglicher Konsum," 176.

27. "Anweisung über die Pflichten eines Bürgermeisters vom Görlitzer Stadtschreiber Johannes Frauenfeld 1476," reproduced in Richard Jecht, "Die Pflichten eines mittelalterlichen Bürgermeisters," *Deutsche Geschichtsblätter* 18 (1909): 89–102, esp. 92.

28. If the cover of the account book of the Florentine family Valori bears the admonition "*Questo libro non si mostri a nessuno*" (This book is not to be shown to anyone) this applies equally to private memorial and household books of the fifteenth and sixteenth centuries north of the Alps; Braunstein, "Towards Intimacy," 552. On secrecy in Matthias Schwarz's bookkeeping methods, see Weitnauer, *Venezianischer Handel der Fugger*, 36.

29. StAB Ratsbücher A 5, f. 110v (1455); similarly, K 23, f. 8v (1506) and K 24, f. 32r (1521); see also Hans-Rudolf Hagemann, *Basler Rechtsleben im Mittelalter*, vol. 1 (Basel, 1983), 277–78. On the council ordinance of 1506, see Rosemarie Grether, "Die Basler Ratsordnung von 1506," *Jahresberichte des Staatsarchiv Basel-Stadt* (1969): 21–51. On proceedings against Strasbourg officials for violating council secrecy, see Strasbourg, ASV, series VI, 488, no. 6.

30. Friedrich Wagner, "Nürnbergische Geheimschrift im 15. und vom Anfang des 16. Jahrhunderts," *Archivalische Zeitschrift* 9 (1884): 14–62, esp. 16.

31. On accounting in Basel at the end of the Middle Ages, see the detailed study by Gerhard Fouquet, *Bauen für die Stadt. Finanzen, Organisation und Arbeit in kommunalen Baubetrieben des Spätmittelalters* (Cologne, 1999). On the council committees, see Hans Füglister, *Handwerksregiment. Untersuchungen und Materialien zur sozialen und politischen Struktur der Stadt Basel in der ersten Hälfte des 16. Jahrhunderts* (Basel, 1981), 178–81, and Rudolf Wackernagel, *Geschichte der Stadt Basel*, 3 vols. (Basel, 1907–54), vol. 2/1, 239. The accounts were read out by the mayor or by the *Oberstzunftmeister*, the administrative head of the guilds. The control of accounts was the target of several heated political controversies. On this issue, see StAB Ratsbücher B 1, f. 178r; Wackernagel, *Geschichte der Stadt Basel*, vol. 2/1, 241–42; and Füglister, *Handwerksregiment*, 166–69, 182.

32. A number of municipal controversies centered not just on the duty of council members to submit proper accounts but also on the selection and manipulation involved. Hans Rappo, a member of the Greater Council of Bern who in 1470 accused members of the Inner Council of having granted secret loans and misappropriated funds, insisted that not everything had been read out, an action that cost him his coun-

cil seat and a fine of ten florins. See Regula Schmid, *Reden, rufen, Zeichen setzen: Politisches Handeln während des Bernr Twingherrenstreits 1469–1471* (Zurich, 1995), 160 ff.

33. Oskar Pausch, ed., *Das älteste deutsch-italienische Sprachbuch* (Vienna, 1972), 208.

34. Harms, *Stadthaushalt*, vol. 3, 80. For similar gifts to the clerk upon the completion of the accounts, see also Venningen, *Hausbuch*, f. 239 (1464).

35. *The Travel Journal of Antonio de Beatis*, ed. John R. Hale (London, 1979); Michel de Montaigne, *Journal de Voyage*, ed. François Rigolot (Paris, 1992), 15.

36. For the time being, see the remarks and bibliography in Gerhard Fouquet, "Das Festmahl in den oberdeutschen Städten des Spätmittelalters: Zu Form, Funktion und Bedeutung öffentlichen Konsums," *AKG* 74 (1992): 83–123; and Mack P. Holt, "Wine, Community and Reformation in 16th-Century Burgundy," *Past & Present* 138 (1992): 58–93. On the meaning of gifts of wine in fifteenth-century Bern, see Schmid, *Reden, Rufen, Zeichen setzen*, 89, 198–206.

37. Bernhard Harms, "Die Steuern und Anleihen im öffentlichen Haushalt der Stadt Basel 1361–1500: Ein Beitrag zur mittelalterlichen Finanzstatistik," *Zeitschrift für die gesamte Staatswissenschaft* 63 (1907): 627–81; Josef Rosen, "Der Staatshaushalt Basels von 1360–1535," in his *Finanzgeschichte im späten Mittelalter: Gesammelte Beiträge 1971–89* (Wiesbaden, 1991), 13–32; Hans-Jörg Gilomen, "Anleihen und Steuern in der Finanzwirtschaft spätmittelalterlicher Städte," in Sébastien Guex, Martin Körner, and Jakob Tanner, eds., *Staatsfinanzierung und Sozialkonflikte* (Zurich, 1994), 137–58, esp. 143–44. An entry in the *Urfehdenbücher* for 1514, for example, documents dissatisfaction with the town council's wine policies. A certain Konrat Vogler was released from jail after taking an oath of peace (*Urfehde*) because he had "said some words against my lords the councilors regarding the sale of wine" (*ettwas wort geredt wider min herren des win kouffs halb*); StAB Ratsbücher o 2, f. 152.

38. On these two assembly rooms as meeting places for the Basel patriciate, see the comments in Wackernagel, *Geschichte der Stadt Basel*, vol. 2/1, 380–81, and *BChr*, vol. 1, 82.

39. See, for example, the Basel council's weekly accounts of expenses, the *Wochenausgabebücher*, henceforth cited as WAB; WAB 9, f. 658 (1462); WAB 12, f. 692 and 694 (1502); WAB 10, f. 477 (1471), WAB 11, f. 653 (1485) and f. 927 (1490), WAB 11, f. 1146 (1509).

40. For example, WAB 10, f. 630 (1473), WAB 11, f. 226 (1477), WAB 12, f. 279 (1515). Gifts of wine were also common practice during sessions of the law courts. The account books for the Alsatian town of Obernai document in detail gifts of wine to various local and visiting officials during the trials of members of the *Bundschuh* conspiracy in 1493; printed in Albert Rosenkranz, *Der Bundschuh* (Heidelberg, 1927), vol. 2, documents, 3–4.

41. StadtAF B 2, 1, Kopialbuch 4, f. 257; repeated one year later in B 13a, 4a (Ratserkanntnisse,1494–1502), f. 49r.

42. StAB Öffnungsbuch 7, f. IXr (1477); see also WAB f. 651 (1485), WAB 12, f. 719 (1502),WAB 13, f. 276 (1515).

43. StAB Ratsbücher, K 23, Ratsordnungen, f. 3r; printed with commentary in Rosemarie Grether, "Die Baseler Ratsordnung von 1506," *Jahresberichte des Staats-*

archiv Basel-Stadt (1969): 21–51. The guild account books also contain scattered mentions of gifts of wine to new town councilors; see, for example, StAB Zunftakten, Safranzunft 66, f. 487 (1509). On similar gifts of wine at the assumption of council office in Strasbourg and their regulation, see Eheberg, *Verfassungsgeschichte,* vol. 1, 14.

44. StAB Ratsbücher, K 23, Ratsordnungen, f. 6r.

45. StaatsAB Finanz G 9, Wochenausgabebücher 1452–62, f. 1.

46. On wine prices in Basel in the fifteenth and sixteenth centuries, see the overview in Knut Schulz, *Handwerksgesellen und Lohnarbeiter: Untersuchungen zur oberrheinischen und oberdeutschen Stadtgeschichte des 14. bis 17. Jahrhunderts* (Sigmaringen, 1985), 410–14.

47. StAB Protokolle, Öffnungsbuch 7, f. IXr.

48. The gift of wine to the rector is mentioned in WAB 12, f. 718 (1502) and WAB 14, f. 940 (1528); one cask of wine to the barefooted friars is noted in WAB 12, f. 11 (1490).

49. For example, WAB 11 f. 587 and f. 597 (1473); WAB 11, f. 207 (1477) and f. 630 (1485).

50. WAB 12, f. 367 and 367a.

51. WAB 14, f. 57.

52. WAB 10, f. 520, 511.

53. WAB 10, f. 604 and WAB 11, f. 175. On Basel's role in the war against Charles the Bold and on perceptions of this conflict in the cities, see Claudius Sieber-Lehmann, *Spätmittelalterlicher Nationalismus: Die Burgunderkriege am Oberrhein und in der Eidgenossenschaft* (Göttingen, 1995).

54. For example, WAB 12, f. 1149 (1509) and WAB 13, f. 611 (1520). For an overview of Basel coinage and grain and wine measurements, see Kurt Weissen, *"An der Stuer ist ganz nuett bezalt": Landesherrschaft, Verwaltung und Wirtschaft in den fürstbischöflichen Ämtern in der Umgebung Basels (1435–1525)* (Basel, 1994), here lv.

55. An abbess of Säckingen was a great exception, as was the countess of Thierstein, who received wine worth 112 pfennigs in October 1473; WAB 10, f. 5 and f. 625.

56. StAB Protokolle, Öffnungsbuch 7, f. IXr.

57. On this banquet, see Fouquet and Dirlmeier, "Alltäglicher Konsum," 182–83. They point out the bishop's multifaceted and often underestimated patronage and presence in the city in the later fifteenth century.

58. Wimpfeling was a guest at the bishop's court during Shrovetide 1504. See Peter Ochsenbein, "Zwei unbekannte Briefe Jakob Wimpfelings über den Fastnachtsbesuch der Zürcher in Basel Ende Januar 1504," in "*Totum me libris dedo*": *Festschrift zum 80. Geburtstag von Adolf Seebaß*, ed. Alain Moirandat (Basel, 1979), 145–62, esp. 152. Cf. the municipal gift to representatives of the Swiss Confederacy on the same occasion (WAB 12, f. 811). Such gifts from the bishop to Swiss delegations visiting the city were probably less unusual than Wimpfeling suggests: cf. the bishop's gifts of wine during a similar visit in 1507, mentioned in the notes of Ludwig Kilchman, in *BChr,* ed. August Bernoulli et al., 10 vols. (Basel, 1879–1976), vol. 6, 441–560, here 450.

59. Eidformel der Stadtknechte in StAB Ratsbücher K 1, f. 1v, repeated f. 41v. These tips could reach substantial sums. When the Basel officer Heinrich Meltinger reached Lucerne in 1513 with the city's troops bound for Novara, the town council pre-

sented him with welcome wine worth ten florins. As he noted in his accounts, he gave one florin to "their sergeants and couriers" (*iren weibeln und botten*); StAB Politisches, M 1, 5, no. 299, f. 2r. For similar welcome gifts, see M 1, 5, no. 288. Cf. Ernst Gagliardi, *Novara und Dijon* (Zurich, 1907), 107.

60. StAB Ratsbücher A 5, f. 108v (1457). See also an older ordinance, A 3, f. 70v (1412).

61. Eheberg, *Verfassungsgeschichte*, no. 214, 450. See also Berchtold Haller, ed., *Bern in seinen Ratsverlässen 1465–1565*, vol. 3 (Bern, 1902), 204 f., and the new 1521 Zurich regulation on gifts of wine in Emil Egli, ed., *Actensammlung zur Geschichte der Zürcher Reformation 1519–1533* (Zurich, 1879), 92 (no. 265, August 6, 1521).

62. Matthias Lexer, ed., *Endres Tuchers Baumeisterbuch der Stadt Nürnberg 1464–1475* (Stuttgart, 1862; reprint, Amsterdam, 1968), 289; WAB 10, f. 19 and 374 (1463 and 1469).

63. Bernhard Harms, *Stadthaushalt*, vol. 3, 305 (1521). On the costs, see vol. 2, 488 (1489): *Item geben von etlichen schenckkannen ze machen und ze pletzen 18 lb 12 ß*. This sum of 4,464 pfennigs for several jugs of gift wine corresponds to 110 days' wages for a comparatively well-paid journeyman in the building trades; a full-time employee of the Basel hospital earned between 2,700 and 3,400 pfennigs a year in cash; Schulz, *Handwerksgesellen und Lohnarbeiter*, 334 and 368–69. On the value of metal objects in comparison to income from wage labor, see my overview in *Ökonomie ohne Haus: Zum Wirtschaften der Armen in Nürnberg am Ende des 15. Jahrhunderts* (Göttingen, 1993), 182 ff.

64. WAB 12, f. 703. Other jugs apparently did not survive the festivities unscathed. See the repairs on wine jugs mentioned in WAB 12, f. 705. On the extensive festivities on the occasion of the alliance, see the expenses listed in Harms, *Stadthaushalt*, vol. 3, 109–10.

65. StAB Ratsbücher, Erkanntnisbuch 2/3, f. 17v.

66. Literally, *Solich Eren lütt deren ein Statt mocht genyessen*; StAB Ratsbücher, Erkanntnisbuch 1, f. 223r. Despite the general wording, the ordinance apparently referred primarily to visitors from the Swiss Confederacy; the entry dated early July 1503 bears the heading "*des winschenckens halb unsern Eydtgen(ossen).*"

67. Harms, *Stadthaushalt*, vol. 2, 338; on the campaign of pillage, see also Walter Schaufelberger, *Der alte Schweizer und sein Krieg* (Zurich, 1952), 122.

68. On the fluctuations in municipal spending on gifts of wine and gifts more generally, see the graphs in the Appendix. In the years between 1450 and 1530, annual expenses for gift wine generally ranged from 19,000 to 29,000 pfennigs. Periods of relatively high spending on wine gifts (1512–23, for example) alternated with more frugal times, such as the years between 1498 and 1506. None of these obvious phases corresponds clearly with the normative regulations on municipal gifts of wine. The restrictive council resolutions of 1503 were passed not after a period of conspicuously expensive gifts, but rather after several years of low or lower than average spending on gift wine.

69. Harms, *Stadthaushalt*, vol. 2, 215. On Felix V, see Bernard Andenmattern and Agostino Paravicini Bagliani, eds., *Amédée VIII—Félix V. Premier Duc de Savoie et Pape (1383–1451)* (Lausanne, 1992).

70. *BChr*, vol. 2 (Leipzig, 1880), 8, and vol. 4, *Chronikalien der Ratsbücher 1356–1548* (Leipzig, 1890), 72–73. Such a goblet of honor was also presented to each newly installed bishop of Basel upon his first solemn entry into the city; Harms, *Stadthaushalt*, vol. 2, 297 and 410, and vol. 3, 137.

71. *BChr*, vol. 4, *Chronikalien der Ratsbücher 1356–1548*, 72–73; and Harms, *Stadthaushalt* vol. 2, 224–25. Cf. the very similar gifts presented to the emperor in Schlettstadt, Augsburg, and Nuremberg; Geny, *Schlettstadter Stadtrechte*, 498–99; *Chroniken der deutschen Städte*, vol. 22 (Leipzig, 1892), 238 and 11, 463 (emperor's visit of 1471), 484 (1485), 501 and 553 (1489). For a compilation of additional accounts of municipal receptions of rulers in the fifteenth century, see Anna-Maria Drabek, "Reisen und Reisezeremoniell der römisch-deutschen Herrscher im Spätmittelalter," Ph.D. diss., University of Vienna, 1964, 6 n. 216.

72. See, for example, Viktor Menzel, *Deutsches Gesandtschaftswesen im Mittelalter* (Hanover, 1892), 144 ff.; Winfried Dotzauer, "Die Ankunft des Herrschers: Der fürstliche 'Einzug' in die Stadt (bis zum Ende des Alten Reiches)," *AKG* 53 (1973): 245–88, and the literature mentioned there; similarly, Drabek, "Reisen und Reisezeremoniell," 57. Extensive examples appear in Jakob Grimm, "Über Schenken und Geben," in Jakob Grimm, *Abhandlungen zur Mythologie und Sittenkunde* (Berlin, 1865), 181 ff. On the legal form of hosting royalty and its development in the later Middle Ages, see Carl-Richard Bruehl, *Fodrum, gistum, servitium regis: Studien zu den wirtschaftlichen Grundlagen des Königtums im Frankenreich und in den fränkischen Nachfolgestaaten vom 6. bis zur Mitte des 14. Jahrhunderts* (Cologne, 1968), and Hans-Conrad Peyer, *Von der Gastfreundschaft zum Gasthaus: Studien zur Gastlichkeit im Mittelalter* (Hanover, 1987), 158 ff. and 179 ff.

73. Literally, "alles nach lut deß alten harkommens und bruchs"; StAB Protokolle, Öffnungsbuch 7, f. IXr. Such internal gift ordinances have come down to us from several cities. Cf., for example, the detailed lists from Florence (dated 1450 and 1473) stipulating how valuable which gifts for which visitors should be; Richard Trexler, ed., *The Libro Ceremoniale of the Florentine Republic* (Geneva, 1978), 62 and 81; and the 1550 Schlettstadt regulations on wine gifts, Geny, *Schlettstädter Stadtrechte*, 499 ff.

74. Harms, *Stadthaushalt*, vol. 3, 21; cf. the descriptions in the chronicles of the council books in *BChr*, 4, 82–83, and the examples in Drabek, "Reisen und Reisezeremoniell," 54–55, esp. n. 207.

75. *Chroniken der deutschen Städte*, vol. 25, *Beilagen zur Chronik des Clemens Sender* (Leipzig, 1896), 403–9.

76. Harms, *Stadthaushalt*, vol. 2, 450 (1483–84). On Augsburg in 1457 and 1471, see *Chroniken der deutschen Städte*, vol. 22 (Leipzig, 1892), 121–22 and 233.

77. Harms, *Stadthaushalt*, vol. 2, 359. See the annual account for 1469–70: "Item 121 fl geschenckt her Peter von Hagenbach landtvogt," vol. 2, 345. This is a very large sum, presumably a gift upon assuming office. On Hagenbach, see Hildburg Brauer-Gramm, *Der Landvogt Peter von Hagenbach* (Göttingen, 1957), and Sieber-Lehmann, *Spätmittelalterlicher Nationalismus*, 45 ff.

78. Harms, *Stadthaushalt*, vol. 3, 145.

79. See Felix. R. Burckhardt, *Der Basler Münsterschatz* (Basel, 1933), 15 and 355 ff.;

and Ernst Ungerer, *Elsässische Altertümer in Burg und Haus, Kirche und Kloster: Inventare vom Ausgang des Mittelalters bis zum 30jährigen Krieg aus Stadt und Bistum Strassburg*, 2 vols. (Strasbourg, 1911–17), vol. 2, 171; see also Johann M. Fritz, *Goldschmiedekunst der Gotik in Mitteleuropa* (Munich, 1982), 80 ff., with numerous additional examples.

80. Venningen, *Hausbuch* f. 3 (March 24, 1465). On similar marks of origin on cups in fifteenth-century silver inventories, see Fritz, *Goldschmiedekunst*, 83.

81. Harms, *Stadthaushalt*, vol. 3, 157. This was the legate's second visit to the city. For a detailed account of his activities in Basel, see Rudolf Wackernagel, "Mitteilungen über Raymundus Peraudi und kirchliche Zustände seiner Zeit in Basel," *BZGA* 2 (1903): 171–273. On Peraudi's political mission, see also his circulars to the Swiss Confederacy in StAB Politisches, M 1,1, nos. 35 and 36 of August 1504.

82. One finds numerous instances, for example in the household account book of Anton Tucher. See Loose, *Anton Tuchers Haushaltsbuch 1507–1517*; for similar material on wills in Constance, see Paul Baur, *Testament und Bürgerschaft: Alltagsleben und Sachkultur im spätmittelalterlichen Konstanz* (Sigmaringen, 1989), 228. For extensive bibliography and material from Nuremberg, see Valentin Groebner, *Ökonomie ohne Haus: Zum Wirtschaften der Armen in Nürnberg am Ende des 15. Jahrhunderts* (Göttingen, 1993), 244 ff.

83. See, for example, Sigrid Bösken, *Die Mainzer Goldschmiedezunft* (Mainz, 1971), 120. On gilding techniques and Nuremberg ordinances, see Theodor Hampe, ed., *Nürnberger Ratsverlässe über Kunst und Künstler*, vol. 1 (Leipzig, 1904), 116, 118, 131–38, and 148, StAN Rep. 60b, Ratsbücher 5, f. 110v. On controversies surrounding counterfeit silver and gold-plated objects, see *StChr*, ed. Karl Hegel et al., vol. 11 (Leipzig, 1874), 531, 571, and 572.

84. Luca Landucci, *Diario fiorentino dal 1450 al 1516*, ed. Iodoco dal Badia (Florence, 1883), 62–63. He adds, ambiguously, "Certainly, it was a rich and magnificent gift. In praise of God." (*Per certo f un ricco e magno dono. A lalde di Dio.*)

85. StadtAF C 1, Landes- und Reichsakten 1, no. 8, cited in what follows as Mennel, Imperial Diet. The results of the Imperial Diet were summarized in a separate paper-covered brochure later bound together with the other documents, f. 69 ff. On the negotiations, see Anton Braun, "Die Verhandlungen zwischen Maximilian I. und den Reichsständen auf dem Imperial Diet in Freiburg/Br. 1498," Ph.D. diss., University of Freiburg, 1898.

86. Mennel, Imperial Diet, f. 2r.

87. Mennel, Imperial Diet, f. 2v–8v, 12–14r, 16v. This order was read aloud to the council and passed on 28 May.

88. Mennel, Imperial Diet, f. 16r and 16v. A wasted investment: Heinrich von Fürstenberg fell a year later at the battle of Dornach fighting against the Swiss Confederacy; "Anonymer Chronik des Schwabenkrieges," in *BChr*, vol. 6 (Leipzig, 1902), 5–23, 12. The index is an appended paper brochure, with new foliation, f. 3v ff. After two empty sheets, it contains a list of which gifts the city presented when to the visitors to the Imperial Diet and how much they cost. Judging by the form, this was probably a compilation of extracts from the municipal accounts, but it breaks off after 2 June. Freiburg's fifteenth-century municipal accounts have been lost; only those after 1520 have survived.

89. Mennel, Imperial Diet f. 17v.

90. On Mennel, see Dieter Mertens, "Geschichte und Dynastie—Zu Methode und Ziel der 'Fürstlichen Chronik' Jakob Mennels," in Kurt Andermann, ed., *Historiographie am Oberrhein im späten Mittelalter und in der frühen Neuzeit* (Sigmaringen, 1988), 121–53.

91. StadtAF B 1, 2 (Geschichtbuch), f. 24v. On the political framework, see Peter Moraw, "Der Reichstag zu Worms von 1495," in the exhibition catalogue *1495—Kaiser Reich Reformen: Der Reichstag zu Worms, Ausstellung des Landeshauptarchivs Worms in Verbindung mit der Stadt Worms zum 500jährigen Jubiläum des Wormser Reichstag von 1495* (Worms, 1995), 25–37.

92. The chronicle note on the Thuringian landgrave, who during a dispute with the city of Erfurt not only tried to cut the citizens off from their supplies of wood, charcoal, and grain, but also angrily returned a gift of beer, remains a rare exception; Ludwig F. Hesse, ed., *Konrad Stolles thüringisch-erfurtische Chronik* (Stuttgart, 1854), 155.

93. StAB Ratsbücher B 1, Erkanntnisbuch 1, f. 7r. Cf. the political adaptation of gifts from the city of Metz to Burgundian princes and diplomats in various political constellations (1448 and 1465) in Dieter Heckmann, "Metz und der franko-burgundische Konflikt in Oberlothringen (1440–1500)," *Rheinische Vierteljahrsblätter* 51 (1987): 115–28, esp. 121–22.

94. Harms, *Stadthaushalt*, vol. 2, 281.

95. "Die Chronik des Bürgermeisters Ulrich Schwarz," 102–3, printed in Georg Panzer, *Ulrich Schwarz, der Augsburger Zunftbürgermeister, 1422–1478* (Bamberg, 1914), 92–107. Hektor Mülich's account appears in *Chroniken der deutschen Städte*, vol. 22 (Leipzig, 1892), 228–29; on the preceding conflict, see 221. On Schwarz, see below, Chapter 4.

96. On a similar case, see Klaus Militzer, "Die feierlichen Einritte der Kölner Erzbischöfe in die Stadt Köln im Spätmittelalter und in der frühen Neuzeit," *Jahrbuch des kölnischen Geschichtsvereins* 55 (1984): 77–116. On the entry of Archbishop Hermann von Hessen, security measures in the city, and the legal complications caused by municipal breaches of etiquette, see 97 ff. On gifts from French cities to the king in the sixteenth century, see Davis, *Gifts*, 94–96.

97. Schwarz, *Chronik*, 103.

98. Harms, *Stadthaushalt*, vol. 2, 351 and 341.

99. Gerd Brinkhus, *Eine bayrische Fürstenspiegelkompilation des 15. Jahrhunderts* (Munich, 1978), 89. See also Eugen Gehr, "Die Fürstenlehren des Johannes von Indersdorf für Herzog Albrecht III. von Baiern München (1436–1460)," Ph.D. diss., University of Freiburg im Breisgau, 1979, 11.

100. WAB 10, f. 588 and 593. On fictitious diplomacy and supposed envoys of Christian princes from the Orient, see, for example, the description of the splendid embassy of the king of Persia (*herlich potschaft von dem künig von Persia*), which was traveling through Italy, in the chronicle of the Augsburger Hektor Mülich for 1460; *Chroniken der deutschen Städte*, vol. 22, 162.

101. Venningen, *Hausbuch*, f. 374 and f. 406.

102. WAB 10, f. 481 and 532; in the yearly account, Harms, *Stadthaushalt*, vol. 2, 351 and 359. On the terminology, cf. Dietrich Kurze, "Johannes Lichtenberger: Eine

Studie zur Geschichte der Prophetie und Astrologie," Ph.D. diss., University of Berlin, 1955, 6–7.

103. Harms, *Stadthaushalt*, vol. 3, 48 (1495–96) and vol. 2, 481 (1487–88). A journeyman tailor employed by the Basel hospital earned between 18 and 24 pfennigs a day in the last third of the fifteenth century. See Michaela von Tscharner-Aue, *Die Wirtschaftsführung des Basler Spitals bis zum Jahr 1500* (Basel, 1983), 178 ff. The accounts provide scarcely any details about the spectacles that these travelers offered, but the Solothurn treasurer's accounts (*Seckelmeisterbücher*) for 1490 noted a gift of five shillings to a man from Augsburg who arrived in town leading a woman by a chain; Hans Morgenthaler, "Kulturgeschichtliche Notizen aus den solothurnischen Seckelmeisterrechnungen des 15. Jahrhunderts," *Anzeiger für schweizerische Alterthumskunde* NF 21 (1919): 187–89 and NF 22 (1919): 57–60, esp. 58.

104. *BChr*, vol. 4, 73; in contrast, the annual accounts record six florins given to two such (unnamed) dignitaries; Harms, *Stadthaushalt*, vol. 2, 373.

105. On the role of the heralds in the late Middle Ages, see the overview of the literature in Werner Paravicini, *Die ritterlich-höfische Kultur des Mittelalters* (Munich, 1994), 77–85; as well as Paul-Joachim Heinig, "Die Türhüter und Herolde Kaiser Friedrichs III.," in Heinig, ed., *Kaiser Friedrich III. (1440–1493) in seiner Zeit* (Cologne, 1995), 355–75; and Gerd Melville, "Die Herolde im europäischen Spätmittelalter," in Peter Moraw, ed., *Hof, Hoftag und Imperial Diet im späteren Mittelalter* (Sigmaringen, 1999). See also Karl Schottenloher, "Kaiserliche Herolde des 16. Jahrhunderts als Berichterstatter," *Historisches Jahrbuch* 49 (1929): 460–71, and Theodor Kolde, "Der Reichsherold Kaspar Sturm und seine literarische Tätigkeit," *Archiv für Reformationsgeschichte* 4 (1907): 117–61.

106. WAB 10, f. 50; similarly, Harms, *Stadthaushalt*, vol. 2, 338, WAB 9, f. 650; WAB 9, f. 583 (1461); WAB 10, f. 631 (1473).

107. See, for example, Harms, *Stadthaushalt*, vol. 2, 382 (1474–75) and 441 (1482–83), WAB 11, f. 226 (1477).

108. In June 1496 a *parcifal* of Maximilian's still received 240 pfennigs in Basel, but a year later such an official appears in the records with a gift of only 156 pfennigs, while the accounts for 1498–99, the years of the Swabian War, note that neutral Basel presented Maximilian's herald with a mere 144 pfennigs; WAB 12, f. 344; Harms, *Stadthaushalt*, vol. 3, 73, 86.

109. The yearly accounts for 1518–19 note that the city had given 254 pfennigs to a "speaker who serves a prince" (eynem sprecher so eyns fursten diener ist), and on September 7 and October 5, 1521, the weekly expense book notes that 300 pfennigs each had been presented to foreign heralds; Harms, *Stadthaushalt*, vol. 3, 288; WAB 13, f. 24 and 34.

110. On the topos of gifts to minstrels and musicians, see the material-rich study by Sabine Zak, *Musik als "Ehr und Zier" im mittelalterlichen Reich: Studien zur Musik im höfischen Leben, Recht und Zeremoniell* (Neuss, 1979), 31, 139, 232, 288; on municipal gifts of wine to minstrels in the fifteenth century, see 129 and 168. A bibliography and a not particularly satisfying overview is provided by Jürgen Brandhorst, "Spielleute—Vaganten und Künstler," in Bernd-Ulrich Hergemöller, *Randgruppen der spätmittelalterlichen Gesellschaft* (Warendorf, 1990), 115–33. For more detail see Ernst Schubert,

Fahrendes Volk im Mittelalter (Bielefeld, 1995), 115 ff. and 145 ff. On Basel, see Fritz Ernst, "Die Spielleute im Dienst der Stadt Basel im ausgehenden Mittelalter," *BZGA* 44 (1945): 79–236, 225.

111. Venningen, *Hausbuch*, f. 426; on further gifts cf. Fouquet and Dirlmeier, "Alltäglicher Konsum," 143–44; for contemporary assessments of Venningen, see 116.

112. Venningen, *Hausbuch*, f. 118, f. 230, f. 332 (during a visit to Strasbourg in 1466).

113. Groebner, *Ökonomie ohne Haus*, 27 ff. In 1478 Basel, Freiburg, Colmar, and Breisach complained in a letter to Sigmund of Austria about the rising exchange rate of the florin in silver money and inferior coins. Bernhard Harms, *Die Münz- und Geldpolitik der Stadt Basel im Mittelalter* (Tübingen, 1907), 157–58 and 197 ff. Maximilian did not grant Basel the right to mint its own florins until 1516; *Basler Urkundenbuch*, vol. 9, 391 and Harms, *Münz- und Geldpolitik*, 133.

114. WAB 10, f. 578 and 586.

115. WAB 10, f. 596, f. 609, f. 633 (1473).

116. Cf. Sieber-Lehmann, *Spätmittelalterlicher Nationalismus*, 58. The emperor's visit to Basel in September 1473 played a particular role here; that year the expenses under the rubric *Verschenckt* (given as a gift) reached a level never seen again in the entire period of our study—600,000 pfennigs.

117. Harms, *Stadthaushalt*, vol. 2, 381–82 and 389.

118. In 1478–79 the yearly accounts record an additional two florins in gold to the bishop of Trier's pipers; Harms, *Stadthaushalt*, vol. 2, 410. According to the yearly accounts for 1502–3, in Basel Maximilian's pipers received seven florins in gold, or "8 lb 17 ß 11 d" in coins; ibid., vol. 3, 136. As far as I can tell, these were the only exceptions.

119. WAB 11, f. 214, f. 224, f. 632; WAB 12, f. 358; WAB 12, f. 5, f. 318, f. 367 a.

120. On the use of heraldic shields to identify municipal musicians, which began in the fourteenth century, see Zak, *Musik*, 122–23 and 142; for Basel, see Ernst, "Spielleute," 86 ff. Basel musicians also received gifts when they traveled; for evidence of presents to Basel minstrels in Swiss cities, see Ernst, "Spielleute," 108 and 112–13.

121. See Schubert, *Fahrendes Volk*, 115 ff.; on Wimpfeling, see Bruno Singer, *Die Fürstenspiegel in Deutschland im Zeitalter des Humanismus und der Reformation* (Munich, 1981), 191; on the eternal punishment for gifts to musicians, see also Singer, *Fürstenspiegel*, 261.

122. See, for example, the 1495 and 1498 prohibitions on gifts to musicians in StadtA Freiburg/Br. B 13a, 4a (Ratserkanntnisse 1494–1502), f. 25v, and C 1, Landes- und Reichsakten 1, no. 8, f. 71r.

123. Ernst, "Spielleute," 214.

124. See StAB Ratsbücher B 1, Erkanntnisbuch 1, f. 220v (February 1505), which states that musicians from the Swiss Confederacy should be given preferential treatment in the bestowing of gifts; see also Ernst, "Spielleute," 137, 152–53, and 159 ff.

125. WAB 13, f. 250, f. 283 (1515); WAB 13, f. 592, f. 605 (1520); WAB 14, f. 967 (1528).

126. On the Lucerne figure of Fritschi, see the reprint from the chronicles of the council records (*Ratsbücher*) in *BChr* 4, 92–97 and 160–62, and Gerhard Fouquet, "Das Festmahl in den oberdeutschen Städten des Spätmittelalters: Zu Form, Funktion und

Bedeutung öffentlichen Konsums," *AKG* 74 (1992): 83–123, esp. 109–12. Extracts of chronicles on Swiss visiting diplomacy have been compiled by Leo Zehnder in his *Volkskundliches aus der älteren Schweizer Chronistik* (Basel, 1976), 315–24; see also Wackernagel, *Geschichte*, vol. 3, 4 ff.

127. Cf. the remark in the annual accounts for 1508–9 referring to the detailed lists in the *Ratsbuch*; Harms, *Stadthaushalt*, vol. 3, 195.

128. Cf., for example, WAB 11, f. 16 (1490); WAB 12, f. 731 (1502), and, similarly, WAB 13, f. 664 (1520) and f. 728 (1521). See, for example, *Gerold Edlibachs Chronik*, ed. J. M. Usteri (Zurich, 1847), 237–40; *Johannes Stumpfs Schweizer- und Reformationschronik*, part 1, ed. Ernst Gagliardi, H. Müller, and E. Büser (Basel, 1952), 50–51 (with an incorrect date); "Anonyme Chronik des Schwabenkriegs," in *BChr*, vol. 6, 19; Ludwig Schwinkhart, *Chronik 1506 bis 1521*, ed. Hans von Greyerz (Bern, 1941), 249, etc.

129. WAB 12, f. 693 and 695. The only similar donation of a window to appear in the municipal accounts before 1501 was from fiscal year 1468–69. Harms, *Stadthaushalt*, vol. 2, 338. On the role of these panes of glass, see Hermann Meyer, *Die schweizerische Sitte der Fenster- und Wappenschenkung vom 15. bis 18. Jahrhundert* (Frauenfeld, 1884); P. Ganz, "Über die Schweizer Glasmalerei und ihre Bedeutung für die Kunstgeschichte," in *Jahresberichte der öffentlichen Kunstsammlung Basel* (Basel, 1905), and P. Boesch, *Die Glasmalerei in der Schweiz* (Basel, 1955).

130. See, for example, Harms, *Stadthaushalt*, vol. 3, 136, 137, 146–47, and 157; WAB 12, f. 742, and passim.

131. Cf. WAB 12, f. 1162 (1509), repeated in the annual accounts; Harms, *Stadthaushalt*, vol. 3, 203 and, similarly, 210 (1510–11). For extensive donations of windows to Appenzell, Glarus, and Underwalden in fiscal year 1513–14, see Harms, *Stadthaushalt*, vol. 3, 236. See also WAB 13, f. 251 (January 1515), WAB 13, f. 706 and WAB 14, f. 18, f. 70 (1521). Further donations of windows to Schaffhausen, Zurich, Lucerne, and Wettingen in fiscal year 1521–22 are mentioned in Harms, *Stadthaushalt*, vol. 3, 318. Incidentally, this standard sum also appears in the case of the windows that the Basel saffron guild presented in 1506 to the Spitalkirche; Paul Koelner, "Die Kuchibücher der Safranzunft," *Basler Jahrbuch* (1929): 202–69, 247 n. 60. On return gifts, see, for example, WAB 12, f. 1130. The gift was made in conjunction with the remodeling of the Basel town hall, which took place at the same time. On the custom of donating panes of stained glass, see Barbara Giesecke, *Die Glasmalereien im Basler Rathaus* (Basel, 1994), and the remarks of Ulrich Barth in the same volume, "Zur Baugeschichte des Rathauses," 17–32, esp. 19.

132. Michaela von Tscharner-Aue, *Die Wirtschaftsführung des Basler Spitals bis zum Jahr 1500* (Basel, 1983), 183; the gingerbread and *latwergen* (another spiced sweet) from Klingenthal appear yearly. See Venningen, *Hausbuch*, f. 133 (1460), f. 360 (1467), etc. Gifts in and from abbeys at NewYear's are frequently mentioned in the sources, although late medieval reformers were sometimes highly critical of them. For examples, see Martin Straganz, ed.,"Die ältesten Statuten des Klarissenklosters zu Brixen," in *Franziskanische Studien* 6 (1919): 143–70, 160. I thank Jeffrey Hamburger for bringing this article to my attention.

133. Venningen, *Hausbuch*, f. 174 (1461), 179 (1462), 181, 416, and passim. Such gifts

of food appear often in the household book; they document the tightly woven net of reciprocal courtesies that connected the bishop with the city's secular and clerical institutions and officials. The language of other courtesies had stronger religious connotations. In September 1470, Venningen noted that he had given 36 pfennigs to the courier who brought him a scourge (f. 412). Such scourges as instruments of penitential practice were not uncommon gifts in the fourteenth and fifteenth centuries, particularly in the monastic milieu. See Jeffrey Hamburger, "The Liber miraculorum of Unterlinden: An Icon in Its Convent Setting," in Robert Ousterhout and Leslie Brubaker, eds., *The Sacred Image East and West* (Urbana, Ill., 1995), 145–90, esp. 162–63, and *The Visual and the Visionary* (New York, 1998).

134. Venningen, *Hausbuch*, f. 352 and 375; Loose, *Anton Tuchers Haushaltsbuch*, 117.

135. Venningen, *Hausbuch*, f. 313; WAB 10, f. 596.

136. Venningen, *Hausbuch*, f. 413; WAB 12, f. 5; WAB 13, f. 638. That the Baselers—who at this time were recipients of French money, or *kronenfresser* (crown gobblers) as unflattering popular parlance put it—made presents to papal couriers in French currency was not without a certain piquancy; see below, Chapter 5.

137. On the history of the word *Bote*, see Menzel, *Deutsches Gesandtschaftswesen*, 58. On council messages, see Grether,"Die Baseler Ratsordnung von 1506," 38, and Hans Füglister, *Handwerksregiment: Untersuchungen und Materialien zur sozialen und politischen Struktur der Stadt Basel in der ersten Hälfte des 16. Jahrhunderts* (Basel, 1981), 187.

138. For an overview and literature for further reading see Heinz-Dieter Heimann, "Brievedregher: Kommunikations- und alltagsgeschichtliche Zugänge zur modernen Postgeschichte und Dienstleistungskultur," in *Kommunikation und Alltag in Spätmittelalter und Früher Neuzeit* (Vienna, 1992), 241–92; "Neue Perspektiven für die Geschichte der Post," *HZ* 253 (1991): 661–74; and"Zur Visualisierung städtischer Dienstleistungskultur: Das Beispiel der kommunalen Briefboten," in Hermann Maué, ed., *Visualisierung städtischer Ordnung* (Nuremberg, 1993), 22–36. Also rich in material are Otto Lauffer, "Der laufende Bote im Nachrichtenwesen der früheren Jahrhunderte," *Beiträge zur deutschen Volks- und Altertumskunde* 1 (1954): 19–60; Henri Gachot, "Laufende botten," *Archiv für deutsche Postgeschichte* 2 (1964); Adalbert Korzendorfer, "Regensburger Handel und Nachrichtenverkehr im Ausgang des Mittelalters," *Archiv für Post und Telegraphie* 51 (1923): 467 ff.; Luise Sporhan-Krempel, *Nürnberg als Nachrichtenzentrum zwischen 1400 und 1700* (Nuremberg, 1968); and Klaus Gerteis, "Reisen, Boten, Posten: Korrespondenz im Mittelalter und früher Neuzeit," in Hans Pohl, ed., *Die Bedeutung der Kommunikation für Wirtschaft und Gesellschaft* (Stuttgart, 1989), 19–39.

139. Francis Rapp, "Politique et administration strasbourgeoise," in Gerhard Bauer, ed., *Stadtsprachenforschung, unter besonderer Berücksichtigung der Verhältnisse der Stadt Strassburg in Spätmittelalter und früher Neuzeit* (Göppingen, 1988), 327–72, esp. 342; Arnold Esch, "Alltag der Entscheidung: Berns Weg in den Burgunderkrieg," *Berner Zeitschrift für Geschichte und Heimatkunde* 50 (1988): 3–64, esp. 29; on letters, political correspondence, and information networks in the Upper Rhine region in the

1470s, see Sieber-Lehmann, *Spätmittelalterlicher Nationalismus*, 356–62. In comparison, for the ten years between 1431 and 1440, the Nuremberg municipal accounts record expenses for 850 official journeys by couriers; Sporhan-Krempel, *Nürnberg als Nachrichtenzentrum*, 23.

140. Jecht, "Die Pflichten eines mittelalterlichen Bürgermeisters", 89–102, esp. 100–101.

141. Schulz, *Handwerksgesellen und Lohnarbeiter*, 373–74; WAB 10, f. 664; Lauffer, "Der laufende Bote," 25–26 and 30; Heimann, "Brievedregher," 275 and 286.

142. StAB Ratsbücher, K 1, f. 2 und f. 42.

143. Johann Brucker, *Strassburger Zunft- und Polizeiordnungen des 14. und 15. Jahrhunderts* (Strasbourg, 1889), 142 and 138; on the symbols and cases, see Lauffer, "Der laufende Bote," 43–48; Heimann, "Brievedregher," 281–84, and in more detail, his essay "Visualisierung," 29–34, with additional literature and visual examples.

144. Wackernagel, *Geschichte*, vol. 2/1, 244 and 311. On municipal colors as a system of political symbols in the cities of the Upper Rhine in the fifteenth century, see Sieber-Lehmann, *Spätmittelalterlicher Nationalismus*, 378 ff., which points out the connections between the increasing "uniforming" of municipal servants and mercenary soldiers and the prohibition on uniform clothing among journeyman artisans, for example. On similar admonitions at the end of the fifteenth century, cf. Geny, *Schlettstadter Stadtrechte*, 357–58; and Lauffer, "Der laufende Bote," 39 (for further examples for Cologne, Regensburg, and the cities of the Swiss Confederacy, see 38).

145. WAB 12, f. 710 (1502); Harms, *Stadthaushalt*, vol. 3, 193 (1508), and similarly, 200 (1509). The courier Dietrich Dietschi is given money for a jacket, but the color is not mentioned. See also Harms, *Stadthaushalt*, vol. 3, 214 and 215 (1511), 235 (1514). On similar gifts in August 1515, see WAB 13, f. 287 and Emil Usteri, *Marignano: Die Schicksalsjahre 1515/16 im Blickfeld der historischen Quellen* (Zurich, 1974), 355.

146. WAB 13, f. 290; Harms, *Stadthaushalt*, vol. 3, 236 (1513–14); WAB 13, f. 303 (December 1, 1515). See also WAB 13 f. 305 (1515) and StAB Ratsbücher B 2/3, f. 140v (1517).

147. See Sieber-Lehmann, *Spätmittelalterlicher Nationalismus*, 381, for further examples. At municipal marksmanship competitions, the winning contestants were also increasingly given gifts in the municipal colors. For examples see WAB 13, f. 664 (1520) and f. 728 (1521).

148. On the remodeling of the Basel town hall, see Ulrich Barth, "Baugeschichte," in Staatskanzlei des Kantons Basel Stadt, ed., *Das Basler Rathaus* (Basel, 1983), 7–23, and the same author's "Baugeschichte und Renovation seit dem Bundesbeitritt 1501," in *Basler Rathaus: Dokumentation der Restaurierung*, text volume (Basel, 1985), 27–43. The standard-bearer, or *Weppner*, on the town hall's market-side facade, which the sculptor Hans Thurner apparently completed in 1510–11, was commissioned with special emphasis on municipal symbols; StAB Ratsbücher B 2, Erkanntnisbuch II, f. 47 (1509). On the figure of the courier now in the town hall courtyard, see C. H. Baer, "Die erhaltenen Architekturteile der alten Rathausbauten," in *Die Kunstdenkmäler des Kantons Basel-Stadt*, vol. 1 (Basel, 1932), 363–478, esp. 390. The tale that this figure represents a messenger who ran from Basel to Strasbourg in 24 hours on an especially important mission and then fell down dead is an eighteenth-century legend. See Georg

Kreis, "Namenlose Eidgenossen: Zur Frühgeschichte der schweizerischen Denkmalskultur," *Zeitschrift für schweizerische Archäologie und Kunstgeschichte* 55 (1998): 13–24.

149. Politisches M 1, 6 (July to November 1513), no. 327. In 1513 the Basel courier was carrying substantial amounts of money from mercenaries in addition to letters. It was apparently common practice for couriers to transport not just letters but also large cash sums. See Schaufelberger, *Der alte Schweizer und sein Krieg*, 92; and Arnold Esch, "Mit Schweizer Söldnern auf dem Marsch nach Italien: Das Erlebnis der Mailänder Kriege 1510–1515 nach bernischen Akten," *Quellen und Forschungen aus italienischen Archiven und Bibliotheken* 70 (1990): 348–439, esp. 400.

150. In 1475, the finder of a lost letter received a handsome reward. Harms, *Stadthaushalt*, vol. 2, 386; on Erzberg, see vol. 3, 266.

151. Heinrich Brennwald, *Schweizerchronik*, ed. Rudolf Luginbühl, 2 vols. (Basel, 1910), vol. 2, 314; Morgenthaler, "Kulturgeschichtliche Notizen," 188; Heimann, "Brievedregher," 286 and 289; similarly, Lauffer, "Der laufende Bote," 53. Cf. also the stipulations of the Strasbourg courier ordinance stating that no one could alter (*verkenden*, here in the sense of to reproduce with intent to defraud) or otherwise misappropriate (*veruntreuen*) courier cases and symbols. Heimann, "Visualisierung," 32.

152. "Warum trägt ein bott ein büchs oder schilt am mantel hangen anderst, als allein dasz man sehe, dasz er ein botschaft ist?" Quoted in Grimm, *Wörterbuch*, 2, 278, and Lauffer, "Der laufende Bote," 45.

153. Harms, *Stadthaushalt*, vol. 3, 231, 266, 305, 316. The new jacket in 1522 is mentioned on 324, and he is named as a courier in 1525 on 361; Urfehde StAB Ratsbücher o 2, f. 322.

154. Usteri, *Marignano*, 195; on the practice of intercepted letters and false messengers, see 85, 239–40, and 288–89; on false information, see 495 ff. In his chronicle, Ludwig Schwinkhart mentions such a false messenger at Novara in 1513; *Chronik 1506 bis 1521*, 97. For a nice example of a deliberately false piece of news from 1474, see Sieber-Lehmann, *Spätmittelalterlicher Nationalismus*, 356 n. 56.

155. Norbert Schindler, *Widerspenstige Leute: Studien zur Volkskultur der frühen Neuzeit* (Frankfurt am Main, 1992), 59.

156. An example of such a list can be found in the so-called Easter Book of the city of Bern for 1485; Schmid, *Reden, Rufen, Zeichen setzen*, 154.

157. Haller, Ratsmanuale Bd. 3, S. 110. Cf. the search for the rabble-rouser Peter Dietrich in the Bernese countryside in 1470. The Bern magistrate (*Amtmann*) was charged with gathering information for a "wanted poster." In addition to the addresses of relatives of the wanted man, he was principally interested in details of clothing; Schmid, *Reden, Rufen, Zeichen setzen*, 208–9. Cf. the stipulations of the Bamberg penal code (Halsgerichtsordnung) of 1495 on searching for suspects; Joachim Köhler, *Die Carolina und ihre Vorgängerinnen*, vol. 2, *Die Bambergische Halsgerichtsordnung* (Halle, 1902), 17.

158. Rosenkranz, *Der Bundschuh*, vol. 2, 269–70, 272, and 278 ff.; on the letter "H" as an identifying mark of the Bundschuh conspirators, see 284.

159. Text of the document of bestowal in *Der Bundschuh*, vol. 2, 120.

160. The "H"—symbol of the *Bundschuh* conspirators—was also known to the Basel authorities; it appears in a letter of warning sent by the Basel town council to

Strasbourg around this same time; Rosenkranz, *Der Bundschuh*, 271. On similar letters on clothing in the courtly context, see Jean-Pierre Jourdan, "La lettre et l'étoffe: Etude sur les lettres dans le dispositif vestimentaire à la fin du Moyen Age," *Médiévales* 29 (1995): 23–46. On the popular dissemination of the "Chronik der Entstehung und Entdeckung des Bundschuhs" in Basel by means of a print by Pamphilius Gengenbach, which makes several references to the conspirators' "secret word-signs" (*haimlich wortzaichen*), see Karl Goedecke, ed., *Pamphilus Gengenbach* (Hanover, 1854), 28–31, 388, 389, and 399–400. See my "Describing the Person, Describing the Face in Renaissance Europe: Identity Papers, Vested Figures, and the Limits of Identification, 1400–1600," in *Documenting Individual Identity: The Development of State Practices in the Modern World*, ed. Jane Caplan and John Torpey (Princeton, N.J., 2001).

Chapter 2

1. Bernhard Harms, *Der Stadthaushalt Basels im ausgehenden Mittelalter*, 3 vols. (Tübingen, 1909–13), vol. 2, 53 (1392). On the acquisition of Kleinbasel, see Werner Meyer, "Der Zusammenschluss von Gross- und Kleinbasel im Spätmittelalter," in Brigitte Meles and Beat von Wartburg, eds., *Leben in Kleinbasel 1392—1892—1992* (Basel, 1992), 12–37; WAB 11, f. 178 (1477). See also the supplement accorded to the town clerk for a journey to a spa in 1481; Harms, *Stadthaushalt*, vol. 2, 425.

2. Venningen, *Hausbuch*, for example, f. 416 (gifts to the Basel town guards at Christmas 1470), f. 431 (1471), f. 442 (1472), etc.; on the gift to Fricker, see Harms, *Stadthaushalt*, vol. 3, 145. At this point, the 73-year-old Fricker was no longer the official town clerk of Bern, but he was still a member of the Inner Council (*Kleiner Rat*) and a key political figure in the city. On his career and influence, see Regula Schmid, *Reden, Rufen, Zeichen setzen: Politisches Handeln während des Bernr Twingherrenstreits 1469–1471* (Zurich, 1995), 38–39; and Urs-Martin Zahnd, "Studium und Kanzlei: Der Bildungsweg von Stadt- und Ratsschreibern in eidgenössischen Städten des ausgehenden Mittelalters," in Rainer-Christoph Schwinges, ed., *Gelehrte im Reich. Zur Sozial- und Wirkungsgeschichte akademischer Eliten des 14. bis 16. Jahrhunderts* (Berlin, 1997), 453–76, and the bibliography provided there.

3. On the concept of office (*Amt*), see the overview and extensive bibliography in Udo Wolter, "Amt und Offizium in mittelalterlichen Quellen vom 13.–15. Jahrhundert," *Zeitschrift der Savigny-Stiftung für Rechtsgeschichte, kanonistische Abteilung* 74 (1988): 246–80; Dietmar Willoweit, "Die Entwicklung und Verwaltung der spätmittelalterlichen Landesherrschaft," in Kurt G. A. Jeserich et al., eds., *Deutsche Verwaltungsgeschichte*, vol. 1 (Stuttgart, 1983), 66–142, esp. 82ff. Karl Kroeschell, "Amt," in *Handwörterbuch der deutschen Rechtsgeschichte*, vol. 1 (Berlin, 1978), 150–54. On the broad early use of the term, see the examples in the entry "Amt" in *Deutsches Rechtswörterbuch (Wörterbuch der älteren deutschen Rechtssprache)*, vol. 1 (Weimar, 1914), 544–57.

4. Max Weber, *Wirtschaft und Gesellschaft: Grundriss der verstehenden Soziologie*, 5th ed. (Tübingen, 1976), 126.

5. Gustav Schmoller, *Strassburg zur Zeit der Zunftkämpfe und die Reformation seiner Verfassung und Verwaltung im 15. Jahrhundert* (Strasbourg, 1875), 45 ff.; similarly "a new financial administration, . . . the modern state, begins with the written recording of all official procedures" (71–72). The texts of the two voluminous ordinances of 1405 and 1433 are printed in Karl Theodor Eheberg, *Verfassungs-, Verwaltungs- und Wirtschaftsgeschichte der Stadt Strassburg bis 1681*, vol. 1, *Urkunden und Akten* (Strasbourg, 1899), 11 ff. and 85 ff. On Schmoller and his influence, see the contributions in Pierangelo Schiera and Friedrich Tenbruck, eds., *Gustav Schmoller in seiner Zeit: Die Entstehung der Sozialwissenschaften in Deutschland und Italien* (Berlin, 1989).

6. Georg von Below, "Die städtische Verwaltung des Mittelalters als Vorbild der späteren Territorialverwaltung," *HZ* 75 (1895): 396–421; see also Karl Bücher, "Das städtische Beamtentum im Mittelalter," in *Beiträge zur Wirtschaftsgeschichte* (Tübingen, 1922), 358–72.

7. See Gustav Schmoller, "Der deutsche Beamtenstaat vom 16. bis 18. Jahrhundert," in his *Umrisse und Untersuchungen zur Verfassungs-, Verwaltungs- und Wirtschaftsgeschichte* (Leipzig, 1898), 292 ff.; similarly, Schmoller, *Grundriß der allgemeinen Volkswirtschaftslehre* (Leipzig, 1908), vol. 1, 332 ff. On stylized portrayals of the medieval burgher in the nineteenth century, see Klaus Schreiner, "Kommunebewegung und Zunftrevolution: Zur Gegenwart der mittelalterlichen Stadt im historisch-politischen Denken des 19. Jahrhunderts," in Franz Quarthal and Wilfried Setzler, eds., *Stadtverfassung—Verfassungsstaat—Pressepolitik: Festschrift für Eberhard Naujoks* (Sigmaringen, 1980), 39–168, and the same author's "Die Stadt des Mittelalters als Faktor bürgerlicher Identitatsbildung," in *Stadt im Wandel: Katalog zur Landesausstellung Niedersachsen 1985*, vol. 4 (Braunschweig, 1985), 517–41.

8. Schmoller, *Strassburg*, 72.

9. Weber, *Wirtschaft*, 131–40.

10. "Nothing could be further from our intentions than the belief that the whole of historical reality can be 'captured' in the conceptual scheme developed below"; Weber, *Wirtschaft*, 124. The irresistibility of grand ordering concepts lies, it seems, in a paradox: the more vehemently Weber rejects a "real historical" interpretation of his classifications, the closer he moves them as heuristic metaempirical devices.

11. On critiques of older views, see Willoweit ("Die Entwicklung und Verwaltung der spätmittelalterlichen Landesherrschaft," vol. 1, 82–141), who warns against the "latent determinism of older and more recent scholarly literature" (84 ff.), and "a powerful push towards normativity" (132–33). On the prohibitions on gifts, see 133–34. See also the same author's "Allgemeine Merkmale der Verwaltungsorganisation in den Territorien," in Jeserich et al., *Deutsche Verwaltungsgeschichte*, vol. 1, 289–344.

12. Willoweit, "Entwicklung," 133 ff.; Michael Stolleis, "Grundzüge der Beamtenethik (1550–1650)," in Roman Schnur, ed., *Die Rolle der Juristen bei der Entstehung des modernen Staates* (Berlin, 1986), 273–302, esp. 290 ff. On prohibitions on accepting gifts in the oath formulas of the late Middle Ages, see Erich Wyluda, *Lehnrecht und Beamtentum: Studien zur Entstehung des preussischen Beamtentums* (Berlin, 1969), 147–48.

13. For a clear-eyed view of this dilemma in the study of late medieval institutions and their regulations, see Peter Moraw, "'Regierung' und 'Verwaltung' des deutschen

Königs im Reich," in Werner Paravicini and Karl Ferdinand Werner, eds., *Histoire comparé de l'administration (IV-XVIIIe siècles)* (Munich, 1980), 149–67, esp. 157.

14. Alain Guery, "Le roi dépensier: Le don, la contrainte, et l'origine du système financier de la monarchie française d'Ancien Régime," *Annales E.S.C.* 39 (1984): 1241–69. See also Wim Blockmans, "Patronage, Brokerage and Corruption as Symptoms of Incipient State Formation in the Burgundian-Habsburg Netherlands," in Anthoni Maczak, ed., *Klientelsysteme im Europa der frühen Neuzeit* (Munich, 1988), 117–26; Sharon Kettering, *Patrons, Brokers and Clients in Seventeenth-Century France* (Oxford, 1986), esp. 192–206, and "Gift-giving and Patronage in Early Modern France," *French History* 2 (1988): 131–51. On municipal administrations, see Andrea Zorzi, "I Fiorentini e gli uffici publici del primo Quattrocento: Concorrenza, abusi, illegalitá," *Quaderni storici* 22 (1987): 725–51, and "Ordine publico e amministrazione della giustizia nelle formazioni politiche toscane fra Tre e Quattrocento," in *Italia 1350–1450: Tra crisi, trasformazione e sviluppo* (Pistoia, 1993), 419–74; and William J. Connell, "Clientelismo e Stato territoriale: Il potere fiorentina a Pistoia nel XV secolo," *Societa e Storia* 14 (1991): 523–41.

15. Giorgio Chittolini, "The 'Private,' the 'Public', the State," in Giorgio Chittolini, Anthony Molho, and Pierangelo Schiera, eds., *The Origins of the State in Italy, 1300–1600* (Chicago, 1995), 34–61, esp. 51–52.

16. John of Salisbury, *Policraticus*, ed. Cary J. Nederman (Cambridge, 1990), 96–97; the maxim comes from the *Corpus Iuris Civilis*, Digests 1,16,6. See also Jean-Philippe Genet, "Ecclesiastics and Political Theory in Late Medieval England," in Barrie Dobson, ed., *The Church, Politics and Patronage in the Fifteenth Century* (Gloucester, 1984), 23–44. On the Latin terminology of gifts and bribery in ancient and medieval legal texts, see Joseph Weitzel, *Begriff und Erscheinungsformen der Simonie bei Gratian und den Dekretisten* (Munich, 1967), 151–52; for a detailed account, see John T. Noonan, *Bribes* (New York, 1986), 31 ff., 117–18, 124–25, and 139 ff. On the dual nature of *munus*, see also Guèry, "Le roi dépensier," 1259–60.

17. This is conditioned by the history of these historical disciplines themselves. See the relevant reflections of Frantisek Graus, "Verfassungsgeschichte des Mittelalters," *HZ* 243 (1986): 529–89.

18. On this problem, see the introduction to Ronald Asch and Adolf Birke, eds., *Princes, Patronage and the Nobility: The Court at the Beginning of the Modern Age 1450–1650* (Oxford, 1991).

19. The heterogeneity of these sources is emphasized by Michael Stolleis, "Grundzüge der Beamtenethik (1550–1650)," in Roman Schnur, ed., *Die Rolle der Juristen bei der Entstehung des modernen Staates* (Berlin, 1986), 273–302, esp. 274–80.

20. Willoweit, "Entwicklung," 82–141; similarly, Wolter, "Amt und Offizium," 278. Stolleis emphasizes that complaints about second occupations and corruption continued throughout the early modern period: "Absolutism never managed to solve the problem of corrupt officials"; "Grundzüge der Beamtenethik," 290. For a similar view, see Wilhelm Brauneder, "Korruption als historisches Phänomen," in *Korruption und Kontrolle*, ed. Christian Brünner (Vienna, 1981), 75–104, esp. 83–84. Cf. the case study on the criteria for appointments to office in the Austrian territories of the Upper Rhine region in 1511 in Manfred Hollegger, "Zur 'Beamtenethik' um 1500: Standards

von Räten, Beamten, Amtleuten und Dienern Maximilians I.," in H. Ebner et al., eds., *Geschichtsforschung in Graz* (Graz, 1990), 139–45.

21. Jakob van Klaveren, entry "Korruption," in *Handwörterbuch der deutschen Rechtsgeschichte*, vol. 2 (Berlin, 1980), 1163–69. The classification of corruption as a "middle-class phenomenon" that depends upon the form of state, which the same author develops elsewhere ("Die historische Erscheinung der Korruption in ihrem Zusammenhang mit der Staats- und Gesellschaftsstruktur betrachtet," *VSWG* 44 [1957]: 289–324), is not very convincing; see the sharp critique of Jean-Claude Wacquet in *De la corruption: Morale et pouvoir à Florence aux XVIIe et XVIIIe siècles* (Paris, 1984), 10 ff. The phenomenon of corruption also appears in a similarly ahistorical form ("almost as old as humanity"), as a sort of eternal "temptation" to which anyone can succumb, in the otherwise excellent and richly documented study by Maurice Arnould, "L'origine historique des pots-de-vin," Académie Royale de Belgique, *Bulletin de la classe des lettres et des sciences morales et politiques*, 5th series, 62 (1976): 216–67, here 217 and 225.

22. Moraw, "'Regierung' und 'Verwaltung,'" 157.

23. On the modern definition of the term, see Daniel H. Lowenstein, "Legal Efforts to Define Political Bribery," in A. J. Heidenheimer et al., eds., *Political Corruption: A Handbook* (New Brunswick, N.J. 1989), 29–38; see also Werner Rügemer, *Wirtschaften ohne Korruption?* (Frankfurt, 1996). On the problems of an open historical terminology, see Noonan, *Bribes*, xi ff.; Robert Harding, "Corruption and the Moral Boundaries of Patronage in the Renaissance," in Guy Fitch Little and Stephen Orgel, eds., *Patronage in the Renaissance* (Princeton, N.J., 1981), 47–71; and Roberto Mancini, "La corruzione: Usi e abusi di un termine storiographico," *Ricerche Storiche* 21 (1991): 3–33.

24. On the uniform criterion of oath of office, see Ernst Pitz, *Schrift- und Aktenwesen der städtischen Verwaltung im Spätmittelalter* (Cologne, 1959), 158–59; on Basel, see Knut Schulz, *Handwerksgesellen und Lohnarbeiter* (Sigmaringen, 1985), 370 ff. On conditions in Strasbourg, cf. Francis Rapp, "Politique et administration strasbourgeoise," in Gerhard Bauer, ed., *Stadtsprachenforschung, unter besonderer Berücksichtigung der Verhältnisse der Stadt Strassburg in Spätmittelalter und früher Neuzeit* (Göppingen, 1988), 327–72, with bibliography; for Nuremberg, see Paul Sander, *Die reichsstädtische Haushaltung Nürnbergs, dargestellt auf Grund ihres Zustands von 1431–1440* (Leipzig, 1902). I have discussed the payment structure of municipal officials in Nuremberg in more detail elsewhere; see Groebner, *Ökonomie ohne Haus* (Göttingen, 1993), 131–77.

25. On the partial payment of wages in clothing, see, for example, WAB 10, f. 62 (1463) or WAB 12, f. 716 (1502). The Basel council records (*Ratsbücher*) for 1490 note in detail all income that was owed to the town guards and their immediate superior, the *Oberstknecht*; StAB Ratsbücher A 5, f. 137v; printed with incorrect page numbers in *Basler Rechtsquellen*, ed. Christian Schnell, 2 vols. (Basel, 1859–65), vol. 1, 378–79. For similar lists for Bern, see Berchtold Haller, ed., *Bern in seinen Ratsmanualen 1465–1565*, 3 vols. (Bern, 1902), vol. 3, 551–52, and for Séléstat, Joseph Gény, ed., *Schlettstadter Stadtrechte* (Heidelberg, 1902), 322.

26. Venningen, *Hausbuch*, for example, f. 442. See also Gerhard Fouquet and Ulf

Dirlmeier, "'Weger wer, ich hett sie behaltten': Alltäglicher Konsum und persönliche Beziehungen in der Hofhaltung des Basler Bischofs Johannes von Venningen (1458–1478)," in Werner Paravicini, ed., *Alltag bei Hofe* (Sigmaringen, 1995), 171–96, esp. 181 and 183. On similar circumstances at the court of the dukes of Burgundy, on gifts as part of wages, and service at court as a second source of income in the fifteenth century, see Holger Kruse, *Hof, Amt und Gagen: Die täglichen Gagenlisten des burgundischen Hofes 1430–1467 und der erste Hofstaat Karls des Kühnen 1456* (Bonn, 1996), 281–82. On the Medici court in the sixteenth and seventeenth centuries, see Marcello Fantoni, *La corte del Granduca: Forme e simboli del potere mediceo fra Cinque e Seicento* (Rome, 1994), 101–2, where the author speaks of "quasi una regolare forma di sovraremunerazione."

27. Oskar Pausch, *Das älteste italienisch-deutsche Sprachbuch: Eine Überlieferung aus dem Jahre 1424 nach Georg von Nürnberg* (Vienna, 1972), 251; further gifts of wine upon the conclusion of agreements appear on 243, 256, and 258. On the term, see "Litkouf," *HRG*, vol. 2, cols. 1842 f. (Berlin, 1978); "Leitkauf," *Deutsches Rechtswörterbuch*, vol. 8, 1216; see also Vinzenz Bartlome, *Die Rechnungsbücher des Wirtes Hans von Herblingen* (Bern, 1988), 98–99.

28. Venningen, *Hausbuch*, f. 316 (1466), f. 354 (1467), and passim.

29. Venningen, *Hausbuch*, f. 434; Thierstein received an annuity of 100 Rhenish florins; on costly gifts to his wife, see 439 and 477.

30. Venningen, *Hausbuch*, f. 306 (1466); Harms, *Stadthaushalt*, vol. 3, S. 309. In August 1476, Venningen gave his servant Marx Rich first ten and later an additional three florins as a parting gift when he entered the service of the duke of Lorraine. "God grant him good fortune," he added, "for he needs it"; Venningen, *Hausbuch*, f. 468.

31. The city of Basel gave rejected applicants for municipal office a sort of parting gift or compensation. In 1515 a foreigner who had applied for a position as watchman and a trumpeter seeking work were given 76 pfennigs each as a tip, more than three good days' wages for an artisan; Harms, *Stadthaushalt*, vol. 3, 225. See also the similar earlier account in vol. 2, 266 (1451–52).

32. StAB Zunftakten, Safranzunft 66, f. 487 (1509); Venningen, *Hausbuch*, for example, f. 262 (1464), 399 (1469), 416 (1470), 431 (1471), 442 (1472), 451 (1473), etc.; StAB Ratsbücher A 5, f. 137v.

33. StAB Ratsbücher A 5, f. 137v. Cf. the Strasbourg regulations in Eheberg, *Verfassungsgeschichte*, 35–36.

34. StAB Ratsbücher A 5, f. 138 r.

35. See the rules of the court set out in the so-called *Blaues Buch*, printed in *Basler Rechtsquellen*, vol. 1, 156 (1457) and the reformulation of 1497 in StAB Ratsbücher B1, Erkanntnisbuch 1, f. 132r and f. 154r; on the Strasbourg regulations, see Eheberg, *Verfassungsgeschichte*, 464–65.

36. Eheberg, *Verfassungsgeschichte*, 372, 463, 464–65, and passim; StAB Ratsbücher A 5, f. 115r, K 1, f. 39v, etc. The oath formula for the *Schultheiss* appears in K 1, f. 2v; *Basler Rechtsquellen*, vol. 1, 397–98. Similarly, the 1498 oath formula for court messengers in Sélestat not merely admonished them to place fines immediately in the box designated for this purpose but also required them to keep precise records, noting the date and time of payment; Gény, *Schlettstadter Stadtrechte*, 665. See also Benoît Garnot, *Juges, notaires, et policiers délinquants, XIVe-XXe siècle* (Dijon, 1997).

37. For greater detail and numerous examples, see Groebner, *Ökonomie*, 130–37.

38. This was no mere example of picturesque "customary law"; the sums involved could be quite substantial. The official occasionally received a formal transfer fee for his rights to the garments of the executed, as occurred, for example, in 1500–1501, when the chief town guard was paid 130 pfennigs for the clothing of an executed man; Harms, *Stadthaushalt*, vol. 3, 104. These 130 pfennigs corresponded to the weekly income of a well-paid journeyman artisan.

39. Ratsbücher B 1, f. 6v and 18v (Basel 1482–83); on the sale of secondhand clothes by the Strasbourg executioner, see Louis Dacheux, ed., "Jacobus Wencker Extractus ex Protocollis vulgo Les Annales de Sebastien Brant," in *Fragments des anciennes chroniques d'Alsace*, vol. 3, *Les chroniques Strasbourgiennes* (Strasbourg, 1892), 209–79, esp. 227. The council decree of 1509 did not forbid this practice but stipulated that the executioner's wife should set up her stand separately from the other women at the flea market, so that she was recognizable. On moonlighting by Freiburg beadles, see StadtAF B XIIIa, 4a, f. 27v.

40. See, for example, Archives de la ville de Strasbourg série III, BB 24, 1; StadtAF B 5, XIII, no. 4, f. 27r; Friedrich J. Mone, "Kanzlei- und Gerichtsgebühren im 15. und 16. Jahrhundert," *ZGO* 12 (1862): 435 ff.; and Folkmar Thiele, *Die Freiburger Stadtschreiber im Mittelalter* (Freiburg im Breisgau, 1973), 94–97, 103–4, and 107 (oath of the town clerk, 1494). Of the extensive literature on Peutinger, his offices, and his work as royal councilor to Maximilian in spring 1506, see Heinrich Lutz, *Konrad Peutinger: Eine politische Biographie* (Augsburg, 1958), 50 ff.; Wolfgang Zorn, "Die soziale Stellung der Humanisten in Augsburg und Nürnberg," in Otto Herding und Robert Stupperich, eds., *Die Humanisten in ihrer sozialen Umwelt* (Boppard, 1976), 35–49; and Ulrich Meier, "'Ad incrementum rectae gubernationis': Zur Rolle der Kanzler und Stadtschreiber in der politischen Kultur von Augsburg und Florenz," in Rainer-Christoph Schwinges, *Gelehrte im Reich: Zur Sozial- und Wirkungsgeschichte akademischer Eliten des 14. bis 16. Jahrhunderts* (Berlin, 1997), 477–503. On the economic situation of town clerks, see Gerhart Burger, *Die südwestdeutschen Stadtschreiber im Mittelalter* (Böblingen, 1960); Ferdinand Elsener, "Notare und Stadtschreiber: Zur Geschichte des schweizerischen Notariats," in Elsener, *Studien zur Rezeption des gelehrten Rechts* (Sigmaringen, 1989), 11–151; Eberhard Isenmann, *Die deutsche Stadt im Spätmittelalter* (Stuttgart, 1988), 143 ff.; and Zahnd, "Studium und Kanzlei."

41. Erasmus of Rotterdam, *Institutio Principis*, 189–90. On the coexistence of salary, pensions, and gifts in the remuneration of French officeholders at court and in the urban trades, see also Natalie Zemon Davis, *Gifts and Bribes in Sixteenth-Century France* (Lancaster, 1995), 51–54.

42. On Spatzinger, see Archives de la ville de Strasbourg série III, BB 24, 1; Georg Steer et al., eds., *Die "Rechtssumme Bruder Bertholds,"* vol. 4 (Tübingen, 1987), 1830. Compiled in southern Germany in the second half of the fourteenth century, the *Rechtssumme* became one of the most "influential use texts of the German late Middle Ages." More than 70 complete manuscripts and 12 incunabula have come down to us, most of them produced between 1450 and 1470. See Helmut Weck, "Die handschriftliche Überlieferung der 'Rechtssumme,'" in Georg Steer et al., eds., *Die "Rechtssumme Bruder Bertholds,"* vol. 3 (Tübingen, 1986), 221–51, esp. 233 ff.

43. Eheberg, *Verfassungs-, Verwaltungsgeschichte*, 175–77 (1456); Haller, *Bern*, vol. 3, 404.

44. Ordnung und Eidformel der Unzüchter, 15. Jahrhundert, *Basler Rechtsquellen*,

vol. 1, 435; StAB Ratsbücher B 1, f. 59v (July 1486), printed, with some transcription errors (*uffgericht* instead of *ussgericht*, the quotation marks around *erkannt* are missing) in *Basler Rechtsquellen*, vol. 1, 209. One year earlier the Zurich town council had also issued a mandate against the practice of officials lowering, waiving, or negotiating fines ("ützit zu schenken, abzulassen oder zu tädingen"); Ernst Gagliardi, ed., *Dokumente zur Geschichte des Bürgermeisters Hans Waldmann*, vol. 1 (Basel, 1911), 263.

45. On the adjustment or deferment of payments, see the overview in Gerd Schwerhoff, *Köln im Kreuzverhör: Kriminalität, Herrschaft und Gesellschaft in einer frühneuzeitlichen Stadt* (Cologne, 1991), 275, with bibliography; on "mercy" (*Gnade*) as part of a regulatory system of price surveillance and the waiving of sanctions, see my "Towards an Economic History of Customary Practice: Bread, Money and the Economy of the Bazaar," *German History* 12 (1994): 119–36. On the Basel example, see StAB Protokolle, Öffnungsbuch 7, f. 118r. The *Erkanntnisbücher* relate extensive negotiations before political visits by princes regarding the names and number of such candidates for pardon as requested by the high-ranking guest; after entry into the Swiss Confederacy, high-ranking Swiss allies assumed the role of intercessors for convicted miscreants. On this issue, see StAB Ratsbücher B 1, for instance, f. 67v (1486) and f. 209r; in 1501 the town council granted the request of the Swiss to pardon certain named escaped men convicted of manslaughter, albeit reluctantly ("obwol im das swer sey").

46. Venningen, *Hausbuch*, f. 99 (1477); Gagliardi, *Dokumente zur Geschichte*, vol. 2, 29–30; on the official Zurich pardon request, see vol. 1, 368. Gifts to municipal officials in conjunction with the waiving of sanctions are documented far more clearly elsewhere. In 1490–91, the account books of the city of Lille recorded the expense of 120 livres of municipal coins to "Guy d'Arleux, equerry, provost of Lille, so that he may not execute his sentence against the brewers"; Alain Derville, "Les pot-de-vins dans le dernier tiers du XVe siècle," in Wim Blockmans, ed., 1477. *Le privilège général et les privilèges regionaux de Marie Bourgogne pour le Pays-Bas* (Kortrijk, 1986), 449–71, esp. 469.

47. StAB Protokolle, Öffnungsbuch 1, f. 337 (1448); the council resolved that an arrestee should not be required to pay the town guards more than 24 pfennigs in *bintgelt*.

48. StAB Ratsbücher o 2, f. 206, f. 346. Scheffer was arrested again in 1519 for his violent nocturnal activities, f. 253. The former Basel courier Lienhart Meyer was imprisoned in the tower in July 1514 for calling the town guards "the executioner's hounds" (*des henckers jagdhund*) and making other derogatory remarks about municipal officials; ibid., f. 111. On the assaults and corruption of Basel beadles, see also Hans-Rudolf Hagemann, *Basler Rechtsleben im Mittelalter*, vol. 1 (Basel, 1983), 276, with numerous examples.

49. Andrea Bendlage and Peter Schuster, "Hüter der Ordnung: Bürger, Rat und Polizei in Nürnberg im 15. und 16. Jahrhundert," *MVGN* 82 (1995); 37–56, esp. 43–44; on Drotzech, see 46. The prohibition on demanding gifts was repeated in 1487, 1490, and twice in 1491 in the council decrees, 44; on violence by beadles, see 41 ff. The guardians of order were repeatedly admonished to hand over anything in the way of clothing, money, or valuables found on the person of prisoners to the jailers and not to

keep any of it for themselves. See StadtAF B XIIIa, 4a, f. 27v (1496); and on Nuremberg, see Groebner, *Ökonomie,* 169–70.

50. StadtAF B 3, 3, f. 37v and 63r; for council decrees concerning the violence of beadles, see B XIII, 4 a, f. 25v and f. 27v (1496). On the reorganization of the town guards and their payment in 1495–96, see StadtAF B 1, 2 (Geschichtbuch 1492–1562), f. 93r–94r. For a general prohibition on loans, see StAB Ratsbücher K 2, Amtseide, f. 10r and v (1469). Cf. the case of the Nuremberg market inspector Sinterspiess, who was placed in the stocks in 1490 for taking bribes and then expelled from the city. The transcripts of interviews with butchers mention not just gifts of their wares but also "loans" that Sinterspiess received; Groebner, *Ökonomie,* 173.

51. StAB Ratsbücher A 5, f. 138r.

52. StAB Ratsbücher K 1, f. 2r; Eheberg, *Verfassungsgeschichte,* 175; for similar mentions in the *Ratsordnung* of 1405, see Eheberg, *Verfassungsgeschichte,* 34, 35–36, and 37.

53. Ernst Mummenhoff, *Das alte Nürnberger Rathaus* (Nuremberg, 1931), 74–75; see also Sander, *Die reichsstädtische Haushaltung,* 72–73.

54. Erich Ennen, ed., "Joannes Wals Rechenschaff van Basel und Ulme," *Annalen des historischen Vereins für den Niederrhein* 17 (1866): 102–18, here 108, 110–11, 113.

55. Harms, *Stadthaushalt,* vol. 2, 266.

56. *BChr,* vol. 4, 83; Harms, *Stadthaushalt,* vol. 3, 85. The usual practice, according to an account from the city of Frankfurt on gifts on the occasion of the emperor's visit in 1517, was to give ten florins to the doorkeepers and an additional florin to the head doorkeeper; Johannes Janssen, ed., *Frankfurter Reichskorrespondenz nebst anderen verwandten Actenstücken 1376–1519,* part 2, vol. 2 (Freiburg im Breisgau, 1872), 904. The city of Augsburg's official list of all gifts (*Vereerungen* and *Schanckungen*) given at the Imperial Diet of 1530 also mentions ten florins for the imperial doorkeepers, and the same sum went to the imperial valets (*camerdiener*). *StChr,* ed. Karl Hegel et al. , vol. 25 (Leipzig, 1869–1917), 406.

57. Carl August Barack, ed., *Des Teufels Netz* (Stuttgart, 1863), 274–75. On compulsory gifts to doorkeepers and advisers, without which no one could gain access to the prince, see also Johannes Rothe, *Ratsgedichte,* ed. Herbert Wolf (Berlin, 1971), 95. See also Paul-Joachim Heinig, "Die Türhüter und Herolde Kaiser Friedrichs III," in Heinig, ed., *Kaiser Friedrich III. (1440–1493) in seiner Zeit* (Cologne, 1995), 355–75.

58. I cite the German translation of 1529 here; Eneas Silivius Piccolomini, *Von höfen/ hoffleuten vund dienern der Fürsten,* trans. Wolff Hasen (n.p., 1529), f. 34. Cf. the description of the doorkeeper as a greedy Cerberus in John of Salisbury's *Policraticus,* which provides one of the models for this tradition; Peter von Moos, *Geschichte als Topik: Das rhetorische Exemplum der Antike zur Neuzeit und die Historiae im "Policraticus" Johanns von Salisbury* (Hildesheim, 1996). The motif of the fees necessary to gain access to the papal court is common in satires critical of the church; on its adaption in the Reformation pamphlet literature of the 1520s, see Oskar Schade, ed., *Satiren und Pasquille aus der Reformationszeit,* 3 vols. (Hanover, 1855–58; reprint, Hildesheim, 1966), vol. 2, 105–7. On these "door-openers," see also Natalie Zemon Davis, *The Gift in Sixteenth-Century France* (Madison, 2000), 73–74.

59. Hartmut Vogel, "Sporteln und Sporteldelikte: Eine Untersuchung über die historische Entwicklung und gegenwärtige Bedeutung der Sporteldelikte, verbunden mit einem Abriß zur Geschichte des Sportelwesens," Jur. diss., University of Göttingen, 1960.

60. An early fifteenth-century Basel town council ordinance sought to regulate the relationships between madames (*husfrowen*), who provided lodgings for *varend töchtern und frowen* (literally: property daughters and women), that is, prostitutes, and the women dependent upon them. These *husfrowen* had previously demanded unduly large gifts (*gar groß unglimplich schenckin*), but the council ruled that they should no longer do so and no longer take gifts from their lodgers (*das sollent si hinnanthin nit me tun und kein schenke von inen nemmen*); instead, they should receive one-third of the earnings of the "daughters" to whom they offered protection; *Basler Rechtsquellen*, vol. 1, 87–88. For more on the relations of dependency between municipal prostitutes and brothel-keepers, see Beate Schuster, *Die freien Frauen. Dirnen und Frauenhäuser im 15. und 16. Jahrhundert* (Frankfurt am Main, 1995), 134–57.

61. Maurice Arnould, "L'origine historique des pots-de-vin," Académie Royale de Belgique, *Bulletin de la classe des lettres et des sciences morales et politiques*, 5e série, 62 (1976): 216–67, esp. 230. Cf. the terms for forced gifts and pensions in the sixteenth and seventeenth century in Fritz Redlich, *The German Military Enterpriser and His Work Force*, 2 vols. (Wiesbaden, 1964), vol. 1, 331–43; for France, see also Davis, *The Gift*, 87–88.

62. StAB, Zunftakten, Safranzunft 66, f. 430 (1504), and Safranzunft 69, f. 155; Ernst Gagliardi, *Der Anteil der Schweizer an den italienischen Kriegen 1494–1516*, vol. 1 (Zurich, 1919), 660 (1507).

63. See the graphs in the Appendix.

64. *Chroniken der deutschen Städte*, vol. 25, supplements to the chronicle of Clemens Sender, 408.

65. *BChr*, vol. 2, 53 and 58. See also Hildburg Brauer-Gramm, *Der Landvogt Peter von Hagenbach* (Göttingen, 1957), 93–94; August Bernoulli, ed., "Balci Descriptio Helvetiae," in *Quellen zur Schweizer Geschichte*, vol. 6 (Basel, 1884), 73–105, esp. 78–79.

66. "Von schencken wegen" in StAB Ratsbücher A 5, f. 106r (um 1450); see also Gerhard Fouquet, "Das Festmahl in den oberdeutschen Städten des Spätmittelalters: Zu Form, Funktion und Bedeutung öffentlichen Konsums," *AKG* 74 (1992): 83–123, esp. 119.

67. Bob Scribner, "Mündliche Kommunikation und Strategien der Macht in Deutschland im 16. Jahrhundert," in *Kommunikation und Alltag in Spätmittelalter und früher Neuzeit* (Vienna, 1992), 183–97.

68. See *BChr*, vol. 5, 287–88 (Henman Offenburg), the portrayal in the anonymous chronicle of the Swabian War (490), and that of Heinrich Appenwiler (vol. 4, 259 ff. and 263–64); guild chronicles such as that of Hans Brüglinger (vol. 4, 174 ff.) make no mention whatsoever of the case. In an explicitly political manner, the annual accounts for 1444–45 juxtapose the various gifts of wine and money to threatening guests with the costs for compensation payments to the aggrieved aristocrats and emphasize that the wine was drunk by both the enemy Swiss and their allies in the

Basel guilds; none of the chroniclers describe the events in such a politically aggressive form; Harms, *Stadthaushalt*, vol. 2, 234. On the context, see Friedrich Meyer, *Die Beziehungen zwischen Basel und den Eidgenossen in der Darstellung der Historiographie des 15. und 16. Jahrhunderts* (Basel, 1951), 39 ff.

69. *BChr*, vol. 3, 105–6: "*accesserunt capitaneos eorum, propinantes eis zuckarum et malvasiam.*"

70. *BChr*, vol. 3, 227. Many thanks to Claudius Sieber, who drew my attention to this and the previous passage.

71. The yearly account for 1504–5, at least, lays great stress on the malmsey wine; Harms, *Stadthaushalt*, vol. 3, 157. On the Baden pension letter of 1503 and the diplomatic activities associated with it, see Chapter 4.

72. Quoted in Aloys Schulte, *Geschichte der grossen Ravensburger Handelsgesellschaft 1380–1530*, vol. 3 (Stuttgart, 1923), 451; see also vol. 1, 470–73.

73. Ibid., vol. 3, 453.

74. *Chroniken der deutschen Städte*, vol. 22 (Leipzig, 1892), supplements to the chronicle of Hektor Mülich, 417–19; on Schwarz see below, Chapter 4.

75. On the Strasbourg brokers in 1494, see Johann Brucker, *Strassburger Zunft- und Polizeiordnungen des 14. und 15. Jahrhunderts* (Strasbourg, 1899), 532; on Conz and the cloak, see Carl August Barack, ed., *Chronik der Grafen von Zimmern*, vol. 2 (Tübingen, 1896), 262.

76. *Chroniken der deutschen Städte*, vol. 5 (Leipzig, 1866), supplements to the chronicle of Burkard Zink, 386.

77. Gagliardi, *Dokumente zur Geschichte*, vol. 2, 29–30; on Zurich's official request to Milan for clemency, which mentions Schenk, see vol. 1, 368. The records of the papal Cour Temporelle in Avignon mention an Italian lawyer, who is referred to as *Ricardus de Multidenariis*; Jacques Chiffoleau, *Les justices du pape: Delinquance et criminalité dans la région d'Avignon au XIVe siècle* (Paris, 1984), 56. See also Bernard Guenée, *Tribunaux et gens de justice à la fin du Moyen Age* (Paris, 1963), 183, 257–58, and 288.

78. Eheberg, *Verfassungs-, Verwaltungsgeschichte*, 450; and StaB Ratsbücher, Erkanntnisbuch 1, f. 223r. In his reconstruction of the regular personnel of the imperial court in the fifteenth century, Paul-Joachim Heinig makes use of municipal bookkeeping on gifts in Frankfurt and Nuremberg. See his "How Large Was the Court of Emperor Frederick III?" in Ronald Asch and Adolf Birke, eds., *Princes, Patronage and the Nobility: The Court at the Beginning of the Modern Age, 1450–1650* (Oxford, 1991), 136–56, esp. 141–47.

79. StAB Ratsbücher K 1, f. 2; see Chapter 1.

80. For details see Hans Füglister, *Handwerksregiment: Untersuchungen und Materialien zur sozialen und politischen Struktur der Stadt Basel in der ersten Hälfte des 16. Jahrhunderts* (Basel, 1981), 190–91.

81. StAB Ratsbücher A 5, f. 92v, f. 93v, and Rosemarie Grether, "Die Basler Ratsordnung von 1506," *Jahresberichte des Staatsarchiv Basel-Stadt 1969*, 21–51, esp. 46–47.

82. StAB Ratsbücher A 5, f. 25v (1385).

83. See, for example, Gagliardi, *Dokumente zur Geschichte*, vol. 1, 384; on Waldmann as a recipent of pensions, see the next chapter.

84. StAB K 23, f. 10v and 11v.

85. StAB Ratsbücher, Erkanntnisbuch 2/3, f. 37v.

86. Ibid., f. 95v.

Chapter 3

1. StAB Ratsbücher A 1, f. 41 and A 5, f. 21v (1372) and A 1, f. 51 (1385). Both formulas add that those gifts accepted not by the officeholder himself but by his wife, children, relatives or servants also fell under the prohibition.

2. StAB Ratsbücher, A 1, f. 48, and *Basler Rechtsquellen*, vol. 1 (Basel, 1859), 67 and 69; StAB Ratsbücher K 1, f. 1r, 2v, 3r, 10; and L 1, Ratsbesatzungen 1436–1501, and without changes, L 2, Ratsbesatzungen 1505–1600; K 1, f. 35r and 63r; K 2; K 23, Ratsordnungen, f. 18v and f. 31v (1499); *Basler Rechtsquellen*, vol. 2 (Basel, 1865), 459–506, see, for example, 464, 497, and 502. On the new council ordinances and oath formulas after 1521 and 1529, respectively, see StAB Ratsbücher K 24, f. 4v and passim.

3. StAB Ratsbücher A 3, Leistungsbuch 2, f. 89v and 90r. See also Hans-Rudolf Hagemann, *Basler Rechtsleben im Mittelalter*, vol. 1 (Basel, 1983), 276, which reports a further case from 1412. See also Gottfried Studer, ed., *Die Berner Chronik des Conrad Justinger* (Bern, 1871), 123.

4. The regulations stipulated "pfert, gewande, harnesch, pfennige, silber, gold, saltz, alles wiltpret, es sye essende spise oder anders, clein und grosz, gelte oder geltes wert, das den man erweichen mag oder die gemeine statt ze hindern oder einige personen zu fürdern oder zu hindern in iren sachen"; StaB Ratsbücher A 1, f. 41 and 51; A 5, f. 25v and, slightly altered, K 23, f. 18v. Gifts in the form of foods were not, however, generally above suspicion. The prohibition on *miet* frequently appears in conjunction with a prohibition on accepting food; the oath of Basel informants on morals offenses not only forbade them to accept *miet* and *gab*, but also to eat with others in taverns or other places; K 1, f. 91r. See also *Basler Rechtsquellen*, vol. 1, 156–57, 397, 401–2, and the court rules of 1539 and 1557 (315 and 424).

5. Karl Theodor Eheberg, *Verfassungs-, Verwaltungs- und Wirtschaftsgeschichte der Stadt Strassburg bis 1681*, vol. 1, *Urkunden und Akten* (Strasbourg, 1899), 85 ff. (1433); the definition appears on 92. On closer inspection, this Strasbourg definition proves to be composed of several older stipulations; see, for example, the entry for July 25, 1300, in W. Wiegand et al., eds., *Urkundenbuch der Stadt Strassburg*, vol. IV/2 (Strasbourg, 1888), 21; supplements to the chronicle of Jakob Twinger von Königshofen, 39, in *StChr*, ed. Karl Hegel et al., vol. 8 (Leipzig, 1870). The prohibition of *miet* runs through all of the later oath formulas for Strasbourg officials. Cf., for example, the text of the oath of 1482, the basis of the city's charter in the early modern period, printed in *Chroniken der Deutschen Städte*, vol. 8, 947–48.

6. Eheberg, *Verfassungsgeschichte*, 93, 94, 95, 265, 443, and 445–46. On frequent official permits to receive gifts, see Otto Winckelmann, "Strassburgs Verfassung und Verwaltung im 16. Jahrhundert," *ZGO* 18 (1903): 493–537, 600–39, esp. 606; and Friedrich J. Mone, ed., "Sponheimische Beamtenverordnung 1437," *ZGO* 6 (1855): 385–95, esp. 389–90.

7. Oath formula for Bern officeholders, printed in the appendix to Regula Schmid, *Reden, rufen, Zeichen setzen: Politisches Handeln während des Berner Twingherrenstreits 1469–1471* (Zurich, 1995), 278 f.; StAFr B 3, 3, f. 3v, 6r, 8v, extracts reproduced in Folkmar Thiele, *Die Freiburger Stadtschreiber im Mittelalter* (Freiburg im Breisgau, 1973), 107–8; Joseph Gény, *Schlettstädter Stadtrechte* (Heidelberg, 1902), 481–82 (1498); Joachim Köhler, *Die Carolina und ihre Vorgängerinnen*, vol. 2, *Die Bambergische Halsgerichtsordnung* (Halle, 1902), 5 ff.; Ulrich Tengler, *Der new Leyenspiegel von rechtmassigen ordnungen in burgerlichen und peynlichen Regimenten* (Strasbourg, 1514), f. 3r (judges' oath), f. 4v (assessors), f. 5r (court and town clerks). See also Hubert Drüppel, *Judex Civitatis: Zur Stellung des Richters in der hoch- und spätmittelalterlichen Stadt* (Cologne, 1981), 290–91.

8. See the entries for "miet" and "miet-wân" in Matthias Lexer, *Mittelhochdeutsches Wörterbuch*, 3 vols. (Leipzig, 1872), vol. 2, 2134 and 2136; in the *Deutsches Rechtswörterbuch/Wörterbuch der älteren deutschen Rechtssprache*, vol. 9 (Cologne, 1993), 614 ff.; and in the *Schweizerisches Idiotikon*, vol. 4 (Frauenfeld, 1901), 565 ff. On treatments of the Genelun/Judas motif, see Karl Stackmann, "Karl und Genelun: Das Thema des Verrats im Rolandslied des faffen und Konrad und seinen Bearbeitungen," *Poetica* 8 (1976): 258–80.

9. Karl A. Eckhardt and H. Hübner, eds., *Deutschenspiegel* (Hanover, 1939), 150; Karl A. Eckhart, ed., *Sachsenspiegel Landrecht* (Göttingen, 1955), 41; and H. Gengler, ed., *Schwabenspiegel* (Erlangen, 1853), Art. 71. See also Robert Scheyhing, *Eide, Banngewalt und Amtsleihe* (Cologne, 1960); on judges' oaths of office and references to Judas, see 170–75.

10. In the *Decretum Gratiani*, false witness—represented by Judas—is treated immediately following the duties of the judge and the prohibition on accepting gifts (c. 83 and cc. 78–82 respectively, C. XI, q. 3); Scheyhing, *Eide*, 187. High medieval deeds of donation frequently contain a clause with a curse referring to the torments of Judas Ischariot; H. Martin, "The Judas Ischariot Curse," *American Journal of Philology* 37 (1916): 435–51; Carl August Barack, *Des Teufels Netz* (Stuttgart, 1863), 231–32 and 283; Archives municipales de Strasbourg, II, VDG 117, f. 137r–153v, and with the same wording in a corrected transcript with marginal notes in f. 157v–195r; reproduced in Peter-Johannes Schuler, "Reformation des geistlichen Gerichts zu Strassburg. Eine Reformschrift aus der Mitte des 15. Jahrhunderts," *Francia* 9 (1981): 177–214. See also Schuler's "Die 'armen lüt' und das Gericht," in Peter Claasen, ed., *Recht und Schrift im Mittelalter* (Sigmaringen, 1977), 221–36.

11. Hans Gille and Ingeborg Spriewald, eds., *Die Gedichte des Michel Beheim*, 3 vols. (Berlin, 1968), vol. 2, 147 and 155. The German New Testament printed for the first time by Johann Mentelin in Strasbourg around 1467 translates Matthew 27:9 as follows: "Vnd sy namen die 30 silberin den werde des gemieten den sy hetten gemiet von den sunen israels"; W. Kurrelmeyer, *Die erste deutsche Bibel*, vol. 1 (Tübingen, 1904), 108.

12. Eheberg, *Verfassungsgeschichte*, 93 and 450.

13. Gille and Spriewald, *Die Gedichte des Michael Behaim*, vol. 2, 160; on the sweets, see Ernst Matthias, "Der Nürnberger Meistersänger Kunz Has," *MVGN* 7 (1888): 169–236, esp. 182; Carl August Barack, ed., *Ein Lobgedicht auf Nürnberg aus dem*

Jahre 1490 von dem Meister-Sänger Kunz Has (Nuremberg, 1858), 36. Cf. John T. Noonan, *Bribes* (New York, 1984), 139 ff.

14. Richard Jecht, "Die Pflichten eines mittelalterlichen Bürgermeisters; Das Traktat des Görlitzer Stadtschreibers Johannes Frauenfeld 1476," *Deutsche Geschichtsblätter* 18 (1909): 89–102, esp. 94; Johannes Rothe, *Ratsgedichte*, ed. Herbert Wolf (Berlin, 1971), 47. On the metaphor of the body politic, see the extensive overview of the literature in Dietmar Peil, *Untersuchungen zur Staats- und Herrschaftsmetaphorik in literarischen Zeugnissen von der Antike bis zur Gegenwart* (Munich, 1983); on civil servants as hands, see 420–21, 331–32, and 333–37. On the late medieval reception of John of Salisbury, see Amnon Linder, "The Knowledge of John of Salisbury in the Later Middle Ages," *Studi medievali* 18 (1977): 315–66; and Jean-Philippe Genet, "Ecclesiastics and Political Theory in Late Medieval England," in Barrie Dobson, ed., *The Church, Politics and Patronage in the Fifteenth Century* (Gloucester, 1984), 23–44.

15. On the metaphor of greased or oiled hands, see Frederic C. Tubach, *Index Exemplorum* (Helsinki, 1969), 191–92; Thomas Crane, ed., *The Exempla of Jacques de Vitry* (London, 1890), 15; Noonan, *Bribes*, 179, 262–63, and, for the use of the phrase in the fourteenth century, 270.

16. On the various applications of the "pfennig salve," see Ignaz von Zingerle, *Die deutschen Sprichwörter im Mittelalter* (Vienna, 1864), 112–13; Adalbert von Keller, ed., *Fasnachtsspiele aus dem 15. Jahrhundert*, vol. 2 (Stuttgart, 1853), 1000; Aloys Schulte, *Geschichte der grossen Ravensburger Handelsgesellschaft 1380–1530*, 3 vols. (Stuttgart, 1921–23), vol. 3, 9; Johann von Morsheim, *Spiegel des Regiments*, ed. Karl Goedecke (Stuttgart, 1856), 16. On the author, see Manfred Lemmer, "Johann von Morschheim," in Kurt Ruh et al. eds., *Verfasserlexikon der deutschen Literatur des Mittelalters*, vol. 4 (Berlin, 1983).

17. Hubert Drüppel, *Judex Civitatis: Zur Stellung des Richters in der hoch- und spätmittelalterlichen Stadt* (Cologne , 1981), 234; cf. Berent Schwineköper, *Der Handschuh im Recht, Ämterwesen, Brauch und Volksglauben*, 2nd ed. (Sigmaringen, 1981), 62; on gloves and bribe money, see 130 and 135; biblical quotation translated from the text of Kurrelmeyer, *Die erste deutsche Bibel*, vol. 1, 102.

18. Rothe, *Ratsgedichte*, 71–72.

19. Michael Evans, "Two Sources for Maimed Justice," *Source: Notes in the History of Art* 2 (1982): 12–15. On the illustrated manuscripts, see Fritz Saxl, "Aller Tugenden und Laster Abbildung," in Arpad Weixlgaertner and Leo Planiscig, eds., *Festschrift für Julius Schlosser* (Zurich, 1927), 116–21, and "A Spiritual Encyclopaedia of the Later Middle Ages," *JWCI* 5 (1942): 82–142.

20. Erasmus of Rotterdam, *Institutio principis christiani* (Paderborn, 1968), 116–17; Dennis E. Curtis and Judith Resnik, "Images of Justice," *Yale Journal*, 96 (1987): 1727–72, esp. 1751; Michael Evans, "Two Sources for Maimed Justice," 14; Andreas Alciatus, *Emblematum Libellus* (Paris, 1542), 135–36; illustration from Thomas Murner, *Die Schelmenzunft*, ed. M. Spanier (Berlin, 1925), 60. Erasmus has the prince make a particular remark about officials as his larcenous and violent hands: "non possum meorum omnium continere manus." Erasmus, *Institutio principis christiani*, 162. Cf. Natalie Zemon Davis, *The Gift in Sixteenth-Century France* (Madison, Wisc., 2000),

90–92, which, however, does not address the medieval prehistory of this pictorial tradition.

21. Sebastian Franck, *Erste namenlose Sprichwörtersammlung vom Jahre 1532*, ed. Friedrich Latendorf (Hildesheim, 1970), 49; on accusations of corruption using this expression, see *Chroniken der deutschen Städte*, vol. 3 (Leipzig, 1869), 132. The Nuremberg chronicler Heinrich Deichsler noted similarly in 1505 about the trial of a municipal official that he had "looked through his finger with his companion" (durch die vinger gesehen mit seinem gesellen); *Chroniken der deutschen Städte*, vol. 11, 689.

22. Theodor von Karajan, ed., *Michel Beheims Buch von den Wienern 1462–1465* (Vienna, 1843), 206–7. See Albert Müller, "Stigma und Stigmatisierungstechniken im Spätmittelalter: Zur symbolischen Bekämpfung aufständischer Untertanen am Beispiel Michel Beheims 'Buch von den Wienern,'" in *Alltag der Symbole, Symbole des Alltags: Festschrift für Harry Kühnel zum 65. Geburtstag* (Vienna, 1995), 323–47, esp. 331.

23. Now in the Bibliotheca Casanatense in Rome, Codex Cas. 1404, f. 33r. See the precise list of illustrations in Saxl, "Aller Tugenden und Laster Abbildungen," 116–21, esp. 120, and the parallel discussion in his "Spiritual Encyclopaedia of the Later Middle Ages," 82–142, esp. 100, Plate 24.

24. See the compilation in Frederic C. Tubach, *Index Exemplorum* (Helsinki, 1969), 224; on the motif of the judgment of Cambyses in German chess books of the fourteenth and fifteenth centuries, see Ernst Sievers, "Ein mitteldeutsches Schachbuch," *Zeitschrift für deutsches Altertum* 17 (1874): 189–221, esp. 214; Ferdinand Vetter, ed., *Das Schachzabelbuch Kunrats von Ammenhausen* (Frauenfeld, 1892), 195–96; and Gerard F. Schmidt, ed., *Das Schachzabelbuch des Jacobus de Cessolis* (Berlin, 1961), 46. For the direct connection to *miet*, see Adalbert von Keller, ed., *Gesta Romanorum* (Leipzig, 1841), 22, and Hermann Österley, ed., *Die Gesta Romanorum* (Berlin, 1872), 29. See, more recently, Brigitte Weiske, *Gesta Romanorum: Untersuchungen zu Konzeption und Überlieferung*, 2 vols. (Tübingen, 1992).

25. Hugo van der Velden, "Cambyses for Example," *Simiolus* 23 (1995): 5–39; on the context of Gerard David's painting, see the same author's "Cambyses Reconsidered: Gerard David's *exemplum iustitiae* in the Bruges Town Hall," ibid., 40–63; for numerous further examples, see Dennis E. Curtis and Judith Resnik, "Images of Justice," 1753; and Otto von Simson, "Gerard Davids Gerechtigkeitsbild und der spätmittelalterliche Humanismus," in Friedrich Piel and Jörg Träger, eds., *Festschrift für Wolfgang Braunfels* (Tübingen, 1977), 349–56.

26. Barack, *Des Teufels Netz*, 269 ("Aber doert hands pin am end / daz Got boes amptlüt schend"), and 268 ("Die armen tuot man schinden"); Morsheim, *Spiegel des Regiments*, 18–19. Cf. Noonan, *Bribes*, on the use of the motif in the sermons of Hugh Latimer before Edward VI, 315; see also Noonan, *Bribes*, 298.

27. Sebastian Brant, *Das Narrenschiff: Nachdruck der Erstausgabe 1494* (Tübingen, 1968), 324. See Simson, "Gerard Davids Gerechtigkeitsbild," 2–3, which points to the direct parallels between the woodcut in the 1495 edition of Brant's *Narrenschiff* and Gerard David's Brussels picture. On the pictorial tradition of Marsyas in the late Middle Ages and the Renaissance, see the overview in Reinhold Baumstark and Peter Volk, eds., *Apoll schindet Marsyas: Über das Schreckliche in der Kunst*, exhibition catalogue,

Bayrisches Nationalmuseums (Munich, 1995). The punishment of Sisamnes also appears in the illustrations to the German edition of Petrarch's *De remediis utriusque fortunae* (*Von der artzney bayder glück*), which was originally supposed to appear in Augsburg in 1521 with a preface by Sebastian Brants. It comments upon chapter 47, "Von den titeln der empter" (On titles of office). See Franciscus Petrarcha, *Von der Artzney bayder Glück*, ed. Manfred Lemmer (Leipzig, 1983), Afterword, 195–96.

28. Quoted in Rosemarie Aulinger, *Das Bild des Imperial Diets im 16. Jahrhundert* (Göttingen, 1980), 277. Cf. also Edgar Wind, "The Flaying of Marsyas," in his *Pagan Mysteries in the Renaissance* (New Haven, Conn., 1958).

29. Guido Kisch, *Recht und Gerechtigkeit in der Medaillenkunst*, Abhandlungen der Heidelberger Akademie der Wissenschaften, phil. hist. Klasse (Heidelberg, 1955), 69 and 123; and Edward Gans and Guido Kisch, "The Cambyses Justice Medal," *Art Bulletin* 29 (June 1947): 121–23.

30. Enea Silvio Piccolomini, *Von höfen/hoffleuten vund dienern der Fürsten* (n.p., 1529), f. 27. Similarly, in another passage, he notes that the tablecloths at court were so dirty that one could not use them to clean one's hands after a meal but was forced to wipe them on one's clothes instead. That was why courtiers' garments were usually greasy in front (f. 23). On the dissemination of Piccolomini's writings, see Paul Weinig, *Aeneam suscipite, Pium recipite: Aeneas Silvius Piccolomini: Studien zur Rezeption eines humanistischen Schriftstellers im Deutschland des 15. Jahrhundert* (Wiesbaden, 1998).

31. John Najemy, "The Republic's Two Bodies: Body Metaphors in Italian Renaissance Political Thought," in Alison Brown, ed., *Language and Images in Renaissance Italy* (Oxford, 1995), 237–62, esp. 241–42; on monsters, see 246.

32. As one example among many, see the tale in Walter Map, *De Nugis curialium*, ed. C. N. Brooke et al. (Oxford, 1983), 213–14 (the queen tries to seduce the knight Galo with gifts) and 225 (she seeks to avenge herself for Galo's rejection by means of a gift promised her by the king). The epigram "femina quae accipit se vendit; femina quae dat se dedit" already appears in Franciscan sermons of the early fourteenth century. The version quoted here comes from Juan Luis Vives, *De institutione femine Christianae*, vol. 1, ed. C. Fantazzi and C. Matheeusen, 2 vols. (Leiden, 1996), 134. For a different version by Andreas Capellanus, see P. G. Walsh, ed., *Andreas Cappellanus on Love* (London, 1982). See also Michael Camille, *The Medieval Art of Love* (London, 1998), chapter 2.

33. John of Salisbury, *Policraticus*, ed. Cary Nederman (Cambridge, 1990), V, 10 (90–91 and 185); see also Noonan, *Bribes*, 158. John of Salisbury varies an even older motif here; cf. Sallust, *De coniuratione Catilina* 1, 11.

34. Literally, "si sint mietnemer" (they are takers of *miet*); Franz Pfeiffer, ed., *Das Buch der Natur von Konrad von Megenberg* (Stuttgart, 1861), 196–97. Megenberg's work, which was written in the mid-fourteenth century, enjoyed extraordinarily wide dissemination in the fifteenth century and went through seven editions between 1475 and 1499. On Konrad's references to Vincent of Beauvais, Thomas of Cantimpré, and Albertus Magnus, see Manfred Günther Scholz, "Quellenkritik und Sprachkompetenz im 'Buch der Natur,'" in *Festschrift für Walter Haug und Burkart Wachinger*, vol. 2 (Tübingen, 1992), 925–41; on the role of Helinand of Froidmont and Vincent of Beauvais in the dissemination of *Policraticus*, see Amnon Linder, "The Knowledge of John of Salisbury in the Later Middle Ages," *Studi medievali* 18 (1977): 315–66, esp. 324–25.

35. Oskar Pausch, *Das älteste italienisch-deutsche Sprachbuch. Eine Überlieferung aus dem Jahre 1424 nach Georg von Nürnberg* (Vienna, 1972), 55, where the Venetian word *el chastron* is translated as "Büttel, Scherge" (beadle, catchpole). The Munich manuscript of the language textbook compiled in 1424 lays it on even thicker with an ironic Italian-German dialogue: "Du pist alz diemutigt ich gelaub du seist v(er)sniten / E no son chastrado ma e son obediente p(er) natura—ich pin nicht auss gesniten aber ich pin naturleich unt(er)tenigt" (You are all too submissive, I think you must be castrated / No, I am not castrated but I am obedient by nature).

36. *Policraticus*, III, 6, V, 10 and VIII, 12 (19–21; see also 90 and 185). He already takes up the theme of deception and lying as a poisoned drink in the first section of book I (9).

37. Eugen Gehr, "Die Fürstenlehren des Johannes von Indersdorf für Herzog Albrecht III. von Baiern München (1436–1460)," Ph.D. diss., University of Freiburg im Bresigau, 1979; Gerd Brinkhus, *Eine bayrische Fürstenspiegelkompilation des 15. Jahrhunderts* (Munich, 1978), 84, 93–94; Jakob Wimpfeling, "Agatharchia," in Bruno Singer, *Der Fürstenspiegel in Deutschland im Zeitalter des Humanismus und der Reformation* (Munich, 1981), 229–49, esp. 241 and 246; see also 184–85; Erasmus, *Institutio principis christiani*, 124–27 and 144–45; Baldessare Castiglione, *The Book of the Courtier* (Harmondsworth, 1976), 288–89; on the androgynous courtier as a dangerous figure, see 61, 94–97, 109–10; see also Agrippa von Nettesheim, *De incertitudine et vanitate scientiarium atque artium, Declamatio*, ed. Joachim Wolgast (Berlin, 1993), 161–62, 169, on prostitution and patronage see 148–49. On this topos, cf. Jonathan Goldberg, *Sodometries: Renaissance Texts, Modern Sexualities* (Princeton, N.J., 1992), 57–59. On the dissemination of Castiglione's work, see Peter Burke, *The Fortunes of the "Courtier"* (Oxford, 1995).

38. Robert Steele, ed., *Secretum secretorum cum glossis et notulis* (Oxford, 1920), and M. A. Manzalaoui, ed., *Secretum Secretorum: Nine English Versions* (Oxford, 1977). On the dissemination and history of the text, see Pseudo-Aristotle, *The Secret of Secrets: Sources and Influence*, ed. W. F. Ryan and Charles B. Schmitt (London, 1982), and William Eamon, *Science and the Secrets of Nature: Books of Secrets in Medieval and Early Modern Culture* (Princeton, N.J., 1994), 45–53; on German translations, see Hiltgart von Hürnheim, *Mittelhochdeutsche Prosaübersetzung des Secretum Secretorum*, ed. Reinhold Moeller (Berlin, 1963); Wolfgang Hirth, "Studien zu den Gesundheitslehren des sogenannten Secretum Secretorum," Ph.D. diss., University of Heidelberg, 1969; and Friedrich Wurms, "Studien zu den lateinischen und deutschen Prosafassungen des Secretum Secretorum," Ph.D. diss., University of Hamburg, 1970. On the dissemination of individual passages in the form of "familiar quotations," see Carl Selmer, "Eine spätmittelhochdeutsche und lateinische pseudoaristotelische Spruchsammlung," *PMLA* 56 (1941): 627–32.

39. Brinkhus, *Bayrische Fürstenspiegelkompilation*, 93, with sources of the exact quotes; *Aristotelis Heimlichkeit*, illustrated manuscript on paper of 1476, from the collection of the Basel jurist and book collector Remigius Faesch, in UB Basel, call number O II 26. On the deleterious effects of consorting with women, see f. 13v; on the necessity of secret informers, f. 13r; on corrupt couriers, f. 35v–36r.

40. *Aristotelis Heimlichkeit*, f. 14r.

41. Wilhelm Dick, *Die Gesta Romanorum* (Leipzig, 1890), 10–11; on the German

version, see Hermann Österley, ed., *Die Gesta Romanorum* (Berlin, 1872), 11; on the dissemination of the motif, see Tubach, *Index Exemplorum*, 295 (no. 3830), and Wilhelm Hertz, "Die Sage vom Giftmädchen," in his *Gesammelte Abhandlungen*, ed. Friedrich von der Leyen (Stuttgart, 1905).

42. Morsheim, *Spiegel des Regiments*, 14 f.; Geiler von Kaysersberg, *De arbore humana: Von dem menschlichen Baum* (Strasbourg, 1521), f. 159v. He continues, noting that the holy fathers had recommended that men should avoid the society of bishops and women, for both brought fear and misery. On the history of the motif, see Helmuth Kiesel, *Bei Hof, bei Höll: Untersuchungen zur literarischen Hofkritik von Sebastian Brant bis Friedrich Schiller* (Tübingen, 1979).

43. "Ich schem mich und verdreust mich die ding so kündig sein / zu erzeln mit was scheltworten diser alt und dückisch verborgen / oder heymliche weg vergifftet hab," Petrarch, *Von der Artzney bayder Glück*, book 1, chap. 57.

44. In the life of Judas from the 1330 lectionary in the Schaffhausen municipal library, Judas secretly (*haimlich*) murders the son of a king, and as the custodian of the money of Jesus' disciples he also acts in secret (*gehaim*); quoted in Friedrich Ohly, *Der Verfluchte und der Erwählte* (Opladen, 1976), 140–43. One finds the same choice of words in the rhymed life of Judas in Alfred Heinrich, ed., *Johannes Rothes Passion* (Breslau, 1906), 108 and 109, and in the story of Judas in the Alsatian *Legenda Aurea* of the later fourteenth century; Ulla Williams and Werner Krapp-Williams, eds., *Die Elsässische Legenda Aurea*, vol. 1, *Das Normalcorpus* (Tübingen, 1980), 216 and 217. This text was extraordinarily widely disseminated (54 manuscripts from the Upper Rhine and South German region alone, and 13 printed editions before 1521). On the popularity of the Judas legend in the late Middle Ages, see Paul Franklin Baum, "The Medieval Legend of Judas Iscariot," *PMLA* 31 (1916): 481–632; Paul Lehmann, "Judas Ischariot in der lateinischen Legendenüberlieferung des Mittelalters," in his *Erforschung des Mittelalters*, vol. 2, (Stuttgart, 1959), 229–85; Peter Dinzelbacher, *Judastraditionen* (Vienna, 1977); and Franz Josef Worstbrock, "Judaslegende," in Kurt Ruh, ed., *Verfasserlexikon der Literatur des Mittelalters*, vol. 4 (1983), 882–87. See also Christoph Huber, "Mittelalterliche Ödipus-Varianten," in Johannes Janota et al., eds., *Festschrift Walter Haug und Burghart Wachinger*, vol. 1 (Tübingen, 1992), 165–99. Cf. the image of Judas on the Herrenberg Altar of Jörg Ratgeb (1519), where he is shown with twisted posture, a fly in front of his mouth (the devil), fashionable dress, attributes of vice (dice and playing cards), and an erect penis; Dinzelbacher, *Judastraditionen*, Plate 6, 33.

45. Gille and Spriewald, *Die Gedichte des Michel Beheim*, vol. 2, 160–63. See also Stephan von Landskron, *Die Hymelstrasz*, ed. Gerardus Johannes Jaspers (Augsburg, 1494; reprint, Amsterdam, 1979), f. 2v. On the close association between *avaritia* and *simonia* in late medieval catechetic literature, see also Noonan, *Bribes*, 265. In fifteenth-century German Bible translations, the word *Geytigkait* stands not for parsimony (*Geiz*), but rather for sexual desire and greed for money, honor, and worldly pleasures; Ernst Gössel, "Der Wortschatz der ersten deutschen Bibel," Ph.D. diss., University of Giessen, 1933, 18–19.

46. Gille and Spriewald, *Die Gedichte des Michel Beheim*, vol. 2, 160; Morsheim, *Spiegel des Regiments*, 4, 9.

47. For an example, see the Alsfeld Passion play, in which Judas, whom Caiphas is

paying his wages, complains, "The penny is red! This one is sick!" (Der pennigk ist roit! Disser ist krangk!) Others have holes, are black, are made completely of lead, or have "the wrong marking" (eyn falsch zeychen); quotes from Karl Tscheuschner, "Die deutsche Passionsbühne und die deutsche Malerei des 15. und 16. Jahrhunderts in ihren Wechselbeziehungen," *Repertorium für Kunstwissenschaft* 27 (1904): 289–307, esp. 306–7.

48. Nikolaus von Dinkelsbühl, "Von den czehen poten ein tractat" (1423), printed in Karin Baumann, *Aberglaube für Laien: Zur Programmatik und Überlieferung mittelalterlicher Superstitionenkritik* (Würzburg, 1981), 495–680, esp. 638; on unjust or corrupt judges, see 645–46, on usury; 650–51. Nikolaus was one of the most influential doctors of the Church in the German-speaking region during the late Middle Ages. On the dissemination of his texts in Latin and German editions, see the overview and bibliography in Klaus Grubmüller, "Geistliche Übersetzungsliteratur im 15. Jahrhundert," in Hartmut Boockmann, ed., *Kirche und Gesellschaft im Heiligen Römischen Reich des 15. und 16. Jahrhunderts* (Göttingen, 1994), 59–74.

49. Anonymous handbook for confessors (*Beichtspiegel*), *Die zehen gepot gots,* printed in Baumann, *Aberglaube für Laien,* 681–831, here 821.

50. Munich, Bayrische Staatsbibliothek Ms. clm 8729 and clm 11969, printed in Egino Weidenhiller, *Untersuchungen zur deutschsprachigen katechetischen Literatur des späten Mittelalters, nach den Handschriften der bayrischen Staatsbibliothek* (Munich, 1965), 56–78, here 60–61. The *Speculum* clearly points to an urban context and audience, for instance, when the betrayal of secrets and oath-breaking are explained using the example: "furthermore, when he reveals something secret from the council" (item so er etwas haimlichs offenbart aus dem radt), 71. On the definition of simony and heresy (*Ketzerei*), see Georg Steer et al., eds., *Die "Rechtssumme Bruder Bertholds,"* 4 vols. (Tübingen, 1980–87), vol. 3, 1390–91, and vol. 4, 1964–93; the sale of secular office is also addressed there, vol. 4, 1978. On the canon law debates surrounding simony, see Anton Leinz, *Die Simonie* (Freiburg im Breisgau, 1901), and Joseph Weitzel, *Begriff und Erscheinungsformen der Simonie bei Gratian und den Dekretisten* (Munich, 1967). See the overview of simony as heresy, 33–38, and on the equation of simony with a crime against the crown beginning in the twelfth century (because of its origins and *perversitate,* simony was considered the worst of ecclesiastical offenses), see 66. On early fourteenth–century polemics against Pope Boniface VIII as a simoniac, usurer, and sodomite, see Noonan, *Bribes,* 254–63; on the use of the term by Wyclif and Hus, see 279 ff. and 291 ff.

51. Quoted in Karin Schneider, *Der "Trojanische Krieg" im späten Mittelalter: Deutsche Trojaromane des 15. Jahrhunderts* (Berlin, 1968), 36, 88–89, and 100; Ulrich Füetrer, *Der Trojanerkrieg: Aus dem "Buch der Abenteuer,"* ed. Edward G. Fichtner (Munich, 1968); Horst Brunner, ed., *Die deutsche Trojaliteratur des Mittelalters und der Frühen Neuzeit* (Wiesbaden, 1990), on "Symon," see 292. Cf. Hans Fromm, "Aeneas der Verräter," in *Festschrift Walter Haug und Burghart Wachinger,* vol. 2, 139–63.

52. Thomas Murner, *Die Schelmenzunft,* ed. M. Spanier (Berlin, 1925), 41.

53. Cf. Lothar Graf zu Dohna, *Reformatio Sigismundi: Beiträge zum Verständnis einer Reformschrift des 15. Jahrhunderts* (Göttingen, 1960), 77; and Clemens Bauer, "Der Wucher-Begriff der Reformatio Sigismundi," in *Aus Stadt- und Wirtschaftsgeschichte*

Südwestdeutschlands: Festschrift für Erich Maschke zum 75. Geburtstag (Stuttgart, 1975), 110–17.

54. See the extensive treatment in Peter von Moos, "Das Öffentliche und das Private im Mittelalter," in Gerd Melville and Peter von Moos, eds., *Das Öffentliche und das Private in Mittelalter und Früher Neuzeit* (Cologne, 1997), 3–83. Many thanks to Peter von Moos for permitting me to read his essay before publication.

55. Heinrich Koller, ed., *Reformation Kaiser Sigmunds* (Stuttgart, 1964), 60, 106, 152 (priests as sodomites), 100 (*miet* as election bribe), 143 and 195 (*miet* as bribery of the bishop), 200 (*miet* as perverted alms), see also 134, 139, and passim; on the formulation in the printed edition of 1476, see 135. See also Dohna, *Reformatio Sigismundi*; Karl Mommsen, "Die Reformatio Sigismundi und die Schweiz," *SZG* 20 (1970): 71–91; further literature in Hartmut Boockmann, "Zu den Wirkungen der 'Reform Kaiser Siegmunds,'" in Bernd Moeller et al., eds., *Studien zum städtischen Bildungswesen des späten Mittelalters und der frühen Neuzeit* (Göttingen, 1983), 112–35; on the expansion of the concept of simony, see Bauer, *Der Wucher-Begriff*, 111–12.

56. See the overview of reform writings from the Upper Rhine region in Klaus Lauterbach, *Geschichtsverständnis, Zeitdidaxe und Reformgedanke an der Wende zum 16. Jahrhundert: Das oberrheinische "buchli der hundert capiteln" im Kontext des spätmittelalterlichen Reformbiblizismus* (Freiburg im Breisgau, 1985), 47 ff.; on the urban field of influence of the *Reformatio* and the striking parallels to the dissemination and reception of the *Schachzabelbuch* as a textbook on the estates, see Koller, *Reformation Kaiser Sigmunds*, 36–37 and 38–39, and Lauterbach, *Geschichtsverständnis*, 46 ff. The text has been edited by Annelore Franke and Gerhard Zschäbitz as *Das Buch der Hundert Kapitel und der vierzig Statuten des sogenannten Oberrheinischen Revolutionärs* (Berlin, 1974).

57. Wilhelm Rem, "Cronica Newer geschichten," in *Chroniken der deutschen Städte*, vol. 25 (Leipzig, 1896), 12–13, and 86. Rem emphasizes the "unspeakable" nature of the events, 12.

58. "Chronik des Jörg Bräu," in *Chroniken der deutschen Städte*, vol. 29 (Leipzig, 1906), 20–21. Anna Laminit at any rate received a visit from Luther on his way home from Rome in 1511; Martin Luther, *Tischreden*, vol. 6 (Weimar, 1921), no. 7005, 320; briefer version in vol. 4 (Weimar, 1916), no. 4925, 582–83. On the confidence woman Anna Laminit, see Lyndal Roper, *The Holy Household: Women and Morals in Reformation Augsburg* (Oxford, 1988), 262–63, with additional bibliography.

59. Reformation pamphlet literature took up this expanded definition of simony and usury and further broadened it; see, for example, the association of *simonei* with Judas's thirty pieces of silver and his practices in the pamphlet "Ain strafred und ein unterricht wie des bapst junger auf geiz hond zu gericht," which was published around 1524 and has Judas himself report on the particular character of his *simonei*. Reproduced in Oskar Schade, ed., *Satiren und Pasquille aus der Reformationszeit*, 3 vols. (Hanover, 1855–58, reprint, Hildesheim, 1966), vol. 2, 177–89.

60. Lauterbach, *Geschichtsverständnis*, 211; see also 270.

Chapter 4

1. Rochus von Liliencron, ed., *Die historischen Volkslieder der Deutschen*, vol. 2 (Leipzig, 1866), no. 129, 23–27. On Crusade propaganda against Charles the Bold, see Claudius Sieber-Lehmann, *Spätmittelalterlicher Nationalismus: Die Burgunderkriege am Oberrhein und in der Eidgenossenschaft* (Göttingen, 1995), 251 ff.; on Montigel, see 253; on the author, see Frieder Schanz in Kurt Ruh et al., eds., *Verfasserlexikon der deutschen Literatur des Mittelalters*, vol. 6, 682–83.

2. Ernst Walder, "Das Torechte Leben von 1477 in der bernischen Politik 1477 bis 1481," *Berner Zeitschrift für Geschichte und Heimatkunde* 45 (1983), 74–134, esp. 103.

3. Supplement to "Chronik des Hektor Mülich: Prozess und Hinrichtung des Ulrich Schwarz," in *StChr*, vol. 22 (Leipzig, 1892), 438–40. Cf. the references to *gemein* and *eigen nutz* in the extensive letter of justification that the council sent to the emperor after Schwarz's execution, 441–42. On a parallel use of the pair of terms in Fricker's chronicle of the *Twingherrenstreit*, see Regula Schmid, *Reden, rufen, Zeichen setzen: Politisches Handeln während des Berner Twingherrenstreits 1469–1471* (Zurich, 1995), 122–26.

4. *Chroniken der deutschen Städte*, vol. 22, 421.

5. Printed in Anhang II, "Fortsetzungen zur Chronik des Hektor Mülich," in *Chroniken der deutschen Städte*, vol. 22, 368–75. On Schwarz, see Georg Panzer, *Ulrich Schwarz, der Zunftbürgermeister von Augsburg 1422–1478* (Bamberg, 1914), and Jörg Rogge, *Für den Gemeinen Nutzen: Politisches Handeln und Politikverständnis von Rat und Bürgerschaft in Augsburg im Spätmittelalter* (Tübingen, 1996), 48–99, esp. 76 ff.

6. Cf. Hartmut Boockmann, "Spätmittelalterliche deutsche Stadt-Tyrannen," *Blätter für deutsche Landesgeschichte* 119 (1983): 73–91; and the remarks in Gerhard Fouquet, "Die Affäre Niklas Muffel: Die Hinrichtung eines Nürnberger Patriziers im Jahre 1469," *VSWG* 84 (1996): 459–500.

7. See the complaints and grievances of the provincial estates (*Landschaft*) in March 1489 in Ernst Gagliardi, ed., *Dokumente zur Geschichte des Bürgermeisters Hans Waldmann*, 2 vols. (Basel, 1911–13), vol. 2, 9–11, in the "Höngger" and the so-called *Stadtzürcher Bericht* on the uprising, 468–69, 406; the text of the sumptuary edict is in vol. 1, 310–15.

8. The text of the bill of indictment is printed in Gagliardi, *Dokumente*, vol. 2, 32–33; see also vol. 1, clxx–clxxi, 178, 452, 504. On April 22, 1489, council messengers from Bern reported on these rumors; vol. 2, 377.

9. Interrogation of Hans Wunderlich, text in Gagliardi, *Dokumente*, vol. 2, 97.

10. Translator's note: The present-day meaning of *ketzer* is "heretic." There is a parallel to the English word *bugger*, which in the medieval period also referred to a heretic and took on its current meaning only in the early modern period.

11. For a detailed description of the execution, see the so-called *Stadtzürcher Bericht* in Gagliardi, *Dokumente*, vol. 2, 445–46; notes on Waldmann's property and its sale, 85 f., 217–25, 256–59; on the banquet that at once marked the end of the revolt and was a gift to the new mayor, see 366.

12. Paul Hinschius, *System des katholischen Kirchenrechts mit besonderer Rücksicht auf Deutschland*, 6 vols. (Berlin, 1878; reprint, Graz, 1959), here vol. 2, 412–17. The Basel

municipal accounts accordingly record the proceeds from ecclesiastical livings, out of which the university professors were paid, as *pensiones.* See, for example, Bernhard Harms, ed., *Der Stadthaushalt Basels im ausgehenden Mittelalter: Die Jahresrechnungen 1360–1535*, 3 vols. (Tübingen, 1909–13), vol. 3, 220 (1511–12). For an overview, see Josef Rosen, "Die Universität Basel im Stadthaushalt 1460–1535," in his *Finanzgeschichte Basels im späten Mittelalter: Gesammelte Beiträge 1971–1989* (Wiesbaden, 1991), 34–115, 70–73; and Guy Marchal, *Die Statuten des weltlichen Kollegiatstifts St. Peter in Basel* (Basel, 1972), 341–42, 383–84.

13. On Strasbourg, see Peter-Johannes Schuler, "Reformation des geistlichen Gerichts zu Strassburg: Eine Reformschrift aus der Mitte des 15. Jahrhunderts," *Francia* 9 (1981): 177–214, quotations on 196 and 206; Peter S. Lewis, ed., *Ecrits politiques de Jean Juvénal des Ursins*, vol. 1 (Paris, 1978), 533; quoted here from Peter S. Lewis, "Les pensionnaires de Louis XI," in Bernard Chevalier and Philippe Contamine, eds., *La France à la fin du 15ᵉ siècle* (Paris, 1985), 167–81, esp. 169.

14. Cf. *Schweizerisches Idiotikon*, vol. 4, 1394, where *pensioner* is defined as a person "who receives some pay from someone and yet is obliged to do nothing for it (die etwas besoldung von eim hat und dennoht etwas ze tuen nit verpflicht ist); for the military sphere, see Fritz Redlich, *The German Military Enterpriser and His Work Force: A Study in European Economic and Social History*, 2 vols. (Wiesbaden, 1964–65), vol. 1, 327–30.

15. Sieber-Lehmann, *Spätmittelalterlicher Nationalismus*, 228; Karl Stettler, *Ritter Niklaus von Diesbach, Schultheiss von Bern* (Bern, 1924), 128.

16. Cf. Stettler, *Ritter Niklaus von Diesbach*, 132. Diebold Schilling, *Berner Chronik*, vol. 1 (Bern, 1893), 164–65. On Schilling as a pension recipient, see Peter Rück, "Diebold Schilling für des Kaisers Sache," in *Die Schweizer Bilderchronik des Luzerners Diebold Schilling* (Lucerne, 1981), 559–84.

17. *EA*, series 1245–1798, various places of publication, 1839–90, hereafter to be referred to as *EA*. *EA* II, 916, supplement 52 (1474); *EA* II, 526 (1475); on this topic see also Sieber-Lehmann, *Spätmittelalterlicher Nationalismus*, 231–32, and Ernst Walder, "Zur Entstehungsgeschichte des Stanser Verkommnisses und des Bundes der acht Orte mit Freiburg im Uechtland und Solothurn von 1481," *SZG* 32 (1982): 263–92. On the long series of similar ordinances against Austrian pensions in the 1470s and 1480s, see *EA* II, 473, 484, 487, 498, 514, and passim.

18. Gagliardi, *Dokumente*, vol. 1, 113 (no. 99).

19. Bern, Ratsmemorial no. 15, f. 26, 31, 67, quoted in Emmanuel von Rodt, *Die Feldzüge Karls des Kühnen, Herzogs von Burgund, und seiner Erben*, vol. 1 (Schaffhausen, 1843), 199. Many thanks to Claudius Sieber for this reference.

20. Ratsmanual 22, f. 115v and 27, f. 113, both printed in Gagliardi, *Dokumente*, vol. 1, cxi–cxii.

21. Lucerne, Ratsprotokolle 6, f. 202r; quoted in Elisabeth Wechsler, *Ehre und Politik: Ein Beitrag zur Erfassung politischer Verhaltensweisen in der Eidgenossenschaft (1440–1500)* (Zurich, 1991), 235 (1487).

22. Gagliardi, *Dokumente*, vol. 1, 173 (no. 143) and 205–6 (no. 144 aa); on the Austrian payments, see 405 (no. 237), 412 (no. 241) and 422–4 (nos. 245a and b).

23. Gagliardi, *Dokumente*, vol. 1, 429 f. (no. 248); Friedrich Hegi, "Die schweiz-

erischen Provisionäre des Erzherzogs Sigmund von Österreich im Jahre 1488," *Anzeiger für schweizerische Geschichte* 39 (1908): 280–82, esp. 280.

24. Gagliardi, *Dokumente*, vol. 1, 348–57, on payments in cloth (*in certa seta*), 356, 391–401; quotation on 396. Similarly, the Austrian agent in Zurich, Lanz, conveyed to the Innsbruck chancellery an urgent appeal from Swiss pension recipients to keep the written receipts secret; Hegi, "Die schweizerischen Provisionäre," 279.

25. Heinrich Brennwald, *Schweizerchronik*, ed. Rudolf Luginbühl, 2 vols. (Basel, 1910), vol. 2, 307; Petermann Etterlin, *Kronica von der loblichen Eydtgenoschaft, jr harkommen und sust seltzam stritten und geschichten* (Basel, 1507), ed. Eugen Gruber (Aarau, 1965), 277.

26. See the introductory remarks in Gagliardi, *Dokumente*, and, most recently, Valentin Groebner, "'Gemein' und 'geheym': Pensionen, Geschenke und Sichtbarmachung des Unsichtbaren," *SZG* 49 (1999): 445–68.

27. See, for example, Francois de Capitani, *Adel, Bürger und Zünfte im Bern des 15. Jahrhunderts* (Bern, 1982); Hans Conrad Peyer, "Die wirtschaftliche Bedeutung der fremden Dienste für die Schweiz vom 15. bis 18. Jahrhundert," in Jürgen Schneider, ed., *Wirtschaftskräfte und Wirtschaftswege: FS für Hermann Kellenbenz* (Stuttgart, 1978), vol. 2, 701–15, and "Die Anfänge der schweizerischen Aristokratien," in Kurt Messmer and Peter Hoppe, *Luzerner Patriziat* (Lucerne, 1976), 3–28; Martin Koerner, "Les répercussions de l'expansion territoriale sur les finances friburgeoises au XVIe siècle," in Gaston Gaudard, Carl Pfaff, and Roland Ruffieux, eds., *Fribourg, ville et territoire* (Fribourg, 1981), 124–38, and "Der Einfluss der europäischen Kriege auf die schweizerischen Finanzen im 16. Jahrhundert," in Ohmar Pickl, ed., *Krieg, Militärausgaben und wirtschaftlicher Wandel* (Graz, 1980), 37–45; Roger Sablonier, "Etat et structures militaires dans la Confédération autour des années 1480," in *500ème anniversaire de la bataille de Nancy 1477* (Nancy, 1979), 429–47; on Zurich, see Hermann Romer, *Herrschaft, Reislauf und Verbotspolitik: Beobachtungen zum rechtlichen Alltag der Zürcher Solddienstbekämpfung im 16. Jahrhundert* (Zurich, 1995), 94–96.

28. Gagliardi, *Dokumente*, vol. 2, 163–65 and (from the duke of Milan) 175–76; Friedrich Hegi, *Die geächteten Räte des Erzherzogs Sigmund von Österreich und ihre Beziehungen zur Schweiz 1487–1499* (Innsbruck, 1910), 313, 589; for payments in the 1490s, see 471.

29. Gagliardi, *Dokumente*, vol. 1, 44, 57–58, and vol. 2, 367–68.

30. Gagliardi, *Dokumente*, vol. 2, 118–19 (no. 294); report from Bern, vol. 2, 366.

31. Ernst Gagliardi, "Mailänder und Franzosen in der Schweiz, 1495–1499," *Jahrbuch für schweizerische Geschichte* 39 (1914): 1–283, esp. 145–46 and 40 (1916): 1–276; cf. Christian Dietrich, *Die Stadt Zürich und ihre Landsgemeinden während der Bauernunruhen von 1489 bis 1525* (Bern, 1985), 305 n. 83.

32. Gagliardi, "Mailänder und Franzosen," vol. 39, 84–85; cf. also Brennwald, *Schweizerchronik*, vol. 2, 498–99; on the lifting of the prohibition on pensions and the accompanying rumors, see also Hans Morf, "Zunftverfassung, Obrigkeit und Kirche in Zürich von Waldmann bis Zwingli," Ph.D. diss., University of Zurich, 1968, 66 ff.

33. Gagliardi, "Mailänder und Franzosen," vol. 39, 17. See Christian Erni, "Bernische Ämterbefragungen 1495–1522," *Archiv des Historischen Vereins des Kantons Bern* 39 (1947): 3–123, esp. 45; and Catherine Schorer, "Berner Ämterbefragungen.

Untertanenrepräsentation und- mentalität im ausgehenden Mittelalter," *Berner Zeitschrift für Geschichte und Heimatkunde* 51 (1989): 217–53, esp. 233.

34. EA 3/1, 512 and 516. Cf. the description of the activities of the French *bailli* of Dijon at the Swiss Assembly of August 1495 in Lucerne in Ernst Gagliardi, *Der Anteil der Schweizer an den italienischen Kriegen 1494–1516*, vol. 1 (Zurich, 1919), 222–23, and the 1496 list of recipients of imperial pensions, 473. The list names, among others, the Zurich town clerk Ludwig Ammann, the Bernese Thüring Fricker, and the chronicler Petermann Etterlin.

35. Gagliardi, *Anteil der Schweizer*, 283–84, 373. The later prohibitions especially emphasize the connection between the prohibition and the system of enlistment in foreign mercenary armies (*Reislauf*); see also Erni, "Bernische Ämterbefragungen," 47.

36. *EA* 3/2, 11, 21–22, 28–29.

37. Romer, *Herrschaft*, 37; see the overview of prohibitions on pensions and *Reislauf* in Gagliardi, *Anteil der Schweizer*, 492–93.

38. Katharina Simon-Muscheid, "'Schweizergelb' und 'Judasfarbe': Nationale Ehre, Zeitschelte und Kleidermode um die Wende vom 15. zum 16. Jahrhundert," *ZHF* 22 (1995): 317–43, and Gagliardi, *Anteil der Schweizer*, 409–59.

39. *EA* 3/2, 41.

40. Gagliardi, *Anteil der Schweizer*, 484 ff.; see the compilation of contemporary testimonies, 456–59; and Brennwald, *Schweizerchronik*, vol. 2, 384. On the trials of individual pension brokers and military entrepreneurs in Zurich, see Dietrich, *Die Stadt Zürich*, 106.

41. *EA* 3/2, 42 (May 5, 1500); 54 (Zurich, June 23, 1500); 79 (on the session held in Freiburg on November 13, 1500); 88 and 100 (on the Swiss Assembly of January and February 1501); draft regulation on pensions, dated September 16, 1501, 141; unsuccessful consultations concerning pensions and salaries in Schwyz, December 7, 1501, 162.

42. Gagliardi, *Anteil der Schweizer*, 510–11, 513, 521–22, 523; Erni, *Bernische Ämterbefragungen*, 55–58; Karl Dändliker, "Die Berichterstattungen und Anfragen der Zürcher Regierung an die Landschaft in der Zeit vor der Reformation," *Jahrbuch für Schweizer Geschichte* 21 (1896): 41 ff., and *Geschichte der Stadt und des Kantons Zürich*, 2 vols. (Zurich, 1910), vol. 2, 258 ff.; Dietrich, *Die Stadt Zürich*, 106–7; Morf, "Zunftverfassung," 67.

43. The text of the Baden ordinance is printed in *EA* 3/2, 1314–16; see also *EA* 3/2, 234 (Baden, July 20, 1503). For an overview of the diplomatic maneuvering, see Gagliardi, *Anteil der Schweizer*, 549–62.

44. On Schilling see Gagliardi, *Anteil der Schweizer*, 479 n. 377; on Basel see Hans–Georg Wackernagel, "Aus der Frühzeit der Universität," *BZGA* 49 (1950): 8–24, 15, and Peter Ochsenbein, "Politische Publizistik am Oberrhein," in Heinz Rupp and H.–G. Roloff, eds., *Akten des VI. Intern. Germanistenkongresses Basel, 1980*, part 4 (Bern, 1980), 230–36, esp. 236; Brennwald, *Schweizerchronik*, vol. 2, 488.

45. *EA* 3/2, 726–33; Gagliardi, *Novara und Dijon, Höhepunkt und Verfall der schweizerischen Grossmacht* (Zurich, 1907), 204–12; Bruno Amiet, "Die solothurnischen Bauernunruhen in den Jahren 1513 und 1514 und die Mailänderfeldzüge," *Zeitschrift für schweizerische Geschichte* 21 (1941): 653–728; on Lucerne see Messmer and Hoppe, *Luzerner Patriziat*, 70–71; on Bern see Christian Bierbrauer, *Freiheit und Gemeinde im*

Berner Oberland 1300–1700 (Bern, 1991), 239 ff.

46. Bierbrauer, *Freiheit und Gemeinde*, 243; Erni, "Bernische Ämterbefragungen," 70 ff.; and Schorer, "Berner Ämterbefragungen," 223–24, 229.

47. Gagliardi, *Novara und Dijon*, 268–78; *EA* 3/2, 770 ff.

48. Erni, "Bernische Ämterbefragungen," 78–83. The city was so much on the defensive that it even offered to let representatives of the rebellious countryside interrogate the president of Villeneuve. On his fate, see Gagliardi, *Novara und Dijon*, 299 ff.

49. For an extensive account, see Dietrich, *Die Stadt Zürich*, 112 ff.; see also the printed excerpts from witness testimony and accusations in Emil Usteri, *Marignano: Die Schicksalsjahre 1515/16 im Blickfeld der historischen Quellen* (Zurich, 1974), 446–52, 426, and 512.

50. *EA* 3/2, 964; on the debates in autumn and winter 1515, see also 922, 936, 945.

51. "Got welle, das ers trewlichen verdien"; quoted in Usteri, *Marignano*, 106–7. On further lists of recipients of imperial pensions and the problems of transferring money, see 32, 39–40, 134.

52. Quoted in Usteri, *Marignano*, 134 n. 25. In the account of the chronicler Schwinkhart, the Zurich peasant revolts were indeed unleashed in 1515 by gifts and wicked promises from the imperial envoy Dr. Reichenbach; Ludwig Schwinkhart, *Chronik 1506 bis 1521*, ed. Hans von Greyerz (Bern, 1941), 185.

53. Morf, "Zunftverfassung," 51–52; on Berger's career, see 74 ff.

54. StAB Politisches, M 2, no. 41, testimonies before the mayor and council of Lucerne, March 15, 1515, no. 43. On French promises of money in the spring and summer of 1515, see the detailed account in Usteri, *Marignano*, 30 ff.; see also 335–36 and passim.

55. Gagliardi, *Anteil der Schweizer*, 443–44 (1500); *EA* 3/2, 852–53, 856, 861–62; Usteri, *Marignano*, 47, 66, 69. Cf. the remarks on the new coins that Maximilian had minted in 1516 to pay his Swiss mercenaries: "and one piece was estimated at three crowns" (vnd derselbigen stücken eins ward geschetzt für dry kronen); Schwinkhart, *Chronik*, 194–95.

56. StAB Eidgenossenschaft E 1, f. 116 v (1507); E 4, f. 163r (1520).

57. Brennwald, *Schweizerchronik*, vol. 2, 479, 483–84.

58. StAB Politisches, M 2, no. 39 (January 21, 1515, instruction to the Zurich and Basel envoys to the trial of Burkart Sässeli), f. 1r; *EA* 3/2, 766; Schwinkhart, *Chronik*, 155, similarly, 185–86.

59. Staatsarchiv Bern, U.P. 232, 281. Many thanks to Guy Marchal for drawing my attention to this passage. Marchal is currently preparing a publication of his own on Hetzel and his son; see also Arnold Esch, "Mit Schweizer Söldnern auf dem Marsch nach Italien: Das Erlebnis der Mailänderkriege 1510–1515 nach bernischen Akten," *Quellen und Forschungen aus italienischen Archiven und Bibliotheken* 70 (1990): 348–439, 429. Cf. the allusion to the Judas motif in Thüring Fricker's chronicle of the Twingherrenstreit of 1471. On Fricker's technique of denunciation by means of a "net of associations," see Schmid, *Reden, rufen, Zeichen setzen*, 62.

60. Gagliardi, "Mailänder und Franzosen," vol. 39, 144 (1496), and *Anteil der Schweizer*, 414. Translator's note: "Fleischbank" is the word Martin Luther used in his translation of Proverbs 7:22, where the English Bible speaks of "to the slaughter."

61. Brennwald, *Schweizerchronik*, vol. 2, 498; see also Gagliardi, *Anteil der Schweizer*, 551–52; Thomas Murner, *Die Schelmenzunft*, ed. M. Spanier (Berlin, 1925), 60; Schorer, "Berner Ämterbefragungen," 234 and 237; Erasmus, *Adagia*, II 6, 23. The original text of Zwingli's sermon has not survived; see Emil Egli and Georg Finsler, eds., *Huldreich Zwinglis sämtliche Werke*, vol. 1 (Berlin, 1905), 73. We know the sermon only from Heinrich Bullinger, *Reformationsgeschichte*, ed. J. J. Hottinger and H. Vögeli, 3 vols. (Frauenfeld, 1838), vol. 1, 51. Cf. the use of *fleyschpank* as a metaphor for handing over, betrayal, and the sale of flesh in Schwinkhart, *Chronik*, 106, 245, and Schilling, *Berner Chronik*, 433.

62. May 1500, *EA* 3/2, S. 42; see also 3/1, 318 and 324. A report of September 1489 speaks of pensions as dangerous "secret gifts and payments" (heimlichen schenckungen und dienstgelder); *EA* 3/1, S. 332. Cf. *EA* 3/2, 22 and 28–29.

63. *EA* 3/2, 476, 767, 768, 1169–70.

64Emil Egli, *Actensammlung zur Geschichte der Zürcher Reformation 1519–1533* (Zurich, 1879), 11.

65. Brennwald, *Schweizerchronik*, vol. 2, 479 (1500); report of March 16, 1508, by the Freiburg courier Niklaus Lumbard, quoted in Gagliardi, *Anteil der Schweizer*, 724; cf. Brennwald, *Schweizerchronik*, vol. 2, 524–25. On the sack of gold as a body, see also Joachim Köhler, ed., *Die Carolina und ihre Vorgängerinnen*, vol. 2, *Die Bambergische Halsgerichtsordnung* (Halle, 1902), S. Abb. 21, lix, and 114–15. The printed edition of the Bamberg criminal code (*Halsgerichtsordnung*) of 1507 turned the coin-filled vessel into an allegory when a greedy and corrupt judge tortured a money bag.

66. Morf, "Zunftverfassung," 71. On pensions as Italian poison, see also Usteri, *Marignano*, 221.

67. Heinz von Bechwinden, "Reimchronik über den Schwabenkrieg 1499," in Theodor Lorentzen, ed., "Zwei Flugschriften aus der Zeit Maximilian I.," *Neue Heidelberger Jahrbücher* 17 (1913), 139–228, here 182 (*ratzen*), 170–72, 175, 191, 193. On the identification of the author as the Tübingen humanist Heinrich Bebel, see Johannes Haller, *Die Anfänge der Universität Tübingen 1477–1537* (Stuttgart, 1927), and Peter Seibert, *Aufstandsbewegungen in Deutschland 1476–1517 in der zeitgenössischen Reimliteratur* (Heidelberg, 1978), 115–16, 127–28. On the context, see Guy Marchal, "Die Antwort der Bauern: Elemente und Schichtungen des eidgenössischen Geschichtsbewußtseins am Ausgang des Mittelalters," in Hans Patze, ed., *Geschichtsschreibung und Geschichtsbewußtsein im späten Mittelalter* (Sigmaringen, 1987), 758–90, esp. 764. In his *soliloquium*, published in 1505, the Strasbourg humanist Wimpfeling writes that the crude and money-hungry Swiss confederates were worse than the Turks and Hussites; Peter Ochsenbein, "Jakob Wimpfelings literarische Fehde mit den Baslern und Eidgenossen," *BZGA* 79 (1979): 37–65; Guy Marchal, "Bellum justum contra iudicium belli: Zur Interpretation von Jakob Wimpfelings antieidgenössischer Streitschrift 'Soliloquium pro Pace Christianorum,' in Nicolai Bernhard and Quirinus Reichen, eds., *Gesellschaft und Gesellschaften: Festschrift für Ulrich Im Hof* (Bern, 1982), 114–37.

68. Brennwald, *Schweizerchronik*, vol. 2, 346–47. On the history of the motif, see Claudius Sieber-Lehmann and Thomas Wilhelmi, *In Helvetios: Fremd-und Feindbilder in antieidgenössischen Texten von 1386 bis 1532* (Bern, 1998).

69. On the Burgundian wars, see Sieber-Lehmann, *Spätmittelalterlicher National-*

ismus, 148–49, 294 ff.; Hohenburg's confession is reproduced in Heinrich Witte, "Der letzte Puller von Hohenburg: Ein Beitrag zur politischen und Sittengeschichte des Elsasses und der Schweiz im 15. Jahrhundert sowie zur Genealogie des Geschlecht der Puller," *Beiträge zur Landes- und Volkskunde von Elsass-Lothringen* 4 (1895): 1–143, esp. 33; see also Elisabeth Wechsler, *Ehre und Politik: Ein Beitrag zur Erfassung politischer Verhaltensweisen in der Eidgenossenschaft (1440–1500) unter historisch-anthropologischen Aspekten* (Zurich, 1991), 183. On the strict canon law meaning of the term, see Winfried Trusen, "Rechtliche Grundlagen des Häresiebegriffs und des Ketzerverfahrens," in Silvana Seidel Menchi et al., eds., *Ketzerverfolgung im 16. und frühen 17. Jahrhundert* (Wiesbaden, 1992), 1–20 and bibliography; on the accusation of buggery as an anti–Italian stereotype in humanist lampoons around 1500, see Ingrid Rowland, "The Revenge of the Regensburg Humanists," *Sixteenth Century Journal* 25 (1994): 305–22.

70. Hans Krut of Zurich had already been arrested in 1485 for allegedly calling Waldmann a traitor and a sodomite and was sentenced to death by drowning; Gagliardi, *Dokumente*, vol. 1, 270–71.

71. The two witness testimonies are printed in Gagliardi, "Mailänder und Franzosen," 10–11 n. 2.

72. Quoted in Wechsler, *Ehre und Politik*, 208, and Gagliardi, "Mailänder und Franzosen," 121–22. On farther-reaching threatening comparisons between Waldmann and the Lucerne mayor Seiler, against which the latter complained to the town council in November 1497, see Gagliardi, "Mailänder und Franzosen," 174 n. 1.

73. *EA* 3/2, 791, May 1514; Wechsler, *Ehre und Politik*, 236.

74. Quoted in Usteri, *Marignano*, 251. The word *ketzer* retained this particular meaning in the early years of the Reformation. When the Glarn chronicler Fridolin Bäldi noted of the military campaign to Pavia in 1525 that it had been against the *ketzer*, he was more interested in denouncing the enemy as sodomites than in religious matters. See Esch, "Mit Schweizer Söldnern," 435.

75. Gagliardi, *Dokumente*, vol. 2, 350, 506; on Hohenburg, see vol. 1, lv–lvi. See also Heinrich Witte, "Der letzte Puller von Hohenburg," 72 ff. On rumors in Lucerne and Zurich concerning gifts of money to Waldmann and the then mayor Göldli in connection with Richard von Hohenburg's execution, see Gagliardi, *Dokumente*, vol. 2, 85, 189–90.

76. Gagliardi, "Mailänder und Franzosen," vol. 40, 144.

77. Winfried Schulze, "Vom Gemeinnutz zum Eigennutz: Über den Normenwandel in der ständischen Gesellschaft der frühen Neuzeit," *HZ* 243 (1986): 591–626, esp. 597 ff. Cf. Winfried Eberhard, "Der Legitimationsbegriff des 'Gemeinen Nutzens' im Streit zwischen Herrschaft und Genossenschaft im späten Mittelalter," in Jörg Fichte et al., eds., *Zusammenhänge, Einflüsse, Wirkungen: Kongressakten zum Symposium des Mediävistenverbands in Tübingen 1984* (Berlin, 1986), 241–54, and the same author's "'Gemeiner Nutzen' als oppositionelle Leitvorstellung im Spätmittelalter," in Manfred Gerwing and Godehart Ruppert, eds., *Renovatio et Reformatio: Festschrift für Ludwig Hödl* (Münster, 1985), 195–214.

78. Gagliardi, *Anteil der Schweizer*, 674.

79. Report of the Basel commanders, July 9, 1512, StAB Politisches M 1, 4, no. 218.

80. Staatsarchiv Bern, Ratsmanual no. 15, f. 26, 31, 67. Which term was used to refer to the payments was always controversial; on the language used to refer to foreign pensions in Zurich in 1512, cf. Morf, "Zunftverfassung," 48–49.

81. Berchtold Haller, *Bern in seinen Ratsmanualen 1465–1565*, 3 vols. (Bern, 1902), vol. 3, 253.

82. The song about Hans Waldmann, which describes the events of 1489 from the perspective of the insurgent communes on Lake Zurich, does not mention the pensions but rather speaks of the unjust rule (*falschen gewalt*) of the mayor and his advisers, which was Waldmann's undoing; Liliencron, *Die historischen Volkslieder*, vol. 2, no. 174, 269–73, here 271, 273. On the "Waldmann Treaty" and the "Milanese Treaty," which granted certain communal rights to the rural population, see Dietrich, *Die Stadt Zürich*, 112 ff.; and Mireille Othenin-Girard, "Aufstand der Zürcher Landschaft 1489 unter besonderer Berücksichtigung der Beschwerden," *Zürcher Taschenbuch* 107 (1987): 32–54.

83. Morf, "Zunftverfassung," 75–76. On the interrelationships between the military entrepreneurs and the patrician elites, see Esch, "Mit Schweizer Söldnern"; Romer, *Herrschaft*, 47 ff., 123–24, 229–38. Cf. the comment by Jakob Schmid, who was arrested in Zurich in 1519, on the proceedings against pensions: "now they expel a man from the council who took money from the French or some other foreign lord, and tomorrow they put him back in again"; Egli, *Actensammlung*, 14, no. 79. On the unsanctioned acceptance of pensions from the duke of Württemberg by a Zurich bailiff (*Landvogt*), see 15, no. 81; for similar accounts see Otto Sigg, "Aspekte zum Zürcher Solddienst des 16. Jahrhunderts," in Hans Berger et al., eds., *Mundo multa miracula: Festschrift für Hans Conrad Peyer* (Zurich, 1992), 107–14.

84. In March 1521, Zurich introduced a special ordinance according to which gifts to municipal diplomats and troops should go primarily to officeholders; only any remaining surplus was to be distributed among the common people; Egli, *Actensammlung*, 36, no. 154.

85. Quoted in Esch, "Mit Schweizer Söldnern," 377; see the texts of the cards in Paul Heitz, ed., *Neujahrswünsche des 15. Jahrhunderts* (Strasbourg, 1909). A witness later testified to Glaser's words; Glaser was executed on July 23, 1515, after the Köniz uprising. Sixty crowns were equivalent to about 75 florins, a large sum; characteristic here is the insistence on the rhetoric of the traditional New Year's gift. Glaser (or the witness) added at this point that the money had been given to him, "that I may give it to whomever I choose." Only peace and honor were at stake, not obligations or reciprocity.

86. Printed in Usteri, *Marignano*, 32; see Rück, Schilling, and the references to controversial imperial New Year's gifts in Zurich in the spring of 1521 in Egli, *Actensammlung*, 36, no. 155.

87. Cf. Usteri, *Marignano*, 39–40, 106–7.

88. Quoted in Etterlin, *Kronica*, Introduction, 14. He received a strict reprimand from the town council for this comment.

89. Gagliardi, *Anteil der Schweizer*, 815; Bierbrauer, *Freiheit und Gemeinde*, 110; Haller, *Bern in seinen Ratsmanualen*, vol. 2, 89. See also Valerius Anshelm, *Berner*

Chronik, ed. Historischer Verein des Kantons Bern, 6 vols. (Bern, 1884–1901), vol. 4, 180.

Chapter 5

1. Rudolf Wackernagel, *Geschichte der Stadt Basel*, 3 vols. (Basel, 1907–54), vol. 3, 97–104; on Basel's "uniqueness," see 103.

2. StAB Eidgenossenschaft E 1, f. 40a.

3. StAB Eidgenossenschaft E 1, f. 96. The relevant passages in the text were later underlined in red chalk.

4. StAB Politisches M 1,1, no. 6, f. 1v.

5. StAB Eidgenossenschaft E 1, f. 100v. The instruction is undated but must have been written down between July 10 and August 7, 1503.

6. Bernhard Harms, ed., *Der Stadthaushalt Basels im ausgehenden Mittelalter: Die Jahresrechnungen 1360–1535*, 3 vols. (Tübingen, 1909–13), vol. 3, 146. The reading out of the accounts for 1504–5 revealed another formal gift of wine to couriers from the Swiss Confederacy "when the ordinance about the pensions was sworn to because of times of war and the pensions" (als man die ordnung des kriegszlouffen und pension halb geschworen hatt)—namely, six liters of malmsey (157). On the Basel records of the pension letter see also *Basler Urkundenbuch*, ed. August Bernoulli et al., vol. 9 (Basel, 1905), no. 305, 251.

7. StAB Politisches M 1, 1, nos. 40–46.

8. StAB Eidgenossenschaft E 1, f. 116v and 117r.

9. StAB Ratsbücher, Erkanntnisbuch 2/3, f. 37v. According to the yearly account for 1507–8, Mayor Offenburg presented 15 crowns "that the French gave him" to the municipal treasury; the following year 2,568 pfennigs "that were presented to us" were recorded without further explanation as well as 6,096 pfennigs, which Cardinal Schiner had presented to the city's couriers in Lucerne. Harms, *Stadthaushalt*, vol. 1, 372 and 380.

10. Harms, *Stadthaushalt*, vol. 1, 381, and vol. 3, 203.

11. These included some rather substantial amounts: the municipal delegations to the duke of Savoy received a total of 193 crowns as a gift (*geschenckt*), and the bishop of Sitten and Maximilian's councilors gave 30 florins to the town clerk and the master of the guilds (*Zunftmeister*); Harms, *Stadthaushalt*, vol. 3, 385. On the official pensions, see 389, 394; cf. Wackernagel, *Geschichte*, vol. 2/1, 100; and Josef Rosen, *Finanzgeschichte Basels im späten Mittelalter: Gesammelte Beiträge 1971–1989* (Wiesbaden, 1991), 269.

12. In the spring of 1513, Basel's envoy at the Swiss Assembly in Zurich had to insist that his portion of the Milanese pension should be paid out after much delay; StAB Eidgenossenschaft E 2, f. 14r.

13. Josef Rosen, "Eine mittelalterliche Stadtrechnung: Einnahmen und Ausgaben Basels 1360–1535," in his *Finanzgeschichte Basels im späten Mittelalter: Gesammelte Beiträge 1971–1989* (Wiesbaden, 1991), 116–33, esp. 128.

14. Harms, *Stadthaushalt*, vol. 3, 220–21.

15. Harms, *Stadthaushalt*, vol. 3, 239. The city's outlays, which lay between 22,000 and 27,000 lbs. in the years 1510–14, rose to 44,263 lbs. in the yearly accounts for 1514–15 and remained over 40,000 lbs. a year until 1519. And while in these years the municipal treasury generally showed a surplus, at least according to its own balance sheets, in 1520–21, expenses of 60,327 lbs. contrasted with income of only 43,646 lbs. Rosen, "Eine mittelalterliche Stadtrechnung," 128.

16. Of the 50,120 pfennigs (converted into coins) of papal gratifications, 2,918 pfennigs remained and flowed back into the municipal treasury because "a number of men did not wish to accept such money" (etlicher halb so solich gelt nit haben wellen nemmen); Harms, *Stadthaushalt*, vol. 3, 200.

17. Harms, *Stadthaushalt*, vol. 3, 389 and 393–95. See also *BChr*, ed. August Bernoulli et al., 10 vols. (Basel, 1879–1976), vol. 6, 39 and 42.

18. StAB Ratsbücher B 2/3, f. 37v, supplement.

19. StAB Ratsbücher B 2/3, f. 95v; see also f. 132r.

20. On Jakob Meyer, see *HBLS*, vol. 5, 97–98; on his military functions in the years 1510–13, see StAB Politisches M 1, 2, no. 69, 74, 82, 86, and M 1, 3, nos. 164, 170 and (Dijon, 1513) M 2, no. 2. For a more detailed description of this group as an "outside leadership stratum" with an overview of envoy missions, see Hans Füglister, *Handwerksregiment: Untersuchungen und Materialien zur sozialen und politischen Struktur der Stadt Basel in der ersten Hälfte des 16. Jahrhunderts* (Basel, 1981), 186–92.

21. StAB B 2/3, f. 94. A copy of the two pension letters to Meyer issued by Schiner can be found in f. 92–93. The heading "How all pensions from princes, lords or cities were forbidden" (Wie all Pensionen von fürsten, herren oder stätten verboten) was clearly added later.

22. StAB B 2/3, f. 99r. The pension letter of January 7, 1513 to the city is in *Basler Urkundenbuch*, vol. 9, 364, no. 399; see the confirmation of receipt of the pension, dated March 10, 1513, in StAB Missiven A 25, f. 8v.

23. Harms, Stadthaushalt, vol. 3, 227.

24. StAB Missiven A 25, f. 30; Politisches L 1, 13 (incorrectly dated July 24 rather than July 28, 1513; the date of the second letter, July 2, can only be the date of receipt).

25. StAB Ratsbücher B 2/3, f. 99r.

26. StAB Eidgenossenschaft E 2, f. 139; July 1514, f. 239. See also Emil Usteri, *Marignano: Die Schicksalsjahre 1515/16 im Blickfeld der historischen Quellen* (Zurich, 1974), 106.

27. Harms, *Stadthaushalt*, vol. 3, 241.

28. StAB Eidgenossenschaft E 2, f. 122 f. On the negotiations of the alliance with France known as the *Ewige Richtung*, see StAB Missiven A 25, f. 180 ff., and the detailed description in Usteri, *Marignano*, 586–87, which particularly emphasizes Basel's hesitancy to join.

29. See the last section in this chapter.

30. StAB Missiven A 25, f. 12r, a letter from the council to Massimiliano Sforza regarding the *pensione privata* to Peter Offenburg; StAB Politisches M 1, 4 (July 23, 1512).

31. Harms, *Stadthaushalt*, vol. 3, 394 and 377.

32. Receipts for *pensione privata* to the city. *Basler Urkundenbuch*, vol. 9, no. 451, 396 (1517) and no. 465, 412 (1518), and receipts in StAB Missiven A 25, f. 228r; on this

topic, see also Rosen, *Finanzgeschichte Basels*, 269. The mediator was the Lucerne mayor (*Schultheiss*) Jakob von Hertenstein; Missiven A 25, f. 218r (October 24, 1517).

33. StAB Politisches M 1, 7, no. 381.

34. StAB Eidgenossenschaft E 2, f. 92r. There appear to have been greater difficulties with payment the following year; see E 3, f. 222v and 223v. See also StAB Missiven A 25, f. 177v.

35. StAb Politisches M 1, 7, no. 382.

36. StAB Ratsbücher O 2, Urfehdenbuch, f. 109. He was released from custody on January 29 after taking an oath (*Urfehde*) and paying a fine.

37. Friedrich Waga, ed., *Die Welschgattung* (Breslau, 1910), 193, 227–28, 220, 215–16.

38. *Die Welschgattung*, 174–75 (poisonous vapors), 180 and 242 (secret sin).

39. See Valerius Anshelm, *Berner Chronik*, 6 vols. (Bern, 1884–1901), vol. 3, 256. The attack provoked the so-called cold winter campaign of Swiss Confederate volunteers in Ticino.

40. *Berner Chronik*, 192–93, 194, 199 (warning against France and French pensions), 214 (poison), 257 (scorpion, see also the woodcut on p. 26), 265. On the scorpion, cf. Gengenbach's *Narrenschiff vom Bundschuch*, printed in 1514 in Basel, which describes the scorpion as the emblem (*warzeichen*) of the insurgents. Karl Goedecke, ed., *Pamphilus Gengenbach* (Hanover, 1854), 388.

41. Pamphilus Gengenbach, *Der welsch Flusz* (Basel, 1513), reproduced in Goedecke, *Pamphilus Gengenbach*, 3–11, here 4–5. See also *Basler Buchillustrationen 1500–1545*, exhibition catalogue of the Universitätsbibliothek Basel (Basel, 1984), no. 196, 160–62; copies of this pamphlet have survived in Zurich, Colmar, Basel, and Augsburg. On the card game called "flux" or "flüsslis," see *Basler Buchillustrationen*, 160, and Goedecke, *Pamphilus Gengenbach*, 533.

42. Goedecke, *Pamphilus Gengenbach*, 5–6.

43. Ibid., 8.

44. Ibid., 10. On Gruyer's expulsion from Basel in late March 1513, see Ernst Gagliardi, *Novara und Dijon, Höhepunkt und Verfall der schweizerischen Grossmacht* (Zurich, 1907), 28, and StAB Missiven A 25, f. 11r.

45. Zwingli, "Das Fabelgedicht vom Ochsen" and "Der Labyrinth," in Huldreich Zwingli, *Gesammelte Werke*, ed. Emil Egli and Georg Finsler, vol. 1 (Berlin, 1905), 3–22, 53–60.

46. Pamphilus Gengenbach, *Der Alt Eydgenosz*, in Goedecke, *Pamphilus Gengenbach*, 12–22, esp. 14, 16, 20–21. Cf. the play of similar tendency written in Zurich in 1514 in Friedrike Christ–Kutter, ed., *Das Spiel von den alten und den jungen Eidgenossen* (Bern, 1963). See also Guy Marchal, "Die 'Alten Eidgenossen' im Wandel der Zeiten," in *Innerschweiz und frühe Eidgenossenschaft*, vol. 2 (Olten, 1990), 309–406, esp. 319 ff.

47. Pamphilus Gengenbach, *Der Nollhart* (Stuttgart, 1977), 41, 51, 68.

48. Pamphilus Gengenbach, *Die X Alter Dyser Welt*, in Goedecke, *Pamphilus Gengenbach*, 54–76. Originally printed in 1518 in Augsburg, with several reprints by 1520.

49. Gengenbach, *Nollhart*, 84. Pamphilus Gengenbach was born in Basel in 1480 as the son of the printer Ulrich Gengenbach. After a brief period as a journeyman printer in Nuremberg, he returned to Basel, where he is mentioned in the documents beginning in 1507. In 1509 he is first mentioned as a printer and the owner of the Little

Horse Tavern (Zum Rösslein) there. He was a member of the Basel guild of the "Gartner." His first independent works date from 1513. See Karl Lendi, *Der Dichter Pamphilus Gengenbach* (Bern, 1926).

50. Harms, *Stadthaushalt*, vol. 1, 426, 431, 437–38. On the written receipts of French pensions by the mayors Jakob Meyer zum Hasen and Wilhelm Zeigler in the years 1518–20, see *Basler Urkundenbuch*, vol. 9, 412, 424, 436.

51. Harms, *Stadthaushalt*, vol. 1, S. 444.

52. The anonymous Basel chronicler of the Reformation period, presumably a chaplain in Basel, begins his chronicle of the years 1521–26, which he probably started in 1525, with this break with old custom (*alt härkomens*); *BChr*, vol. 7, 247.

53. This was the case in May 1519. StAB Eidgenossenschaft E 4, f. 4r, 14r, 50r. See also Emil Dürr, ed., *Aktensammlung zur Geschichte der Basler Reformation 1519–1534*, vol. 1 (Basel, 1921), 8–9.

54. StAB Ratsbücher B 3, f. 195; printed in Dürr, *Aktensammlung*, vol. 1, 21–22.

55. StAB Ratsbücher B 3, f. 196; in addition the members of the *Sechser* each received six crowns privately. Two additional detailed accounts appear in Dürr, *Aktensammlung*, vol. 1, 24–26. See also Harms, *Stadthaushalt*, vol. 3, 307–8, which lists gifts to the town guards and official council letter–carriers (each received two crowns).

56. StAB Politisches M 1, 7, nos. 422 and 423.

57. Wackernagel, *Geschichte*, vol. 3, 309–10; the instruction to Dichtler appears in StAB Eidgenossenschaft E 5, f. 68r; see also the outlays for his mission at the Lucerne Swiss Assembly in WAB 14, f. 33r; renewed strict prohibition on enlisting mercenary soldiers for the pope appears in Missiven A 26, f. 237. Verdicts against a number of persons for entering foreign military service (and in some cases also for accepting pensions from the duke of Württemberg) appear in *Basler Urkundenbuch*, vol. 9, 434 (1519) and in the Urfehdebücher O 2, f. 290–92 (July 1521) and f. 316–18.

58. StAB Eidgenossenschaft E 5, f. 113, and Dürr, *Aktensammlung*, vol. 1, 28–29.

59. Wackernagel, *Geschichte*, vol. 3, 310; Füglister, *Handwerksregiment*, 263.

60. Anonymous chronicle from the Reformation period, in *BChr*, vol. 7 (Leipzig, 1915), 247–306, esp. 247–48, 251, 255, 256–57; *Chronik des Fridolin Ryff*, in *BChr*, vol. 1, 29.

61. Wackernagel, *Geschichte*, vol. 2/1, 104; vol. 3, 310–12; Friedrich Meyer, *Die Beziehungen zwischen Basel und den Eidgenossen in der Darstellung der Historiographie des 15. und 16. Jahrhunderts* (Basel, 1951), 146. More restrained is the earlier account in Peter Ochs, *Geschichte der Stadt und Landschaft Basel*, vol. 5 (Basel, 1796; 1821), 364–69.

62. Füglister, *Handwerksregiment*, 263–66; cf. Wackernagel, *Geschichte*, vol. 3, 310 ff., esp. 312.

63. Emil Dürr, ed., *Aktensammlung zur Geschichte der Basler Reformation 1519–1534*, vol. 1 (Basel, 1921), 29–32; StAB Ratsbücher B 6, Decreta et Mandata, f. 5r–6r. These texts expressly mention that the incriminated individuals had accepted more than fifteen crowns; see also *BChr*, vol. 1, 29, and the comments of the editor, 30.

64. *Basler Urkundenbuch*, vol. 9, no. 524, S. 459–60.

65. StAB Missiven A 26, f. 10, report from Basel to Fribourg on the investigations. Ruman said in his own defense that he had not meant anyone in particular, but only that a number of people were rumored to have accepted money.

66. Harms, *Stadthaushalt*, vol. 3, 231, 250, 292, 303, for the last time in 1523 as "fronfasten lipding" (an annuity paid four times a year), 325.

67. StAB Ratsbücher O 2, f. 301–2.

68. StAB Ratsbücher O 2, f. 308, released on January 15, 1522; f. 311, April 1, 1522.

69. StAB Ratsbücher f. 306, printed in Dürr, *Aktensammlung*, vol. 1, 32.

70. StAb Ratsbücher K 24, Ratsordnungen 1521–29, f. 4v. Gifts for a "good year" were excepted from the regulation, though. That same year an addition was made to the oath formula for Basel citizens stating that they should accept no pensions or gifts from princes or lords; StAb Ratsbücher K 23, f. 32v; Dürr, *Aktensammlung*, vol. 1, no. 82, 32.

71. Holbein was only accepted into the painters' guild (Himmelzunft) as a master in September 1519 and did not became a citizen of Basel until June 1520; see John Rowlands, *Holbein: The Paintings of Hans Holbein the Younger* (Oxford, 1985), 31–32. On the *verding*, the official commission to Holbein, see the certificates and file notes in Rudolf Riggenbach, "Die Wandgemälde des Rathauses zu Basel aus dem 15. und 16. Jahrhundert," in *Die Kunstdenkmäler des Kantons Basel-Stadt*, vol. 1, with additions by François Maurer (Basel, 1932; reprint, Basel, 1971), 517–646, esp. 591. On the commission, see Riggenbach, 538; Holbein received 120 florins in all or 150 lbs. as his fee; Harms, *Stadthaushalt*, vol. 3, 327. On the demolition and reconstruction of the hall in the nineteenth century, see François Maurer, "Der Basler Großratssaal im 19. Jahrhundert," *BZGA* 73 (1973): 129–56; Paul Roth, "Die Wandgemälde im Basler Großratssaal," in *Basler Stadtbuch*, 1960, 70–72; on Hans Holbein's frescoes in the great council hall, see Ulrich Barth, "Baugeschichte," in Staatskanzlei des Kantons Basel Stadt, ed., *Das Basler Rathaus* (Basel, 1983), 10 ff., and the same author's "Baugeschichte und Renovation seit dem Bundesbeitritt 1501," in *Basler Rathaus: Dokumentation der Restaurierung* (Basel, 1985), 27–43.

72. *Iuste iudicate filii hominum.* Gert Kreytenberg, "Hans Holbein der Jüngere: Die Wandgemälde im Basler Ratssaal," Zeitschrift des deutschen Vereins für Kunstwissenschaft 24 (1970): 77–100, esp. 80, 83–84. Here too the basis was Valerius Maximus: the two histories are related one after the other; Riggenbach, "Wandgemälde," 533, 588–89.

73. Meyer is the young painter's first documented patron; apparently in conjunction with his appointment as mayor, he had his portrait painted by the eighteen-year-old Holbein in 1516; in 1517 and 1519 he arranged commissions for him from the mayor of Lucerne, Hertenstein, one of the intermediaries in the payment of French pensions to Basel. In 1520, Holbein painted the so-called Solothurn Madonna (now in the Öffentliche Kunstsammlung, Basel) for the Basel town clerk Hans Gerster, a close associate of Meyer; in 1526 he painted another madonna for Jakob Meyer. See Rowlands, Holbein, 21–22, 31, 64; and Maria Netter, "Hans Holbeins Madonna des Bürgermeisters Jakob Meyer zum Hasen und ihre Geheimnisse," Basler Jahrbuch (1951): 109–25. Several authors have hinted at a connection between Holbein's decoration of the town hall and the pension uprisings. For an overview see Christian Müller, "New Evidence for Hans Holbein the Younger's Wall Paintings in Basel Town Hall," Burlington Magazine 139 (1991): 21–25.

74. The picture itself is now lost, but the text has come down to us in the collec-

tion of Basel inscriptions printed in 1622 by Johannes Gross; Gert Kreytenberg, "Hans Holbein der Jüngere," 80. A direct connection between Anacharsis's spider web and the portrayal of Curius Dentatus is probable: in Holbein's or Rhenanus's most likely model, the histories of Valerius Maximus, the two exempla were linked; Riggenbach, Wandgemälde, 533.

75. In 1817, before the demolition of the old great council hall, the picture was still in such good condition that the Basel painter Hieronymus Hess could make a detailed copy of it. A large fragment showing the heads of the ambassadors has also survived and is now in the Öffentliche Kunstsammlung, Basel; Riggenbach, Wandgemälde, 583–84; on Hess's copy, see 587–88, and Kreytenberg, "Hans Holbein," 80 (text of the inscriptions) and 92.

76. The reference to learned pictorial programs appears frequently: for Nuremberg, for instance, the chronicler Meisterlin noted that the town hall was painted with histories from Valerius Maximus, Plutarch, and Aulus Gellius: "the histories were intended to encourage the councilors and judges to act justly"; Chroniken der deutschen Städte, vol. 3, 154–55. In reality, however, it was medieval traditions and not classical sources that provided the direct models for the pictures, as Hugo van der Velden has demonstrated. See his "Cambyses for Example / Cambyses Reconsidered: Gerard David's Exemplum Iustitiae in the Bruges Town Hall," Simiolus 23 (1995): 5–63, 16–17. See also Ursula Lederle, "Gerechtigkeitsdarstellungen in deutschen und niederländischen Rathäusern," Ph.D. diss., University of Heidelberg, 1937; Karl Simon, Abendländische Gerechtigkeitsbilder (Frankfurt am Main, 1948), 50 ff.; Dennis E. Curtis and Judith Resnik, "Images of Justice," Yale Journal 96 (1987): 1727–72; Ulrich Meier, "Vom Mythos der Republik. Formen und Funktionen mittelalterlicher Rathausikonographie in Deutschland und Italien," in Andrea Löther et al., eds., Mundus in imagine: Festgabe für Klaus Schreiner (Munich, 1996), 345–88; and Susan Tiptoe, Res publica bene ordinata: Rathausdekorationen in der Frühen Neuzeit (Hildesheim, 1996).

77. O vos regentes obliti privatorum publica curate. Kreytenberg, "Hans Holbein," 80, 85, 88. On the pictures added by Holbein in 1530 and their political references, see 80 and 90.

78. Mercenaries from Basel fought on both sides in the battle for Milan in November 1519; the vanquished on the French side were captured and plundered by their victorious compatriots. See Anshelm, Berner Chronik, vol. 6, 75; and Ryff, *BChr*, vol. 1, 28–29: "the cardinal's men took from those they captured in the city everything they had."

79. Official suits brought by Meyer, StAB Gerichtsarchiv O 9, f. 70v and 79v; verdict, A 55, August 2, 1522, printed in Dürr, Aktensammlung, vol. 1, 42, 43, 46. See also Ratsbücher o 2, f. 318, and for detailed testimony by Basel mercenaries on statements by Vorster and Schenkli, Gerichtsarchiv, Schultheissengericht der Mehrern Stadt, Kundschaften D 23, f. 198v, 200v, 207v–210v.

80. Kunstmuseum Basel, Kupferstichkabinett, Inv. no. U.I.58. See also Christiane Andersson, Dirnen—Krieger—Narren: Ausgewählte Zeichnungen von Urs Graf (Basel, 1978), with a different interpretation of the motif, Plate 24 and pp. 28–29; similarly, the exhibition catalogue Dürer—Holbein—Grunewald: Meisterzeichnungen der

deutschen Renaissance aus Berlin und Basel (Basel, 1997), cat. no. 22.2. On Graf's biography and his conflicts and imprisonment in Basel, see Andersson, Dirnen—Krieger—Narren, 8 ff., and Emil Major, Urs Graf: Ein Beitrag zur Geschichte der Goldschmiedekunst des 16. Jahrhunderts (Strasbourg, 1907).

81. Kunstmuseum Basel, Kupferstichkabinett, Inv. no. U.XI.17; exhibition catalogue Dürer—Holbein—Grunewald, no. 22.6, 314.

82. Franz Bächtiger, "Andreaskreuz und Schweizerkreuz: Zur Feindschaft zwischen Landsknechten und Eidgenossen," Jahrbuch des Bernischen Historischen Museums 51/52 (1971–72), 205–70, esp. 232 ff.; Andersson, Dirnen—Krieger—Narren, 30–31, with references to the relevant passages in Brant and Murner; Thomas Murner, Die Schelmenzunft, ed. M. Spanier (Berlin, 1925), 133.

83. StAB Gerichtsarchiv, Schultheissengericht der Mehrern Stadt, Kundschaften D 23, f. 208v.

84. StAB Gerichtsarchiv, Schultheissengericht der Mehrern Stadt, Kundschaften D 23, f. 200v.

Chapter 6

1. Erasmus, *The Correspondence of Erasmus*, trans. R. A. Mynors and D. F. S. Thompson, ed. James K. McConica, in *Collected Works of Erasmus*, vol. 3 (Toronto, 1974), 43–44, n. 312; I quote here from Natalie Zemon Davis, *The Gift in Sixteenth-Century France* (Madison, 2000), 36.

2. Davis, *The Gift*, 37–38, and "Beyond the Market: Books as Gifts in Sixteenth-Century France," *Transactions of the Royal Historical Society*, series 5, 33 (1989): 69–88; for other gifts, cf. Paula Findlen, "The Economy of Scientific Exchange in Early Modern Italy," in Bruce Moran, ed., *Patronage and Institutions* (Woodbridge, 1991), 5–24.

3. Lisa Jardine, *Erasmus, Man of Letters: The Construction of Charisma in Print* (Princeton, N.J., 1993), 27–54.

4. Erasmus of Rotterdam, *Adages*, trans. and ed. R. A. B. Mynors, *Collected Works*, V, 32 (Toronto, 1989), 168–69; Adage, I 1, 1 and I 8, 81.

5. Erasmus, *Opus Epistolarum*, ed. Percy Stafford Allen, 12 vols. (Oxford, 1906–58), vol. 10, 254, 2826.69: *argenteum poculum inauratum*, and 2929.10–11. Many thanks to Jan van Heerwarden for this reference.

6. On the varied reception of these texts, see Peter Burke, *The Fortunes of the "Courtier"* (Oxford, 1995), and Lisa Jardine, *Erasmus, Man of Letters.*

7. On the Strasbourg brokers in 1494, see Johann Brucker, *Strassburger Zunft- und Polizeiordnungen des 14. und 15. Jahrhunderts* (Strasbourg, 1889), 532; Oskar Pausch, *Das älteste italienisch-deutsche Sprachbuch* (Vienna, 1972), 246–47: "per amore—darumb daz er ein ander mal desto lieber zu dir chum"; on the *amor* between Waldmann and his negotiation partners, see Chapter 4, n. 24.

8. Cf. the popular "Was nutz bringt, das liebt mann" (One loves that which is useful) from Sebastian Franck's 1532 collection of proverbs; Franck, *Erste namenlose*

Sprichwörtersammlung vom Jahre 1532, ed. Friedrich Latendorf (Hildesheim, 1972), 74. I have tried to describe the functions of these brokers in greater detail elsewhere. See my "Mobile Werte, informelle Ökonomie: Zur 'Kultur der Armut' in der Stadt des späten Mittelalters und der frühen Neuzeit," in Michael Borgolte and Otto Gerhard Oexle, eds., *Armut im Mittelalter* (Sigmaringen, 2001), forthcoming.

9. Gagliardi, "Mailänder und Franzosen in der Schweiz, 1495–1499," *Jahrbuch für schweizerische Geschichte* 39 (1914), 1–283, esp. 146–47 and 40 (1916), 1–276. Not just the transport but also the safekeeping or temporary storage of money gifts had to be repaid with further gifts of money; the Basel annual accounts for 1515–16 register a gift of 2,448 pfennigs from the three Basel envoys Meltinger, Offenburg, and Gallizian to the town guards, who were given the money that the Basel diplomats had received from the French in Milan for safekeeping. Bernhard Harms, *Der Stadthaushalt Basels im ausgehenden Mittelalter*, 3 vols. (Tübingen, 1909–13), vol. 3, 253.

10. Harms, *Stadthaushalt*, vol. 3, 227, 277.

11. Regula Schmid, *Reden, rufen, Zeichen setzen: Politisches Handeln während des Berner Twingherrenstreits 1469–1471* (Zurich, 1995), 179, 249; StAB Ratsbücher O 2, f. 306 and 308.

12. *EA* 3/2, S. 719; Ludwig Schwinkhart, *Chronik 1506 bis 1521*, ed. Hans von Greyerz (Berne, 1941), 258. On the history of the term *florence*, see Michael Rocke, *Forbidden Friendships: Homosexuality and Male Culture in Renaissance Florence* (Oxford, 1996).

13. StA Innsbruck, Maximiliana I 40, 25, quoted in Ernst Gagliardi, *Der Anteil der Schweizer an den italienischen Kriegen 1494–1516* (Zurich, 1919), vol. 1, 608 n. 32. On the Antichrist as the rule of dissimulation, see my "Der öffentliche Leichnam, reproduziert: Der Gekreuzigte und die Medien städtischer Gewalt im ausgehenden Mittelalter," in Agostino Paravicini Bagliani, ed., *Le cadavre au Moyen Age* (Turnhout, 1999), 383–403.

14. Gadi Algazi, *Herrengewalt und Gewalt der Herren im späten Mittelalter* (Frankfurt am Main, 1996), 22–23, 223, 250–51.

15. See, for instance, Hans Sachs, "Der Eygen nutz, das grewlich thier, mit sein zwölff eygenschaffften," in Sachs, *Werke*, ed. Adalbert von Keller, vol. 3 (Tübingen, 1870), 491–501. In this poem written in 1527, Sachs furnishes the monster of self-interest with political qualities. Its first quality is the greed of officials, who oppress their subjects with "heavy taxes, dues and simony" (*schwerer steur*, *fron* and *simoney*) (494), then come excessive customs duties and tolls, corrupt privileges and bribes, and only after these, excessive credits, the profits of the trading companies, and cheating by merchants and artisans. Cf. the examples in chapters seven and eight of Karl Goedecke, *Pamphilus Gengenbach* (Hanover, 1854), 54–67.

16. Cf. Erasmus of Rotterdam, "Convivium fabulosum / Das geschichtenreiche Gastmahl," in *Colloquia familiaria / Vertraute Gespräche*, ed. and trans. Werner Welzig (Darmstadt, 1967), 277–313, esp. 292 ff. (turnips), 298 ff. (gifts from the king), 302 (allocation of office), 304 ff. See also Private Smith, *A Key to the Colloquies of Erasmus* (Cambridge, 1927), 38, and, in more detail, Elsbeth Gutmann, *Die Colloquia Familiaria des Erasmus von Rotterdam* (Basel, 1968), 60–61.

17. Huldreich Zwingli, *Sämtliche Werke*, ed. Emil Egli and Georg Finsler (Berlin, 1905), vol. 1, 73.

18. Zwingli, *Sämtliche Werke*, vol. 1, 181–84.

19. Emil Egli, *Actensammlung zur Geschichte der Zürcher Reformation 1519–1533* (Zurich, 1879), 103–4. Cf. the new regulation on municipal gifts of wine in August of the same year, 92. On the allusions to Waldmann at the Reformed Zurich *schenki* or distribution of gifts in 1522, see Thomas Schärli, "Zürich im Übergang von der spätmittelalterlichen Universalkirche zur frühneuzeitlichen Staatskirche," in *Zwinglis Zürich 1484–1531*, ed. Staatsarchiv Zürich (Zurich, 1984), 14–48, esp. 31.

20. Egli, *Actensammlung*, 118 (no. 337) and 146–47 (no. 407), with extensive supplements and witness testimony. See Georg Gerig, *Reisläufer und Pensionenherren in Zürich 1519–1523* (Zurich, 1947), 55–56, and Hermann Romer, *Herrschaft, Reislauf und Verbotspolitik: Beobachtungen zum rechtlichen Alltag der Zürcher Solddienstbekämpfung im 16. Jahrhundert* (Zurich, 1995), 50–51, 118–19, 181, and 237–38.

21. Zwingli, *Sämtliche Werke*, vol. 3, 104–5 and 106.

22 Zwingli, *Sämtliche Werke*, vol. 3, 586–89. The original text has not survived, however, only the version in Bullinger's *Reformationschronik.*

23. Egli, *Actensammlung*, 489; the text of Zwingli's deposition from the council ledgers (*Ratsmanualen*), 491–92; the new ordinance of December 13, 519–20. On the pension trial of 1526 and the death sentence against Jakob Grebel, see Georg Gerig, *Reisläufer und Pensionsherren in Zürich 1519–1523* (Zurich, 1947), 53 ff.; Hans Morf, "Zunftverfassung, Obrigkeit und Kirche in Zürich von Waldmann bis Zwingli," Ph.D. diss., University of Zurich, 1968, 64–76; Christian Dietrich, *Die Stadt Zürich und ihre Landsgemeinden während der Bauernunruhen von 1489 bis 1525* (Bern, 1985), 72 ff.; Walter Jacob, "Politische Führungsschicht und Reformation: Untersuchungen zur Reformation in Zürich 1519–1528," Ph.D. diss., University of Zürich, 1969, 17–25; on Zwingli's instrumentalization of pensions, see also the remarks in Ulrich Gäbler, *Huldrych Zwingli* (Munich, 1983), 19; for a detailed account of the trial, see Leo Schelbert, "Jacob Grebel's Trial Revised," *Archiv für Reformationsgeschichte* 60 (1969): 33–64.

24. Schelbert, "Jacob Grebel's Trial Revised," 60–61.

25. Johannes Stumpf, *Schweizer- und Reformationschronik*, ed. Ernst Gagliardi, H. Müller, and E. Büser, part 1 (Basel, 1952), 35, 137–45; see his comments on 78 and 81 regarding the attempts at prohibiting pensions in 1507 and 1508. On the author and the period when he was writing, see Richard Feller and Edgar Bonjour, *Geschichtsschreibung der Schweiz vom Spätmittelalter zur Neuzeit*, vol. 1 (Basel, 1962), 180 ff.

26. Schwinkhart, *Chronik*, 83 (1512–13), 190–91 (1516), 233 (1520); on the limited efficacy of French pension payments in 1507, see 19; Ryff in *Basler Chronik*, vol. 1, 26, 32–33, 34.

27.Valerius Anshelm, *Berner Chronik*, 6 vols. (Bern, 1884–1901), vol. 5, 247. Franz Moser, "Valerius Anshelms Staats- und Geschichtsauffassung," *Archiv des Historischen Vereins des Kantons Bern* 39 (1948): 273–89; and Arnold Esch, "Wahrnehmung sozialen und politischen Wandels in Bern an der Wende vom Mittelalter zur Neuzeit," in Jürgen Miethke and Klaus Schreiner, eds., *Sozialer Wandel im Mittelalter* (Sigmaringen, 1994), 177–193, esp. 185 ff.

28. Anshelm, *Chronik*, vol. 1, 87 ff. and 106 ff. On Waldmann, see vol. 1, 336; on the alliance with France, see vol. 2, 23ff.; on the Swabian war, see 205; on French missions, vol. 3, 26 and passim; on accusations of corruption, 443 ff., with particular

emphasis on treason and "muet und gaben," 447–48; prohibition of secret pensions, 466; unrest in Lucerne, 468–69.

29. Anshelm, *Chronik*, vol. 4, 205–6.

30. Anshelm, *Chronik*, vol. 3, 26; vol. 4, 106, 307. See, for example, Anshelm's oft-cited remark that Swiss flesh was cheaper than veal; vol. 3, 43.

31. Adolf Fluri, ed., "Die Lücken in Anshelms Chronik," *Anzeiger für schweizerische Geschichte* 39 (1908): 283–95, 293; and Anshelm, *Chronik*, vol. 5, 155.

32. Anshelm's frequently cited descriptions of the luxurious dress of pension recipients and those involved in the mercenary trade also refer to the moral rhetoric of the 1530s and 1540s rather than to conditions between the Burgundian wars and the Reformation, the period in which he places them.

33. See Lyndal Roper, *The Holy Household: Women and Morals in Reformation Augsburg* (Oxford, 1988). On the regulation of heterosexual relations in the Swiss Reformation, see Susanna Burghartz, "Das starke Geschlecht und das schwache Fleisch," in Michael Erbe et al., eds., *Dissens und Toleranz im Wandel der Geschichte: Festschrift zum 65. Geburtstag von Hans R. Guggisberg* (Mannheim, 1996), 89–106, and *Zeiten der Reinheit-Orte der Unzucht: Ehe und Sexualität in Basel waehrend der fruehen Neuzeit* (Paderborn, 1999), 37–72.

34. Natalie Zemon Davis, *Gifts and Bribes in Sixteenth-Century France*, Iredell Lecture, University of Lancaster, 1995, 9–11, and *The Gift in Sixteenth-Century France*, 109–14, 121–24.

35. Johannes Dierauer, *Geschichte der Schweizerischen Eidgenossenschaft*, 3rd ed. (Gotha, 1920), vol. 2, 312 ff.; Ernst Gagliardi, *Novara und Dijon, Höhepunkt und Verfall der schweizerischen Grossmacht* (Zurich, 1907), 8–9, and "Mailänder und Franzosen in der Schweiz, 1495–1499," *Jahrbuch für schweizerische Geschichte* 39 (1914): 1–283, esp. 54, and 40 (1916): 1–276, esp. 265; "degeneration" into a "widespread disease," vol. 39, 55–56.

36. Emil Dürr, "Eidgenössische Grossmachtpolitik im Zeitalter der Mailänderkriege," in *Schweizer Kriegsgeschichte*, vol. 2 (Berne, 1933), 521–708, here 543–47; Christian Erni, "Bernische Ämterbefragungen 1495–1522," *Archiv des Historischen Vereins des Kantons Bern* 39 (1947): 3–123, here 15.

37. See Giorgio Chittolini, "L'onore dell' officiale," in Sergio Bertelli, Nicolai Rubinstein, and Craig Hugh Smyth, eds., *Florence and Milan: Comparisons and Relations* (Florence, 1989), 101–33, and "The 'Private,' the 'Public,' the State," in G. Chittolini, Anthony Molho, and Pierangelo Schiera, eds., *The Origins of the State in Italy, 1300–1600* (Chicago, 1995), 34–61.

38. Ernst Gagliardi, ed., *Dokumente zur Geschichte des Bürgermeisters Hans Waldmann*, 2 vols. (Basel 1911–13), vol. 2, 24–25, 344, 420–21, 494–96; Petermann Etterlin, *Kronica von der loblichen Eydtgenoschaft, jr harkommen und sust seltzam stritten und geschichten* (Basel, 1507), ed. Eugen Gruber (Aarau, 1965), 226 ff.; Heinrich Brennwald, *Schweizerchronik*, ed. Rudolf Luginbühl (Basel, 1910), 311 ff.; "Chronik des Clemens Sender," in *Chronik der deutschen Städte*, vol. 23 (Leipzig, 1894), 42.

39. Max Weber, *Wirtschaft und Gesellschaft: Grundriss der verstehenden Soziologie*, 5th ed. (Tübingen, 1976), 129.

40."Harpokratem quisquis huc intrat praestet oportet. Nam nostra arcanum promere jura vetant"; Gert Kreytenberg, "Hans Holbein der Jüngere: Die Wandgemälde im Basler Ratssaal," *Zeitschrift des deutschen Vereins für Kunstwissenschaft* 24 (1970): 77–100, esp. 80.

41. Ernst Kantorowicz, "Mysteries of State: An Absolutist Concept and Its Late Medieval Origins," *Harvard Theological Review* 48 (1955): 65–92; and Jacques Chiffoleau, "Dire l'Indicible: Remarques sur la catégorie du Nefandum du XIIe au XVe siècle," *Annales ESC* 45 (1990): 289–324.

Bibliography

Manuscript Sources

Basel, Staatsarchiv

Finanz G 9, 10, 11, 12, 13, 14
Gerichtsarchiv: Schultheissengericht der mehrern Stadt, Kundschaften D 23
Politisches L 1, L 2.1, M 1.1–1.7, M 2
Protokolle Öffnungsbuch 1, 7
Ratsbücher A1, A 3, A 5, A 6, A 7, B1, B 2+3, B 6, K1, K2, K 23, K 24, L 1, L 2, M 1, M 2, N 1, N 10, O 2
Zunftakten Safranzunft 46, 66

Basel, Universitätsbibliothek

Aristotelis Heimlichkeit. Illustrierte Papierhandschrift 1476, Sig. O II 26

Freiburg im Breisgau, Stadtarchiv

B 1.2, B 2.4, B 3.3, B 13 a.4a, B 13 a.5
C 1, Landes- und Reichsakten 1, Nr. 8

Porrentruy, Staatsarchiv

Archives de l'ancien Evéché de Bâle, *Hofrechnungen, Hausbuch des Basler Bischofs Johann von Venningen, 1458–1478*

Strasbourg, Archives de la ville de Strasbourg

II, VDG, 117
III, BB 24, 1
VI, 488, Nr. 6

PRIMARY LITERATURE

Alberti, Leon Battista. *The Family in Renaissance Florence: A Translation of I Libri della Famiglia.* Trans. Renée Neu Watkins. Columbia, S.C., 1969.

Anshelm, Valerius. *Berner Chronik.* Ed. Historischer Verein des Kantons Bern. 6 vols. Bern, 1884–1901.

Barack, Carl August, ed. *Chronik der Grafen von Zimmern.* 4 vols. Tübingen, 1892–96.

———. *Des Teufels Netz.* Bibliothek des Literarischen Vereins Stuttgart, 70. Stuttgart, 1863.

Basler Rechtsquellen. Ed. Christian Schnell. 2 vols. Basel, 1859–65.

Basler Urkundenbuch. Ed. August Bernoulli et al. 11 vols. Basel, 1890–1910.

BChr. Ed. August Bernoulli et al. 10 vols. Basel, 1879–1976.

Bernoulli, August, ed. "Balci Descriptio Helvetiae." In *Quellen zur Schweizer Geschichte.* Vol. 6, 73–105. Basel, 1884.

Brant, Sebastian. *Das Narrenschiff.* Basel, 1494. Reprint. Tübingen, 1968.

Brennwald, Heinrich. *Schweizerchronik.* Ed. Rudolf Luginbühl. 2 vols. Quellen zur Schweizergeschichte Neue Folge: Chroniken, 1. Basel, 1910.

Brucker, Johann. *Strassburger Zunft-und Polizeiordnungen des 14. und 15. Jahrhunderts.* Strasbourg, 1889.

Castiglione, Baldassare. *The Book of the Courtier.* Trans. George Bull. Harmondsworth, 1976.

Dacheux, Louis, ed. "Jacobus Wencker Extractus ex Protocollis vulgo Les Annales de Sebastien Brant." In *Fragments d'anciennes chroniques d'Alsace,* vol. 3, *Les chroniques Strasbourgeoises,* 209–79. Strasbourg, 1892.

Dürer, Albrecht. "Tagebuch der Reise in die Niederlande." In A. Dürer, *Schriften und Briefe.* Leipzig, 1989.

Dürr, Emil, ed. *Aktensammlung zur Geschichte der Basler Reformation 1519–1534.* Vol. 1. Basel, 1921.

EA, series 1245–1798. Various places of publication, 1839–90. Vol. 3/2, Lucerne, 1896.

Eckhardt, Karl A., ed. *Sachsenspiegel Landrecht.* Göttingen, 1955.

Eckhardt, Karl A., and Hermann Hübner, eds. *Deutschenspiegel.* Hanover, 1939.

Egli, Emil, ed. *Actensammlung zur Geschichte der Zürcher Reformation 1519–1533.* Zurich, 1879.

Egli, Emil and Georg Finsler, eds. *Huldreich Zwinglis sämtliche Werke.* Vol. 1. Berlin, 1905.

Eheberg, Karl Theodor. *Verfassungs-, Verwaltungs- und Wirtschaftsgeschichte der Stadt Strassburg bis 1681.* Vol. 1, *Urkunden und Akten.* Strasbourg, 1899.

Erasmus of Rotterdam. *Adages.* Trans. and ed. R. A. B. Mynors. Collected Works V, 32. Toronto, 1989.

———. *Colloquia familiaria / Vertraute Gespräche.* Ed. and trans. Werner Welzig. Darmstadt, 1995.

———. *Institutio principis christiani / Fürstenerziehung.* Ed. and trans. Werner Welzig. Paderborn, 1968.

———. *Opus epistolarum Desiderii Erasmi Roterodami / denuo recognitum et auctum per Percy Stafford Allen.* 12 vols. Oxford, 1906–58.

Etterlin, Petermann. *Kronica von der loblichen Eydtgenoschaft, jr harkommen und sust seltzam stritten und geschichten.* Ed. Eugen Gruber. Quellenwerk zur Entstehung der Schweizerischen Eidgenossenschaft III, 3. Basel, 1507. Reprint. Aarau, 1965.

Franke, Annelore, and Gerhard Zschäbitz, eds. *Das Buch der Hundert Kapitel und der vierzig Statuten des sogenannten Oberrheinischen Revolutionärs.* Berlin, 1974.

Füetrer, Ulrich. *Der Trojanerkrieg: Aus dem "Buch der Abenteuer."* Ed. Edward G. Fichtner. Munich, 1968.

Gagliardi, Ernst, ed. *Dokumente zur Geschichte des Bürgermeisters Hans Waldmann.* 2 vols. Basel, 1911–13.

Geiler von Kaysersberg, [Johannes]. *De arbore humana: Von dem menschlichen Baum.* Strasbourg, 1521.

———. "Predigt zum Narrenschiff." In J. Scheible, ed., *Das Kloster,* vol. 1, 545–47. Stuttgart, 1845.

Gengenbach, Pamphilus. *Der Nollhart.* Stuttgart, 1977.

———. *Der welsch Flusz.* Basel, 1513.

Gengler, Hermann, ed. *Schwabenspiegel.* Erlangen, 1853.

Geny, Joseph, ed. *Schlettstadter Stadtrechte.* Oberheinische Stadtrechte, 3. Heidelberg, 1902.

Gille, Hans, and Ingeborg Spriewald, eds. *Die Gedichte des Michel Beheim.* 3 vols. Berlin, 1968.

Goedecke, Karl, ed. *Pamphilus Gengenbach.* Hanover, 1854.

Greiff, B., ed. *Tagebuch des Lukas Rem aus den Jahren 1495–1541: Ein Beitrag zur Handelsgeschichte der Stadt Augsburg.* Augsburg, 1861.

Grether, Rosemarie. "Die Basler Ratsordnung von 1506." *Jahresberichte des Staatsarchiv Basel-Stadt* (1969): 21–51.

Haller, Berchtold, ed. *Bern in seinen Ratsmanualen 1465–1565.* 3 vols. Bern, 1902.

Harms, Bernhard, ed. *Der Stadthaushalt Basels im ausgehenden Mittelalter: Die Jahresrechnungen 1360–1535.* 3 vols. Tübingen, 1909–13.

Hesse, Ludwig F., ed. *Konrad Stolles thüringisch-erfurtische Chronik.* Stuttgart, 1854.

Jecht, Richard, ed. "Die Pflichten eines mittelalterlichen Bürgermeisters: Das Traktat des Görlitzer Stadtschreibers Johannes Frauenfeld 1476." *Deutsche Geschichtsblätter* 18 (1909): 89–102.

John of Salisbury. *Policraticus.* Ed. Cary Nederman. Cambridge, 1990.

Koelner, Paul. "Die Kuchibücher der Safranzunft." *Basler Jahrbuch* (1929): 202–69.

Köhler, Joachim, ed. *Die Carolina und ihre Vorgängerinnen.* Vol. 2, *Die Bambergische Halsgerichtsordnung.* Halle, 1902.

Koller, Heinrich, ed. *Reformation Kaiser Sigmunds.* MGH, Staatsschriften des späteren Mittelalters, 6. Stuttgart, 1964.

Kress von Kressenstein, Georg. "Das Schenkbuch einer Nürnberger Patriziersfrau von 1416–1438." *Anzeiger für die Kunde der deutschen Vorzeit,* NF 23 (1876): 37–42, 70–74.

Kurrelmeyer, W., ed. *Die erste deutsche Bibel.* Vol. 1. Bibliothek des Literarischen Vereins Stuttgart, 234. Tübingen, 1904.

Landucci, Luca. *Diario fiorentino dal 1450 al 1516.* Ed. Iodoco dal Badia. Florence, 1883.

Latendorf, Friedrich, ed. *Sebastian Franck: Erste namenlose Sprichwörtersammlung vom Jahre 1532.* Hildesheim, 1970.

Lemmer, Manfred, ed. *Franciscus Petrarcha, Von der Artzney bayder Glück.* Leipzig, 1983.

Lexer, Matthias, ed. *Endres Tuchers Baumeisterbuch der Stadt Nürnberg 1464–1475.* Stuttgart, 1862. Reprint. Amsterdam, 1968.

Liliencron, Rochus von, ed. *Die historischen volkslieder der Deutschen.* 3 vols. Leipzig, 1864–69.

Loose, Wilhelm, ed. *Anton Tuchers Haushaltsbuch 1507–1517.* Stuttgart, 1877.

Lorentzen, Theodor, ed. "Zwei Flugschriften aus der Zeit Maximilian I." *Neue Heidelberger Jahrbücher* 17 (1913): 139–228.

Manzalaoui, M. A., ed. *Secretum Secretorum: Nine English Versions.* Oxford, 1977.

Melville, Gerd. "Die Herolde im europäischen Spätmittelalter." In Peter Moraw, ed., *Hof, Hoftag und Reichstag im späteren Mittelalter*, 33–51. Sigmaringen, 1999.

Moeller, Reinhold, ed. *Hiltgart von Hürnheim: Mittelhochdeutsche Prosaübersetzung des Secretum Secretorum.* Berlin, 1963.

Mollwo, Carl, ed. *Das rote Buch der Stadt Ulm.* Stuttgart, 1905.

Montaigne, Michel de. *Journal de voyage.* Ed. François Rigolot. Paris, 1992.

Morgenthaler, Hans. "Kulturgeschichtliche Notizen aus den solothurnischen Seckelmeisterrechnungen des 15. Jahrhunderts." *Anzeiger für schweizerische Altertumskunde* NF 21 (1919): 187–89 and NF 22 (1919): 57–60.

Morsheim, Johann von. *Spiegel des Regiments.* Ed. Karl Goedecke. Stuttgart, 1856.

Murner, Thomas. *Die Schelmenzunft.* Ed. M. Spanier. Berlin, 1925.

Nettesheim, Agrippa von. *De incertitudine et vanitate scientiarium atque artium, Declamatio.* Ed. Joachim Wolgast. Berlin, 1993.

Ölhafen, Carl von, ed. "Eine Hochzeit zu Nürnberg zu Anfang des 16. Jahrhunderts." *Anzeiger für die Kunde der deutschen Vorzeit* 24 (1877): 242–47.

Österley, Hermann, ed. *Die Gesta Romanorum.* Berlin, 1872.

Pastor, Ludwig, ed. *Die Reise des Kardinals Luigi d'Aragona durch Deutschland, die Niederlande, Frankreich und Oberitalien 1517–1518, beschrieben von Antonio de Beatis.* Freiburg im Breisgau, 1921.

Pausch, Oskar. *Das älteste italienisch-deutsche Sprachbuch: Eine Überlieferung aus dem Jahre 1424 nach Georg von Nürnberg.* Vienna, 1972.

Pfeiffer, Franz, ed. *Das Buch der Natur von Konrad von Megenberg.* Stuttgart, 1861.

Piccolomini, Enea Silvio. *Von höfen / hoffleuten vnd dienern der Fürsten: Verteutscht durch Herr Wolff Hasen.* Flugschriftensammlung Gustav Freytag, no. 840. N.p., 1529.

Riggenbach, Bernhard, ed. *Das Chronikon des Konrad Pellikan.* Basel, 1877.

Rosenkranz, Albert. *Der Bundschuh.* Vol. 2, *Quellen.* Heidelberg, 1927.

Sachs, Hans. "Der Eygen nutz, das grewlich thier, mit sein zwölff eygenschafften." In H. Sachs, *Werke*, ed. Adalbert von Keller, vol. 3, 491–501. Tübingen, 1870.

Schade, Oskar, ed. *Satiren und Pasquille aus der Reformationszeit.* 3 vols. Hanover, 1855–58. Reprint. Hildesheim, 1966.

Schmidt, Gerard F., ed. *Das Schachzabelbuch des Jacobus de Cessolis.* Berlin, 1961.

Schuler, Peter-Johannes. "Reformation des geistlichen Gerichts zu Strassburg: Eine Reformschrift aus der Mitte des 15. Jahrhunderts." *Francia* 9 (1981): 177–214.
Schultz, Alwin, ed. *Der Weisskönig: Jahrbuch der Kunsthistorischen Sammlungen des allerhöchsten Kaiserhauses.* vol. 6. Vienna, 1888.
Schwarz, Ulrich. *Die Chronik des Bürgermeisters U. S.* In Georg Panzer, *Ulrich Schwarz, der Augsburger Zunftbürgermeister 1422–1478.* Bamberg, 1914.
Schwinkhart, Ludwig. *Chronik 1506 bis 1521.* Ed. Hans von Greyerz. Bern, 1941.
Sieber-Lehmann, Claudius, and Thomas Wilhelmi, eds. *In Helvetios—Wider die Kuhschweizer: Fremd- und Feindbilder in antieidgenössischen Texten von 1386 bis 1532.* Bern, 1998.
StChr. Ed. Karl Hegel et al. 37 vols. Leipzig, 1869–1917.
Steer, Georg et al., eds. *Die "Rechtssumme Bruder Bertholds."* 4 vols. Tübingen, 1980–87.
Stumpf, Johannes. *Johannes Stumpfs Schweizer- und Reformationschronik.* Ed. Ernst Gagliardi, H. Müller, and E. Büser. Part 1. Basel, 1952.
Tengler, Ulrich. *Der new Leyenspiegel von rechtmassigen ordnungen in burgerlichen und peynlichen Regimenten.* Strasbourg, 1514.
Waga, Friedrich, ed. *Die Welschgattung.* Breslau, 1910.
Weitnauer, Alfred, ed. *Venezianischer Handel der Fugger nach der Musterbuchhaltung des Matthäus Schwarz.* Munich, 1931.
Welti, Emil, ed. *Die Rechtsquellen des Kantons Bern.* Vol. 1. Sammlung schweizerischer Rechtsquellen, II. Aarau, 1902.
Williams, Ulla, and Werner Krapp-Williams, eds. *Die Elsässische Legenda Aurea.* 2 vols. Tübingen, 1980–82.
Wimpfeling, Jakob. *Agatharchia.* In Bruno Singer, *Der Fürstenspiegel in Deutschland im Zeitalter des Humanismus und der Reformation,* 229–49. Munich, 1981.
Wolf, Herbert, ed. *Johannes Rothes Ratsgedichte.* Texte des späten Mittelalters und der frühen Neuzeit, 25. Berlin, 1971.
Zingerle, Ignaz von. *Die deutschen Sprichwörter im Mittelalter.* Vienna, 1864.

Secondary Literature

Adorno, Theodor W. *Minima Moralia.* Trans. E. F. N. Jephcott. London, 1984.
Algazi, Gadi. *Herrengewalt und Gewalt der Herren im späten Mittelalter: Herrschaft, Gegenseitigkeit und Sprachgebrauch.* Frankfurt, 1996.
Amiet, Bruno. "Die solothurnischen Bauernunruhen in den Jahren 1513 und 1514 und die Mailänderfeldzüge." *Zeitschrift für schweizerische Geschichte* 21 (1941): 653–728.
Arnould, Maurice. "L'Origine historique des pots-de-vin." *Académie Royale de Belgique, Bulletin de la classe des lettres et des sciences morales et politiques,* 5th ser., 62 (1976): 216–67.
Asch, Ronald, and Adolf Birke, eds. *Princes, Patronage and the Nobility: The Court at the Beginning of the Modern Age, 1450–1650.* Oxford, 1991.

Aulinger, Rosemarie. *Das Bild des Reichstags im 16. Jahrhundert.* Göttingen, 1980.

Bächtiger, Franz. "Andreaskreuz und Schweizerkreuz: Zur Feindschaft zwischen Landsknechten und Eidgenossen." *Jahrbuch des Bernischen Historischen Museums* 51/52 (1971–72): 205–70.

———. "Erörterungen zum 'alten und jungen Eidgenossen.'" *Bernisches Historisches Museum, Jahrbuch* (1969–70): 35–70.

Baer, C. H. "Die erhaltenen Architekturteile und Einrichtungsstücke der alten Rathausbauten" In Baer, *Die Kunstdenkmäler der Schweiz: Die Kunstdenkmäler des Kantons Basel-Stadt,* vol. 1, 363–478. Basel, 1932. Reprint revised by Francois Maurer. Basel, 1971.

———. "Die Geschichte der Rathaus-Bauten." In Baer, *Die Kunstdenkmäler der Schweiz: Die Kunstdenkmäler des Kantons Basel-Stadt,* vol. 1, 339–61. Basel, 1932. Reprint revised by Francois Maurer. Basel, 1971.

Barth, Ulrich. "Baugeschichte." In Staatskanzlei des Kantons Basel Stadt, ed., *Das Basler Rathaus,* 7–23. Basel, 1983.

———. "Baugeschichte und Renovation seit dem Bundesbeitritt 1501." In *Basler Rathaus: Dokumentation der Restaurierung: Textband,* 27–43. Basel, 1985.

Barthélémy, Dominique, and Jacques Chiffoleau. "Les Sources cléricales et la notion de clandestinité au Moyen Age." In Jacques Chiffoleau et al., eds., *Histoire et Clandestinité du Moyen Age à la Première Guerre mondiale,* 19–39. Albi, 1979.

Bauer, Clemens. "Der Wucher-Begriff der Reformatio Sigismundi." In *Aus Stadt- und Wirtschaftsgeschichte Südwestdeutschlands: Festschrift für Erich Maschke zum 75. Geburtstag,* 110–17. Stuttgart, 1975.

Baum, Paul Franklin. "The Medieval Legend of Judas Iscariot." *PMLA* 31 (1916): 481–632.

Baumann, Karin. *Aberglaube für Laien: Zur Programmatik und Überlieferung mittelalterlicher Superstitionenkritik.* Würzburg, 1981.

Baur, Paul. *Testament und Bürgerschaft: Alltagsleben und Sachkultur im spätmittelalterlichen Konstanz.* Sigmaringen, 1989.

Bendlage, Andrea, and Peter Schuster. "Hüter der Ordnung: Bürger, Rat und Polizei in Nürnberg im 15. und 16. Jahrhundert." *MVGN* 82 (1995): 37–56.

Berg, Dieter. "Mediävistik—eine 'politische Wissenschaft.'" In Wolfgang Küttler et al., eds., *Geschichtsdiskurs,* vol. 1, 317–30. Frankfurt, 1993.

Berges, Wilhelm. *Die Fürstenspiegel des hohen und späten Mittelalters.* Leipzig, 1938.

Berking, Helmut. *Schenken: Zur Anthropologie des Gebens.* Frankfurt, 1996.

Bernays, Isaac. "Die Diplomatie um 1500." *HZ* 138 (1927): 1–23.

Bierbrauer, Christian. *Freiheit und Gemeinde im Berner Oberland 1300–1700.* Bern, 1991.

Blockmans, Wim. "Patronage, Brokerage and Corruption as Symptoms of Incipient State Formation in the Burgundian-Habsburg Netherlands." In Anthoni Maczak, ed., *Klientelsysteme im Europa der frühen Neuzeit,* 117–26. Munich, 1988.

Boockmann, Hartmut. "Das 15. Jahrhundert und die Reformation." In *Kirche und Gesellschaft im Heiligen Römischen Reich des 15. und 16. Jahrhunderts,* 9–25. Göttingen, 1994.

———. "Geschäfte und Geschäftigkeit auf dem Reichstag im späten Mittelalter." *HZ* 246 (1988): 294–325.

———. "Spätmittelalterliche deutsche Stadt-Tyrannen." *Blätter für deutsche Landesgeschichte* 119 (1983): 73–91.

———. "Zu den Wirkungen der 'Reform Kaiser Siegmunds.'" In Bernd Moeller et al., eds., *Studien zum städtischen Bildungswesen des späten Mittelalters und der frühen Neuzeit*, 112–35. Göttingen, 1983.

———. "Zur Mentalität spätmittelalterlicher gelehrter Räte." *HZ* 233 (1981): 295–316.

Boone, Marc. "Dons et pots-de-vin: Aspects de la sociabilité urbaine au Bas Moyen Age: Les cas gantois pendant la période bourguignonne." *Revue du Nord* 70 (1988): 471–87.

Bouchard, Constance B. *Holy Entrepreneurs. Cistercians, Knights, and Economic Exchange in Twelfth-Century Burgundy.* Ithaca, N.Y., 1991.

Bourdieu, Pierre. *The Logic of Practice.* Trans. Richard Nice. Cambridge, 1980.

———. *Outline of a Theory of Practice.* Trans. Richard Nice. Cambridge, 1977.

Brady, Thomas. *Turning Swiss: Cities and Empire 1450–1550.* Cambridge, 1985.

Brauer-Gramm, Hildburg. *Der Landvogt Peter von Hagenbach.* Göttingen, 1957.

Braunstein, Philippe. "Towards Intimacy: The Fourteenth and Fifteenth Centuries." In Georges Duby, ed., Arthur Goldhammer, trans., *A History of Private Life: Revelations of the Middle Ages.* Cambridge, Mass., 1991.

Bray, Alan. "Homosexuality and the Signs of Male Friendship in Elizabethean England." *History Workshop Journal* 29 (1990): 1–19.

Brunner, Horst, ed. *Die deutsche Trojaliteratur des Mittelalters und der Frühen Neuzeit.* Wiesbaden, 1990.

Buc, Philippe. "Conversion of Objects." *Viator* 28 (1997): 99–143.

Bücher, Karl. "Der öffentliche Haushalt der Stadt Frankfurt im Mittelalter." *Zeitschrift für die gesamte Staatswissenschaft* 6 (1896): 1–19.

Burghartz, Susanna. "Frauen-Politik-Weiberregiment: Schlagworte zur Bewältigung der politischen Krise von 1691 in Basel." In Anne-Lise Head-König and Albert Tanner, eds., *Frauen in der Stadt / Les femmes dans la ville*, 113–34. Zurich, 1993.

———. "Das starke Geschlecht und das schwache Fleisch." In Michael Erbe et al., eds. *Dissens und Toleranz im Wandel der Geschichte: Festschrift zum 65. Geburtstag von Hans R. Guggisberg*, 89–106. Mannheim, 1996.

Burke, Peter. *The Fortunes of the "Courtier."* Oxford, 1995.

Camille, Michael. *The Medieval Art of Love: Subjects and Objects of Desire.* London, 1998.

Capitani, Francois de. *Adel, Bürger und Zünfte im Bern des 15. Jahrhunderts.* Bern, 1982.

Chartier, Roger. "L'histoire culturelle entre 'linguistic turn' et retour au sujét." In Hartmut Lehmann, ed., *Wege zu einer neuen Kulturgeschichte*, Göttinger Gespräche zur Geschichtswissenschaft, 1, 31–60. Göttingen, 1995.

Chiffoleau, Jacques. "Dire l'indicible: Remarques sur la catégorie du Nefandum du XIIe au XVe siècle." *Annales ESC* 45 (1990): 289–324.

Chittolini, Giorgio. "L'onore dell' officiale." In Sergio Bertelli, Nicolai Rubinstein, and Craig Hugh Smyth, eds., *Florence and Milan: Comparisons and Relations*, 101–33. Florence, 1989.

———. "The 'Private,' the 'Public,' the State." In G. Chittolini, Anthony Molho, and Pierangelo Schiera, eds., *The Origins of the State in Italy,1300–1600*, *Journal of Modern History* 67, supplement, 34–61. Chicago, 1995.

Connell, William J. "Clientelismo e Stato territoriale: Il potere fiorentina a Pistoia nel XV secolo." *Societa e Storia* 14 (1991): 523–41.

Curtis, Dennis E., and Judith Resnik. "Images of Justice." *Yale Journal* 96 (1987): 1727–72.

Dändliker, Kurt. "Die Berichterstattungen und Anfragen der Zürcher Regierung an die Landschaft in der Zeit vor der Reformation." *Jahrbuch für Schweizer Geschichte* 21 (1896) and 23 (1898).

Davis, Natalie Zemon. "Beyond the Market: Books as Gifts in Sixteenth Century France." *Transactions of the Royal Historical Society*, 5th ser., 33 (1989): 69–88.

———. *The Gift in Sixteenth-Century France.* Madison, 2000.

———. "Gifts and Bribes in Sixteenth-Century France." Iredell Lecture, University of Lancaster, 1995.

Derrida, Jacques. *Given Time I: Counterfeit Money.* Trans. Peggy Kamuf. Chicago, 1993.

Derville, Alain. "Pots-de-vin, cadeaux, racket, patronage: Essai sur les mécanismes de décision dans l'état bourguignon." *Revue du Nord* 56 (1974): 341–64.

———. "Les Pots-de-vins dans le dernier tiers du XVe siècle." In Wim Blockmans, ed., *1477: Le privilége géneral et les priviléges regionaux de Marie Bourgogne pour les Pays-Bas*, 449–71. Kortrijk, 1985.

Dierauer, Johannes. *Geschichte der Schweizerischen Eidgenossenschaft.* 3rd ed. 4 vols. Gotha, 1920.

Dietrich, Christian. *Die Stadt Zürich und ihre Landsgemeinden während der Bauernunruhen von 1489 bis 1525.* Bern, 1985.

Dinzelbacher, Peter. *Judastraditionen.* Vienna, 1977.

Dobson, Barrie, ed. *The Church, Politics and Patronage in the Fifteenth Century.* Gloucester, 1984.

Dohna, Lothar Graf zu. *Reformatio Sigismundi: Beiträge zum Verständnis einer Reformschrift des 15. Jahrhunderts.* Göttingen, 1960.

Douglas, Mary. "No Free Gifts." Foreword to Marcel Mauss, *The Gift.* London, 1990.

Drabek, Anna-Maria. "Reisen und Reisezeremoniell der römisch-deutschen Herrscher im Spätmittelalter." Ph.D. diss., University of Vienna, 1964.

Drüppel, Hubert. *Judex Civitatis: Zur Stellung des Richters in der hoch- und spätmittelalterlichen Stadt.* Cologne, 1981.

Dürr, Emil. "Eidgenössische Grossmachtpolitik im Zeitalter der Mailänderkriege." In *Schweizer Kriegsgeschichte*, vol. 2, 521–708. Bern, 1933.

Eamon, William. *Science and the Secrets of Nature: Books of Secrets in Medieval and Early Modern Culture.* Princeton, N.J., 1994.

Eberhard, Winfried. "'Gemeiner Nutzen' als oppositionelle Leitvorstellung im Spätmittelalter." In Manfred Gerwing and Godehart Ruppert, eds., *Renovatio et Reformatio: Festschrift für Ludwig Hödl*, 195–214. Münster, 1985.

———. "Der Legitimationsbegriff des 'Gemeinen Nutzens' im Streit zwischen Herrschaft und Genossenschaft im späten Mittelalter." In Jörg Fichte et al., eds., *Zusammenhänge, Einflüsse, Wirkungen: Kongressakten zum Symposium des Mediävistenverbands in Tübingen 1984*, 241–54. Berlin, 1986.

Elwert, Georg. "Ausdehnung der Käuflichkeit und Einbettung der Wirtschaft." In K. Heinemann, ed., *Soziologie wirtschaftlichen Handelns*, Kölner Zeitschrift für Soziologie und Sozialpsychologie Sonderheft, 300–321. Opladen, 1987.

Erni, Christian. "Bernische Ämterbefragungen 1495–1522." *Archiv des Historischen Vereins des Kantons Bern* 39 (1947): 3–123.

Ernst, Fritz. "Die Spielleute im Dienst der Stadt Basel im ausgehenden Mittelalter." *BZGA* 44 (1945): 79–236.

———. "Über Gesandtschaftswesen und Diplomatie an der Wende vom Mittelalter zur Neuzeit." *AKG* 33 (1950): 64–95.

Esch, Arnold. "Alltag der Entscheidung: Berns Weg in den Burgunderkrieg." *Berner Zeitschrift für Geschichte und Heimatkunde* 50 (1988): 3–64.

———. "Mit Schweizer Söldnern auf dem Marsch nach Italien: Das Erlebnis der Mailänderkriege 1510–1515 nach bernischen Akten." *Quellen und Forschungen aus italienischen Archiven und Bibliotheken* 70 (1990): 348–439.

———. "Überlieferungs-Change und Überlieferungs-Zufall als methodisches Problem des Historikers." *HZ* 240 (1985): 529–70.

———. "Wahrnehmung sozialen und politischen Wandels in Bern an der Wende vom Mittelalter zur Neuzeit." In Jürgen Miethke and Klaus Schreiner, eds., *Sozialer Wandel im Mittelalter*, 177–93. Sigmaringen, 1994.

Evans, Michael. "Two Sources for Maimed Justice." *Source: Notes in the History of Art* 2 (1982): 12–15.

Fantoni, Marcello. *La corte del Granduca: Forme e simboli del potere mediceo fra Cinque e Seicento*. Rome, 1994.

Feller, Richard, and Edgar Bonjour. *Geschichtschreibung der Schweiz vom Spätmittelalter zur Neuzeit*. vol. 1. Basel, 1962.

Fink, August. *Die Schwarzschen Trachtenbücher*. Munich, 1963.

Fischer, Thomas. *Städtische Armut und Armenfürsorge im 15. und 16. Jahrhundert. Sozialgeschichtliche Untersuchungen am Beispiel der Städte Basel*. Freiburg im Breisgau, 1979.

Fouquet, Gerhard. "Das Festmahl in den oberdeutschen Städten des Spätmittelalters. Zu Form, Funktion und Bedeutung öffentlichen Konsums." *AKG* 74 (1992): 83–123.

———. "Finanzen, Organisation und Arbeit in kommunalen Baubetrieben des Spätmittelalters." Habilitation thesis, typescript. Siegen, 1994.

Fouquet, Gerhard, and Ulf Dirlmeier. "'Weger wer, ich hett sie behaltten': Alltäglicher Konsum und persönliche Beziehungen in der Hofhaltung des Basler Bischofs Johannes von Venningen (1458–1478)." In Werner Paravicini, ed., *Alltag bei Hofe*. Residenzenforschung, 5, 171–96. Sigmaringen, 1995.

Friedrich-Ebert-Stiftung, ed. *Korruption in Deutschland: Ursachen, Erscheinungsformen, Bekämpfungsstrategien*. Berlin, 1995.

Fritz, Johann M. *Goldschmiedekunst der Gotik in Mitteleuropa*. Munich, 1982.

Fromm, Hans. "Aeneas der Verräter." In Johannes Janota et al., eds., *Festschrift Walter Haug und Burghart Wachinger*, vol. 2, 139–63. Tübingen, 1992.

Füglister, Hans. *Handwerksregiment: Untersuchungen und Materialien zur sozialen und politischen Struktur der Stadt Basel in der ersten Hälfte des 16. Jahrhunderts*. Basel, 1981.

Gäbler, Ulrich. *Huldrych Zwingli*. Munich, 1983.

Gagliardi, Ernst. *Der Anteil der Schweizer an den italienischen Kriegen 1494–1516*. Vol. 1. Zurich, 1919.

———. "Mailänder und Franzosen in der Schweiz, 1495–1499." *Jahrbuch für schweizerische Geschichte* 39 (1914): 1–283 and 40 (1916): 1–276.

———. *Novara und Dijon, Höhepunkt und Verfall der schweizerischen Grossmacht.* Zurich, 1907.

Gehr, Eugen. "Die Fürstenlehren des Johannes von Indersdorf für Herzog Albrecht III von Baiern München 1436–1460." Ph.D. diss., University of Freiburg, 1979.

Gerig, Georg. *Reisläufer und Pensionenherren in Zürich 1519–1523.* Zurich, 1947.

Gerteis, Klaus. "Reisen, Boten, Posten: Korresondenz im Mittelalter und früher Neuzeit." In Hans Pohl, ed., *Die Bedeutung der Kommunikation für Wirtschaft und Gesellschaft*, VSWG Beihefte, 87, 19–39. Stuttgart, 1989.

Godelier, Maurice. *L'Enigme du don.* Paris, 1996.

Gouldner, Alwin. *Reziprozität und Autonomie.* Frankfurt, 1984.

Graus, Frantisek. "Verfassungsgeschichte des Mittelalters." *HZ* 243 (1986): 529–89.

Greyerz, Hans von. "Der Jetzerprozess und die Humanisten." *Archiv des Historischen Vereins des Kantons Bern* 31 (1932): 243–99.

Grimm, Jakob. "Über Schenken und Geben." In Jakob Grimm, *Abhandlungen zur Mythologie und Sittenkunde*, 173–210. Berlin, 1865.

Groebner, Valentin. "Insides Out: Clothes, Dissimulation and the Arts of Accounting in the Autobiography of Matthaeus Schwarz (1498–1574)." *Representations* 66 (1999): 52–72.

———. *Ökonomie ohne Haus: Zum Wirtschaften der Armen in Nürnberg am Ende des 15. Jahrhunderts.* Veröffentlichungen des Max-Planck-Instituts für Geschichte, 108. Göttingen, 1993.

———. "Towards an Economic History of Customary Practice: Bread, Money and the Economy of the Bazar." *German History* 12 (1994): 119–36.

Guenée, Bernard. *Tribunaux et gens de justice à la fin du Moyen Age.* Paris, 1963.

Guery, Alain. "Le Roi dépensier." *Annales E.S.C.* 39 (1984): 1241–69.

Haferland, Harald. *Höfische Interaktion: Interpretationen zu höfischer Epik und Didaktik um 1200.* Munich, 1988.

Hagemann, Hans-Rudolf. *Basler Rechtsleben im Mittelalter.* Vol. 1. Basel, 1983.

Hamburger, Jeffrey. "The Liber miraculorum of Unterlinden: An Icon in Its Convent Setting." In Robert Ousterhout and Leslie Brubaker, eds., *The Sacred Image East and West*, 145–90. Urbana, Ill., 1995.

Hannig, Jürgen. "Ars donandi: Zur Ökonomie des Schenkens im früheren Mittelalter." In Richard van Dülmen, ed., *Armut, Liebe, Ehre: Studien zur historischen Kulturforschung*, 11–37. Frankfurt, 1988.

Harding, Robert. "Corruption and the Moral Boundaries of Patronage in the Renaissance." In Guy Fitch Little and Stephen Orgel, eds., *Patronage in the Renaissance*, 47–71. Princeton, N.J., 1981.

Harms, Bernhard. *Die Münz- und Geldpolitik der Stadt Basel im Mittelalter.* Tübingen, 1907.

———. "Die Steuern und Anleihen im öffentlichen Haushalt der Stadt Basel 1361–1500: Ein Beitrag zur mittelalterlichen Finanzstatistik." *Zeitschrift für die gesamte Staatswissenschaft* 63 (1907): 627–81.

Hegi, Friedrich. *Die geächteten Räte des Erzherzogs Sigmund von Östereich und ihre Beziehungen zur Schweiz 1487–1499.* Innsbruck, 1910.

———. "Die schweizerischen Provisionäre des Erzherzogs Sigmund von Österreich im Jahre 1488." *Anzeiger für schweizerische Geschichte* 39 (1908): 277–82.

Heimann, Heinz-Dieter. "Brievedregher: Kommunikations- und alltagsgeschichtliche Zugänge zur modernen Postgeschichte und Dienstleistungskultur." In *Kommunikation und Alltag in Spätmittelalter und Früher Neuzeit.* Österr. Akademie der Wissenschaften, phil.-hist. Klasse, Sitzungsberichte 569, 241–92 Vienna, 1992.

———. "Zur Visualisierung städtischer Dienstleistungskultur: Das Beispiel der kommunalen Briefboten." In Hermann Maué, ed. *Visualisierung städtischer Ordnung,* 22–36. Anzeiger des Germanischen Nationalmuseums, 1993. Nuremberg, 1993.

Heinig, Paul-Joachim. "Die Türhüter und Herolde Kaiser Friedrichs III." In P.-J. Heinig, ed., *Kaiser Friedrich III. (1440–1493) in seiner Zeit,* 355–75. Cologne, 1995.

Heitz, Paul, ed. *Neujahrswünsche des 15. Jahrhunderts.* Strasbourg, 1909.

Hergemöller, Bernd-Ulrich, ed. *Randgruppen der spätmittelalterlichen Gesellschaft.* Warendorf, 1990.

Hertz, Wilhelm. "Die Sage vom Giftmädchen." In Wilhelm Hertz, *Gesammelte Abhandlungen,* ed. Friedrich von der Leyen. Stuttgart, 1905.

Hinschius, Paul. *System des katholischen Kirchenrechts mit besonderer Rücksicht auf Deutschland.* 6 vols. Berlin, 1878. Reprint. Graz, 1959.

Hollegger, Manfred. "Zur 'Beamtenethik' um 1500: Standards von Räten, Beamten, Amtleuten und Dienern Maximilians I." In H. Ebner et al., eds., *Geschichtsforschung in Graz,* 139–45. Graz, 1990.

Holt, Mack P. "Wine, Community and Reformation in 16th-Century Burgundy." *Past & Present* 138 (1992): 58–93.

Howell, Martha. "Fixing Movables: Gifts by Testament in Late-Medieval Douai." *Past & Present* 150 (1996): 3–45.

Huber, Christoph. "Mittelalterliche Ödipus-Varianten." In Johannes Janota et al., eds. *Festschrift WalterHaug und Burghart Wachinger,* vol. 1, 165–99. Tübingen, 1992.

Isenmann, Eberhard. *Die deutsche Stadt im Spätmittelalter.* Stuttgart, 1988.

Jacob, Walter. "Politische Führungsschicht und Reformation: Untersuchungen zur Reformation in Zürich 1519–1528." Ph.D. diss., University of Zurich, 1969.

———. "Zwingli und 'der' geheime Rat." *Zwingliana* 13 (170): 234–44.

Jardine, Lisa. *Erasmus, Man of Letters: The Construction of Charisma in Print.* Princeton, N.J., 1993.

Jourdan, Jean-Pierre. "La Lettre et l'étoffe: Etude sur les lettres dans le dispositif vestimentaire à la fin du Moyen Age." *Médiévales* 29 (1995): 23–46.

Kantorowicz, Ernst. "Mysteries of State: An Absolutist Concept and Its Late Medieval Origins." *Harvard Theological Review* 48 (1955): 65–92.

Kellenbenz, Hermann. "Buchhaltung der Fuggerzeit." *VSWG* 58 (1971): 221–29.

Kettering, Sharon. "Gift-Giving and Patronage in Early Modern France." *French History* 2 (1988): 131–51.

———. *Patrons, Brokers and Clients in Seventeenth-Century France.* Oxford, 1986.

Kirchgässner, Bernhard. "Studien zur Geschichte des kommunalen Rechnungswesens der Reichsstädte Südwestdeutschlands vom 13. – 16. Jahrhundert." In Centro Pro Civitate, ed., *Finances et comptabilité urbaines du XIIIe au XVIe siècle,* 236–54. Brussels, 1964.

———. "Zur Frühgeschichte des modernen Haushalts, vor allem nach Quellen der

Reichsstädte Esslingen und Konstanz." In Erich Maschke and Jürgen Sydow, eds., *Städtisches Haushalts- und Rechnungswesen*, 9–44. Sigmaringen, 1977.

Klapisch-Zuber, Christiane. "Le complexe de Griselda: Dot et dons de mariage." In C. Klapisch-Zuber, *La maison et le nom: Stratégies et rituels dans l'Italie de la Renaissance*, 185–213. Paris, 1990.

Klaveren, Jakob van. "Korruption." In *Handwörterbuch der deutschen Rechtsgeschichte*, vol. 2, cols. 1163–69. Berlin, 1980.

Kohlhaussen, Heinrich. *Nürnberger Goldschmiedekunst des Mittelalters und der Dürerzeit 1240–1540*. Berlin, 1968.

Körner, Martin. "Der Einfluss der europäischen Kriege auf die schweizerischen Finanzen im 16. Jahrhundert." In Ohmar Pickl, ed., *Krieg, Militärausgaben und wirtschaftlicher Wandel*, 37–45. Graz, 1980.

———. *Luzerner Staatsfinanzen 1451–1798: Strukturen, Wachstum, Konjunkturen*. Lucerne, 1981.

———. "Les Répercussions de l'expansion territoriale sur les finances fribourgeoises au XVIe siècle." In Gaston Gaudard, Carl Pfaff, and Roland Ruffieux, eds., *Fribourg, ville et territoire*, 124–38. Fribourg, 1981.

———. *Solidarités financières suisses au XVIe siècle: Contribution à l'histoire monétaire, bancaire et financière des cantons suisses et des états voisins*. Lausanne, 1980.

Kreytenberg, Gert. "Hans Holbein der Jüngere: Die Wandgemälde im Basler Ratssaal." *Zeitschrift des deutschen Vereins für Kunstwissenschaft* 24 (1970): 77–100.

Kruse, Holger. *Hof, Amt und Gagen: Die täglichen Gagenleistungen des burgundischen Hofes 1430–1467 und der erste Hofstaat Karls des Kühnen 1456*. Bonn, 1996.

Kurze, Dietrich. "Popular Astrology and Prophecy in the 15th and 16th Century: Johannes Lichtenberger." In Paola Zambelli, ed., *Astrologi hallucinati: Stars and the End of the World in Luther's Time*, 177–93. Berlin, 1986.

Lauffer, Otto. "Der laufende Bote im Nachrichtenwesen der früheren Jahrhunderte." *Beiträge zur deutschen volks- und Altertumskunde* 1 (1954): 19–60.

Lauterbach, Klaus. *Geschichtsverständnis, Zeitdidaxe und Reformgedanke an der Wende zum 16. Jahrhundert: Das oberrheinische "buchli der hundert capiteln" im Kontext des spätmittelalterlichen Reformbiblizismus.* Freiburg im Breisgau, 1985.

Lederle, Ursula. "Gerechtigkeitsdarstellungen in deutschen und niederländischen Rathäusern." Ph.D. diss., University of Heidelberg, 1937.

Lehmann, Paul. "Judas Ischariot in der lateinischen Legendenüberlieferung des Mittelalters." In Paul Lehmann, *Erforschung des Mittelalters*, vol. 2, 229–85. Stuttgart, 1959.

Lendi, Karl. *Der Dichter Pamphilus Gengenbach*. Bern, 1926.

Lévi-Strauss, Claude. "Introduction de l'oeuvre de Mauss." In Marcel Mauss, *Sociologie et Anthropologie*, iii–xlii. Paris, 1950.

Lewis, Peter S. "Les Pensionnaires de Louis XI." In Bernard Chevalier and Philippe Contamine, eds., *La France à la fin du 15e siècle*, 167–81. Paris 1985.

Lexer, Matthias. *Mittelhochdeutsches Wörterbuch*. 3 vols. Leipzig, 1872.

Lhotsky, Alphons. "Dr. Jakob Mennel: Ein Vorarlberger im Kreise Kaisr Maximilians I." *Alemannia: Zeitschrift für Geschichte, Heimat- und volkskunde Vorarlbergs.* Heft 1/2 (1936): 1–15.

Lieb, Norbert. *Die Fugger und die Kunst im Zeitalter der Gotik und der frühen Renaissance.* Munich, 1952.

Linder, Amnon. "The Knowledge of John of Salisbury in the Later Middle Ages." *Studi medievali* 18 (1977): 315–66.

Little, Lester K. *Religious Poverty and the Profit Economy in Medieval Europe.* Ithaca, N.Y., 1978

Lowenstein, Daniel H. "Legal Efforts to Define Political Bribery." In A. J. Heidenheimer et al., eds., *Political Corruption: A Handbook*, 29–38. New Brunswick, N.J., 1989.

Lutz, Heinrich. *Konrad Peutinger: Eine politische Biographie.* Augsburg, 1958.

Lytle, Guy F. "Friendship and Patronage in Renaissance Europe." In F. W. Kent and Patricia Simons, eds., *Patronage: Art and Society in Renaissance Italy*, 47–61. Oxford, 1987.

Major, Emil. *Urs Graf: Ein Beitrag zur Geschichte der Goldschmiedekunst des 16. Jahrhunderts.* Studien zur deutschen Kunstgeschichte, 77. Strasbourg, 1907.

Mancini, Roberto. "La corruzione: Usi e abusi di un termine storiographico." *Ricerche Storiche* 21 (1991): 3–33.

Marchal, Guy. "Die 'Alten Eidgenossen' im Wandel der Zeiten." In Historischer Verein der Fünf Orte, ed., *Innerschweiz und frühe Eidgenossenschaft*, vol. 2, 309–406. Olten, 1990.

———. "Die Antwort der Bauern: Elemente und Schichtungen des eidgenössischen Geschichtsbewußtseins am Ausgang des Mittelalters." In Hans Patze, ed. *Geschichtsschreibung und Geschichtsbewußtsein im späten Mittelalter*, 758–90. Sigmaringen, 1987.

———. "Bellum justum contra iudicium belli: Zur Interpretation von Jakob Wimpfelings antieidgenössischer Streitschrift 'Soliloquium pro Pace Christianorum. In Nicolai Bernhard and Quirinus Reichen, eds., *Gesellschaft und Gesellschaften: Festschrift für Ulrich Im Hof*, 114–37. Bern, 1982.

———. *Die Statuten des weltlichen Kollegiatstifts St. Peter in Basel.* Quellen und Forschungen zur Basler Geschichte, 4. Basel, 1972.

Marcus, Kenneth. "A Question of Corruption: The Case of Martin Nuttel, 1543–44." *German History* 11 (1993): 127–40.

Martin, H. "The Judas Ischariot Curse." *American Journal of Philology* 37 (1916): 435–51.

Mauss, Marcel. *The Gift: The Form and Reason for Exchange in Archaic Societies.* Trans. W. D. Halls. New York, 1990.

Meier, Ulrich. "Vom Mythos der Republik: Formen und Funktionen mittelalterlicher Rathausikonographie in Deutschland und Italien." In Andrea Löther et al., eds., *Mundus in imagine: Festgabe für Klaus Schreiner*, 345–88. Munich, 1996.

Meyer, Friedrich. *Die Beziehungen zwischen Basel und den Eidgenossen in der Darstellung der Historiographie des 15. und 16. Jahrhunderts.* Basel, 1951.

Meyer, Werner. "Der Zusammenschluss von Gross- und Kleinbasel im Spätmittelalter." In Brigitte Meles and Beat von Wartburg, eds., *Leben in Kleinbasel 1392—1892—1992*, 12–37. Basel, 1992.

Michalski, Sergiusz. *The Reformation and the Visual Arts: The Protestant Image Question in Western and Eastern Europe.* London, 1989.

Militzer, Klaus. "Die feierlichen Einritte der Kölner Erzbischöfe in die Stadt Köln im Spätmittelalter und in der frühen Neuzeit." *Jahrbuch des kölnischen Geschichtsvereins* 55 (1984): 77–116.

Mommsen, Karl. *Eidgenossen, Kaiser und Reich. Studien zur Stellung der Eidgenossenschaft innerhalb des Heiligen Römischen Reichs.* Basler Beiträge zur Geschichtswissenschaft, 72. Basel, 1958.

———. "Die Reformatio Sigismundi und die Schweiz." *SZG* 20 (1970): 71–91.

Moos, Peter von. "Gefahren des Mittelalterbegriffs." In *Modernes Mittelalter: Neue Bilder einer populären Epoche*, ed. Joachim Heinzle, 33–63. Frankfurt, 1994.

———. *Geschichte als Topik: Das rhetorische Exemplum der Antike zur Neuzeit und die Historiae im "Policraticus" Johanns von Salisbury.* 2nd ed. Hildesheim, 1996.

———. "Das Öffentliche und das Private im Mittelalter: Für einen kontrollierten Anachronismus." In Gerd Melville and Peter von Moos, eds., *Das Öffentliche und das Private in Mittelalter und Früher Neuzeit*, 3–83. Cologne, 1998.

Moraw, Peter. "Die Entfaltung der Territorien." In Gabriel Silagi, ed., *Landesherrliche Kanzleien im Spätmittelalter*, 61–108. Münchner Beiträge zur Mediävistik und Renaissanceforschung, 35. Munich, 1984.

———. "'Regierung' und 'Verwaltung' des deutschen Königs im Reich." In Werner Paravicini and Karl Ferdinand Werner, eds., *Histoire comparé de l'administration (IV-XVIIIe siècles)*, Beihefte der Francia, 9, 149–67. Munich, 1980.

———. "Der Reichstag zu Worms von 1495." In *1495—Kaiser Reich Reformen: Der Reichstag zu Worms*, Ausstellung des Landeshauptarchiv Worms in Verbindung mit der Stadt Worms zum 500jährigen Jubiläum des Wormser Reichstag von 1495, 25–37. Worms, 1995.

Morf, Hans. "Zunftverfassung, Obrigkeit und Kirche in Zürich von Waldmann bis Zwingli." Ph.D. diss., University of Zurich, 1968.

Moser, Franz. "Valerius Anshelms Staats- und Geschichtsauffassung." *Archiv des Historischen Vereins des Kantons Bern* 39 (1948): 273–89.

Müller, Albert. "Stigma und Stigmatisierungstechniken im Spätmittelalter. Zur symbolischen Bekämpfung aufständischer Untertanen am Beispiel Michel Beheims 'Buch von den Wienern.'" In *Alltag der Symbole, Symbole des Alltags. Festschrift für Harry Kühnel zum 65. Geburtstag*, 323–47. Vienna, 1995.

Müller, Christian. "New Evidence for Hans Holbein the Younger's Wall Paintings in Basel Town Hall." *Burlington Magazine* 139 (1991): 21–25.

Müller, Jan-Dirk. *Gedechtnus. Literatur und Hofgesellschaft um Maximilian I.* Munich, 1982.

Mummenhoff, Ernst. *Das Rathaus in Nürnberg.* Nuremberg, 1891.

Najemy, John. "The Republic's Two Bodies: Body Metaphors in Italian Renaissance Political Thought." In Alison Brown, ed., *Language and Images in Renaissance Italy*, 237–62. Oxford, 1995.

Niccoli, Ottavia. *Prophecy and the People in Renaissance Italy.* Princeton, N.J., 1990.

Noonan, John T. *Bribes.* New York, 1984.

Ochsenbein, Peter. "Jakob Wimpfelings literarische Fehde mit den Baslern und Eidgenossen." *BZGA* 79 (1979): 37–65.

———. "Politische Publizistik am Oberrhein." In Heinz Rupp and H.-G. Roloff, eds.,

Akten des VI. Intern. Germanistenkongresses Basel 1980, part 4, 230–36. Bern, 1980.

———. "Zwei unbekannte Briefe Jakob Wimpfelings über den Fastnachtsbesuch der Zürcher in Basel Ende Januar 1504." In Alain Moirandat, ed., *"Totum me libris dedo": Festschrift zum 80. Geburtstag von Adolf Seebaß*, 145–62. Basel. 1979.

Oexle, Otto Gerhard. "Das Mittelalter und das Unbehagen an der Moderne: Mittelalterbeschwörungen in der Weimarer Republik und danach." In Susanna Burghartz et al., eds., *Spannungen und Widersprüche. Gedenkschrift für Frantisek Graus*, 125–55. Sigmaringen, 1992.

Panzer, Georg. *Ulrich Schwarz, der Zunftbürgermeister von Augsburg 1422–1478*. Bamberg, 1914.

Parry, Jonathan. "The Gift, the Indian Gift, and the 'Indian Gift.'" *Man* 21 (1986): 453–73.

Petillat, André. "Le Don: Espace imaginaire normatif et secret des auteurs." *Anthropologie et Sociétés* 19 (1995): 17–44.

Peyer, Hans Conrad. "Die Anfänge der schweizerischen Aristokratien." In Kurt Messmer and Peter Hoppe, *Luzerner Patriziat*, 3–28. Lucerne, 1976.

———. *Von der Gastfreundschaft zum Gasthaus: Studien zur Gastlichkeit im Mittelalter*. Hanover, 1987.

———. "Die wirtschaftliche Bedeutung der fremden Dienste für die Schweiz vom 15. bis 18. Jahrhundert." In Jürgen Schneider, ed., *Wirtschaftskräfte und Wirtschaftswege: FS für Hermann Kellenbenz*, vol. 2, 701–15. Stuttgart, 1978.

Pitz, Ernst. *Schrift- und Aktenwesen der städtischen Verwaltung im Spätmittelalter: Köln—Nürnberg—Lübeck*. Mitteilungen aus dem Stadtarchiv von Köln, 45. Cologne, 1959.

Pocock, J. G. A. *Die andere Bürgergesellschaft: Studien zur Dialektik von Tugend und Korruption*. Frankfurt, 1993.

———. *The Machiavellian Moment*. Princeton, N.J., 1975.

Pseudo-Aristotle. *The Secret of Secrets: Sources and Influence*. Ed. Walter F. Ryan and Charles B. Schmitt. London, 1982.

Queller, Donald F. *The Office of the Ambassador in the Middle Ages*. Princeton, N.J., 1967.

Rapp, Francis. "Politique et administration strasbourgeoise." In Gerhard Bauer, ed., *Stadtsprachenforschung, unter besonderer Berücksichtigung der Verhältnisse der Stadt Strassburg in Spätmittelalter und früher Neuzeit*, 327–72. Göppingen, 1988.

Redlich, Fritz. *The German Military Enterpriser and His Work Force: A Study in European Economic and Social History*. 2 vols. VSWG Beihefte 47 and 48. Wiesbaden, 1964–65.

Richter, Melvin. "Reconstructing the History of Political Languages: Pocock, Skinner, and the Geschichtliche Grundbegriffe." *History and Theory* 29 (1990): 38–70.

Riggenbach, Rudolf. "Die Wandgemälde des Rathauses zu Basel aus dem 15. und 16. Jahrhundert." In *Die Kunstdenkmäler des Kantons Basel-Stadt*, vol. 1, 517–646. Basel, 1932. Reprint with additions by Francois Maurer. Basel, 1971.

Rippmann, Dorothee. *Bauern und Städter: Stadt-Land-Beziehungen im 15. Jahrhundert*. Basel, 1990.

———. "'Frauenwerk' und Männerarbeit: Gesinde, Tagelöhner und Tagelöhnerinnen

in der mittelalterlichen Stadt." *BZGA* 95 (1995): 5–42.
Rogge, Jörg. *Für den Gemeinen Nutzen: Politisches Handeln und Politikverständnis von Rat und Bürgerschaft in Augsburg im Spätmittelalter.* Tübingen, 1996.
Romer, Hermann. *Herrschaft, Reislauf und Verbotspolitik: Beobachtungen zum rechtlichen Alltag der Zürcher Solddienstbekämpfung im 16. Jahrhundert.* Zurich, 1995.
Roper, Lyndal. *The Holy Household: Women and Morals in Reformation Augsburg.* Oxford, 1988.
Rosen, Josef. *Finanzgeschichte Basels im späten Mittelalter: Gesammelte Beiträge 1971–1989.* Wiesbaden, 1991.
Rosenwine, Barbara. *To Be the Neighbor of St. Peter: The Social Meaning of Cluny's Property, 909–1049.* Ithaca, N.Y., 1989.
Roth, Paul. "Die Wandgemälde im Basler Großratssaal." *Basler Stadtbuch,* 1960, 70–72.
Rowland, Ingrid. "The Revenge of the Regensburg Humanists." *Sixteenth Century Journal* 25 (1994): 305–22.
Rowlands, John. *Holbein: The Paintings of Hans Holbein the Younger.* Oxford, 1985.
Rublack, Ulinka. "Pregnancy, Childbirth and the Female Body in Early Modern Germany." *Past & Present* 150 (1996): 84–110.
Russell, Jocelyn. *Diplomats at Work.* London, 1992.
Sahlins, Marshall. *Stone Age Economics.* Chicago, 1972.
Sander, Paul. *Die reichsstädtische Haushaltung Nürnbergs, dargestellt auf Grund ihres Zustands von 1431–1440.* Leipzig, 1902.
Saxl, Fritz. "Aller Tugenden und Laster Abbildung." In Arpad Weixlgaertner and Leo Planiscig, eds., *Festschrift für Julius Schlosser,* 116–21. Vienna, 1926.
———. "A Spiritual Encyclopaedia of the Later Middle Ages." *JWCI* 5 (1942): 82–142.
Schaufelberger, Walter. *Der Alte Schweizer und sein Krieg: Studien zur Kriegsführung vornehmlich im 15. Jahrhundert.* Zurich, 1952.
Schelbert, Leo. "Jacob Grebel's Trial Revised." *Archiv für Reformationsgeschichte* 60 (1969): 33–64.
Scheyhing, Robert. *Eide: Banngewalt und Amtsleihe.* Cologne, 1960.
Schindler, Norbert. *Widerspenstige Leute. Studien zur volkskultur in der frühen Neuzeit.* Frankfurt, 1992. English version: *Rebellion, Community and Custom: Popular Culture in Early Modern Germany.* Trans. Pamela E. Selwyn. Cambridge, 2002. Forthcoming.
Schmid, Regula. *Reden, rufen, Zeichen setzen: Politisches Handeln während des Berner Twingherrenstreits 1469–1471.* Zurich, 1995.
Schmoller, Gustav. "Der deutsche Beamtenstaat vom 16. bis 18. Jahrhundert." In G. Schmoller, *Umrisse und Untersuchungen zur Verfassungs-, Verwaltungs- und Wirtschaftsgeschichte.* Leipzig, 1898.
———. *Grundriß der allgemeinen volkswirtschaftslehre.* Vol. 1. Leipzig, 1908.
———. "*Strassburg zur Zeit der Zunftkämpfe und die Reformation seiner Verfassung und Verwaltung im 15. Jahrhundert.* Strasbourg, 1875.
Schneider, Karin. *Der "Trojanische Krieg" im späten Mittelalter: Deutsche Trojaromane des 15. Jahrhunderts.* Berlin, 1968.
Schönberg, Gustav. *Finanzverhältnisse der Stadt Basel im 14. und 15. Jahrhundert.* Tübingen, 1879.

Schorer, Catherine. "Berner Ämterbefragungen: Untertanenrepräsentation und -mentalität im ausgehenden Mittelalter." *Berner Zeitschrift für Geschichte und Heimatkunde* 51 (1989): 217–53.

Schreiner, Klaus. "Kommunebewegung und Zunftrevolution: Zur Gegenwart der mittelalterlichen Stadt im historisch-politischen Denken des 19. Jahrhunderts." In Franz Quarthal and Wilfried Setzler, eds., *Stadtverfassung—Verfassungsstaat—Pressepolitik: Festschrift für Eberhard Naujoks*, 39–168. Sigmaringen, 1980.

———. "Die Stadt des Mittelalters als Faktor bürgerlicher Identitatsbildung." In *Stadt im Wandel: Katalog zur Landesausstellung Niedersachsen, 1985*, vol. 4, 517–41. Braunschweig, 1985.

Schubert, Ernst. *Fahrendes Volk im Mittelalter.* Bielefeld, 1995.

Schuler, Peter Johannes. "Die 'armen lüt' und das Gericht." In Peter Claasen, ed., *Recht und Schrift im Mittelalter*, 221–36. Sigmaringen, 1977.

Schuller, Wolfgang. "Probleme historischer Korruptionsforschung." *Der Staat* 16 (1977): 373–92.

Schulte, Aloys. *Geschichte der grossen Ravensburger Handelsgesellschaft 1380–1530.* 3 vols. Stuttgart, 1921–23.

Schulz, Knut. *Handwerksgesellen und Lohnarbeiter: Untersuchungen zur oberrheinischen und oberdeutschen Stadtgeschichte des 14. bis 17. Jahrhunderts.* Sigmaringen, 1985.

Schulze, Winfried. "Vom Gemeinnutz zum Eigennutz: Über den Normenwandel in der ständischen Gesellschaft der frühen Neuzeit." *HZ* 243 (1986): 591–626.

———. *Vom Gemeinnutz zum Eigennutz: Über den Normenwandel in der ständischen Gesellschaft der Frühen Neuzeit.* Schriften des Historischen Kollegs, 13. Munich, 1987.

Scribner, Bob. "Mündliche Kommunikation und Strategien der Macht in Deutschland im 16. Jahrhundert." In *Kommunikation und Alltag in Spätmittelalter und früher Neuzeit*, Veröffentlichungen des Instituts für Realienkunde 15 / Österreichische Akademie der Wissenschaften, Philosophisch-historische Klasse, Sitzungsberichte, 596, 183–97. Vienna, 1992.

Sieber-Lehmann, Claudius. *Spätmittelalterlicher Nationalismus: Die Burgunderkriege am Oberrhein und in der Eidgenossenschaft.* Göttingen, 1995.

Simmel, Georg. "Dankbarkeit: Ein soziologischer Versuch." In Georg Simmel, *Schriften zur Soziologie*, 210–18. Frankfurt, 1983.

———. *Soziologie: Untersuchungen über die Formen der Vergesellschaftung.* Ed. Otthein Rammstedt. Frankfurt, 1992.

Simon, Karl. *Abendländische Gerechtigkeitsbilder.* Frankfurt, 1948.

Simon-Muscheid, Katharina. "'Schweizergelb' und 'Judasfarbe': Nationale Ehre, Zeitschelte und Kleidermode um die Wende vom 15. zum 16. Jahrhundert." *ZHF* 22 (1995): 317–43.

Simson, Otto von. "Gerard Davids Gerechtigkeitsbild und der spätmittelalterliche Humanismus." In Friedrich Piel and Jörg Träger, eds., *Festschrift für Wolfgang Braunfels*, 349–56. Tübingen, 1977.

Singer, Bruno. *Die Fürstenspiegel in Deutschland im Zeitalter des Humanismus und der Reformation.* Munich, 1981.

Siraisi, Nancy. *Medieval and Early Renaissance Medicine.* Chicago, 1990.

Skinner, Quentin. *The Foundations of Modern Political Thought.* Vol. 1, *The Renais-*

sance. Cambridge, 1978.

Spiegel, Gabrielle M. "History, Historicism, and the Social Logic of the Text in the Middle Ages." *Speculum* 65 (1990): 59–86.

Spufford, Peter. *Money and Its Use in Medieval Europe.* Cambridge, 1988.

Steinmetz, Max. "Johann Virdung von Hassfurt, sein Leben und seine astrologischen Flugschriften." In Hans-Joachim Köhler, ed., *Flugschriften als Massenmedium der Reformationszeit,* 353–72. Stuttgart, 1980.

Stöcklin, Josef. "Johann VI. von Venningen, Bischof von Basel." Ph.D. diss., University of Basel,1902.

Stolleis, Michael. "Grundzüge der Beamtenethik (1550–1650)." In Roman Schnur, ed., *Die Rolle der Juristen bei der Entstehung des modernen Staates,* 273–302. Berlin, 1986.

———. *Staat und Staatsräson in der frühen Neuzeit: Studien zur Geschichte des öffentlichen Rechts.* Frankfurt, 1990.

Stromer, Wolfgang von. *Oberdeutsche Hochfinanz.* Wiesbaden, 1970.

Struve, Tilman. *Die Entwicklung der organologischen Staatsauffassung im Mittelalter.* Stuttgart, 1978.

Thiele, Folkmar. *Die Freiburger Stadtschreiber im Mittelalter.* Freiburg im Breisgau, 1973.

Trusen, Winfried. "Rechtliche Grundlagen des Häresiebegriffs und des Ketzerverfahrens." In Silvana Seidel Menchi et al., eds., *Ketzerverfolgung im 16. und frühen 17. Jahrhundert,* 1–20. Wiesbaden, 1992.

Tscharner-Aue, Michaela von. *Die Wirtschaftsführung des Basler Spitals bis zum Jahr 1500.* Basler Beiträge, 12. Basel, 1983.

Tscheuschner, Karl. "Die deutsche Passionsbühne und die deutsche Malerei des 15. und 16. Jahrhunderts in ihren Wechselbeziehungen." *Repertorium für Kunstwissenschaft* 27 (1904): 289–307.

Tubach, Frederic C. *Index Exemplorum.* Helsinki, 1969.

Usteri, Emil. *Marignano: Die Schicksalsjahre 1515–16 im Blickfeld der historischen Quellen.* Zurich, 1974.

van der Velden, Hugo. "Cambyses for Example / Cambyses Reconsidered: Gerard David's *exemplum iustitiae* in the Bruges Town Hall." *Simiolus* 23 (1995): 5–63.

Vogel, Hartmut. "Sporteln und Sporteldelikte: Eine Untersuchung über die historische Entwicklung und gegenwärtige Bedeutung der Sporteldelikte, verbunden mit einem Abriß zur Geschichte des Sportelwesens." Jur. diss., University of Göttingen, 1960.

Wackernagel, Rudolf. *Geschichte der Stadt Basel.* 3 vols. Basel, 1907–54.

———. "Mitteilungen über Raymundus Peraudi und kirchliche Zustände seiner Zeit in Basel." *BZGA* 2 (1903): 171–273.

Wacquet, Jean-Claude. *De la Corruption: Morale et pouvoir à Florence aux XVIIe et XVIIIe siècles.* Paris, 1984.

Walder, Ernst. "Diebold Schillings drei Redaktionen der Berner Chronik der Burgunderkriege." *Berner Zeitschrift für Geschichte und Heimatkunde* 48 (1986): 87–117

———. "Das Torechte Leben von 1477 in der bernischen Politik 1477 bis 1481." *Berner Zeitschrift für Geschichte und Heimatkunde* 45 (1983): 74–134.

———. "Zur Entstehungsgeschichte des Stanser Verkommnisses und des Bundes der acht Orte mit Freiburg im Uechtland und Solothurn von 1481." *SZG* 32 (1982): 263–92.

Warburg, Aby. "Heidnisch-Antike Weissagungen in Wort und Bild zu Luthers Zeiten." In Aby Warburg, *Gesammelte Schriften*, vol. 2, 487–535. Leipzig, 1932.

Weber, Max. *Wirtschaft und Gesellschaft: Grundriss der verstehenden Soziologie.* 5th ed. Tübingen, 1976.

Wechsler, Elisabeth. *Ehre und Politik: Ein Beitrag zur Erfassung politischer Verhaltensweisen in der Eidgenossenschaft (1440–1500) unter historisch-anthropologischen Aspekten.* Zurich, 1991.

Weck, Helmut. "Die handschriftliche Überlieferung der 'Rechtssumme.'" In Georg Steer et al., eds., *Die "Rechtssumme Bruder Bertholds,"* vol. 3, 221–51. Tübingen, 1986. Pp.

Weidenhiller, Egino. *Untersuchungen zur deutschsprachigen katechetischen Literatur des späten Mittelalters, nach den Handschriften der bayrischen Staatsbibliothek.* Munich, 1965.

Weiner, Annette B. *Inalienable Possessions: The Paradox of Keeping-While-Giving.* Berkeley, Calif., 1992.

Weinig, Paul. *Aeneam suscipite, Pium recipite: Aeneas Silvius Piccolomini: Studien zur Rezeption eines humanistischen Schriftstellers im Deutschland des 15. Jahrhundert.* Wiesbaden, 1998.

Weiske, Brigitte. *Gesta Romanorum: Untersuchungen zu Konzeption und Überlieferung.* 2 vols. Fortuna Vitrea 3/4. Tübingen, 1992.

Weissen, Kurt. "*An der Stuer ist ganz nuett bezalt*": *Landesherrschaft, Verwaltung und Wirtschaft in den fürstbischöflichen Ämtern in der Umgebung Basels (1435–1525).* Basel, 1994.

Weissmann, Ronald. "The Importance of Being Ambiguous: Social Relations, Individualism, and Identity in Renaissance Florence." In Susan Zimmerman and R. Weissmann, eds., *Urban Life in the Renaissance*, 269–80. Newark, Del., 1989.

Weitzel, Joseph. *Begriff und Erscheinungsformen der Simonie bei Gratian und den Dekretisten.* Munich, 1967.

West, William N. "Nothing as Given: Economies of the Gift in Derrida and Shakespeare." *Comparative Literature* 48 (1996): 1–18.

White, Stephen D. *Custom, Kinship, and Gifts to Saints: The Laudatio Parentum in Western France 1050–1150.* Chapel Hill, N.C., 1988.

Whitney, Marian. "Queen of Medieval Virtues: Largesse." In Christabel Fiske, ed., *Vassar Medieval Studies*, 181–215. New Haven, Conn., 1923.

Willoweit, Dietmar. "Die Entwicklung und Verwaltung der spätmittelalterlichen Landesherrschaft." In Kurt G. A. Jeserich et al., eds., *Deutsche Verwaltungsgeschichte*, vol. 1, 82–142. Stuttgart, 1983.

Winckelmann, Otto. *Das Fürsorgewesen der Stadt Strassburg vor und nach der Reformation.* 2 vols. Quellen und Forschungen zur Reformationsgeschichte, 5. Strasbourg, 1922.

———. "Strassburgs Verfassung und Verwaltung im 16. Jahrhundert." *ZGO* 18 (1903): 493–537, 600–639.

Wind, Edgar. "The Flaying of Marsyas." In Edgar Wind, *Pagan Mysteries in the Renaissance.* New Haven, Conn., 1958.

Windler, Christian. "Tributes and Presents in Franco-Tunisian Diplomacy." *Journal of Modern History* 4 (2000): 168–99.

Witte, Heinrich. "Der letzte Puller von Hohenburg: Ein Beitrag zur politischen und Sittengeschichte des Elsasses und der Schweiz im 15. Jahrhundert sowie zur Genealogie des Geschlecht der Püller." *Beiträge zur Landes- und volkskunde von Elsass-Lothringen* 4 (1895): 1–143.

Wolter, Udo. "Amt und Offizium in mittelalterlichen Quellen vom 13.–15. Jahrhundert." *Zeitschrift der Savigny-Stiftung für Rechtsgeschichte, kanonistische Abteilung* 74 (1988): 246–80.

Wurms, Friedrich. "Studien zu den lateinischen und deutschen Prosafassungen des Secretum Secretorum." Ph.D. diss., University of Hamburg, 1970.

Zahnd, Urs-Martin. "Studium und Kanzlei: Der Bildungsweg von Stadt- und Ratsschreibern in eidgenössischen Städten des ausgehenden Mittelalters." In Rainer-Christoph Schwinges, ed., *Gelehrte im Reich: Zur Sozial- und Wirkungsgeschichte akademischer Eliten des 14. bis 16. Jahrhunderts,* ZHF Beihefte, 18, 453–76. Berlin, 1997.

Zak, Sabine. *Musik als "Ehr und Zier" im mittelalterlichen Reich: Studien zur Musik im höfischen Leben, Recht und Zeremoniell.* Neuss, 1979.

Zehnder, Leo. *Volkskundliches aus der älteren Schweizer Chronistik.* Basel, 1976.

Zinner, Ernst. *Geschichte und Bibliographie der astronomischen Literatur in Deutschland zur Zeit der Renaissance.* 2nd ed. Stuttgart, 1964.

Zorzi, Andrea. "I Fiorentini e gli uffici publici del primo Quattrocento: concurrenca, abusi, illegalitá." *Quaderni storici* 22 (1987): 725–51.

———. "Ordine publico e amministrazione della giustizia nelle formazioni politiche toscane fra Tre e Quattrocento." In Centro Italiano di Studi di Storia e d'Arte, Pistoia, ed., *Italia 1350–1450: Tra crisi, trasformazione, sviluppo,* 419–74. Pistoia, 1993.

Index

Acknowledgments

After so many meticulously recorded late medieval gifts, often quite ambiguous in character, I cannot help feeling that in adding my own accounting of the generosity that made this book possible, I am getting closer to my fifteenth-century protagonists than I ever wanted to. *Unheimlich*? Not really. It is rather about sending messages. Research on the Middle Ages and the Renaissance is inescapably about the present, about ourselves and the persons and things we care for. And so I hope to convey through these lines my affection, friendship, and gratitude for all those who have contributed to the book. Gadi Algazi, Lucas Burkart, Natalie Zemon Davis, Johannes Fehr, Gerhard Fouquet, Michael Harbsmeier, Stephen Greenblatt, Hans Medick, Guy Marchal, Wolfgang Kaiser, Nils Minkmar, Peter von Moos, Achatz von Müller, Helmut Puff, Francis Rapp, Lyndal Roper, Philipp Sarasin, Dominik Sieber, Claudius Sieber-Lehmann, Norbert Schindler, Nick Stargardt, Ulrike Strasser, and Simon Teuscher helped me with comments, suggestions, criticism, and enthusiasm. I am particularly indebted to the late Bob Scribner and Hartmut Boockmann, who encouraged me to go forward with the project in its early stages. For their support and their patience with a clumsy and often demanding visitor I want to thank the staff of the Archives municipal de Strasbourg, the Stadtarchiv Freiburg im Breisgau, the Universitätsbibliothek Basel, and particularly the Staatsarchiv Basel. A leave from my teaching duties in the Department of History of the University of Basel and ten wonderful and inspiring months as a fellow in the Wissenschaftskolleg in Berlin have helped me to finish the manuscript. I want to express my gratitude to Jeffrey Hamburger and David Nirenberg, who encouraged me to make the book accessible to readers outside the German-speaking realm, and to Jerome Singerman and Erica Ginsburg at the University of Pennsylvania Press for their enthusiasm and many helpful and clarifying suggestions. Pamela Selwyn has been a wonderful translator to work with, and if this book steps beyond earlier drafts as a heavy-handed and somewhat old-fashioned German-style *Habilitationsschrift*, all the credit must go to her.

Portions of Chapters 3, 4, and 7 have previously, and in rather different form, appeared as "Angebote, die man nicht ablehnen kann: Institution, Verwaltung, und die Definition von Korruption am Ende des Mittelalters," in Reinhard Blänkner and Bernhard Jussen, eds., *Institutionen und Ereignis: Über historische Praktiken und Vorstellungen gesellschaftlichen Ordnens* (Göttingen: Vandenhoek and Ruprecht, 1998): 164–84; as "Accountancies and Arcana: Registering the Gift in Late Medieval Cities," in Esther Cohen and Mayke de Jong, eds., *Medieval Transformations: Texts, Power & Gifts in Context* (Brill: Leiden, 2001): 219–44; and as "'Gemein' und 'Geheym': Pensionen, Geschenke, und die Sichtbarmachung des Unsichtbaren in Basel am Beginn des 16. Jahrhunderts," *Schweizerische Zeitschrift für Geschichte* 49 (1999): 445–69. I am grateful to these publications for the opportunity to develop my ideas and permission to republish the essays.

In a strange and sometimes haunting way, we all know that most gifts cannot be requited. It is the unexpected and unrepeatable moment of the giving itself that we owe to the benefactor. If we are taken by gifts, we are taken by surprise.

To my friends in Cambridge, Massachusetts, with my thanks for many gifts and surprises.

www.ingramcontent.com/pod-product-compliance
Ingram Content Group UK Ltd.
Pitfield, Milton Keynes, MK11 3LW, UK
UKHW011822210826
474419UK00010B/148/J